Ben Ali's Tunisia

Ben Ali's Tunisia

Power and Contention in an Authoritarian Regime

ANNE WOLF

OXFORD
UNIVERSITY PRESS

OXFORD
UNIVERSITY PRESS

Great Clarendon Street, Oxford, OX2 6DP,
United Kingdom

Oxford University Press is a department of the University of Oxford.
It furthers the University's objective of excellence in research, scholarship,
and education by publishing worldwide. Oxford is a registered trade mark of
Oxford University Press in the UK and in certain other countries

Published in the United States of America by Oxford University Press
198 Madison Avenue, New York, NY 10016, United States of America

British Library Cataloguing in Publication Data
Data available

Library of Congress Control Number: 2022940614

ISBN 978–0–19–286850–3

DOI: 10.1093/oso/9780192868503.001.0001

Printed and bound by
CPI Group (UK) Ltd, Croydon, CR0 4YY

Links to third party websites are provided by Oxford in good faith and
for information only. Oxford disclaims any responsibility for the materials
contained in any third party website referenced in this work.

To Leopold

Acknowledgements

This book would not have been possible without the involvement of the many Tunisians who were willing to give me immense amounts of time and to recount their sometimes difficult experiences under the Ben Ali regime, and I am grateful to all of them. I am truly appreciative of the many frank discussions I had with ex–Ben Ali officials, who provided testimonies and detailed accounts of the regime's internal working. During this journey, I enjoyed the unconditional support of my supervisor and friend Michael Willis, who always believed in my project, encouraged me to pursue it, and read successive drafts of my work. I am also deeply grateful to George Joffé, who first got me interested in Tunisian politics and has provided persistent mentoring and support over the past twelve years.

Many other friends and colleagues have provided invaluable guidance and feedback. During my time as a doctoral student at St Antony's College, University of Oxford, I benefited from discussions with Eugene Rogan, Mohamed-Salah Omri, Rory McCarthy, Glen Rangwala, Rikke Haugbolle, Noureddine Jebnoun, Walter Armbrust, Clement Henry Moore, and Paul Chaisty. It was an honour to be a Fellow at the Trajectories of Change Programme of the ZEIT-Stiftung, where I attended yearly workshops and enjoyed discussions with Isabelle Werenfells, Anna Hofmann, and Jane Bartels. I was fortunate enough to have Stathis Kalyvas and Charles Tripp as examiners of my doctoral thesis, who provided critical feedback and invaluable counsel on how to turn my work into a book.

I tremendously enjoyed the stimulating and supportive environment at Girton College, University of Cambridge, where I subsequently held a research fellowship and spent much time working on connecting my deeply local and ethnographic research to wider debates in authoritarian politics. I am extremely grateful for Stathis Kalyvas's encouragement to organize a book workshop, where I received in-depth feedback from Ivan Ermakoff, Giovanni Capoccia, Michael Willis, Christopher Barrie, Michael Biggs, Christopher Mittelstaedt, Rikke Haugbolle, Katerina Dalacoura, Rory McCarthy, Mathilde Zederman, and Laurence Whitehead. I could not have organized the event without All Souls College, which generously hosted and financed it.

I finished the book as a Fellow at All Souls College, University of Oxford, where I enormously benefited from discussions with colleagues. I am grateful for having participated in a Project on Middle East Political Science research workshop in 2021, organized by Marc Lynch, where Adria Lawrence kindly discussed my work. Several other people provided comments at this crucial final revision stage. They include Michaela Collord, Morten Valbjørn, Glen Rangwala, and Ivan Ermakoff, who offered feedback on my theoretical frame, alongside Francesco Cavatorta, who very generously read the entire manuscript before submission. At Oxford University Press, I am deeply indebted to Dominc Byatt, who immediately responded to my book proposal with great enthusiasm and found three fantastic reviewers for my manuscript, all of whom provided excellent comments. Last but not least, thanks to Raphaël, who never got tired of discussing the Ben Ali regime, reading chapters, and motivating me.

Contents

List of Figures

List of Abbreviations

ATCE	Tunisian Agency for External Communication
BTS	Tunisian Bank of Solidarity
CCP	Chinese Communist Party
CPR	Congress of the Republic
CPSU	Communist Party of the Soviet Union
CREDIF	Centre for Research, Studies, Documentation, and Information on the Woman
ENA	National School of Administration
EUR	euro (currency)
FLN	National Liberation Front (Algeria)
FNE	National Employment Fund
FNS	National Solidarity Fund
GPC	General People's Congress (Yemen)
LTDH	Tunisian Human Rights League
MDS	Socialist Democratic Movement
MTI	Islamic Tendency Movement
NDP	National Democratic Party (Egypt)
NGO	non-governmental organization
PDP	Progressive Democratic Party
PRI	Institutional Revolutionary Party (Mexico)
PSD	Socialist Destourian Party
RCD	Constitutional Democratic Rally
RETAP	Rally of the Tunisian Students in Paris
RTF	Rally of the Tunisians in France
TND	Tunisian dinar
UDU	Unionist Democratic Union
UGET	General Union of Tunisian Students
UGTE	General Tunisian Union of Students
UGTT	Tunisian General Labour Union
UNFT	National Union of the Tunisian Woman
USD	United States dollar
UTICA	Tunisian Union of Industry, Trade, and Handicraft

A Note on Transliteration

For colloquial Tunisian Arabic, I have opted for French-based transliterations, which are most commonly used by Tunisians themselves, in order to reflect the local variations in language. For example, the Arabic letter ش is transliterated as 'ch' rather than 'sh'. The names of well-known groups, movements, names, and places mirror general use so that they are more easily recognizable. For sources derived from Modern Standard Arabic, I use a simplified version of the guidelines of the *International Journal of Middle East Studies*. In quotations, I have kept the transliterations used in the original documents.

'Who's Who?' in Ben Ali's Regime

Abdallah, Abdelwahab: longtime Ben Ali adviser and palace associate; previously Foreign Affairs Minister and Information Minister; from Monastir.

Abidi, Samir: appointed Communications Minister in December 2010; previously Minister for Youth and Sports; from Gafsa.

Ammar, Habib: military colonel and co-conspirator in the 7 November 1987 coup against Bourguiba, who headed the National Guard; longtime friend of Ben Ali from Sousse but was marginalized shortly after his takeover of power.

Baccouche, Hedi: co-conspirator in Ben Ali's 7 November 1987 coup; Prime Minister from November 1987 to September 1989; Secretary General of the PSD/RCD from November 1987 to September 1989; Director of the PSD from March 1984 to April 1987; from Hammam Sousse.

Ben Ali, Cyrine: Ben Ali's third daughter from his first marriage. Married Marouane Mabrouk.

Ben Ali, Dorsaf: Ben Ali's middle daughter from his first marriage; married Slim Chiboub.

Ben Ali, Ghazoua: Ben Ali's eldest daughter from his first marriage; married Slim Zarrouk.

Ben Ali, Leila: formerly Leila Trabelsi. Ben Ali's second wife, married in 1992; from Tunis.

Ben Ali, Mohamed: Ben Ali's only son from his second marriage, to Leila; born in 2005.

Ben Ali, Nesrine: Ben Ali's eldest daughter with Leila; married Sakher el-Materi.

Ben Dhia, Abdelaziz: longtime Ben Ali adviser; RCD Secretary General between June 1996 and November 1999, Director of the PSD between April 1987 and September 1987, and held various ministerial posts; from Moknine, Mahdia governorate.

Ben Miled, Mounir: prominent businessman and longtime RCD Central Committee member.

Chaabane, Sadok: Ben Ali adviser; in February 1991, appointed Secretary of State to the Prime Minister and in June 1991 nominated as first presidential adviser on human rights; from Sfax.

Chaouch, Ali: RCD Secretary General from December 2000 to August 2005; headed various ministries, including the Interior Ministry between October 1997 and November 1999; from Bou Arada, Siliana governorate.

Cheikhrouhou, Mahmoud: Ben Ali's personal pilot; flew him to Saudi Arabia on 14 January 2011.

Chettaoui, Nabil: head of Tunisair at the time of the uprising; responsible for Ben Ali's presidential plane.

Chiboub, Afif: brother-in-law of Dorsaf, Ben Ali's daughter from his first marriage.

Chiboub, Slim: Ben Ali's son-in-law, married to Dorsaf, Ben Ali's daughter from his first marriage.

Djilani, Hedi: longtime head of the UTICA employers' union; related to Ben Ali through his daughter's marriage to Belhassen Trabelsi.

Dkhil, Rafaa: Trabelsi associate and business partner from Bizerte; RCD Central Committee member.

Eltaief, Kamel: businessman and longtime Ben Ali associate; in February 2002, sentenced to prison after a fallout with the presidential family; from Hammam Sousse.

Essebsi, Beji Caid: longtime RCD Central Committee member, head of Parliament in the 1990s; Foreign Affairs Minister under Bourguiba and elected President of Tunisia in 2014; from Tunis.

Ghannouchi, Mohamed: Prime Minister between November 1999 and February 2011 and a former Finance Minister; from Sousse.

Ghariani, Mohamed: RCD Secretary General between September 2008 and March 2011; previously ambassador to the United Kingdom and headed the RCD student branch; from Kairouan.

Grira, Ridha: Defence Minister at the time of the uprisings and former State Property and Land Affairs Minister; from Sousse.

Gueddich, Mohamed: longtime Ben Ali palace associate and his personal doctor; from Hammamet.

Jegham, Mohamed: head of the Presidential Cabinet from January 1997 until November 1999 and occupied various ministries, including the Defence and Interior Ministries; from Hammam Sousse.

Kallel, Abdellah: close Ben Ali adviser who occupied the Interior Ministry, the Defence Ministry, and the Justice Ministry, amongst other posts; from Sfax.

Karoui, Hamed: Director of the PSD/RCD from October 1987 to August 1988, then Prime Minister from September 1989 to November 1999; from Sousse.

Kefi, Naima: first wife of Ben Ali; divorced in 1988.

Mabrouk, Marouane: Ben Ali's son-in-law; married to Cyrine, Ben Ali's daughter from his first marriage.

Materi, Sakher, el-: Ben Ali's son-in-law; married to Nesrine, Ben Ali's daughter with Leila.

Mdhafer, Zouhair: created and later headed the RCD Centre for Studies and Training; former State Property and Land Affairs Minister.

Mebazza, Fouad: leading RCD figure and Head of Parliament from October 1997 until 15 January 2011, when he became Interim President of Tunisia and also occupied various ministerial posts; born in Tunis.

Mhenni, Hedi: RCD Secretary General between August 2005 and September 2008; appointed Interior Minister in April 2002 and Defence Minister in November 2004; from Sayada, Monastir governorate.

Mohsen, Abbes: RCD Central Committee member between 2008 and 2011; mayor of Tunis from 2000 to 2010; in 1988, nominated Director of Protocol of the President and subsequently worked in the Interior Ministry; from Tunis.

Morjane, Kamel: Foreign Affairs Minister from January 2010 to January 2011; Defence Minister from August 2005 to January 2010, and previously worked at the United Nations; a distant relative of Ben Ali from Hammam Sousse.

Moussi, Abir: lawyer and Vice-President of the RCD Coordination Committee at the time of the uprising; charged with legally defending the party and challenged its dissolution.

Neffati, Chedli: RCD Secretary General between February 1991 and June 1996; headed various ministries, including the Interior Ministry, with a previous career as governor; from Gabes.

Nasfi, Hassouna: Secretary General of the RCD student wing between 2000 and 2003; from Gabes.

Rouissi, Moncer: adviser to Ben Ali when he first took power. Director of his 1989 presidential campaign; occupied various ministerial posts, and was ambassador to France between September 2003 and May 2005; from Degache, Tozeur governorate.

Saada, Ryadh: Director of the RCD Centre for Studies and Training between 1995 and 2008.

Seriati, Ali: Ben Ali's key security chief and head of the presidential guard at the time of the uprising; on 14 January 2011, convinced Ben Ali to board the plane for Saudi Arabia.

Tarhouni, Samir: commander of the Antiterrorism Brigade at the time of the uprising.

Trabelsi, Belhassen: Leila Ben Ali's favourite brother, who became an economic heavyweight and headed Karthago Airlines; from Tunis.

Trabelsi, Imed: Leila Ben Ali's favourite nephew; elected mayor of La Goulette in 2010.

Zarrouk, Naziha: previous RCD Vice-Secretary General, ambassador to Lebanon (2003–2005), and Minister for Women and Family Affairs; from Jemmal, Monastir governorate.

Zarrouk, Slim: Ben Ali's son-in-law; married to Ghazoua, Ben Ali's daughter from his first marriage.

Zenaidi, Mondher: member of the RCD Central Committee and Political Bureauo occupied various ministerial posts, including Transport, Commerce, Tourism, and Public Health, and associate of Belhassen Trabelsi from Tunis.

Zouari, Abderrahim: RCD Secretary General between August 1988 and February 1991 and between November 1999 and December 2000; held several ministerial posts, including Foreign Affairs, and had a previous career as a governor; from Dahmani, Kef governorate.

Introduction

Avenue Bourguiba, downtown Tunis: thousands of people are cheering, dancing; some are crying out in joy, stupefied at what has just happened. It is 14 January 2011 and moments earlier, at 6:45 pm local time, Prime Minister Mohamed Ghannouchi announced he will take over the interim presidency—the first in a series of steps that will lead to the ousting of Zine el-Abidine Ben Ali, the dictator who has ruled the country with an iron fist for almost twenty-five years. 'Given [Ben Ali's] inability to exercise his duties I . . . have taken over the position of President of the Republic', Ghannouchi declares in a tele-vised speech from the Presidential Palace in Carthage. He vows to implement the 'political, economic and social reforms' that the people have demanded during weeks of mass protests—launching the wider 'Arab Uprisings' in the region—and stresses that he will include 'all national sides, political parties, national organizations and components of civil society' in this process.[1]

Just as celebrations burst out on the streets of Tunis, screams of anger and rage can be heard on board the airborne presidential plane, hundreds of miles away. 'What is going on?!' Ben Ali reportedly exclaims in complete shock when he hears that Ghannouchi—one of his longtime associates and a senior figure in his ruling party—has assumed the presidency. Newspapers around the world have already begun proclaiming that Ben Ali—whose flight is en route to Saudi Arabia—has been 'forced to flee Tunisia as protesters claim victory'.[2] Ben Ali had, in fact, planned only on dropping his family off in Jeddah before returning immediately to Tunisia. Furious and panic-stricken, Ben Ali calls Ghannouchi and other senior officials of his regime. He informs them that he will return to Tunisia without delay and demands they rescind any statements to the contrary. Arriving in Jeddah in the early morning of 15 January, Ben Ali duly orders his pilot to prepare the plane once more, fully intent on heading back to Tunisia later that day.[3] But Ben Ali was never to return.

[1] 'Mr. Mohamed Ghannouchi Announces Taking Over as Interim President of Republic', *Presidency of the Government Portal*, 14 January 2011, http://www.pm.gov.tn/pm/actualites/actualite. php?id=1898&lang=en, last accessed 10 August 2022.

[2] Angelique Chrisafis and Ian Black, 'Zine al-Abidine Ben Ali Forced to Flee Tunisia as Protesters Claim Victory', *The Guardian*, 15 January 2011, https://www.theguardian.com/world/2011/jan/14/tunisian-president-flees-country-protests, last accessed 10 August 2022.

[3] Interviews with Mohamed Ghannouchi, Tunis, 2 October 2015; Mahmoud Cheikhrouhou (Ben Ali's personal pilot), Tunis, 1 July 2016; and Nesrine Ben Ali, Viber, 6 February 2017. See also Ben Ali's own account of events: 'Tasrih al-Ra'is Bin Ali—20 Huzayran 2011' ['Declaration of President Ben Ali—20 June 2011'], published via his lawyer, Akram 'Azuri, Beirut, 20 June 2011.

Ben Ali's Tunisia. Anne Wolf, Oxford University Press. © Anne Wolf (2023).
DOI: 10.1093/oso/9780192868503.003.0001

After almost a decade in exile, he died in Jeddah in September 2019, never having set foot again on Tunisian soil.

This book is an in-depth study of the Ben Ali regime, its inner workings, and eventual collapse in 2011. Extensive research has focused on anti-regime protesters in Tunisia and the wider region during the Arab Uprisings, including their demands and the dynamics of mobilization. By contrast, inner regime processes have received relatively little scholarly attention. In this book, I seek to address this gap, offering an entirely new perspective on one of the most important revolutionary episodes in recent history. The book had its genesis, as in some senses did the revolution itself, in Sidi Bouzid—the Tunisian city where demonstrations first took off following the self-immolation of street vendor Mohamed Bouazizi in December 2010. During conversations I had with people there after the revolution, I was confronted with an intellectual puzzle that motivated me to research more deeply into the Ben Ali regime and—ultimately—write this book.

The puzzle

When visiting Sidi Bouzid, one cannot but be struck by the revolutionary heritage inscribed in the city's fabric. Graffiti with anti-regime slogans features prominently on walls throughout the city; a monument was erected in memory of Bouazizi, and—next to it and most visibly—a massive placard depicting the 'martyr' overlooks the city's main square, which was renamed Mohamed Bouazizi Square. Such symbolism aside, I was moved by the great pride people in this marginalized southern province hold for its role in birthing one of the greatest revolutionary moments in recent history. In cafés and in conversation with foreign visitors, locals from all kinds of social backgrounds passionately recount their activism during *al-thaura* ('the Revolution'). This remained so even in the late 2010s, when political and economic crises—and in some cases, civil war and the rise of new authoritarian regimes—had dampened enthusiasm for the Arab Uprisings in most other parts of the country and the wider region. Sidi Bouzid remained impregnated with the spirit of the revolution—at least so it seemed to me.

I was therefore surprised when I first learned that the history of Sidi Bouzid was intimately linked not only to the Tunisian Revolution but also to its main opponent: the regime of longtime dictator Zine el-Abidine Ben Ali. In particular, the city had a deep association with his ruling Constitutional Democratic Rally (RCD) party. As a matter of fact, the Sidi Bouzid governorate had the greatest concentration of RCD members in all of Tunisia: at the time of the uprising, it was home to about 650 RCD cells, each consisting of 200–300 members.[4] Of the governorate's 415,900-strong population,[5] about 39.1% were thus card-carrying RCD members.[6] To find so many RCD members in the very cradle of the Arab Uprisings, a place where locals across social strata and professions continue fervently to defend its legacy, seemed contradictory to me, to say the least. The protests of 2010–2011 are generally understood as having been directed against Ben Ali and the RCD, as well as responding to wider grievances such as police violence and economic stagnation. Thus, it did not make sense to me that the birthplace of the revolution was swamped with RCD members.

One might have expected that RCD followers would vigorously have opposed the revolution—after all, it deposed their leader and resulted in the party's dissolution. But quite to the contrary, I soon uncovered that many RCD activists in Sidi Bouzid had in fact endorsed the mass protests. Grassroots followers commonly participated in the demonstrations, and local party leaders even encouraged them to do so. In interviews, some activists even claimed that the revolts had occurred in the very spirit of the ruling party.[7] This made little sense to me, at least initially—not least because RCD offices had been attacked by protesters in many parts of the country and were considered key symbols of the Ben Ali regime. Yet party followers in Sidi Bouzid fervently insisted that the RCD had a revolutionary legacy, given its roots in Tunisia's Neo-Destour independence movement (Destour meaning 'constitution'). Hence, belonging to the RCD and participating in revolutionary activism was not a contradiction, at least so they claimed.[8] Some locals even went so far as to suggest that it was the RCD that had forced Ben Ali out of power—an event which led to the dissolution of the ruling party itself. As one grassroots activist proclaimed: 'All RCD activists . . . protested and encouraged the protests to turn into a revolution. RCD followers were revolutionaries . . . Who do you think was behind Ben Ali's fall? The [RCD activists] of Sidi Bouzid!'[9]

---

[4] Interviews with Mohamed Ghariani, RCD Secretary General at the time of the revolution, Tunis, 27 May 2016; and with Abir Moussi, Vice-President of the RCD Coordination Committee—the party's highest regional instance—at the time of the revolution, Tunis, 31 May 2016.

[5] The data is for 2011 and was retrieved from *al-Nashra al-Shahriyya li-l-Ihsa'iyyat* [*Monthly Bulletin of Statistics*], Tunis: al-Ma'had al-Watani li-l-Ihsa' [National Institute for Statistics], September 2012, p. 9.

[6] These calculations are based on an estimated average of 250 members per RCD cell.

[7] Interviews with various RCD members in Sidi Bouzid, July and August 2016.

[8] Ibid.

[9] Interview with Souhail, Sidi Bouzid, 25 June 2016.

Crucially, such statements were not facile attempts by isolated party follow-ers to retroactively bolster their legitimacy by inventing some revolutionary activism. For one thing, these accounts were too numerous and were also echoed by people who did not belong to the ruling party.[10] Moreover, evidence for anti-regime resistance by some party figures went beyond oral testimonies. Amongst other examples, in Regueb, a rural town in the Sidi Bouzid gover-norate, a document was circulated amongst RCD followers asking them to resign from the ruling party and calling for nothing less than the party's self-dissolution.[11] The pattern in Sidi Bouzid exemplified a tendency found more widely across Tunisia: RCD followers in other parts of the country also not only failed to countermobilize but in many cases even supported the mass demonstrations.

From a theoretical point of view, RCD followers' dissent against the Ben Ali regime presents a conundrum: one of the key premises of the literature on authoritarian politics is that ruling parties are a force for stability in that they possess a number of positive-feedback mechanisms that strengthen regimes over time. This literature provides few clues as to when and why ruling par-ties turn into arenas for opposition and dissent, possibly even contributing to regime breakdown. Similarly, the scholarship on revolutions and contentious politics offers limited insights into why some RCD followers joined the Arab Uprisings: it focuses on contention against, not *within*, the regime. It is in this light that this book seeks to answer the following questions. Why would some members of Ben Ali's ruling party participate in protests against his regime and, in some instances, even go so far as to call for his downfall and the dissolution of the RCD—their own party? More generally, which factors influ-ence the relation between a dictator and ruling party and with what effects on authoritarian stability and collapse?

Key arguments and theory

I uncovered that—far from pursuing a unified cause—RCD activists who sup-ported the protests did so for a variety of reasons, depending in part on their party rank and regional affiliation. In Sidi Bouzid, as elsewhere in Tunisia, many mid-level and grassroots followers had lost all trust in Ben Ali, given the city's severe socioeconomic marginalization; they were convinced that as long

---

[10] For example, interviews with Salma and Khalid, Sidi Bouzid, July 2016.
[11] Muhammad al-Arabi al-Zuraibi, *al-Regueb min al-Tahrir ila al-Ta'mir* [*al-Regueb: From Liberation to Reconstruction*], Tunis: Dar Al-Qalam Publishing and Distribution, 2016, pp. 225, 227.

as he remained at the helm, matters would only get worse. By contrast, some senior officials in the city hoped that the protests would pressure Ben Ali to pour more financial resources into the local RCD branch. They lamented that being a regional party leader meant nothing. 'I am from the RCD but I have four [family members] with law degrees who are jobless: my wife, my sister, as well as my two brothers!', exclaimed Sidi Bouzid's RCD Vice-President.[12] Five years on from Ben Ali's ouster, he was still angry that other party figures in the city had supported complete regime change, affirming that Ben Ali was about to allocate more money to the RCD in Sidi Bouzid but could not pursue this plan because he was ousted.

Other party activists advanced other reasons for not supporting the regime at a time of crisis. Beyond Sidi Bouzid, in Jendouba, a city 150 kilometres west of Tunis, a mid-level official told me that he and his colleagues engaged in 'passive resistance'—that is, complete inaction—in order to signal to the powerbrokers in Tunis that they wanted internal party reforms. In particular, they charged that local and mid-level representatives no longer had any political leverage, and they hoped that—by withdrawing from pro-regime activism—they would compel Ben Ali and his associates to restore the influence they once held. By contrast, in Tunis, few high officials engaged in any contentious actions against the powerbrokers at all—that is, until 14 January, when Prime Minister Mohamed Ghannouchi announced he had taken over the interim presidency.

Whilst the nature of the changes party followers sought varied, activists' core critiques of the Ben Ali regime were strikingly similar to one another: they deplored that the President had gained vast personal powers and progressively marginalized ruling party activists. In particular, they disapproved of Ben Ali's family, who, they claimed, had accumulated extensive wealth on the back of ordinary Tunisians—including many RCD activists. Party representatives said they lacked any influence vis-à-vis these figures and increasingly felt like puppets in the service of 'the family'. They charged that Ben Ali and his relatives had robbed the RCD of its identity and nationalist cause, and that the President and his kin lacked any political vision and project—that is, other than accumulating more resources for themselves. RCD followers were particularly dismayed that in the years before the revolution, some members of the Ben Ali family had integrated into the ruling party and placed their associates in key positions. They suspected that Ben Ali, who was seventy-four at the time, was trying to groom a relative as a presidential successor through the ruling party.

---

[12] Interview with Abderrazek Daly, Sidi Bouzid, 25 June 2016.

'The RCD had become a family party', one high official said, summing up her indignation.[13]

Given that the literature fails to explain the RCD's revolt against Ben Ali, I decided to draw up a theory of power and contention within ruling parties in authoritarian regimes. It delineates how incumbents seek to fortify their rule and foster party-political stability, as well as when and why they succumb to internal contention and with what effect. This theory responds to the complex picture set out above, in which party followers' diverse interests give rise to intra-party pressures that ultimately destabilized the regime, a pattern that extends beyond the Tunisian case. Chapter 1 outlines this in detail, but the key tenets are as follows: party leaders always seek to accumulate more power but, in the process, marginalize important constituents who may decide to turn against them. Hence, there is nothing automatically self-perpetuating or stabilizing about ruling parties. Regime decay and collapse can owe as much to internal developments as it can be the result of external processes or a combination of both—though internecine factors are more difficult to observe.

At the most basic level, contentious actors can be differentiated according to whether they operate in the elite or amongst the mid-level and grassroots ranks. If a ruling party acts as a constraint in that it controls the power of the leader, it is elite figures who yield most influence, and they may oust an incumbent who does not serve their interests, especially if he has lost support amongst wider party ranks. Because of the persistent threats of elite coups, leaders have an interest in personalizing their power; that is, they want to rule unchecked. Personalist dictators—such as Ben Ali was beginning to be in the 1990s—have sidelined any veto players in the elite and place senior officials under close scrutiny, which makes it challenging for any dissenters at the party's upper echelons to move against their leader.

However, mid-level and grassroots followers typically still enjoy some freedom of action in personalist regimes. And it is at these levels that followers may stage a revolt from within the regime if an incumbent's authority and legitimacy have come under threat. This is especially the case once the grievances they harbour multiply and begin overlapping with no prospect that matters will improve on their own. However, initially followers' contention is mostly inconspicuous, and it does not necessarily lead to the changes they seek as incumbents respond with severe repression and authoritarian reinforcement. But internal dissent does make the event of regime breakdown more likely, specifically during moments of wider political crisis: it exposes a leader as a

---

[13] Interview with Naziha Zarrouk, a previous ambassador to Lebanon and RCD Vice-Secretary General, Tunis, 30 January 2017.

straw man who has lost the support amongst wider regime ranks. This incites other actors to mobilize against the regime, not only invigorating the political opposition but, importantly, also unsettling the incumbent's traditional supporters, who fear being trapped on a sinking ship. This is what happened in Tunisia on 14 January 2011 when Mohamed Ghannouchi—one of Ben Ali's longtime loyalists—took over power.

Methodological considerations

This study is part of a wider attempt undertaken by a new generation of scholars in area studies to draw upon their in-depth country or regional expertise 'to elucidate features of a larger class of similar phenomena'.[14] I operate from the premise that this can best be done by recognizing—indeed, highlighting—the specificity of one's case and all of its breadth—that is, by reporting and analysing trends that are generalizable and those that are not. As a matter of fact, it is typically not immediately apparent which features are case-specific and which ones have wider relevance. This means that the book aims to elucidate phenomena at two levels: (1) those of the Ben Ali regime and the RCD and (2) those of dictatorships and ruling parties more generally. Each chapter starts with a theoretical or empirical puzzle, which I subsequently seek to answer through a narrative-guided approach of 'process tracing'. This qualitative research method draws 'descriptive and causal inferences from diagnostic pieces of evidence', typically involving a close examination of specific events and situations and how they unfold over time.[15] Respect for historical detail and accuracy is paramount in a meticulous technique that uncovers novel empirical phenomena, the specific mechanisms that underlie them, and how they relate to existing causal claims, generating new theoretical insights.[16]

This book draws on a wealth of qualitative interviews carried out across the eighteen months I spent in Tunisia between 2014 and 2018. The interviewees included eight groups: (1) 112 RCD officials and activists of various ranks and positions, including 6 out of its 8 former Secretaries General and all of its three vice-presidents,[17] many of whom I interviewed several times;

---

[14] John Gerring, 'What Is a Case Study and What Is It Good For?', *American Political Science Review*, 2004, 98, 2, p. 341.

[15] David Collier, 'Understanding Process Tracing', *Political Science and Politics*, 2011, 44, 4, p. 824.

[16] John Gerring, 'What Is a Case Study and What Is It Good For?', *American Political Science Review*, 2004, 98, 2, p. 346.

[17] Abdelaziz Ben Dhia, RCD Secretary General between 1996 and 1999, passed away in 2015; Hedi Mhenni, Secretary General between 2005 and 2008, was unavailable for an interview due to health issues.

(2) 18 high-level diplomats and ministers who were not formally members of the ruling party; (3) 6 close relatives of Ben Ali; (4) 7 key actors during the 2010–2011 uprising, including Mohamed Ghannouchi and Ben Ali's personal pilot, who flew him to Saudi Arabia on 14 January 2011; (5) 13 representatives of groups and associations that were closely linked to the RCD, such as the employers' federation and the public administration; (6) 35 opposition activists in politics and civil society, including bloggers, labour union activists, and representatives of the key opposition parties; (7) 19 demonstrators in the 2010–2011 uprising who were otherwise not politically active; and (8) 6 journalists, experts, and scholars of Tunisian politics. Unless they were prominent public officials, I use pseudonyms to safeguard interviewees' anonymity.

Materials gathered in the National Archives in Tunis supplement this interview data, as do documents from the private households of previous RCD activists who agreed to share their material with me. These include official RCD pamphlets, internal party statutes, and electoral campaign material, alongside books and conference material published by the party's ideological education wing. I also accessed regime mouthpieces, most importantly the official RCD daily *Le Renouveau* and the local daily *La Presse*, which authorities also controlled. These sources are particularly useful in reconstructing the evolution of official regime discourse and yield a deeper understanding of key political players, events, and decisions at the time. Moreover, *Le Renouveau* reported in much depth on formal RCD events, party congresses, and the general elections, and this coverage is instrumental in tracing change within the party of a more evolutionary nature, such as the ways in which alliances were constantly redrawn and formalized or when and how new leaders and rules emerged.

To balance the weight of this official regime propaganda, I draw also on dissident magazines and sources found today in 'expanded archives', in particular in cyberspace. Under Ben Ali, social media outlets, including Facebook, Twitter, and YouTube, were important channels through which opponents expressed their discontent. Human rights reports on Tunisia were also published online, and WikiLeaks yielded cables from the US embassy in Tunis that proved informative. My first monograph, on Ben Ali's main political opposition, the Islamist Ennahda party, also provides valuable background.[18] I triangulated these materials in this book to reconstruct specific events and processes and the causal mechanisms underlying them.

---

[18] See, for details, Anne Wolf, *Political Islam in Tunisia: The History of Ennahda*, New York: Oxford University Press, 2017.

Outline of chapters

Chapter 1 sets out the theory applied throughout this book. I argue that the politics of ideas is central to scrutinizing the durability of dictatorships with ruling parties, challenging studies that focus primarily on incumbents' use or threat of force. I hold that the root of dictatorial stability is internal: incumbents always seek to accumulate greater power, but in this process they risk losing the support of their constituency. To counter this threat, dictators have two ideational strategies at their disposal: (1) correctivism and (2) the creation of new normative priorities. Both involve the promotion of innovations, ostensibly for the good of the party or a larger objective but through which incumbents in fact seek to fortify their own rule. For these strategies to succeed, the proposed changes need to resonate with party followers and appear desirable and credible. If this is not the case and followers consider the incumbent's power reinforcement to be unjust and illegitimate, they may rebel against him. Any internecine contention lays the ground for wider political instability and possibly even regime collapse.

Chapter 2 uncovers how in the Tunisian case Ben Ali managed—within just two years of assuming power in 1987—to establish personal control of the RCD, even though he lacked a background in the party. From a theoretical point of view, Ben Ali's quick consolidation of power presents a puzzle: prevailing theories predict that, when a new leader has to bargain with a pre-existing ruling party, the advent of personal autocracy is unlikely. I solve this puzzle by demonstrating how Ben Ali bolstered his power base by propagating a correctivist ideology, a key feature of which was the promise of a political opening, including inside the ruling party. Amongst other strategies, he launched an 'internal critique' within the party: ostensibly aimed at addressing past wrongs, this in fact served Ben Ali's interests by facilitating wider regime transformations. Crucially, it allowed him to alter the RCD's internal rules and procedures, including those pertaining to the election of the president, a process through which he established executive control.

In Chapter 3, I investigate how, in the 1990s, Ben Ali managed to enforce authoritarian stability and even attract substantial domestic and Western support despite halting his political opening and establishing personal rule. I demonstrate that Ben Ali propped up his power base by constructing new normative priorities—in particular, national security and economic growth—as opposed to democratic politics. As part of this strategy, officials used state- and party-controlled media outlets, amongst other channels, to propagate the impression that Tunisia faced a large-scale domestic terrorist threat; though fabricated, this notion was internalized by wide sections of the population, including many RCD activists. Importantly, these new security prerogatives allowed Ben Ali to bolster his power: he promoted the rise of 'Lumpen activists' within the party grassroots, a constituency notorious for monitoring and coercing dissidents. Ben Ali also transferred resources from the party to the Presidential Palace, further reinforcing his grip on the RCD.

Chapter 4 sheds light on why, in the 2000s, Ben Ali's support base began to crumble, including amongst RCD ranks, even though he propagated the same economic and security prerogatives and even launched a tentative political opening. I demonstrate how these policy priorities exhausted themselves, in that people—including many RCD activists—no longer perceived them as credible. The regime had defeated the main Islamist party, the supposed terrorist threat; in addition, the President and his relatives were openly accumulating vast wealth at the expense of ordinary people, including RCD followers, many of whom were struggling to make ends meet. To add insult to injury, Ben Ali began to groom a presidential successor from his own family, further weakening the ruling party. It is for these reasons that a growing number of RCD activists came to question the legitimacy of Ben Ali's rule. Some even engaged in contentious activity against the regime, though at first this was mostly inconspicuous.

I show in Chapter 5 that during the 2010–2011 Tunisian uprising, internecine contention erupted publicly, becoming a key factor behind the regime's collapse. Instead of organizing rallies in support of Ben Ali, party activists turned into agents of contention: some joined the mass protests, especially at the grassroots level, whereas others decided to pursue passive forms of resistance. Most RCD followers sought political reforms, in particular calling on Ben Ali to strengthen the party and desist from nepotism; they did not seek the total overhaul of the regime, let alone the dissolution of their own party, though some later came to adopt such an agenda. However, their contentious actions exposed Ben Ali's vulnerability, and the overall contingency of the moment prompted a small clique of regime officials to move against the President. Indeed, in contrast to the widely accepted narrative that Ben Ali fled the mass protests, I provide evidence that he was, in fact, ousted in a secret coup d'état.

The conclusion revisits the main theoretical and empirical findings of the book and places them in comparative context. In particular, I show how a range of dictators other than Ben Ali have advanced correctivist strategies to consolidate their power, including Syria's Hafez al-Assad and China's Xi Jinping. I further illustrate how personalist leaders elsewhere have propagated new normative priorities to fortify their rule, at times successfully, but also discussing when and why these attempts at authoritarian regeneration failed or exhausted themselves and with what effects. Indeed, other ruling parties have incubated internal dissent, including in Egypt, Yemen, and Syria during the Arab Uprisings, as well as beyond the region, trends that sometimes contributed to the collapse of authoritarian regimes.

1

The Dictator's Party

A Theory of Power and Contention

Why would some members of Ben Ali's ruling party participate in protests against his regime and, in some instances, even go so far as to call for his downfall and the dissolution of the RCD—their own party? This riddle prompted me to scrutinize the internal workings of the Ben Ali regime and the RCD. It also led me to investigate more generally the factors influencing the relationship between a dictator and a ruling party and the effects on authoritarian stability and collapse. As the introduction has shown, RCD followers protested for a variety of reasons: some demanded internal party reforms or socioeconomic benefits, whilst others sought the fall of the regime. Their revolt illustrates that ruling parties are not necessarily self-perpetuating and stabilizing for authoritarian regimes. Leading scholars, indeed, maintain that ruling parties in authoritarian regimes are 'historically sticky and politically stabilizing'.[1] I suggest that the roots of both authoritarian stability and collapse are *internal* to these regimes and their ruling parties, though internecine factors are more difficult to discern. This chapter draws up a theory for fathoming how leaders seek to fortify their rule and identifying when, why, and how party activists engage in contentious actions against them and with what effects.

I propose that two key variables determine the balance of power between party followers and their incumbent: first, the internal opportunity structure—that is, the extent to which party representatives hold sway over their leader. Party officials may entirely control their incumbent, or they may share power with him on an equal footing; however, a party leader may also escape any accountability, which makes it more challenging to move against him. Second, the incumbent's success at mobilizing internal party support—that is, the extent to which he succeeds in generating legitimacy beliefs amongst followers. I uncover two ideational strategies through which incumbents seek to prop up their power: first, the propagation of a correctivist ideology, and

---

[1] Dan Slater, 'Institutional Complexity and Autocratic Agency in Indonesia', in James Mahoney and Kathleen Thelen (eds.), *Explaining Institutional Change: Ambiguity, Agency, and Power*, Cambridge: Cambridge University Press, 2010, p. 137.

Ben Ali's Tunisia. Anne Wolf, Oxford University Press. © Anne Wolf (2023).
DOI: 10.1093/oso/9780192868503.003.0002

second, the creation of new normative priorities. Both involve the mobilization of ideology—not only or necessarily out of conviction but also, crucially, to redistribute power to their personal advantage and foster regime stability.

Different ideational strategies favour the rise of certain party coalitions and actors over others. Notably, such internal reshuffles always occur, even during generally stable times; indeed, a certain amount of party personnel change is even necessary to pre-empt regime stagnation or decay. However, I propose that marginalized sections of the ruling party may turn into important internal challengers if an incumbent's legitimacy and authority have come under threat. If the party limits the power of the incumbent, elite actors enjoy the most leverage and constitute the key contenders; however, many incumbents eventually become personalist rulers and place them under close scrutiny. In this scenario, the central contentious actors are mid-level and grassroots followers, who often still enjoy some autonomy. Actors like these may decide to revolt against an incumbent if their grievances are left to mount and they believe matters will only get worse. Their dissent makes regime collapse more likely: internecine contention lays bare that the dictator has lost the support of his own constituency. This prompts others—including longtime loyalists seeking to save their own skin—to turn against him.

Who wants the fall of the regime?

Al-sha'b yurid isqat al-nizam! Or: *The people want the fall of the regime!* This slogan, the most famous of the Arab Uprisings, was chanted first in Tunisia, and resounded along Avenue Bourguiba on 14 January, the day the Ben Ali regime fell. These popular revolts inspired an entire generation of new scholarship on Tunisia, which focused on 'people power' and protest dynamics to explain the ousting of Ben Ali and the subsequent dissolution of the RCD.[2] Similar frames have been used to better understand the trajectories of other

---

[2] Key works include Laryssa Chomiak, 'The Making of a Revolution in Tunisia', *Middle East Law and Governance*, 2011, 3, pp. 68–83; Peter J. Schraeder and Hamadi Redissi, 'Ben Ali's Fall', *Journal of Democracy*, 2011, 22, 3, pp. 5–19; Olivier Piot, *La Révolution Tunisienne: Dix Jours qui Ébranlèrent le Monde Arabe*, Paris: Petits Matins, 2011; Ridha Zouaoui, *al-Thawra al-Tunisiyya, Thawrat al-Hamish 'ala al-Markaz* [*The Tunisian Revolution: The Power of the Marginalized*], 'Ala' al-Din: Sfax, 2012; Nouri Gana (ed.), *The Making of the Tunisian Revolution: Contexts, Architects, Prospects*, Edinburgh: Edinburgh University Press, 2013; Alcinde Honwana, *Youth and Revolution in Tunisia*, London: Zed Books, 2013; Salem Labiadh, *Tunis: al-Thawra fi Zaman al-Haymana* [*Tunisia: The Revolution during Times of Domination*], Tunis: Mu'assasat al-Hasad, 2013; Amira Aleya-Sghaier, 'The Tunisian Revolution: The Revolution of Dignity', in Ricardo Larémont (ed.), *Revolution, Revolt and Reform in North Africa: The Arab Spring and Beyond*, Abingdon: Routledge, 2014, pp. 30–52.

countries during the Arab Uprisings.[3] Through such lenses, the protesters in Tunisia were considered agents of change *external* to the Ben Ali regime, engaging in contentious activities from outside the system. United in their quest for freedom, dignity, and jobs, they exposed the vulnerability of one of the world's most repressive dictatorships. The literature on the Arab Uprisings has shed important light on many key dimensions of the protest movement, such as its rural origins, demands, and dynamics of diffusion.[4] However, it did little to help me solve the riddle of my own research: that is, why a sizable number of figures from within Ben Ali's own ruling party—not simply card-carrying adherents and party opportunists, but members who strongly identified with the RCD—decided to participate in demonstrations that led to the regime's collapse.

I next consulted the literature on ruling parties in authoritarian regimes, but it quickly became apparent that this too proved of limited use in investigating my puzzle. One of its main premises is that nominally democratic institutions in dictatorships[5] contribute to the longevity of regimes.[6] Ruling parties—be they single or dominant parties—are considered particularly conducive to authoritarian stability,[7] and leading scholars affirm that they possess

---

[3] See, for example, Charles Tripp, *The Power and the People: Paths of Resistance in the Middle East*, Cambridge: Cambridge University Press, 2013; Jason Brownlee, Tarek Masoud, and Andrew Reynolds, *The Arab Spring: Pathways of Repression and Reform*, Oxford: Oxford University Press, 2015; Adam Roberts, Michael J. Willis, Rory McCarthy, and Timothy Garton Ash (eds.), *Civil Resistance in the Arab Spring: Triumphs and Disasters*, Oxford: Oxford University Press, 2016.

[4] In addition to the works cited above, see Henry E. Hale, 'Regime Change Cascades: What We Have Learned from the 1848 Revolutions to the 2011 Arab Uprisings', *Annual Review of Political Science*, 2013, 16, pp. 331–353; Lahmar Mouldi (ed.), *al-Thawra al-Tunisiyya* [*The Tunisian Revolution*], Doha: Arab Center for Research and Policy Studies, 2014; Mark Beissinger, Amaney Jamal, and Kevin Mazur, 'Explaining Divergent Revolutionary Coalitions: Regime Strategies and the Structuring of Participation in the Tunisian and Egyptian Revolutions', *Comparative Politics*, 2015, 48, 1, pp. 1–21; Zachary C. Steinert-Threlkeld, 'Spontaneous Collective Action: Peripheral Mobilization during the Arab Spring', *American Political Science Review*, 2017, 111, 2, pp. 379–403; Christopher Barrie, 'The Process of Revolutionary Protest: Development and Democracy in the Tunisian Revolution of 2010–2011', Working Paper, 28 August 2018, https://osf.io/preprints/socarxiv/eu5b4/, last accessed 10 August 2022.

[5] Note that I use the terms 'dictatorship' and 'authoritarian regime' interchangeably. I refer to the heads of these regimes as 'incumbent', 'dictator', or 'leader', irrespective of their official title.

[6] Milan W. Svolik, The Politics of Authoritarian Rule, Cambridge: Cambridge University Press, 2012, p. 192. Others have made similar claims. See, for example, Barbara Geddes, 'What Do We Know about Democratization after Twenty Years?', Annual Review of Political Science, 1999, 2, pp. 115–144; Beatriz Magaloni, Voting for Autocracy: Hegemonic Party Survival and Its Demise in Mexico, New York: Cambridge University Press, 2006; Jason Brownlee, Authoritarianism in an Age of Democratization, New York: Cambridge University Press, 2007; Jennifer Gandhi and Adam Przeworski, 'Authoritarian Institutions and the Survival of Autocrats', Comparative Political Studies, 2007, 40, 11, pp. 1279–1301; Jennifer Gandhi, Political Institutions under Dictatorship, Cambridge: Cambridge University Press, 2010.

[7] Barbara Geddes, 'What Do We Know about Democratization after Twenty Years?', *Annual Review of Political Science*, 1999, 2, pp. 115–144; Beatriz Magaloni, *Voting for Autocracy: Hegemonic Party Survival and Its Demise in Mexico*, New York: Cambridge University Press, 2006; Jason Brownlee, *Authoritarianism in an Age of Democratization*, New York: Cambridge University Press, 2007; Jennifer

positive-feedback mechanisms that strengthen regimes over time. Amongst the key functions scholars outline is that ruling parties provide a set of rules to ensure the incumbent cannot amass too much power on his own. Instead of serving primarily the interest of the leader, ruling parties allow a range of elite actors to access lucrative political and economic resources.[8] Similarly, the party's lower echelons provide 'increasing returns to power':[9] officials distribute lucrative perks and privileges to local activists, the value of which increases as followers climb up the party hierarchy, hence creating a long-term interest amongst the grass roots in regime survival.[10] More generally speaking, the authoritarian politics literature has stressed that ruling parties provide a forum for internal regime bargaining, co-optation, and even criticism, as long as it does not touch upon the foundations of political power.[11] Yet with its focus on the usefulness of ruling parties for dictatorships, this literature provides few clues as to why and when a ruling party ceases to be a force for authoritarian stability and instead turns into an arena for opposition and contention—at least amongst some party sections—as was the case in Tunisia.

In a similar vein, before the Arab Uprisings, many scholars of Middle East politics were concerned with how various regime actors fostered what appeared to be particularly durable dictatorships in the region. They highlighted the strength of the military, security services, and ruling parties to

Gandhi and Adam Przeworski, 'Authoritarian Institutions and the Survival of Autocrats', *Comparative Political Studies*, 2007, 40, 11, pp. 1279–1301; Jennifer Gandhi, *Political Institutions under Dictatorship*, Cambridge: Cambridge University Press, 2010; Milan W. Svolik, *The Politics of Authoritarian Rule*, Cambridge: Cambridge University Press, 2012.

[8] Beatriz Magaloni, *Voting for Autocracy: Hegemonic Party Survival and Its Demise in Mexico*, New York: Cambridge University Press, 2006; Scott G. Gehlbach and Philip Keefer, 'Investment without Democracy: Ruling-Party Institutionalization and Credible Commitment in Autocracies', unpublished manuscript, University of Wisconsin, Madison, 2008; Milan W. Svolik, *The Politics of Authoritarian Rule*, Cambridge: Cambridge University Press, 2012; Carles Boix and Milan Svolik, 'The Foundations of Limited Authoritarian Government: Institutions, Commitment, and Power-Sharing in Dictatorships', *Journal of Politics*, 2013, 75, 2, pp. 300–316; Barbara Geddes, Joseph Wright, and Erica Frantz, *How Dictatorships Work*, Cambridge: Cambridge University Press, 2018.

[9] James Mahoney and Kathleen Thelen, 'A Theory of Gradual Institutional Change', in James Mahoney and Kathleen Thelen (eds.), *Explaining Institutional Change: Ambiguity, Agency, and Power*, Cambridge: Cambridge University Press, 2010, p. 7.

[10] See, for example, Milan W. Svolik, *The Politics of Authoritarian Rule*, Cambridge: Cambridge University Press, 2012, pp. 163–164; Barbara Geddes, Joseph Wright, and Erica Frantz, *How Dictatorships Work*, Cambridge: Cambridge University Press, 2018, p. 135.

[11] In addition to the literature cited above, see also Beatriz Magaloni, 'Credible Power-Sharing and the Longevity of Authoritarian Rule', *Comparative Political Studies*, 2008, 41, 4/5, pp. 715–741; Dan Slater, *Ordering Power: Contentious Politics and Authoritarian Leviathan in Southeast Asia*, New York: Cambridge University Press, 2010; Ellen Lust-Okar, 'Elections under Authoritarianism: Preliminary Lessons from Jordan', *Democratization*, 2006, 13, 3, pp. 456–471.

explain how leaders throughout the Arab world had successfully stifled any attempts at democratization.[12] The focus on such formal institutions was particularly pronounced in studies of the Arab republics, where incumbents lacked the kind of religious legitimacy claimed by the region's monarchies.[13] In addition, in the 2000s, a literature emerged that investigated how leaders in the Arab world pursued strategies of 'authoritarian upgrading', that is, how they promoted various economic and political reforms, ostensibly to liberalize their countries but through which they ultimately strengthened their own rule.[14] This body of research is pertinent in so far as it highlights the dynamic and adaptive nature of authoritarian regimes—a key concern of this book. However, it has stopped short of explaining why incumbents choose certain reform paths over others, why some innovations are successful and others fail, and why some that are initially successful may exhaust themselves over time— possibly even destabilizing the regime and fostering internal dissent. This book addresses these issues and more.

Scholars' long preoccupation with regime stability in the Arab world explains the relative novelty of their concern with wider social and cultural dynamics and what has become commonly known as 'people power': many experts on the region embarked upon a self-critique following the Arab Uprisings to better understand why they had failed to see its revolutionary potential.[15] A main conclusion was that they had been so concerned with the

[12] Important works include Eva Bellin, 'The Robustness of Authoritarianism in the Middle East: Exceptionalism in Comparative Perspective', *Comparative Politics*, 2004, 36, 2, pp. 139–157; Steven A. Cook, *Ruling But Not Governing: The Military and Political Development in Egypt, Algeria and Turkey*, Baltimore, MD: Johns Hopkins University Press, 2007; Joseph Sassoon, *Saddam Hussein's Ba'th Party: Inside an Authoritarian Regime*, Cambridge: Cambridge University Press, 2012; Michael Willis, *Politics and Power in the Maghreb: Algeria, Tunisia and Morocco from Independence to the Arab Spring*, London: Hurst Publishing, 2012.

[13] There are, of course, notable exceptions. They include Béatrice Hibou, *The Force of Obedience: The Political Economy of Repression in Tunisia*, Cambridge: Polity, 2011. For an important recent work on the Arab republics, see Joseph Sassoon, *Anatomy of Authoritarianism in the Arab Republics*, Cambridge: Cambridge University Press, 2016.

[14] Key works include Daniel Brumberg, 'Liberalization versus Democracy—Understanding Arab Political Reform', Carnegie Papers—Middle East Series No. 37, 2003; Holger Albrecht and Oliver Schlumberger, '"Waiting for Godot": Regime Change without Democratization in the Middle East', *International Political Science Review*, 2004, 25, 4, pp. 371–392; Ellen Lust-Okar, 'Elections under Authoritarianism: Preliminary Lessons from Jordan', *Democratization*, 2006, 13, 3, pp. 456–471; Steven Heydemann, 'Upgrading Authoritarianism in the Arab World', Brookings Institution Saban Center Analysis Paper No. 13, October 2007; Oliver Schlumberger, *Debating Arab Authoritarianism: Dynamics and Durability in Nondemocratic Regimes*, Stanford, CA: Stanford University Press, 2007; Christopher Alexander, *Stability and Reform in the Modern Maghreb*, London: Routledge, 2010; Morten Valbjørn and André Bank, 'Examining the "Post" in Post-Democratization: The Future of Middle Eastern Political Rule through Lenses of the Past', *Middle East Critique*, 2010, 19, 3, pp. 183–200.

[15] Morten Valbjørn, 'Reflections on Self-Reflections: On Framing the Analytical Implications of the Arab Uprisings for the Study of Arab Politics', *Democratization*, 2015, 22, 2, pp. 218–238; Gregory Gause, 'Why Middle East Studies Missed the Arab Spring', *Foreign Affairs*, July/August 2011, pp. 81–90.

apparent longevity of regimes that they had neglected deeper, micro-level changes on the ground. Ever since, Middle East politics has witnessed a real 'Academic Spring', as scholars have explored entirely new research territories and investigated previously understudied topics. But with their focus on 'the people', they have paid little attention to the causal role that regime actors themselves play in the breakdown of dictatorships. In particular, they have ignored the pressing questions of how and why diverse regime actors responded to—and, in some cases, supported and reinforced—the protest movement. Such focus is key for not only constructing a more accurate picture of the reasons behind the Arab Uprisings but also better understanding trends of authoritarian resurgence in its aftermath. Indeed, regime figures were part of the political change that happened, an insight that helps us understand why many subsequently made a comeback.

Those scholars who decided to bring the regime 'back in' have typically emphasized the role of the military during the Arab Uprisings, arguing that in some countries, the army's 'defection' to the revolutionaries contributed to the breakdown of dictatorships.[16] Such a scenario indeed applies to Egypt, but it has also been used to explain the Tunisian case,[17] though the army there played a very limited role during the revolution itself; it did, however, emerge as a stabilizing force in the immediate aftermath of Ben Ali's ousting. The spread of the narrative that 'the military refused to fire on the protesters and instead defected from the Ben Ali regime'[18]—false as it is[19]—seems to stem principally from a dearth of primary research and cross-checking of what is assumed to

[16] For example, Holger Albrecht, Aurel Croissant, and Fred Lawson, *Armies and Insurgencies in the Arab Spring*, Philadelphia: University of Pennsylvania Press, 2016.

[17] A range of scholars have wrongly asserted that the Tunisian military played a key role in the uprising. They include but are not limited to Gregory Gause, 'Why Middle East Studies Missed the Arab Spring', *Foreign Affairs*, July/August 2011, 90, 4, p. 84; Milan W. Svolik, *The Politics of Authoritarian Rule*, Cambridge: Cambridge University Press, 2012, p. 199; Amin Allal, '"Revolutionary" Trajectories in Tunisia: Processes of Political Radicalisation, 2007–2011', *Revue Française de Science Politique*, 2012, 62, 5, p. 57; Henry E. Hale, 'Regime Change Cascades: What We Have Learned from the 1848 Revolutions to the 2011 Arab Uprisings', *Annual Review of Political Science*, 2013, 16, p. 346; Jason Brownlee, Tarek E. Masoud, and Andrew Reynolds, *The Arab Spring: Pathways of Repression and Reform*, Oxford: Oxford University Press, 2015, p. 38; Sean Burns, *Revolts and the Military in the Arab Spring: Popular Uprisings and the Politics of Repression*, London: I.B. Tauris, 2018.

[18] Risa Brooks, 'Abandoned at the Palace: Why the Tunisian Military Defected from the Ben Ali Regime in January 2011', *Journal of Strategic Studies*, 2012, 36, 2, p. 207.

[19] On 25 January 2011, General Rachid Ammar—the chief of the army at the time of the uprising—was questioned by the Tunis Court of First Instance about his role during the uprising. Throughout the hearing, General Ammar asserted that he never disobeyed Ben Ali. To emphasize the extent to which the army had 'proven its loyalty to the Republican order', he even referenced previous instances during which the military had crushed protests, sometimes violently, including in al-Radeef in 2008. There is no reason to believe that General Ammar was lying about the army's support of Ben Ali—the testimony was delivered at a time that democratic forces in Tunisia held the upper hand and it was highly controversial to admit having stood with Ben Ali until the end. The testimony is also backed by other sources, including recorded phone conversations between Ammar and Ben Ali, with no evidence

be 'established' knowledge.[20] It is also symptomatic of a more general lack of in-depth studies of the factors internal to the Ben Ali regime that contributed to its sudden demise in 2011. This book seeks to address this gap, to offer a new perspective on one of the most important revolutionary movements in recent history. In particular, I scrutinize why a key component of the Ben Ali regime, the RCD—which, in theory, should have provided incentives to its members to perpetuate and defend the system—failed to do so amongst key constituencies and what impact this had on the regime's collapse.

The conflictual potential of ruling parties

Investigating the role that the RCD played in the demise of the Ben Ali regime forced me to enter new academic territory and cross disciplinary boundaries but also to move beyond the available literature. The following sections introduce the end product of this investigation: *a theory of power and contention within ruling parties in dictatorships*. It delineates how incumbents seek to fortify their rule and foster party-political stability, as well as when, why, and how party followers may pursue internal contention and with what effect. The theory draws upon diverse sets of work, including in-depth case studies of ruling parties and related publications on the internal working of authoritarian regimes.[21] These writings—often empirically focused—proved instrumental to illuminate trends I had found on the ground in Tunisia and to locate them within a wider context. Amongst the pioneering works on parties and

---

to the contrary (source: Emir Nader, 'Secret Audio Sheds Light on Toppled Dictator's Frantic Last Hours', *BBC*, https://www.bbc.co.uk/news/world-africa-59972545, last accessed 15 August 2022).

[20] A key reason for the misunderstanding is that the Tunisian police—and not the army—took a key role in the repression of protests; scholars who assert that the military sided with the protests do not provide any evidence to back their account. Note that when General Rachid Ammar was questioned in court on whether he refused to open fire against the demonstrations, he clarified: 'This is a false story and . . . I never received an order to open fire against the demonstrators' (source: author transcript of the court hearing of Rachid Ammar, record number 11-3-55, dated 25 January 2011).

[21] Key works include Simon Leys, *The Chairman's New Clothes: Mao and the Cultural Revolution*, London: Allison & Busby, 1977; Valerie Bunce, *Subversive Institutions: The Design and the Destruction of Socialism and the State*, Cambridge: Cambridge University Press, 1999; Vladimir Tismaneanu, *Stalinism for All Seasons: A Political History of Romanian Communism*, Berkeley: University of California Press, 2003; Charles Kurzman, *The Unthinkable Revolution in Iran*, Cambridge, MA: Harvard University Press, 2009; André Laliberte and Marc Lanteigne (eds.), *The Chinese Party-State in the 21st Century*, London: Routledge, 2011; Joseph Sassoon, *Saddam Hussein's Baath Party: Inside an Authoritarian Regime*, Cambridge: Cambridge University Press, 2012; Mary Elise Sarotte, *The Collapse: The Accidental Opening of the Berlin Wall*, New York: Basic Books, 2014; Sabine Pannen, *Wo ein Genosse ist, da ist die Partei! Der Innere Zerfall der SED-Parteibasis, 1979–1989*, Berlin: Christoph Links, 2018; Daniel Stotland, *Purity and Compromise in the Soviet Party-State: The Struggle for the Soul of the Party, 1941–1952*, London: Lexington Books, 2018.

dictatorships more generally,[22] there are many historic studies that still provide important insights into issues of prime concern to this book, including the role of internal power dynamics in the evolution of authoritarian regimes.[23] In addition, works on 'authoritarian upgrading' in the Arab world offered important leads on incumbents' reform strategies in the 2000s, though they fail to explain why some failed or exhausted themselves.[24] Some post–Arab Uprisings studies of political parties in the Middle East and North Africa are also instructive, but these tend to focus on new actors and do not scrutinize ruling parties in authoritarian contexts in depth.[25] Importantly, a new wave of research within the discipline of historic institutionalism, which focuses on inner institutional change, proved critical to my examination of the Ben Ali regime.[26] Similarly, a number of recent studies in the field of sociology—scrutinizing the internal crumbling of political institutions during periods of heightened contingency—were indispensable.[27] Over the past years, these works—and many more—pushed me to deepen and continuously refine my own analysis

[22] In addition to the literature cited earlier, see also Peter Mair, *Party System Change: Approaches and Interpretations*, Oxford: Oxford University Press, 1997; Stathis N. Kalyvas, 'The Decay and Breakdown of Communist One-Party Systems', *Annual Review of Political Science*, 1999, 2, pp. 323–343; Oliver Schlumberger, *Debating Arab Authoritarianism: Dynamics and Durability in Non-democratic Regimes*, Stanford, CA: Stanford University Press, 2007; Steven Levitsky and Lucan A. Way, *Competitive Authoritarianism: Hybrid Regimes after the Cold War*, Cambridge: Cambridge University Press, 2010; Roger Owen, *The Rise and Fall of Arab Presidents for Life*, Cambridge, MA: Harvard University Press, 2012; Francesco Cavatorta and Lise Storm, *Political Parties in the Arab World: Continuity and Change*, Edinburgh: Edinburgh University Press, 2019.

[23] See, for example, Joseph La Palombara and Myron Weiner (eds.), *Political Parties and Political Development*, Princeton, NJ: Princeton University Press, 1966; Samuel Huntington and Clement H. Moore (eds.), *Authoritarian Politics and Modern Society*, London: Basic Books, 1970; Giovanni Sartori, *Parties and Party Systems: A Framework for Analysis*, Cambridge: Cambridge University Press, 1976; Angelo Panebianco, *Political Parties: Organization and Power*, Cambridge: Cambridge University Press, 1988; Guillermo O'Donnell, *Bureaucratic Authoritarianism: Argentina, 1966–1973, in Comparative Perspective*, Berkeley: University of California Press, 1988; Peter Meyns and Dani Wadada Nabudere (eds.), *Democracy and the One-Party-State in Africa*, Hamburg: Institut für Afrika-Kunde, 1989.

[24] In addition to the works cited earlier, see Robert Springborg, *Mubarak's Egypt: Fragmentation of the Political Order*, Abingdon: Routledge, 2018; Joshua Stacher, *Adaptable Autocrats: Regime Power in Egypt and Syria*, Stanford, CA: Stanford University Press, 2012.

[25] Francesco Cavatorta and Lise Storm, *Political Parties in the Arab World: Continuity and Change*, Edinburgh: Edinburgh University Press, 2018; Francesco Cavatorta, Lise Storm, and Valeria Resta, *Routledge Handbook on Political Parties in the Middle East and North Africa*, Abingdon: Routledge, 2021; Siavush Randjbar-Daemi, Eskandar Sadeghi-Boroujerdi, and Lauren Banko, *Political Parties in the Middle East*, Abingdon: Routledge, 2021.

[26] Key works include John L. Campbell, *Institutional Change and Globalization*, Princeton, NJ: Princeton University Press, 2004; James Mahoney and Kathleen Thelen (eds.), *Explaining Institutional Change: Ambiguity, Agency, and Power*, Cambridge: Cambridge University Press, 2010; James Mahoney and Kathleen Thelen (eds.), *Advances in Comparative-Historical Analysis*, Cambridge: Cambridge University Press, 2015; Giovanni Capoccia, 'When Do Institutions "Bite"? Historical Institutionalism and the Politics of Institutional Change', *Comparative Political Studies*, 2016, 49, 8, pp. 1095–1127.

[27] Ivan Ermakoff, *Ruling Oneself Out: A Theory of Collective Abdications*, Durham, NC: Duke University Press, 2008; Ivan Ermakoff, 'The Structure of Contingency', *American Journal of Sociology*, 2015, 121, 1, pp. 64–125.

of the Ben Ali regime and the RCD, and they provided the backdrop for the theory that follows.

One of the basic premises on which this book stands is that political parties are first and foremost 'distributional instruments laden with power implications.'[28] Indeed, a party's very creation typically reflects an attempt at redistributing resources in society and empowering certain kinds of actors over others—in both democratic and authoritarian contexts. As such, ruling parties[29] in authoritarian regimes mirror—and at the same time organize and reshape—wider power relations, both between regime insiders and outsiders and internally amongst various party followers. They are an integral part of the regime, which, however, entails many other political institutions[30]—such as the government, military, and presidency—and their relations are subject to constant flux, depending on the political priorities and power dynamics of the time, amongst other factors.

Party rules and procedures establish a hierarchy amongst members, for example, by allocating them to specific ranks and stipulating any remuneration and promotion policies. They organize the flow of resources, allowing some members to make large amounts of profit, sometimes on the backs of others. In comparative studies, these power asymmetries have sometimes been described in terms of 'winners' dominating 'losers' or 'rule-makers' controlling 'rule-takers'.[31] But in reality, of course, the dynamics within parties—or other political institutions, for that matter—are much more complex, and various ranks and coalitions—possibly of regional, ideological, ethnic, or religious origin—constantly compete for resources and influence. Indeed, followers always seek to renegotiate and challenge existing power relations to their advantage and to move up the party hierarchy. As such, political parties are fraught with conflict and contention. Internecine strife and struggles give rise to processes of constant change within parties, sometimes incrementally, at other times in transformative ways—though their nature is largely a

---

[28] James Mahoney and Kathleen Thelen, 'A Theory of Gradual Institutional Change', in James Mahoney and Kathleen Thelen (eds.), *Explaining Institutional Change: Ambiguity, Agency, and Power*, Cambridge: Cambridge University Press, 2010, p. 8.

[29] I use the term 'ruling parties' as a broad category encompassing both dominant and hegemonic parties in authoritarian regimes.

[30] I employ the term 'political institutions' to refer to formal institutions such as political parties, legislatures, and the military. Throughout the book, I seek to distinguish between, on the one hand, formal institutions, including formal rules and structures, and, on the other, informal ones, chief amongst them norms and informal practices. Whilst these are sometimes bundled together, my focus is on investigating how formal and informal institutions relate and influence one another and with what effect on regime stability.

[31] For a more detailed discussion on this, see Giovanni Capoccia, 'When Do Institutions "Bite"? Historical Institutionalism and the Politics of Institutional Change', *Comparative Political Studies*, 2016, 49, 8, pp. 5–7.

matter of perspective. Indeed, the overall stability of a party can sometimes be achieved only through vast internal change: for example, the total overhaul of its leadership or ideological underpinnings.[32] This means that there is nothing self-perpetuating or self-reinforcing about ruling parties in dictatorships—far from it. Ruling party decay or collapse can owe as much to internal developments as it can to external processes or it can be due to a combination of both, though any internecine factors are more difficult to observe—especially in authoritarian contexts.

An important implication of ruling parties' dynamic and conflictual nature is that they 'do not necessarily dictate specific functions and render all other functions impossible', as has been noted in a related study.[33] Indeed, ruling parties perform a range of tasks—politically, economically, and socially. These include various seemingly minor day-to-day roles that are, however, crucial to many members and for understanding internal party dynamics, such as creating a sense of belonging and purpose amongst followers. Party membership can also be an entry card for joining a sports club or cultural association or a prerequisite to get a job in the public administration. The multiple roles that ruling parties play defy recent efforts in authoritarian politics to determine their 'primary function',[34] typically with respect to their supposed fostering of regime stability. Moreover, many of the tasks that scholars commonly identify that ruling parties do perform—such as facilitating power-sharing amongst key elites—are tied to lucrative resources and, as such, are inherently contested and subject to change. Whilst power-sharing adds value for some actors, it reduces it for followers who are excluded from these structures. Scholars need to account for this ambiguous and contradictory nature of party functions, as well as their continuous development over time.[35] Scrutinizing which tasks a party performs for specific actors or coalitions during which periods of time is as important as investigating those it fails to carry out and why—and they

---

[32] Notably, the Chinese Communist Party came to embrace economic liberalism after socialist policies had contributed to the weakening and eventual collapse of one-party states in other parts of the world. Joseph Stalin's liquidation of much of the Communist Party leadership during the Great Purge is another prominent though very distinct example of how vast internal party change can contribute to overall regime stability.

[33] Ato Kwamena Onoma, *The Politics of Property Rights Institutions in Africa*, Cambridge: Cambridge University Press, 2010, p. 52.

[34] Milan W. Svolik, *The Politics of Authoritarian Rule*, Cambridge: Cambridge University Press, 2012, p. 88; for comparative examples, see also Beatriz Magaloni, *Voting for Autocracy: Hegemonic Party Survival and Its Demise in Mexico*, New York: Cambridge University Press, 2006; Barbara Geddes, Joseph Wright, and Erica Frantz, *How Dictatorships Work*, Cambridge: Cambridge University Press, 2018.

[35] The contradictory nature of institutions has also been noted in Ato Kwamena Onoma, *The Politics of Property Rights Institutions in Africa*, Cambridge: Cambridge University Press, 2010.

are not always flip sides of the same coin—to understand trends of internecine change and contention.

From this perspective, moreover, much of the discussion about the relative 'strength' or 'weakness' of political institutions in dictatorships is beside the point. Indeed, some scholars have argued that ruling parties tend to be weak, for example, because they lack autonomy.[36] But it is notable that this very 'weakness' may in fact be a source of leadership strength as it may prop up an individual dictator or the party's ruling clique.[37] Some scholars have differentiated between the strength of a party's wider apparatus and that of its leadership to account for their possible variation and contradictory potential.[38] However, power dynamics are complex, especially in the context of large parties with various organizational levels, which often vary greatly in terms of their internal functioning and autonomy. Indeed, at the level of the grass roots, some ruling parties feature a surprisingly large degree of independence, even as higher echelons remain tightly controlled by the leadership.[39] Any study of internal party change and contention in dictatorships has to look out for such 'islands of autonomy', their role, and possible effects—within the party and society at large—during both generally stable times and moments of rapid political change.

Another related discussion on institutional weakness is highly relevant to this book. In particular, scholars have stressed the importance of informal rules and practices in dictatorships, alongside the often loose enforcement of

---

[36] See, for example, Anne Meng, 'Ruling Parties in Authoritarian Regimes: Rethinking Institutional Strength', *British Journal of Political Science*, 2019, doi:10.1017/S0007123419000115; for a more extensive discussion on the frequent weakness of state and party structures in authoritarian regimes, see Steven Levitsky and Lucan A. Way, *Competitive Authoritarianism: Hybrid Regimes after the Cold War*, Cambridge: Cambridge University Press, 2010.

[37] For comparative insights on how some incumbents may benefit from 'weak' party structures, see Vladimir Tismaneanu, 'Personal Power and Political Crisis in Romania', *Government and Opposition*, 1989, 24, 2, pp. 177–198; Immanuel Wallerstein, 'The Decline of the Party in Single-Party African States', in Joseph La Palombara and Myron Weiner (eds.), *Political Parties and Political Development*, Princeton, NJ: Princeton University Press, 1966, pp. 201–214.

[38] Steven Levitsky and Lucan A. Way differentiate between party 'scope'—the size of its infrastructure and extent to which it penetrates society—and 'cohesion'—the degree to which incumbents manage to ensure cooperation amongst party followers. See, for details, Steven Levitsky and Lucan A. Way, *Competitive Authoritarianism: Hybrid Regimes after the Cold War*, Cambridge: Cambridge University Press, 2010, pp. 64–65. In a related vein, Dan Slater distinguishes between a regime's 'infrastructural power'—its power to implement, such as through a highly institutionalized ruling party—and 'despotic power'—its power to decide. See, for more information, Dan Slater, 'Iron Cage in an Iron Fist: Authoritarian Institutions and the Personalization of Power in Malaysia', *Comparative Politics*, 2003, 36, 1, p. 82.

[39] Even the Chinese Communist Party has at times granted a certain degree of autonomy to the grass roots. See, for example, Richard Levy, 'Village Elections, Transparency, and Anticorruption: Henan and Guangdong Provinces', in Elizabeth J. Perry and Merle Goldman (eds.), *Grassroots Elections in China*, Cambridge, MA: Harvard University Press, 2007, pp. 20–47.

any formal stipulations.[40] Yet prevailing theories of institutional change are largely built around studies conducted in democratic settings, where rules are relatively stable and tend to be enforced[41]—though scattered efforts at extending them to authoritarian contexts do exist.[42] They focus on factors such as the degree of compliance with formal rules and the number of veto players to better understand processes of internal change—or their absence.[43] But such a frame is of limited use in authoritarian settings, where both the level of compliance and the number of veto players are low[44]—given the more unequal distribution of power and frequently scant accountability of incumbents, amongst other factors. To understand dynamics of change and contention in ruling parties in dictatorships, we need to look out for how formal and informal rules and practices organize internal affairs. In particular, I propose that we need to scrutinize how party leaders exercise power. Indeed, the party incumbents enjoy most leverage in applying and interpreting any formal rules—if they don't have so much sway, they can simply craft them themselves; likewise, any informal practices of domination at the leadership level greatly affect the inner life of the party. Focusing on incumbents' *power practices*—by which I mean the formal and informal ways through which they seek to defend and fortify their rule—also allows us to better understand how ruling parties themselves become the object of unrest and contention from within. Incumbents' power practices affect internal party change and contention, with the ultimate possibility that this may contribute to regime breakdown. I will elaborate in more detail below.

[40] See, for example, Guillermo O'Donnell, 'On the State, Democratization, and Some Conceptual Problems: A Latin American View with Some Postcommunist Countries', *World Development*, 1993, 21, 8, pp. 1355–1369; Steven Levitsky and Lucan A. Way, *Competitive Authoritarianism: Hybrid Regimes after the Cold War*, Cambridge: Cambridge University Press, 2010; Steven Levitsky and Maria Victoria Murillo, 'Lessons from Latin America: Building Institutions on Weak Foundations', *Journal of Democracy*, 2013, 24, 2, pp. 93–107; Steven Levitsky and Maria Victoria Murillo, 'Variations in Institutional Strength', *Annual Review of Political Science*, 2009, 12, pp. 115–133; Mehran Kamrava, *Fragile Politics: Weak States in the Greater Middle East*, London: Hurst Publishers, 2016.

[41] The most prominent works are James Mahoney and Kathleen Thelen (eds.), *Explaining Institutional Change: Ambiguity, Agency, and Power*, Cambridge: Cambridge University Press, 2010; James Mahoney and Kathleen Thelen (eds.), *Advances in Comparative-Historical Analysis*, Cambridge: Cambridge University Press, 2015.

[42] They include Dan Slater, 'Iron Cage in an Iron Fist: Authoritarian Institutions and the Personalization of Power in Malaysia', *Comparative Politics*, 2003, 36, 1, pp. 81–101; Steven Levitsky and Maria Victoria Murillo, 'Variations in Institutional Strength', *Annual Review of Political Science*, 2009, 12, pp. 115–133; Steven Levitsky and Maria Victoria Murillo, 'Lessons from Latin America: Building Institutions on Weak Foundations', *Journal of Democracy*, 24, 2, 2013, pp. 93–107; Daniel M. Brinks, Steven Levitsky, and Maria Victoria Murillo, *Understanding Institutional Weakness*, Cambridge: Cambridge University Press, 2019.

[43] James Mahoney and Kathleen Thelen (eds.), *Explaining Institutional Change: Ambiguity, Agency, and Power*, Cambridge: Cambridge University Press, 2010.

[44] Similar has been noted in Steven Levitsky and Maria Victoria Murillo, 'Lessons from Latin America: Building Institutions on Weak Foundations', *Journal of Democracy*, 2013, 24, 2, pp. 93–107.

The ideational dimensions of incumbent power

How can we fathom incumbents' 'power practices'? Who are the 'incumbents' under investigation, and what are their immediate and long-term goals? What strategies do they employ to achieve their objectives? And to what extent do specific characteristics of ruling parties allow these strategies to flourish or not? All of these questions pertain, in one way or another, to the study of power in ruling parties. Unfortunately, as Paul Pierson has noted, 'power and influence remain elusive . . . and marginalized concepts'—even as many new tools in sociology and historical institutionalism permit their systematic study.[45] I explore this territory by first identifying the central actors in ruling parties under investigation and the power practices they employ—when, how, and with what effect.

When we think of power in ruling parties, most of us think not of abstract processes and underlying political practices but of people—to be specific, party leaders. They are the most visible actors and often seem to hold great leverage. Indeed, from the outside many appear 'invincible'. But not all party leaders are strong and not all of them rule alone. Their strength depends on a variety of factors, such as wider power dynamics in society, the local context, and geopolitical trends. The incumbent's standing is also subject to the internal rules and practices of the party—both formal and informal. A ruling party can impose limits on the power of a leader, just as it can also be headed by a dictator who himself controls executive power; in the most extreme case, the party is a malleable tool at his own personal service. Parties that act as constraints bestow internal actors other than the incumbent with ample political leverage so as to ensure that he cannot amass too much influence on his own but shares power with others. Sometimes formal laws and regulations stipulate term limits to ensure he won't remain in office indefinitely, or executive committees can dismiss a leader who oversteps his mandate.

This scenario of power-sharing has informed much of the literature on ruling parties in political science.[46] The Institutional Revolutionary Party (PRI) in Mexico and the Chinese Communist Party (CCP) are amongst the most

[45] Paul Pierson, 'Power and Path Dependence', in James Mahoney and Kathleen Thelen (eds.), *Advances in Comparative-Historical Analysis*, Cambridge: Cambridge University Press, 2015, p. 123.

[46] Key works include Beatriz Magaloni, *Voting for Autocracy: Hegemonic Party Survival and Its Demise in Mexico*, New York: Cambridge University Press, 2006; Scott G. Gehlbach and Philip Keefer, 'Investment without Democracy: Ruling-Party Institutionalization and Credible Commitment in Autocracies', unpublished manuscript, University of Wisconsin, Madison, 2008; Milan W. Svolik, *The Politics of Authoritarian Rule*, Cambridge: Cambridge University Press, 2012; Carles Boix and Milan Svolik, 'The Foundations of Limited Authoritarian Government: Institutions, Commitment, and Power-Sharing in Dictatorships', *Journal of Politics*, 2013, 75, 2, pp. 300–316; Barbara Geddes,

prominent examples of parties that have practised such 'oligarchic' leadership, though under Xi Jinping the CCP has taken a more personalist turn. In Tunisia, the ruling party acted as a constraint on Ben Ali's power for the first two years after he assumed office. A ruling party can also curb the power of a leader in informal ways, such as when party activists pressure their incumbent to launch internal reforms—typically when he is weakened, such as in the face of socioeconomic or political crisis. During the Arab Uprisings, Ben Ali announced a series of political reforms and pledged he would not run for another term as President—answering to key demands of not only wide sections of the population but also RCD followers—though these promises were in vain.

However, most ruling parties fail to constrain their leaders, either partially or completely. Scholars have shown that 80% of ruling parties in authoritarian regimes are headed by the dictator in person rather than a separate official.[47] This book is part of a nascent body of literature taking seriously variations in incumbent–party relations and investigating their political consequences.[48] Many dictators seek to turn the ruling party into a malleable tool at their own personal service. Dictators' frequent domination of internal party affairs helps explain why the majority of parties do not outlive their architects' rule. Indeed, between 1946 and 2010, 61% of ruling parties broke down following the death or departure of their founding leader.[49] Though some ruling parties formally bestow their leaders with sweeping powers, many don't. Instead, incumbents acquire them informally during the course of their rule, despite any official restrictions that may exist. Far from sharing power, these 'personalist' dictators themselves control the executive and escape accountability, either fully or in part.[50] This has been the dominant—though not exclusive—scenario in the ruling parties of the Arab republics: in Tunisia, Ben Ali came to control the RCD's decision-making process two years after assuming power; in Yemen,

---

Joseph Wright, and Erica Frantz, *How Dictatorships Work*, Cambridge: Cambridge University Press, 2018.

[47] Barbara Geddes, Joseph Wright, and Erica Frantz, *How Dictatorships Work*, Cambridge: Cambridge University Press, 2018, p. 134.

[48] Notably, Yonatan L. Morse argues that only credible ruling parties manage elite conflicts and secure voter loyalty, and he provides a frame for measuring a party's 'credibility', such as by scrutinizing its decisional autonomy and physical size (see, for details, Yonatan L. Morse, *How Autocrats Compete: Parties, Patrons, and Unfair Elections in Africa*, Cambridge: Cambridge University Press, 2019). In addition, Anne Meng offers a theory of credible commitment under dictatorship that takes seriously the fact that many dictators have personalized power (Anne Meng, *From Personalized Rule to Institutionalized Regimes*, Cambridge: Cambridge University Press, 2020).

[49] Anne Meng, 'Accessing the State: Executive Constraints and Credible Commitment in Dictatorships', *Journal of Theoretical Politics*, 2019, 31, 4, p. 569.

[50] For more details, see Ivan Ermakoff, 'Patrimony and Collective Capacity: An Analytical Outline', *Annals of the American Academy of Political and Social Science*, 2011, 636, p. 188.

President Ali Abdullah Saleh (1990–2012) established a grip over the General People's Congress (GPC); Syria's Bashar al-Assad affirmed his command over the Ba'th party shortly after taking power in 2000. In Iraq, Saddam Hussein (1979–2003) came to dominate the Ba'th party to such an extent that it adopted 'Saddamism' as part of its ideological project. In 2003, in Algeria, President Abdelaziz Bouteflika (1999–2019) won a power battle with Ali Benflis, the General Secretary of the National Liberation Front (FLN), and subsequently reinforced his sway over the party. In Egypt, President Hosni Mubarak (1981–2011) progressively personalized power within the National Democratic Party (NDP) and promoted his son to leading posts.

It is notable that personalist rule does not, per se, tell us much about the relative strength or weakness of a dictator. Though in power-hierarchical terms personalist dictators stand at the very top of the party echelon and answer to nobody but themselves, some are in fact straw men, incapable of weathering social and political turmoil. This was the case in Tunisia, Libya, Egypt, and Yemen during the Arab Uprisings. However, other personalist leaders have proven highly resilient: in Egypt, when the 1967 Six-Day War against Israel resulted in the crushing defeat of Arab forces, President Abd al-Nasser announced his resignation, only to retract it the following day when hundreds of thousands of people rallied in support of his rule. Conversely, an incumbent whose powers are constrained by a ruling party is not necessarily 'weak'. Indeed, some have become highly influential, even surviving wider political or economic crisis. For example, during the tenure of PRI President Ernesto Zedillo, Mexico faced one of its greatest economic crisis in history. But Zedillo persevered and when he left office in 2000 his approval rates stood as high as 60%.[51]

When analysing the formal and informal ways in which dictators seek to defend and fortify their rule, many scholars have noted the importance of coalition-building, though the wider role these alliances play in dynamics of regime stability and internecine contention remains underexplored.[52] These scholars have shown that immediately after assuming power, dictators tend to build horizontal alliances with a diverse set of stakeholders so as to maximize

---

[51] Juan Jesús Aznárez, 'Zedillo Abandona la Presidencia con una Popularidad del 60%', El Pais, 30 November 2000, https://elpais.com/diario/2000/12/01/internacional/975625205_850215.html, last accessed 10 August 2022.

[52] Amongst other examples, Thomas Pepinsky has argued that regimes based on different socioeconomic coalitions are vulnerable to distinct economic and financial crises. See, for details, Thomas Pepinsky, *Economic Crises and the Breakdown of Authoritarian Regimes: Indonesia and Malaysia in Comparative Perspective*, New York: Cambridge University Press, pp. 273–274.

their support base.[53] But if they succeed in 'establishing' their power (in that they become unaccountable to other party officials and 'personalist' dictators), they typically then impose more narrow and vertical forms of rule, which rely on a smaller coalition of supporters.[54]

Scholars have also identified a number of other practices through which incumbents bolster their power base. These include nominating loyalists to key positions. Indeed, many dictators surround themselves with stooges who simply carry out their orders whilst marginalizing potential rivals. They also attempt to alter formal institutional rules and procedures to widen their prerogatives and power; if they can, they may even abolish official constraints on their rule, such as term limits. In addition, party leaders commonly redirect the flow of financial resources to allies in other political institutions, whilst withdrawing them from less favourable constituencies.[55] An incumbent's control of lucrative resources also allows him to pursue a divide-and-rule strategy, pitting potential competitors against one another and thus forestalling the prospect that they may unify forces against him.[56]

Whilst illuminating important ways in which incumbents may strengthen their rule, the literature says relatively little about when, why, and how these power practices fail or exhaust themselves and possibly give rise to internecine struggles and contention. Indeed, most scholars assume a relatively linear power trajectory in which incumbents move from an 'unconsolidated' to a 'consolidated' or 'established' status—that is, if they can.[57] Once an incumbent assumes the latter status, there is 'no return' to the former as the support of his

---

[53] Barbara Geddes, 'Minimum-Winning Coalitions and Personalization in Authoritarian Regimes', paper prepared for presentation at the annual meetings of the American Political Science Association, Chicago, 2–5 September 2004, pp. 2–3.

[54] Ibid. See also H. E. Chehabi and Juan J. Linz (eds.), *Sultanistic Regimes*, Baltimore, MD: Johns Hopkins University Press, 1998, p. 19.

[55] These strategies of power fortification correspond to what Dan Slater has termed an incumbent's 'packing', 'rigging', and 'circumvention'. Note that Paul Pierson has identified a similar set of strategies in formal institutions more generally. See, for details, Dan Slater, 'Iron Cage in an Iron Fist: Authoritarian Institutions and the Personalization of Power in Malaysia', *Comparative Politics*, 2003, 36, 1, p. 82; Paul Pierson, 'Power and Path Dependence', in James Mahoney and Kathleen Thelen (eds.), *Advances in Comparative-Historical Analysis*, Cambridge: Cambridge University Press, 2015, pp. 134–141.

[56] For comparative examples, see Isabelle Werenfels, 'Algeria: System Continuity through Elite Change', in Volker Perthes (ed.), *Arab Elites: Negotiating the Politics of Change*, Boulder, CO: Lynne Rienner, 2004, pp. 173–205; Kathleen Collins, *Clan Politics and Regime Transition in Central Asia*, Cambridge: Cambridge University Press, 2006; Victoria Clark, *Yemen: Dancing on the Heads of Snakes*, New Haven, CT: Yale University Press, 2010.

[57] See, for example, Barbara Geddes, 'Minimum-Winning Coalitions and Personalization in Authoritarian Regimes', paper prepared for presentation at the annual meeting of the American Political Science Association, Chicago, 2–5 September 2004; Milan W. Svolik, *The Politics of Authoritarian Rule*, Cambridge: Cambridge University Press, 2012, p. 56.

ruling coalition 'is no longer necessary for survival', as one influential scholar argues.[58] When explaining how dictators can accumulate such vast power, despite the formal restrictions that may exist, scholars commonly point to collective action problems. They argue that information asymmetries, ambiguities around an incumbent's 'true' intentions, and fear of reprisal are amongst the most important reasons preventing party officials from constraining an incumbent who seeks to personalize his power.[59] Yet arguably, these uncertainties also apply to ruling parties that practise oligarchic leadership and contain an incumbent, at least to some extent. Scholars have also suggested that an incumbent's likely control of the security services and threat—if not use—of force dissuades others from moving against him.[60] However, as has been noted in a related study, the 'apparent obviousness of the [coercion] argument can be deceptive', and the role of the security apparatus in the establishment of personal rule is more frequently asserted rather than demonstrated.[61]

Indeed, why some dictators succeed in accumulating vast personal power where others fail is poorly understood, as is the kind of internal resistance they may encounter on the way. In a similar vein, the internal causes of regime breakdown remain underexplored. Within a linear power trajectory, it is true, a personalist dictator typically falls as a result of an external shock—if he does at all—such as popular mobilization against his regime. But the Tunisian case highlights that a seemingly 'established' dictator such as Ben Ali may also be challenged internally from within his own ruling party—possibly alongside external opposition, which may even be a catalyst for change.

I suggest that the relative strength of an incumbent vis-à-vis his party followers depends on two key variables, which are crucial to exploring wider trends of internecine change and contention. The first is the existing internal opportunity structure—that is, the extent to which the ruling party acts as a constraint on the incumbent or not; in the latter case, the incumbent has personalized his power and escapes accountability, which makes it more difficult to challenge him. Parts of this dimension have been discussed in previous sections. A party constrains a dictator if followers pose a credible threat to him in that they have the ability—either perceived or real—to depose him.

---

[58] Milan W. Svolik, *The Politics of Authoritarian Rule*, Cambridge: Cambridge University Press, 2012, pp. 61, 63.

[59] Ibid., p. 59; Barbara Geddes, Joseph Wright, and Erica Frantz, *How Dictatorships Work*, Cambridge: Cambridge University Press, 2018, pp. 75–76, 67. See also H. E. Chehabi and Juan J. Linz (eds.), *Sultanistic Regimes*, Baltimore, MD: Johns Hopkins University Press, 1998.

[60] For example, Barbara Geddes, Joseph Wright, and Erica Frantz, *How Dictatorships Work*, Cambridge: Cambridge University Press, 2018, pp. 160–161.

[61] Ivan Ermakoff, *Ruling Oneself Out: A Theory of Collective Abdications*, Durham, NC: Duke University Press, 2008, p. xiii.

This is the case if a ruling party practises oligarchic leadership. Many ruling parties have formally enshrined power-sharing practices, but, to be credible, these need to be enforced, which is more rare. A party can also act as a constraint in informal ways, typically when a dictator is weak. This is often the case in the incumbent's first years in power, especially if he needs the support of a pre-existing ruling party to remain in office. A party can also serve as a constraint during episodes of major regime crisis. In such instances, acts of dissent are less costly, and rival party leaders are more likely to move against a leader who does not serve their interests.

The second variable is the incumbent's success at *mobilizing internal party support*, a consideration that touches upon wider questions of his legitimacy and authority. Essentially, it is about the politics of ideas, that is, the normative and ideational aspects underlying dictatorial rule. It is notable that many scholars of authoritarian politics have neglected this dimension of power, amongst other reasons because their increasingly quantitative models are ill suited to explore issues of legitimacy and authority in depth. Some scholars also regard these factors as epiphenomenal, suggesting that they do not constitute an independent force on the course of authoritarian politics.[62] And those who do investigate dictators' legitimation modes and strategies— sometimes including their effect on authoritarian stability—typically focus on how incumbents justify their rule in the eyes of the wider population rather than inside the regime, often in the context of framing and discourse analysis.[63] Building on this body of research, I focus specifically on the politics of ideas within the regime's own ranks. This angle is important for investigating processes of authoritarian regeneration and why some may exhaust themselves

[62] Xavier Marquez, 'The Irrelevance of Legitimacy', *Political Studies*, 2016, 64, 1, pp. 19–34. Many recent rationalist studies of authoritarian stability either downplay or outright ignore the issue of legitimacy. These include Milan Svolik, *The Politics of Authoritarian Rule*, Cambridge: Cambridge University Press, 2012; Barbara Geddes, Joseph Wright, and Erica Frantz, *How Dictatorships Work*, Cambridge: Cambridge University Press, 2018; Anne Meng, *From Personalized Rule to Institutionalized Regimes*, Cambridge: Cambridge University Press, 2020. For a more detailed critique of research that treats norms and ideas as epiphenomenal to authoritarian politics, see Lisa Wedeen, *Ambiguities of Domination: Politics, Rhetoric, and Symbols in Contemporary Syria*, Chicago: University of Chicago Press, 1999, p. 5.

[63] Robert Mayer, 'Strategies of Justification in Authoritarian Ideology', *Journal of Political Ideologies*, 2001, 6, 2, pp. 147–168; Holger Albrecht and Oliver Schlumberger, '"Waiting for Godot": Regime Change without Democratization in the Middle East', *International Political Science Review*, 2004, 25, 4, pp. 371–392; Mariya Y. Omelicheva, 'Authoritarian Legitimation: Assessing Discourses of Legitimacy in Kazakhstan and Uzbekistan', *Central Asian Survey*, 2016, 35, 4, pp. 481–500; Yue Hu, 'Refocusing Democracy: The Chinese Government's Framing Strategy in Political Language', *Democratization*, 2020, 27, 2, pp. 302–320; Christian Von Soest and Julia Grauvogel, 'Identity, Procedures and Performance: How Authoritarian Regimes Legitimize Their Rule', *Contemporary Politics*, 2017, 23, 3, pp. 287–305; Johannes Gerschewski, 'Legitimacy in Autocracies: Oxymoron or Essential Feature?', *Perspectives on Politics*, 2018, 16, 3, pp. 652–665.

over time. In particular, I argue that powerful internecine challengers emerge precisely when wider sections of the ruling party come to view an incumbent's rule as 'unjust' or 'illegitimate'. As such, the ways in which leaders succeed or fail in garnering internal party support—and the circumstances under which such support may fade—are key to understanding periods of political stability better, as well as moments of vast change, including any internal party strife that may lead to regime breakdown.

I uncover two ideational strategies that party leaders use to secure their positions, especially those who do not derive legitimacy through personal charisma or revolutionary activism. Understanding these strategies offers valuable new insights into how some incumbents amass great power whereas others fail and why. The first strategy involves *the propagation of a 'correctivist' ideology*; the second concerns *the creation of new normative priorities*. Correctivism constitutes incumbents' promotion of ideational and structural change, built upon the premise of rectifying past 'mistakes', realizing a regime's 'true' purpose, or returning to its 'proper' roots. Party leaders who pursue a correctivist strategy typically operate from a position of weakness; their support base is limited or uncertain, and followers constrain their rule, at least initially. Correctivist ideology is responsive in that the proposed innovations are desired by many party activists, and typically even by people beyond the regime's traditional constituency, hence allowing incumbents to prop up their support base. At the same time, it may pave the way for party leaders to promote wider structural changes that serve their own interests. Indeed, as part of their correctivist frame, incumbents typically seek to revise some of the party's formal rules and practices, which—they claim—is necessary to realize their ambitious reform programme. And it is precisely this tearing down of old structures and the ensuing contingency of the moment that bolsters the agency of key actors, including party leaders.[64] Moments of political flux may allow incumbents to promote beneficial reforms and ultimately personalize their rule—including by appointing their close loyalists to key positions and abolishing term limits.

Alongside Ben Ali, other dictators have used correctivist frames to promote wide-ranging transformations to the regime and consolidate their power. Upon taking office in Syria, Hafez al-Assad even launched a 'Corrective Movement', which allowed him to prop up his support base and ultimately establish personal rule.[65] Mao Zedong's Cultural Revolution gained widespread popularity in part because it specifically promised to rectify the

---

[64] For more information on how moments of heightened contingency may empower key actors, see Ivan Ermakoff, 'The Structure of Contingency', *American Journal of Sociology*, 2015, 121, 1, pp. 64–125.

[65] See, for details, Raymond A. Hinnebusch, *Syria Revolution from Above*, London: Routledge, 2002.

many transgressions and mistakes committed by the CCP leadership.[66] More-over, in his famous speech at the 20th Congress of the Soviet Union's Com-munist Party in 1956, Nikita Khrushchev criticized Joseph Stalin's abuse of powers, promised to restore the party's true purpose, and launched a political opening—in the process of which he reinforced his own power.[67]

Party leaders pursue the second power practice—the creation of new nor-mative priorities—to redefine a party's wider objectives and raison d'être according to their own interests. To deploy this strategy, incumbents must already hold ample agency and decision-making power, which enables them to promote any new party goals widely, for example, through propaganda initiatives and by recruiting new people to the party who supplant older mem-bers, become beholden to the leader, and support his new objectives. The propagation of new normative priorities is directive in that it mainly serves to legitimize transformations to a regime's formal rules and structures that are already under way or launched in parallel—and through which incumbents seek to bolster their power base. But it may also instigate change within the ruling party on its own and protractedly, especially if the new priorities are widely internalized amongst followers, and give rise to new party values, iden-tities, and actors. Indeed, for this strategy to be successful, the new objectives must become well entrenched in the ruling party. This, in turn, is contingent on a variety of factors, such as the extent to which they 'resonate' with followers and are perceived as legitimate.[68] This depends on whether the innovations are generally in line with party norms and identities but also on the extent to which incumbents advocate them in 'consistent and protracted' ways, including in related 'policy clusters',[69] such as the public administration.

In 1993 in Iraq, President Saddam Hussein launched the Return to Faith Campaign, which was spearheaded by the Ba'th party and promised to revive religious policies. By promoting these new normative priorities, the Presi-dent sought to bolster his rule amongst religiously conservative sections at a time when militant Islamism was on the rise; however, this attempt was only partially successful: many of the traditionally more secular Ba'th leaders opposed the reforms, and some conservatives who integrated into the regime

---

[66] Compare Simon Leys, *The Chairman's New Clothes: Mao and the Cultural Revolution*, London: Allison and Busby, 1977.

[67] William Taubman, *Khrushchev: The Man and His Era*, New York: Norton, 2003.

[68] The literature on framing explores how values and norms may become embedded in institutions, and some of its insights can be applied to the context of ruling parties. See, for details, Giovanni Capoccia, 'When Do Institutions "Bite"? Historical Institutionalism and the Politics of Institutional Change', *Comparative Political Studies*, 2016, 49, 8, p. 1105.

[69] Ibid.

ended up being perpetrators of violence. In a very distinct example in Algeria in the 1970s, President Houari Boumediene launched a range of socialist and constitutional reforms when his rule began to stagnate. These political innovations were highly popular amongst FLN followers, as they strengthened the party and elevated its status in society—and, in the process, reinforced Boumediene's power.[70] An influential study revealed that some personalist dictators in sub-Saharan Africa similarly created new formal rules and structures to bolster their ruling parties, with the ultimate aim of fortifying their own power, though the ideational dimension of such efforts remains unexplored.[71]

Notably, at the time of the Arab Uprisings, presidents in Egypt, Libya, Yemen, and Tunisia were trying to groom relatives as successors, in most cases through a ruling party.[72] This process was couched as part of a wider set of party reforms—typically ostensible democratization, which was often even spearheaded by the would-be successors, who were frequently educated in the West and promised to launch a political opening. The pursuit of selective liberalization reforms, and how these served to prop up leaders' powers, have been central themes in the authoritarian upgrading literature. But many party followers did not believe these prerogatives were sincere and denounced them as serving primarily the presidential family rather than the ruling party. Large sections of the ruling parties in each case opposed a presidential successor from the leader's own family, and some eventually decided to revolt against the incumbent.

I suggest that any new normative priorities—be they ostensible liberalization processes or other reforms—fail to become embedded in the ruling party, or this process may exhaust itself, if they do not echo amongst followers or these do not believe they are credible, even after any promotion strategies the incumbent may pursue. In this case, a mismatch ensues between the incumbent's policies and their perceived legitimacy, which may sow the seeds for wider political crises. Phrased in more general terms, different ideational strategies and priorities give rise to distinct party actors and coalitions whilst marginalizing others, who may turn into important 'agents of contention', especially if wider party sections come to view the incumbent's rule as 'unjust'

---

[70] Michael Willis, *Politics and Power in the Maghreb: Algeria, Tunisia and Morocco from Independence to the Arab Spring*, London: Hurst Publishing, 2012, p. 67.

[71] Anne Meng, *From Personalized Rule to Institutionalized Regimes*, Cambridge: Cambridge University Press, 2020.

[72] Virginie Collombier, 'Gamal Moubarak et le Parti National Démocratique ou la Stratégie du Désastre: Comment Ceux qui Prétendaient Préparer la Succession Présidentielle ont Précipité la Chute du Régime', *Outre-Terre*, 2011, 3, 9, pp. 333–345; Roger Owen, *The Rise and Fall of Arab Presidents for Life*, Cambridge, MA: Harvard University Press, 2012; Hani J. D. Awad, 'Forgotten as History: Politics and Space in the Cairo Peri-Urban Fringe', DPhil thesis, University of Oxford, 2018.

or 'illegitimate'—with the ultimate possibility that they may contribute to regime breakdown. I elaborate on this below.

Patterns of change, agents of contention

Who are the 'agents of contention' in ruling parties? What kind of change do they desire and how do they seek to pursue it? Which contentious actors and strategies, if any, flourish with which power practices of incumbents? Or which may be curbed through them? To what extent are specific contentious actors and strategies associated with distinct modes of change? Fathoming patterns of change and contention within ruling parties is a challenging task, given their fluid and ambiguous nature. The previous section detailed how the defenders of the status quo—the incumbents—themselves rely on vast ideational and structural transformations to bolster their power base; the stability of their rule is, in fact, dependent on such strategic change. But change can be brought about by a range of actors and processes—sometimes indirectly or unwillingly. They include internal party competitors and challengers from rival political institutions, as well as wider domestic and geopolitical trends. Whilst recognizing these complex trends and their possible impact, this section focuses on those party actors who purposefully seek to challenge the status quo—the 'agents of contention'—as they are key to understanding internecine party struggles, including any severe strife that may contribute to regime breakdown. I propose that distinct contentious actors pose different threats to party leaders and are associated with different modes of change.

Not all agents of contention want the same thing; indeed, they constitute in themselves a vastly heterogeneous category within the ruling party. Their only unifying point is that they contest the status quo or aspects of it. By this, I mean that contentious actors advocate for change which the incumbent opposes or which does not serve his interest. However, the motivations behind their contentious actions often vary widely, as do the nature of the reforms they seek—to the extent that different contentious actors may support vastly distinct or even opposed transformations. Their desired changes may revolve around a wide range of issues, such as specific political or economic policies, the party's ideational vision, or internal laws and regulations. Indeed, most of the time agents of contention seek reform in areas of seemingly secondary relevance as this is less risky, especially in an authoritarian context, where any 'subversive' activities, however seemingly minor, typically attract harsh reprisals. Because of the persistent fear of punishment, contentious actors tend to advocate for reforms indirectly or inconspicuously, sometimes even suggesting that the proposed changes are beneficial for the incumbent, even if they are not. Only in rare circumstances do they contest the incumbent directly and in the open, as some RCD activists in Tunisia did, given the risks and potential costs associated with such actions. As a result, authoritarian regimes often appear inherently stable, even as internal opposition is growing, possibly heading towards a culmination point.

On the most basic level, contentious actors can be differentiated according to whether they operate in the elite or at the grassroots level. If the ruling party acts as a constraint upon the incumbent and he has to share power, it is elite figures who enjoy the greatest leverage, and some may turn into important political rivals. The more even the balance of power between the incumbent and other members of the ruling clique, the more influence these potential challengers hold. In such cases, they can pressure the incumbent into launching reforms that serve their strategic interest or veto policies they deem unfavourable. Contentious elite actors bolster their sway in a range of ways, often reminiscent of their counterparts in democracies: they use coalition formation, lobbying, including of the incumbent himself, and rival political and ideological work; they also exploit ambiguities in existing rules and policies to further their interests.[73] Given their great leverage, grassroots followers typically seek to promote any reforms through these elite representatives, thereby further propping up the latter's profile. It is notable that the more sway elite figures hold, the less risky it is for them to promote contentious reforms. In consequence, reforms occur more frequently under such circumstances than in more asymmetric power settings. Most of the time, however, they revolve around seemingly minor issues and, as a result, contribute to regime continuity rather than provoking a political crisis. Indeed, members of the ruling clique tend to refrain from contentious actions that might jeopardize the stability of the party and the regime, in which they have invested heavily—often for decades—and from which they greatly benefit. However, even apparently small-scale and incremental changes can trigger wider transformative processes, especially over time, for example, if they empower rival coalitions or strategic actors.

---

[73] For more details on these change strategies, see James Mahoney and Kathleen Thelen (eds.), *Explaining Institutional Change: Ambiguity, Agency, and Power*, Cambridge: Cambridge University Press, 2010.

Though it is a risky undertaking and therefore rarer, members of the ruling clique sometimes also seek to oust an incumbent who does not serve their interests. Such internal leadership challenges most often take place during incumbents' early years, when their power base is more uncertain and fragile. They can also occur during wider political crisis: in China, CCP General Secretary Zhao Ziyang was dismissed and placed under house arrest by party hardliners who fiercely opposed his support of the 1989 Tiananmen Square protests. Moreover, hawks of the Communist Party of the Soviet Union (CPSU) attempted to oust reformist leader Mikhail Gorbachev in August 1991; they failed, but the internal party turmoil accelerated the demise and eventual formal dissolution of the Soviet Union a few months later.[74]

Because of the ever-present possibility of internal coups and deposals, many party leaders have an interest in personalizing power; that is, they seek to control the executive and escape accountability. But the process of personalizing their rule, in fact, temporarily heightens internal threats as it entails the marginalization of powerful elite competitors who may attempt to turn against the incumbent. Moreover, if incumbents pursue a correctivist strategy and seek to bolster their support base by integrating new constituencies into the party, possibly even promoting them to key posts, wider sections of the old guard become redundant. Some incumbents, especially those who lack political capital of their own, also seek out representatives of these new constituencies for ideational guidance and vision, including for their correctivist frames, hence reducing the role of the party's traditional ideologues. And it is precisely these sidelined party factions who have an interest in removing the incumbent.

How do internal elite challengers go about trying to depose an incumbent and with what effect? Naturally, there are many different possible strategies, and these depend largely on wider power dynamics, such as whether these rivals enjoy the support of key actors, including from outside the party, like the military or foreign allies. Often this is not the case, meaning prospective challengers have to devise creative strategies to counter the incumbent, and these are highly contingent on the specific power practices he employs. If incumbents pursue a correctivist approach to personalize their rule, internal adversaries sometimes advance a competing ideational frame to mobilize a rival support base. For example, shortly after the ascent to

---

[74] See, for details, William Taubman, *Gorbachev: His Life and Times*, New York: Simon and Schuster, 2017.

power of the Syrian Ba'th in 1963, a power battle erupted between party founder Michel Aflaq and rival leader Salah Jadid, whose 'social radicalism' prevailed over Aflaq's 'liberal unionism', allowing him—with the support of the military—to take over in 1966 to launch the party's 'socialist transformation'.[75]

Rival leaders must have alternative claims to authority and legitimacy—or succeed in crafting them—all whilst promoting an impression of the incumbent's rule as 'unjust' and 'illegitimate'. This typically requires backing from powerful actors, such as in the security apparatus, and access to important resources, including party propaganda outlets, which many lack. However, even if they fail to mobilize a rival support base, all is not lost for would-be challengers: incumbents may also empower them indirectly and unwillingly. In particular, incumbents' correctivist strategies and the ensuing structural transformations can inadvertently bolster the agency of key competitors. Periods of heightened contingency prop up the leverage of a range of actors—not just the incumbent.[76] And skilled political challengers may succeed in capitalizing on the fluidity of the moment to promote rival policies and ideas.

However, given the many challenges involved, most of the time elites fail to constrain an incumbent who seeks to personalize power, either partially or completely.[77] And personalist rulers are keen to sideline critical voices—especially from the party's leading ranks—as soon as they have gained the upper hand. They tend to replace them with their own associates from the party or related political institutions, such as the public administration; in some cases, incumbents also promote their relatives to key posts, which bestows a family dimension—possibly including a hereditary component—to their rule. This is what happened in Syria, where President Hafez al-Assad successfully groomed his son, Bashar, as a successor, the latter having taken power in 2000. If personalist leaders create new normative priorities to recraft the party according to their own interests, this may also give rise to distinct coalitions and actors. For example, if incumbents promote new security prerogatives, this may bolster the influence of representatives from the military and Interior Ministry within the party. If they prioritize economic growth,

[75] Raymond Hinnebusch, *Syria: Revolution from Above*, Abingdon: Routledge, 2001, pp. 51–52.

[76] See, for details, Ivan Ermakoff, 'The Structure of Contingency', *American Journal of Sociology*, 2015, 121, 1, pp. 64–125.

[77] See, for details, Barbara Geddes, Joseph Wright, and Erica Frantz, *How Dictatorships Work*, Cambridge: Cambridge University Press, 2018, p. 134; Anne Meng, 'Accessing the State: Executive Constraints and Credible Commitment in Dictatorships', *Journal of Theoretical Politics*, 2019, 31, 4, p. 569.

figures from business and finance may take centre stage. Importantly, these actors remain first and foremost associates of the dictator and execute his orders, despite the professional expertise and personal prerogatives they may bring to the party. But of course they also benefit from their posts, which come with important perks and privileges and through which they can promote their own interests—as long as these do not clash with the incumbent's. Indeed, the party may remain a tool for upward mobility and even of social identification and belonging, at least for some sections of society, despite personalist rule and the marginalization of key elites. Where this is the case, it limits the ability of contentious agents to construct a rival support base across wider party ranks.

So when do agents of contention gain relevance in personalist parties? Who are the key actors and what type of change do they seek—why and how? In the upper echelons of personalist regimes, contentious figures are extremely rare or simply non-existent: incumbents have marginalized veto players in the elite and potentially critical voices are placed under close scrutiny. Sometimes, specific middle or grassroots ranks enjoy more autonomy or even constitute 'islands of independence' and, if so, may turn into central stages for internecine contention. Even if middle and grassroots levels remain under tight leadership control, some followers—though a minority—may still decide to take matters into their own hands, especially given that they lack elite representatives to defend their interests. However, these rank-and-file activists rarely seek reforms in fields of secondary relevance, owing to the potentially high costs for actions that have little or no immediate impact. Instead, contention— if it takes place at all—pertains to issues at the very heart of the regime. I argue that in personalist regimes, mid-level and grassroots followers may engage in contentious action when the authority and legitimacy of the incumbent comes under threat.

Ruling parties perform multiple functions, including at the local level, and grassroots activists may disapprove of their incumbent for various reasons—political, economic, normative, or a combination of these. Sometimes, socioeconomic hardship leads followers to question the incumbent's legitimacy: if the party provides limited opportunities for upward mobility, lower ranks are hit hardest, and this is especially so amongst followers who were vulnerable to start with—often young and rural activists, or those from marginalized ethnic, religious, or regional backgrounds. If internal party resources are sparse because of a wider economic downturn, followers may be relatively forgiving towards their leader, especially if events seem out of his immediate control; some may even applaud an incumbent who appears to be doing his best in a challenging situation. However, this is less so if the incumbent blatantly mismanages economic resources, withholds them deliberately from activists, or—even more problematically—enriches himself on the backs of his followers, possibly alongside his wider family. In such cases, internal resentment and opposition are prone to mount quickly. Followers can furthermore come to question the incumbent's legitimacy on many other grounds, such as when his strategic priorities do not match the party's norms and values. Sometimes, internal opposition arises out of 'focal events', for example, when party activists experience the regime's injustice firsthand or learn of a relative or a friend's mistreatment by the authorities.

Notably, internal disapproval and opposition do not necessarily translate into contentious action, even if such sentiments are widely shared amongst party activists. Indeed, most followers who come to question the legitimacy and authority of their leader choose to do nothing about it. As Paul Pierson noted, the more asymmetric the distribution of power in political institutions, the less likely it is that weaker actors will contest stronger ones, especially if the costs and potential for retaliation are high.[78] Those who still engage in contentious activity typically choose to do so inconspicuously and discreetly. They stage passive or symbolic forms of resistance, possibly slowly withdrawing from politics or allowing their party membership to lapse—already very dangerous undertakings in an authoritarian context. Indeed, often one of the first signs of internal party dissent is falling membership, though incumbents try to keep such trends secret. But despite the risks involved, a minority of followers may still decide to act openly. This occurs if their grievances multiply or become overlapping, if they have nothing to lose or believe matters will only get worse. However, the contentious actions of these internal dissenters—no matter their specific manifestations—rarely result in the change they desire. Far from it: incumbents tend to respond with severe repression, possibly even wider authoritarian reinforcement, though some enact cosmetic reforms in the hope of soothing critical voices. Incumbents also do everything they can to keep internecine contention hidden, well aware that it encourages further acts of dissidence, with the risk that these gradually spiral out of control.

Whilst internecine contention has various effects and can even lead to authoritarian reinforcement, especially in the short term, I propose that it makes the event of regime breakdown more likely. Scholars have pointed out that personalist regimes are particularly susceptible to collapse as a result of mass protests.[79] By contrast, I claim that the roots of personalist rulers'

---

[78] Paul Pierson, 'Power and Path Dependence', in James Mahoney and Kathleen Thelen (eds.), *Advances in Comparative-Historical Analysis*, Cambridge: Cambridge University Press, 2015, p. 126.

[79] For example, Robert H. Dix, 'Why Revolutions Succeed and Fail', *Polity*, 1983, 16, pp. 423–446; Jack A. Goldstone, 'Revolutions and Superpowers', in Jonathan R. Adelman (ed.), *Superpowers and*

vulnerability is internal and that this vulnerability applies only for those leaders whose legitimacy and authority have come under threat from within the regime. In such instances, any political turmoil—be it evoked through mass protests or another 'shock' event—exposes the incumbent as a straw man, who has lost support from his own ruling party. In the event of anti-regime mobilization, disgruntled party activists—especially from the rank and file—may even participate in the demonstrations, as did the RCD activists in Tunisia. However, the political changes they seek tend to be distinct from those of other activists: they often centre on internal reforms and leadership shifts rather than the complete overturning of the regime, though some followers come to adopt such an agenda, especially once the demonstrations gain in relevance and develop their own momentum, with possibly changing protester demands. Some internecine opponents also choose to do nothing in the face of wider crisis. But this in itself still amounts to 'doing something' as it too lays bare the political isolation of the incumbent. By contrast, followers of a relatively unified party, who stand behind their leader, help contain—if not entirely thwart—moments of political turmoil, including mass protests, for example, by policing opponents, spreading pro-regime propaganda, and staging counterdemonstrations.

Far from being self-perpetuating and stabilizing, ruling parties can in fact evolve into major arenas of conflict and unrest. Moments of political turmoil empower internal opponents, who have less to fear during times of crisis: these challengers may then succeed in ousting an incumbent whose legitimacy and authority have come under threat amongst wider party ranks. Contentious activities by grassroots and mid-level followers deeply unsettle loyal party figures, including those in the elite, who do not want to be trapped on a sinking ship. In an attempt to save their own skin, some decide to switch sides, possibly even formally joining the opposition. Their realignment is the final straw breaking the regime's back. This was the scenario in Tunisia on 14 January 2011, when mounting protests and internal regime contention increased elite insecurity to such a level that Prime Minister Mohamed Ghannouchi took over power.

Revolutions, New York: Praeger, 1986, pp. 38–48; Jeff Goodwin and Theda Skocpol, 'Explaining Revolutions in the Contemporary Third World', *Politics and Society*, 1989, 17, 4, pp. 489–509; Alan Knight, 'Revolutions in Twentieth-Century Latin America', in Claude Auroi and Aline Helg (eds.), *Latin America 1810–2010: Dreams and Legacies*, London: Imperial College Press, 2012, p. 145. Some scholars acknowledge that internal factors contribute to personalist rulers' vulnerability; see, for example, H. E. Chehabi and Juan J. Linz (eds.), *Sultanistic Regimes*, Baltimore, MD: Johns Hopkins University Press, 1998; Jack Goldstone, 'Towards a Fourth Generation of Revolutionary Theory', *Annual Review of Political Science*, 2001, 4, pp. 138–187.

2

A Man amongst Others . . . a Man above All

> Ben Ali was a military man . . . but politically he was weak . . . . He
> wasn't good at delivering speeches . . . he had never been an activist of
> the Party. This was his weak spot.
>
> Hassouna, RCD student activist, Bardo, 24 May 2016

On 7 November 1987, a small coalition of party and military officials, including Prime Minister Zine el-Abidine Ben Ali, deposed Tunisia's first president,
Habib Bourguiba, who had led the country to independence in 1956. In an
address to the nation that day, Ben Ali—who took the position of Interim
President—announced a 'new era' and the establishment of a 'democracy fully
respecting the sovereignty of the people'.[1] The incoming officials abolished the
constitution's presidency-for-life provision, which had allowed Bourguiba to
hold onto power for so long, and announced early general elections to enable
people to freely choose their political representatives. They also licensed several new parties and opened up membership in the ruling Socialist Destourian
Party (PSD), the hegemonic party that had emerged out of the independence
movement, including to political currents that were previously outlawed. To
demarcate the beginning of the new era, in 1988, the PSD was renamed the
Constitutional Democratic Rally (RCD).

Yet soon afterwards, in a dramatic about-face, Ben Ali established one-man
rule. He was the uncontested candidate in the 1989 presidential elections
and furthermore gained personal control over the RCD, despite lacking any
background in the party. From a theoretical point of view, Ben Ali's quick
consolidation of power cannot be fully explained: prevailing theories predict
that when a new leader has to bargain with a pre-existing ruling party, such
as the PSD, the establishment of personal rule is unlikely.[2] Those incumbents

---

[1] Ben Ali's speech, delivered on 7 November 1987. An English translation is available at 'Tunisia:
The Overthrow of Bourguiba', *al-Bab*, n.d., https://al-bab.com/albab-orig/albab/arab/docs/tunisia/
declaration_07111987.htm, last accessed 19 August 2017.

[2] Barbara Geddes, Joseph Wright, and Erica Frantz, *How Dictatorships Work*, Cambridge:
Cambridge University Press, 2018, pp. 77, 89, 107; Milan Svolik, *The Politics of Authoritarian Rule*,
Cambridge: Cambridge University Press, 2012, p. 87; Beatriz Magaloni and Ruth Kricheli, 'Political

Ben Ali's Tunisia. Anne Wolf, Oxford University Press. © Anne Wolf (2023).
DOI: 10.1093/oso/9780192868503.003.0003

who nevertheless succeed in accumulating vast powers do so because of their grip over the security forces and threat, if not use, of force.[3] Even though Ben Ali's military background helped him stage a coup in the first place, he subsequently bolstered his sway primarily through the politics of ideas. In particular, he pursued a 'correctivist' strategy, couched in terms of rectifying past 'mistakes' and realizing the regime's 'true' purpose. Correctivist language speaks to party followers—as well as many people beyond the regime's traditional support base. They in fact desire the reforms the new incumbent proposes. But it is precisely in the process of deep internal party change that leaders may induce policies that benefit their own interests.

This chapter uncovers how Ben Ali—within just two years of assuming the presidency—managed to establish personal rule. Whilst tracing how various political processes unfolded over time and were causally linked, I reveal the key correctivist strategies Ben Ali and his associates pursued: they hired 'ideological lobbyists' to garner a wide support coalition, launched a self-critique within the ruling party to instigate internal reform, and created pacts with other political actors. I illustrate how this ideological work facilitated a makeover of the party, such as through the appointment of new figureheads favourable to the new officials—all the way from the grass roots through mid-level to senior representatives. This bottom-up process of power redistribution allowed Ben Ali—once he had garnered sufficient sway—to promote changes to the RCD's rules and practices and ultimately establish one-man rule.

The coup

Any study of an authoritarian regime must begin with its inception. Indeed, the way in which officials first take power and the composition of their seizure group provide important insights into the resources and skills that give them an edge over rival forces.[4] In the case of Tunisia, scholars have highlighted how Ben Ali used the security apparatus to take power, with National Guard troops surrounding the Presidential Palace during the night of 7 November.[5]

Order and One-Party Rule', *Annual Review of Political Science*, 2010, 13, p. 127; Barbara Geddes, 'Minimum-Winning Coalitions and Personalization in Authoritarian Regimes', paper prepared for presentation at the annual meetings of the American Political Science Association, Chicago, 2–5 September 2004, p. 22.

[3] Barbara Geddes, Joseph Wright, and Erica Frantz, *How Dictatorships Work*, Cambridge: Cambridge University Press, 2018, pp. 160–161.

[4] Ibid., p. 33.

[5] For example, Larbi Chouikha and Éric Gobe, *Histoire de la Tunisie depuis l'Indépendance*, Paris: La Découverte, 2015, pp. 44–45; Christopher Alexander, *Tunisia: From Stability to Revolution in the Maghreb*, Abingdon: Routledge, 2016, p. 49.

They have also pointed out that everything was done to ensure the ousting was perceived as conforming to the constitution, and a team of medical doctors testified to Bourguiba's unfitness according to constitutional article 57.[6] Because of these scholars' focus on the security forces and, in particular, the person of Ben Ali, other figures that participated in the coup have received less attention, including those from the ruling party.

However, initially Ben Ali was certainly not the only man in town: another coup conspirer was Hedi Baccouche, PSD Director from March 1984 until April 1987. Baccouche even wrote Ben Ali's 7 November statement in which he declared that he had taken power.[7] Together with Hamed Karoui, another longtime party official who succeeded him as PSD Director, Baccouche also mobilized party followers in the coup's immediate aftermath. Both old friends of Ben Ali from Sousse, Baccouche and Karoui had pushed for his promotion to Prime Minister in October 1987, a position critical for the succession.[8] Moreover, I uncovered that earlier that year, Baccouche had reached out to opposition figures and university professors, organizing clandestine meetings between them and Ben Ali,[9] presumably to prepare for a smooth transfer of power.

However, aside from Hedi Baccouche, no other PSD figures were directly involved in the logistics of the coup—the other key figure being Habib Ammar, a military officer. Several party officials were hoping to succeed Bourguiba, including Mohamed Sayah, a prominent leader and adviser to Bourguiba. Opposing party clans had different successors in mind, few of them favouring Ben Ali, a military man, so the architects of 7 November sought to keep those in the party out of the loop as much as possible. To remove Bourguiba, they relied mainly on personal relations, forged since childhood, thus shifting the centre of power to their native Sousse and giving rise to the so-called Sousse clan. The three coup conspirers even came from the same village within the Sousse governorate, Hammam Sousse, and they subsequently promoted a disproportionate number of officials from the region to leading posts in the state and party.[10] Indeed, in the cabinet that was formed

---

[6] For example, Emma C. Murphy, *Economic and Political Change in Tunisia: From Bourguiba to Ben Ali*, London: Palgrave Macmillan, 1999, p. 165; Amor Boubakri, 'Interpreting the Tunisian Revolution: Beyond Bou'azizi', in Larbi Sadiki (ed.), *Routledge Handbook of the Arab Spring: Rethinking Democratization*, Abingdon: Routledge, 2015, pp. 70–71.

[7] Interviews with Hedi Baccouche, Tunis, 28 September 2015 and 22 July 2017.

[8] Article 57 of the constitution stipulated that the prime minister was to take over power should the president pass away or be unfit to govern.

[9] Interview with Moncer Rouissi, Tunis, 21 July 2017.

[10] Note that dictators commonly rely on regional loyalties to bolster their power base. Amongst other examples, Saddam Hussein promoted a disproportionate number of officials from his home region of

the day after the coup by Hedi Baccouche, who became the new Prime Minister, one in four ministers hailed from Sousse. This stands in sharp contrast with the 1970 and 1986 Bourguiba-era governments of Hedi Nouira and Mohamed Mzali (before the rise of Ben Ali as Interior Minister and Prime Minister), which did not include a single minister from the coastal city.[11]

Leading scholars have theorized Ben Ali's takeover of power as a leadership change within the same 'ruling group'[12]—amongst other factors, because Ben Ali was Prime Minister before he ousted Bourguiba. However, the subsequent power shift to Sousse and, to a certain extent, to the military and security establishment,[13] suggests that the 7 November coup can be best understood as the ascent of a new ruling clique. This differentiation is important in so far as it refocuses the analysis from authoritarian continuation and 'ruling coalition spells'—that is, the 'uninterrupted succession in office of politically affiliated leaders'[14]—to processes of authoritarian reproduction and change. Ben Ali's rise in government, before the coup, had also been recent, and he was considered an outsider, lacking a background in politics, let alone in PSD activism. Moreover, in the context of a hegemonic party, it is often near impossible to oust an incumbent dictator without at least some allies in the party.[15] How new leaders like Ben Ali seek to regenerate legitimacy—and, in some cases, even succeed in establishing personal rule in the context of a hegemonic party—requires investigation.

Strategies of legitimation

In the immediate aftermath of the coup, the architects of 7 November relied on three principal strategies to legitimate their assumption of power. First,

Tikrit to the Ba'th party. See, for details, Lisa Blaydes, *State of Repression: Iraq under Saddam Hussein*, Princeton, NJ: Princeton University Press, 2018, p. 125.
  [11] Author's own calculations.
  [12] Milan Svolik, *The Politics of Authoritarian Rule*, Cambridge: Cambridge University Press, 2012, p. 21; for a similar discussion about the difference between leader-shuffling and regime-change coups, see Barbara Geddes, Joseph Wright, and Erica Frantz, *How Dictatorships Work*, Cambridge: Cambridge University Press, 2018, p. 46.
  [13] Tawfik al-Madani, *Suqut al-Dawla al-Bulisiyya fi Tunis* [*The Collapse of the Police State in Tunisia*], Beirut: Arab Scientific Publishers, 2011, pp. 74–75; Emma C. Murphy, *Economic and Political Change in Tunisia: From Bourguiba to Ben Ali*, London: Palgrave Macmillan, 1999, p. 184.
  [14] Milan Svolik, *The Politics of Authoritarian Rule*, Cambridge: Cambridge University Press, 2012, p. 42.
  [15] Beatriz Magaloni and Ruth Kricheli, 'Political Order and One-Party Rule', *Annual Review of Political Science*, 2010, 13, p. 128; compare also Jason Brownlee, *Authoritarianism in an Age of Democratization*, Cambridge: Cambridge University Press, 2007, pp. 37–40.

they quickly organized grassroots rallies in favour of the new powerbrokers to suggest their takeover enjoyed widespread support. Second, they propped up the political credentials of the new president, Ben Ali, by propagating the myth that he evinced a long history of party activism, even though this was not the case. Third, and most important, they put forth a correctivist frame to enhance their takeover's popular appeal, including to party followers.

Mobilizing the grass roots

The new Tunisian officials began their quest for popular support by mobilizing the PSD grass roots. Early in the morning of 7 November, when news spread that Bourguiba had been ousted and that Ben Ali—a military man—had assumed power, PSD members were completely taken aback. Just like most people, they learned about it from the radio or the television—where Ben Ali's 7 November speech was broadcast—or from friends. Hamza, a regional leader from Bizerte, recalled:

> At 6.30am [on 7 November] a friend called . . . asking me if I had listened to the radio . . . I switched it on and heard [Ben Ali] delivering his speech. I called the *délégué* [the head of one of Tunisia's 264 regional delegations] and he didn't even know about it yet. People were completely taken aback, they didn't know what to do![16]

PSD activists were particularly unsettled because in his first speech to the people, Ben Ali did not clarify which role, if any, the party would play under his presidency. Some worried that he might even decide to dissolve the PSD, given that he had no background in party activism. However, the matter was settled a few hours later—temporarily, at least—when Ben Ali's team delivered a statement calling upon the PSD to participate in the political 'change'.[17] Subsequently, Hedi Baccouche and Hamed Karoui were tasked with mobilizing activists in support of Ben Ali. Karoui explained that he had contacted the PSD regional representatives and requested they 'organize . . . rallies' in favour of

---

[16] Interview with Hamza, Ras Jebel, Bizerte governorate, 9 February 2017.
[17] Interview with Mohamed Ghariani, Tunis, 20 July 2017; 'Attachement à Préserver les Acquis et à Concrétiser les Objectifs du Changement', *Le Renouveau*, 1 August 1998, p. 3.

the new president, later asserting that mobilization occurred 'spontaneously' in an attempt to convey that Ben Ali enjoyed widespread support.[18]

The fact that Baccouche and Karoui managed to organize pro-Ben Ali rallies so swiftly, even though the new president was not a party figure, illustrates that the PSD maintained a high degree of internal discipline, even at this time of political upheaval. Mobilization was facilitated by the confusion of the moment and the party's hierarchical structure in that followers were looking up to their leaders, waiting for instructions on how to react.[19] Widespread awareness of Bourguiba's deteriorating health and belief in the transitional character of the new powerbrokers—a perception Ben Ali had himself promoted through the 7 November speech—made rallying for the new powerbrokers relatively uncontroversial. Many party activists were in fact relieved that Bourguiba's removal had occurred without bloodshed and thought that Ben Ali's assumption of the interim presidency was constitutional, even if they had favoured another successor from the PSD.[20]

The involvement of the PSD structures immediately following the 7 November coup highlights several important points: on the most fundamental level, it illustrates how important the party was to the new powerbrokers. Scholars have long highlighted how a seizure group's control of the security and military apparatus, or parts thereof, facilitates their assumption of power.[21] However, they do not explain how such groups remain in office the morning afterwards if they also depend on the support of a hegemonic party. In such cases, a seizure group's strategies of legitimation, especially towards party followers, are as important as the initial event of the coup. In the case of Tunisia, the architects of 7 November even sought to conceal the very fact that a coup[22] had taken place, instead stressing that their takeover was constitutional. The RCD rallies were crucial in their quest for legitimacy as they outwardly projected

---

[18] Interview with Hamed Karoui, Tunis, 1 February 2017. *L'Action* subsequently also announced 'spontaneous rallies' for Ben Ali. See, for example, 'Une Manifestation Spontanée de Soutien au Président Zine El Abidine Ben Ali', *L'Action*, 8 November 1987, p. 7.

[19] Ivan Ermakoff has called this type of effect, in which a group establishes its sense of direction from one or a small set of actors, 'pyramidical impact'. See, for details, Ivan Ermakoff, 'The Structure of Contingency', *American Journal of Sociology*, 2015, 121, 1, p. 78.

[20] In the 1980s, various PSD factions had come to compete over the succession; one favoured Bourguiba's son, Habib Bourguiba Jr.; another supported Mohamed Mzali—Prime Minister and PSD Secretary General between 1980 and 1986; still another favoured Mohamed Sayah, a longtime party leader and adviser to the President; other party factions had different candidates in mind.

[21] Barbara Geddes, Joseph Wright, and Erica Frantz, *How Dictatorships Work*, Cambridge: Cambridge University Press, 2018, p. 33; compare also Milan Svolik, *The Politics of Authoritarian Rule*, Cambridge: Cambridge University Press, 2012.

[22] Consonant with Milan Svolik, I define a coup d'état 'as the removal of an authoritarian leader by his inner circles that is accompanied by the threat or actual use of force'; Milan Svolik, *The Politics of Authoritarian Rule*, Cambridge: Cambridge University Press, 2012, p. 41.

an image of popular support for the new officials. Indeed, 'legitimacy beliefs have a performative character' in that they 'take shape through the public enactment of allegiance'.[23] The rallies also helped discourage political competitors from challenging the new incumbents by staging a countercoup, for example.[24]

Reinventing Ben Ali's legacy

The new powerbrokers' immediate control of the PSD official publications provided a key resource to disseminate ideas that served their interests. The day after Ben Ali's assumption of power, the official PSD publication *L'Action* featured a series of articles detailing the constitutional provisions of article 57 that had been invoked to remove Bourguiba and stressing that his dismissal had been prompted by a respect for the 'national interest' and 'republican legality'.[25] Everything was done to convey respect for the rule of law. *L'Action* also announced a new PSD leadership in accordance with the party charter: as the Interim President of the republic, Ben Ali would also be the President of the PSD; Hedi Baccouche—who was appointed Prime Minister—would become its Secretary General; Hamed Karoui would remain its Director.[26] Ben Ali's ascent to the head of the ruling party appeared almost like a technicality. Most party activists assumed that his leadership would be transitional and that followers would formally elect their new PSD president at the next party congress.

The new powerbrokers also sought to bolster Ben Ali's political credentials, most importantly by inventing the myth that he possessed considerable Destourian legitimacy. In particular, they propagated the idea that he had played an important role in the fight for independence. Ben Ali's official biography—advertised in all major newspapers following his takeover—proclaimed that 'at the age of sixteen, he had been active in the ranks of the Destourian youth and served as a liaison officer between the regional party structures and the

---

[23] Ivan Ermakoff and Marko Grdesic, 'Institutions and Demotions: Collective Leadership in Authoritarian Regimes', *Theory and Society*, 2019, 48, 2, p. 562.

[24] For more information on how civilians on the streets help deter rival coup plotters from taking action, see Barbara Geddes, Joseph Wright, and Erica Frantz, *How Dictatorships Work*, Cambridge: Cambridge University Press, 2018, pp. 102–103.

[25] 'Dans le Respect de la Légalité et de la Constitution', *L'Action*, 8 November 1987, p. 1; 'Changement Dans la Légalité Constitutionnelle', *L'Action*, 8 November 1987, p. 5; 'Le Premier Alinéa de l'Article de la Constitution de la République Tunisienne', *L'Action*, 7 November 1987, p. 3.

[26] 'Communiqué de la Direction du Parti Socialiste Destourien', *L'Action*, 8 November 1987, p. 3.

armed struggle led by the resistance fighters.'[27] Yet it is unlikely that he held any significant posts, given his young age and limited military training at the time. The biography also underscored that Ben Ali had become a member of the PSD Political Bureau in June 1986 and had later risen to become its Vice-Secretary General—although these positions were given to him automatically by virtue of his appointment as Interior Minister and then Prime Minister, and he did not use them to become active in the party.[28] Everything was done to bolster the authority and legitimacy of the new president.

A correctivist frame

Ben Ali and his supporters next outlined the basic ideological tenets of their regime, which were consonant with those of the ruling party. For decades the PSD's legitimacy had been tied to the struggle for independence, but as Steven Levitsky and Lucan Way have observed, such 'founding legacies are bounded in that their effects weaken and expire over time'.[29] The decay of the PSD, particularly in the last decade of Bourguiba, provided 'an opening for redrawing the parameters of political authority'.[30] The new officials pursued this process through a correctivist frame that formally spoke the language of democracy and multiparty politics[31] but which they portrayed to PSD followers as beneficial to the party and, hence, as desirable for party activists.

In particular, Ben Ali and his supporters promised to re-elevate the PSD to a political leadership role, which it had lost under Bourguiba. Whilst at the regional level, the PSD retained some real independent leverage, including on new appointments and local policies, at the national level, Bourguiba

[27] 'Biographie du Président Zine El Abidine Ben Ali', *L'Action*, 7 November 1987, p. 2 and 8.

[28] Interview with Hedi Baccouche, Tunis, 22 July 2017.

[29] Steven Levitsky and Lucan A. Way, 'Not Just What But When (and How): Comparative-Historical Approaches to Authoritarian Durability', in James Mahoney and Kathleen Thelen (eds.), *Advances in Comparative-Historical Analysis*, Cambridge: Cambridge University Press, 2015, p. 109.

[30] Jason Brownlee, *Authoritarianism in an Age of Democratization*, Cambridge: Cambridge University Press, 2007, p. 41.

[31] In a similar vein, other leaders in the Arab world pursued ostensible democratization reforms in the late 1980s. In 1989, Jordan held parliamentary elections that were considered relatively free and fair. The following year, in Syria, authorities reserved sixty parliamentary seats for 'independents'. In Saudi Arabia, in 1992, officials created a sixty-member consultative body tasked with advising on political affairs. These policies led some observers to proclaim a new era of democratization in the Middle East and North Africa—especially as they came in the context of the decline and subsequent collapse of the Soviet Union. See also Holger Albrecht and Oliver Schlumberger, '"Waiting for Godot": Regime Change without Democratization in the Middle East', *International Political Science Review*, 2004, 25, 4, p. 373.

himself came to take all key decisions personally. The architects of 7 November promised to correct this wrong and restore the PSD's rightful decision-making and executive powers. They announced that party activists were the ones entrusted with realizing political 'change'. This rhetorical tool became one of the basic tenets of the new regime: it suggested the beginning of a new era with wide-ranging reforms whose nature remained, however, vaguely defined and whose projected outcome was open-ended. The new powerbrokers even denominated the party itself as 'author' of the change, a move intended to suggest that their assumption of power had occurred within a Destourian framework—even though the wider party structures had not been involved in the coup.[32]

Notably, in his 7 November speech, Ben Ali had announced the advent of democracy and multiparty politics, but the new powerbrokers were quick to affirm to party followers that the road towards political pluralism would not reduce but actually strengthen the PSD's role. On 10 November, Hedi Baccouche declared to party followers that:

we need to be prepared for the new stage by adopting PSD programmes and policies that respond to the demand for pluralism, in order for the [PSD] to remain the party of national liberation, the party which gathers the majority of citizens, and in order for it to acquire the means of exercising democracy so that it will preserve the privileged place it enjoys in Tunisian society more generally and in politics in particular.[33]

The architects of 7 November cast pluralism as a means of reinvigorating a hegemonic party that had weakened in previous decades. Baccouche's statement illustrates that the new authorities were careful to highlight that the goal was for the PSD to remain the 'majority'[34] party: they would recognize other political voices but assured followers that this plurality would ultimately only benefit the PSD. This strategy was attractive both to PSD hardliners—who wanted to reinforce their political predominance no matter what—and

---

[32] This rhetoric was reiterated in later months and years. See, for example, 'Ben Ali Trace: Nous Voulons Réaliser le Changement dans le Pays et Nous Voulons que le R.C.D. en Soit l'Auteur', *Le Renouveau*, 30 July 1988, p. 8.

[33] 'M. Hédi Baccouche Tient une Réunion avec les Secrétaires Généraux des Comités de Coordination du Parti', *L'Action*, 10 November 1987, p. 10.

[34] Ibid. See also declaration by the Central Committee following its February 1988 meeting, quoted in 'Tunisie: Changement d'Appellation; Le Parti Socialiste Destourien Devient le Rassemblement Constitutionnel Démocratique', *Le Monde*, 1 March 1988, http://www.lemonde.fr/archives/article/1988/03/01/tunisie-changement-d-appellation-le-parti-socialiste-destourien-devient-le-rassemblement-constitutionnel-democratique_4071577_1819218.html, last accessed 27 August 2017.

to followers who believed that a certain degree of pluralism was needed for the party to remain strong. Following encounters with Baccouche and Karoui, the Secretaries General of the Coordination Committee, the party's highest regional organ, published a communiqué in which they announced their 'total backing of the measures [Ben Ali] has taken' and their 'wholehearted adherence to the content of his [7 November] declaration'.[35] Similar statements were echoed by other party institutions.[36] Such official PSD endorsement bolstered the legitimacy of the new powerbrokers.

It is notable that the idea of truly competitive politics was never seriously discussed within the PSD party structures, though it was touted to opposition forces and Western allies, presumably to bolster support for the new regime.[37] Indeed, Ben Ali's 'change' and 'democracy' were sufficiently malleable and indeterminate concepts as to speak to different constituencies, and they were pitched to them in different ways. This had the strategic advantage of allowing the new powerbrokers to gather a broad coalition that went beyond the regime's traditional support base, the PSD.[38] Even many regime insiders said they did not know how much pluralism Ben Ali initially had in mind.

Elaborating on Ben Ali's early intentions, Hedi Baccouche—the central ideologue behind the 'change'—affirmed that a 'savage' or uncontrolled opening was never on the table. He went on, explaining that this was what Tunisia came to witness after 2011—when the country became a liberal democracy—'with [the emergence of] over 216 political parties'.[39] A range of sources confirm the early authoritarian tendencies of the new officials—though after the Arab Uprisings many people asserted that Ben Ali was initially sincere about democracy, probably to justify their own political activities at the time.[40] Amongst other indications, this can be seen in how, in the days following

---

[35] 'Les Secrétaires Généraux des Comités de Coordination Expriment Leur Appui au Président Ben Ali', *L'Action*, 10 November 1987, p. 4.

[36] 'La Cellule Destourienne de l'Agence TAP: l'Ère Nouvelle Sera une Ère de Labeur, de Réalisation, de Sérénité et de Renforcement des Acquis Républicains', *L'Action*, 8 November 1987, p. 7.

[37] Interviews with various opposition leaders, for example, Abdelfattah Mourou, an Islamist leader, La Marsa, July 2013.

[38] Tawfik al-Madani argues that one goal was to reunite with parties that had split from the PSD—such as the Movement of Social Democrats—and bring them back into the regime. See, for details, Tawfik al-Madani, *Suqut al-Dawla al-Bulisiyya fi Tunis* [*The Collapse of the Police State in Tunisia*], Beirut: Arab Scientific Publishers, 2011, p. 80.

[39] Interview with Hedi Baccouche, Tunis, 22 July 2017.

[40] For example, the Association of Former Tunisian Parliamentarians assessed that during the early period of Ben Ali, 'many initiatives were taken that guaranteed the openness of the regime'. See, for details, '*Istintajat al-Qira'a al-Naqdiyya li-Masarat al-Hukm min Sanat 1955 ila Sanat 2010*' ['*Conclusions from the Critical Reading of the Trajectories of Governance from 1955 until 2010*'], Association of Former Tunisian Parliamentarians, July 2017, private archives in Tunis.

the coup, newspaper articles repeatedly proclaimed the 'unanimous support' Ben Ali and his team enjoyed,[41] thus denying their opponents and critics any voice.

Thwarting internal resistance

Far from enjoying uncontested rule, Ben Ali in fact had several important rivals for succession, including Mohamed Sayah—the longtime party leader and adviser to Bourguiba. He placed them under house arrest on 7 November to forestall the possibility that they might stage a countercoup and they were released only once the new president believed they were no longer able to challenge his rule.[42] Naturally, some PSD factions, especially faithful Bourguibists who knew Bourguiba personally and had fought under his leadership against the French, disapproved of Ben Ali's coup and subsequent presidency. Far from a homogeneous block, the party was a site of internecine struggles, and the ascent of Ben Ali and his team had heightened conflicts amongst rival factions, sometimes publicly.

However, those PSD activists who opposed the new powerbrokers had little leverage to contest them on constitutional grounds. Even the most loyal Bourguibists knew that their figurehead had become frail and recognized that a change was necessary. Thus, eventually, most decided, however unwillingly, to accept Ben Ali's rule. They were deeply concerned about how the new President treated Bourguiba, particularly in cutting him off from public life and providing no news about him in the days following the coup. Many PSD followers from Bourguiba's hometown, Monastir, were particularly anxious. One of them, Mohamed, explained:

> We were waiting for news about Bourguiba and what would happen to him. At a certain point some people thought they [Ben Ali's team] might kill him. . . . The first and second days [after the coup] were calm here in Monastir. Then we started asking for news about [Bourguiba]. We were not opposed to his removal, he was old. . . . But we wanted reassurances about his well-being.[43]

Mohamed recalled that on 10 and 11 November 1987, rallies were staged in Monastir and some other localities to demand information about Bourguiba's whereabouts and condition. He said that a particularly loyal group of

---

[41] 'M Zine El Abidine Ben Ali, Président de la République: Soutien Unanime du Peuple', *L'Action*, 8 November 1987, pp. 7, 10.

[42] *L'Action* briefly confirmed the house arrests, calling them 'precautionary measures'. See 'Arrestation à Titre Préventif de Quelques Personnalités', *L'Action*, 7 November 1987, p. 3.

[43] Interview with Mohamed, Monastir, 27 July 2017.

Bourguibists even demonstrated—armed—in front of the PSD headquarters in El Kasbah, Tunis.[44] Though Mohamed despised the fact that Ben Ali, a military man, had taken power, he repeatedly emphasized that these rallies were 'not against Ben Ali, but for Bourguiba'.[45] This illustrates that even many fierce critics of Ben Ali refrained from voicing opposition against him and believed in the constitutionality of his takeover, a tendency that undermined any concerted efforts at mobilizing against the new incumbents. It is noteworthy that even after the Arab Uprisings, many Ben Ali associates still deny the fact that Bourguibist demonstrations took place.[46] These protests also received no media coverage at the time. To the new powerbrokers, any criticism of the way in which they treated Bourguiba signalled disloyalty and threatened their claim of unanimous support.

To forestall the wider spread of demonstrations, the new PSD leaders tried hard to avoid alienating the Bourguibist protesters. They reportedly offered the El Kasbah group 'guarantees' that Bourguiba would be unharmed.[47] And a few days later, Bourguiba was duly transferred to a house in Mornag and later to Monastir, where he spent the rest of his life. The new leaders' responsive and almost collegial attitude towards the Bourguibist protests is indicative of the initial fragility of their power base. The possibility of protests spreading to other localities—at a time when the new officials were trying hard to establish their political legitimacy, especially in the eyes of party followers—bolstered the bargaining power of the PSD demonstrators.

Still, Bourguiba was confined to his residency in Monastir and could receive only a very limited number of visitors, a situation his supporters found difficult to accept. The daughter of one PSD activist who knew Bourguiba personally said that in Monastir, her hometown, people 'couldn't bear that Bourguiba, who led the struggle for independence, found himself locked away'.[48] Some decided to show their disapproval symbolically. In particular, interviewees highlighted how the most loyal Bourguiba followers continued displaying pictures of him in their homes or workplaces, even after authorities mandated these be taken down: a quiet form of protest conveying their persistent allegiance to Tunisia's first President.[49]

---

[44] Ibid.

[45] Ibid.

[46] For example, interviews with Sami, a mid-level leader in Monastir, 25 July 2017; Hedi Baccouche, Tunis, 22 July 2017.

[47] Interview with Mohamed, Monastir, 27 July 2017.

[48] Interview with Samia, Tunis, 29 September 2015.

[49] Note that this practice was common amongst Bourguiba loyalists well beyond Monastir. Interviews with Hamza, Ras Jebel, Bizerte governorate, 9 February 2017; Mohamed, Monastir, 27 July 2017.

Some Bourguibists in Monastir decided to demonstrate their discontent more openly. In the village of Ksar Hellal, a bastion of Bourguiba followers and location of the Neo Destour founding congress on 2 March 1934, the entire local PSD bureau resigned out of loyalty to Bourguiba, provoking early municipal by-elections. These were held in January 1988 alongside legislative by-elections, triggered by the dismissal of two deputies representing the district of Monastir who were considered particularly close to Bourguiba.[50] During the ballots, some protesters shouted 'Long live Bourguiba'—a slogan Ben Ali supporters quickly dismissed by ascribing it to a handful of 'PSD barons' who were 'too jealous' to share their power.[51]

A group of loyal Bourguibists in Monastir even sought to challenge Ben Ali up front through rival electoral lists, publicly questioning his Destourian legitimacy. However, they had little chance of winning, as Mohamed, who ran on such a competitor list for the parliamentary by-elections, explained:

> We were sure that [Ben Ali] would win . . . because we did not have the money to campaign and we knew he might falsify the results. Our participation [in the by-elections] was an act of refusal, it was an act of opposition against Ben Ali. We wanted to show him that he would have to deal with us, that we had a voice in Monastir.[52]

Mohamed further elaborated that on the day of the legislative by-elections, all independent observers were expelled from the polling station. Ben Ali's list was awarded all seats. The same happened during the municipal by-elections. Arguably, Ben Ali and his team considered it particularly important to claim victory in Monastir and its historically significant Ksar Hellal village to convey the impression that even Bourguiba's stronghold had come to embrace the new president, reinforcing his Destourian legitimacy. The falsification of elections was relatively risk-free, given that Ksar Hellal was a small village and the event was not covered by independent journalists.

From the very beginning, indeed, the new leaders did not shy away from blatant authoritarian practices—even if they refrained from the use of force against PSD opponents—as long as their power grabs remained relatively inconspicuous. The multiple acts of resistance discussed in this section demonstrate that opposition was still possible; it remained limited, however, owing

---

[50] One of them was Mansour Skhiri, a former governor of Monastir and head of Bourguiba's Presidential Cabinet.

[51] Asma Larif-Beatrix, 'Chronique Tunisienne (1988)', *Annuaire de l'Afrique du Nord*, 1990, 27, Paris: CNRS, p. 745.

[52] Interview with Mohamed, Monastir, 27 July 2017.

to the correctivist rhetoric advanced by the officials—which resonated with the aspirations of many party activists—and the perceived constitutionality and transitional character of their takeover. Ben Ali's rule was considered legitimate, at least for the time being.

The remaking of the ruling party

Ben Ali and his team bolstered their sway within key state structures, such as the government, without much difficulty in that they simply appointed their loyal officials. But such practices were more difficult to implement in the case of the ruling party, with its deeply entrenched internal rules and traditions. Indeed, scholars have emphasized the great 'cost of reconstructing patronage networks, dismantling or radically transforming ruling parties, and reorienting policy regimes backed by entrenched constituencies', which is why 'authoritarian coalitions tend to be stable'.[53] However, processes of power redistribution may be easier to achieve during the political contingency and flux that accompany leadership and regime shifts—especially when incumbents frame the proposed changes in a way that makes them desirable to party activists. The following sections uncover how Ben Ali officials (1) hired 'ideological lobbyists' to garner broad coalitions for institutional change and (2) negotiated party reforms with key leaders, including through 'self-critique', a practice which (3) paved the way for a vast local and mid-level personnel overhaul in the ruling party.

Ideological lobbyists

Dictators with ample political capital of their own often crack down on intellectuals—a key source of political opposition.[54] But Ben Ali—a military man with no background in the ruling party—needed them to bolster his support base, regenerate political legitimacy, and develop the ideological

---

[53] Steven Levitsky and Lucan A. Way, 'Not Just What But When (and How): Comparative-Historical Approaches to Authoritarian Durability', in James Mahoney and Kathleen Thelen (eds.), *Advances in Comparative-Historical Analysis*, Cambridge: Cambridge University Press, 2015, p. 104; Thomas B. Pepinsky, *Economic Crises and the Breakdown of Authoritarian Regimes: Indonesia and Malaysia in Comparative Perspective*, Cambridge: Cambridge University Press, 2009, pp. 16–17; compare also Barbara Geddes, Joseph Wright, and Erica Frantz, *How Dictatorships Work*, Cambridge: Cambridge University Press, 2018, pp. 130–131.

[54] Mao Zedong even pronounced intellectuals as 'class enemies'; see, for details, Xing Lu, *The Rhetoric of Mao Zedong: Transforming China and Its People*, Columbia: University of South Carolina Press, 2017, pp. 103–104.

underpinnings of his regime. Hence, initially Ben Ali officials made it a priority to integrate public intellectuals and academics into the ruling party and the government, a practice through which they bestowed greater substance upon their claim to be opening up the political scene.

The intellectuals and academics who teamed up with Ben Ali became key 'ideological lobbyists' of the new regime: they took a central role in developing and directing the ideational underpinnings of Ben Ali's correctivist frame, as well as promoting the new powerbrokers to important constituencies domestically and abroad. These included universities—where many of the ideological lobbyists worked—and Western countries, particularly France, where they had often studied and had networks. Their functions ranged from agenda-setting and mediating with other political forces to advocacy for the new regime. Most were lawyers; some were sociologists, of whom many became highly influential. They were carefully chosen by a handful of close advisers to Ben Ali. Besides Hedi Baccouche, the key PSD figure in the coup, they included Abderrahim Zouari, a lawyer appointed head of the Political Bureau responsible for the party's restructuring, and Abdelaziz Ben Dhia, then Dean of the Law Faculty in Tunis and a long-standing Ben Ali ally who became highly influential in subsequent years.

These ideological lobbyists—who typically had backgrounds as leaders in the Tunisian Human Rights League (LTDH), the leftist student scene, labour union, or perspectivist movement[55]—took key positions in the sociocultural and educational arenas, and some rose to become central ideologues of the new regime. Most famously, Mohamed Charfi—a lawyer and former leader of the LTDH, who, under Bourguiba, had spent fifteen months in a penitentiary for his activities in the perspectivist movement—became Education Minister in 1989, a position in which he was tasked with 'modernizing' the education curriculum. Abdelbaki Hermassi, a sociologist who had studied at Berkeley, became Culture and Foreign Affairs Minister, a post which he used to promote Ben Ali's 'modernism' abroad and frame it as being in tune with Western liberalism. These ideological lobbyists served to bestow a liberal face on the regime and to underpin its legality, all whilst also designing the substance of its correctivist frame.

---

[55] The perspectivist movement was of far-left tendency and active on Tunisian university campuses in the 1960s and 1970s. For more information about its origin, ideology, activities, and repression under Bourguiba, see Abdeljalil Bouguerra, *De l'Histoire de la Gauche Tunisienne: Le Mouvement Perspectives, 1963–1975*, Tunis: Cérès, 1993; Olfa Belhassine, 'Tunisie: La Répression au Temps des Perspectivistes', *Justiceinfo*, 28 February 2020, https://www.justiceinfo.net/fr/43917-tunisie-la-repression-au-temps-des-perspectivistes.html, last accessed 10 February 2022.

One of their key innovations immediately after Ben Ali's takeover of power was the creation of '7 November' clubs and federations (named in allusion to the coup), which existed in parallel to the party cells. Hedi Baccouche stressed that everybody was welcome to join the new 7 November institutions or the wider party structures. He stated:

> The [party's] Central Committee decided that all those who believe in the 7th of November and have the predisposition to work for the good of Tunisia and its new, modern orientations are welcome. It is sufficient that their intentions are sincere.[56]

The creation of 7 November institutions was highly strategic: it encouraged people who had never been involved in the PSD to become politically active, thus serving as a key recruitment structure for the new regime and widening its grassroots support coalition. Many of these 7 November activists would eventually join the PSD. Hedi Baccouche remarked on the 'massive influx of . . . patriots of all [political] tendencies' at the time.[57] Whilst this is an overstatement, as the party never absorbed the entire ideological spectrum,[58] a range of interviewees testified that its membership grew significantly in the months following Ben Ali's takeover.[59] By July 1988, the official number of adherents had reached a staggering 1.5 million.[60] The party membership fee was only a couple of dinars per year, making membership readily accessible to any willing person.

Despite their important recruitment function, the 7 November structures stoked fear amongst the PSD's traditional support base. Many worried that the new president might yet decide to establish his own party, despite his assurances that the PSD would remain important and would even lead his 'change'. Increasing talk about a '7 November movement'[61] and the '7 Novemberists'— that is, those who participated in the ousting of Bourguiba—only reinforced

---

[56] 'Interview de M Hedi Baccouche', *Le Renouveau*, 29 July 1988, p. 6.

[57] Ibid.

[58] Activists of the far left and the Islamists commonly maintained some distance from Ben Ali and his associates, voicing suspicions about their 'true' intentions. See, for details, Anne Wolf, *Political Islam in Tunisia: The History of Ennahda*, New York: Oxford University Press, 2017.

[59] For example, interviews with regional official Anouar, Sousse, 27 July 2017, and RCD Executive Bureau member Mounir Ben Miled, Tunis, 24 May 2016.

[60] 'Le R.C.D. par les Chiffres', *Le Renouveau*, 29 July 1988, p. 6. Note that one interviewee alleged that authorities inflated the number by also counting people who had retreated from political life, including some loyal Bourguibists. Interview with Sahbi, Tunis, 24 May 2016.

[61] See, for example, 'Reconnaissance aux Martyrs et aux Résistants', *Le Temps*, 21 March 1989, p. 2.

such suspicion. PSD loyalists' anxieties were increased when some of Ben Ali's close advisers openly suggested he create his own political movement.[62]

A new party?

Uncertainty about the future of the ruling party reached its height in February 1988 on the occasion of the first meeting of the PSD Central Committee under Ben Ali. The Central Committee comprised the top leaders of the party, who held prime responsibility for executing its programmes and resolutions, decided during five-yearly party congresses. The February 1988 Central Committee meeting revealed that PSD activists had reason to believe that Ben Ali wanted to create his own party—a common ambition amongst dictators who seek to consolidate personal power.[63] During his inauguration speech, Ben Ali called on the PSD to 'become an example of the "Popular Democratic Rally"'[64]—a somewhat blurry statement which attendees interpreted as either an allusion to a proposed new party that would absorb the PSD or a suggested new name for the latter.[65] Both options were discussed during the meeting. Naturally, Central Committee members, dominated by the PSD old guard, were fiercely opposed to creating a new party, as was Hedi Baccouche, who chaired the meeting. He recalled:

> Contrary to Ben Ali, I was attached to the party. Some people told him 'you are a great man, you can establish a new party', but in practical terms it was not a good idea. We had a party with its traditions, a reasonable man wouldn't abandon it. . . . So we fought.[66]

The fact that Ben Ali even contemplated creating his own party shows how little he cared about the PSD—despite the party's important historical legacy—and that he really represented the ascent of an entirely new political class. Though Central Committee members vehemently rejected the idea of a new

[62] Most interviewees affirmed that only officials without backgrounds in the PSD provided such counsel, believing this would boost their own career prospects (e.g., interviews with Hamed Karoui, Tunis, 1 February 2017; Sahbi, Tunis, 24 May 2016); however, a minority of historic party figures also advocated for the creation of a new political movement—including Abderrazak Kefi, Information Minister under Bourguiba—to convey an image of 'total reform'.

[63] Barbara Geddes, Joseph Wright, and Erica Frantz, *How Dictatorships Work*, Cambridge: Cambridge University Press, 2018, pp. 79–80.

[64] 'Ben Ali Devant le Comité Central, 26 et 27 Février 1988', *Le Renouveau*, 29 July 1988, p. 5.

[65] Interviews with Mohamed Ghariani, Tunis, 20 July 2017; Hedi Baccouche, Tunis, 28 September 2015.

[66] Interview with Hedi Baccouche, Tunis, 28 September 2015.

party, they were not opposed to altering the name of the PSD to signal a political change. However, they disapproved of Ben Ali's suggested 'Popular Democratic Rally' as it did not include the term 'Destour'. To the old guard, this proposition conveyed a dismissal not only of Bourguiba's legacy but also of the wider independence movement. 'In the end we made a compromise that included the word "Destour"', Habib Baccouche explained, setting out the reasons behind settling on Constitutional Democratic Rally (commonly abbreviated RCD from the French Rassemblement Constitutionnel Démocratique; in Arabic al-Tajammu' al-Dusturi al-Dimuqrati).[67]

The fact that Hedi Baccouche and the Central Committee members restrained Ben Ali from creating his own party and that they significantly influenced the renaming of the PSD illustrates that they had significant agency and bargaining power. Whilst this may seem counterintuitive at first glance, the ousting of Bourguiba had in fact invigorated key party structures. With Bourguiba's decades-long personal grip on the PSD released, these party structures gained independent political leverage and decision-making power. Ben Ali—though formally the President of the ruling party—had to compromise with key party figures and play by the book. The PSD began operating in oligarchic fashion according to its party charter and, hence, could keep Ben Ali's ambitions in check—at least initially.

Whilst the choice of the name RCD suggested some element of historical continuity, through its reference to the Destour movement, it also reflected the party's formal incorporation of the wider political and economic principles laid out by the new president. This normative refashioning was a way to regenerate legitimacy for a ruling party whose founding legacy—the independence struggle—was no longer sufficient to garner a wide support base. The elimination of the 'Socialist' reference highlighted the RCD's commitment to economic liberalism, a strategy the PSD had already come to embrace in the preceding years, after its socialist experiment had failed. More important, the 'Democratic Rally' stipulation signalled the party's adoption of Ben Ali's pluralistic rhetoric, at least formally. However, in stark contrast to the outward democratization discourse, Ben Ali and his team actually used the Central Committee meeting to reaffirm their belief in a majority party. Mohamed Ghariani stated:

> The idea of democracy was discussed. We were in a way obliged to play the game. But Ben Ali gave guarantees . . . that this democracy would not

[67] Ibid.

be at the expense of the party. Thus, the elites knew that their party would remain . . . in power.[68]

Ghariani explained that the 'only matter of real contention' at the meeting concerned the naming of the party; a competitive democracy was something neither the new political leadership nor the Central Committee members desired or believed could happen.[69] To some extent, the 'Rally' component of the new name conveyed this perspective: the main concern for Ben Ali and his associates was that the RCD should remain a mass party capable of 'rallying' people around the new president. To bolster Ben Ali's support base, the Central Committee members formally agreed to 'consolidate and enlarge the structures of the Rally [RCD]'[70] by recruiting people from a range of ideological backgrounds. Whilst sometimes officials restrict the membership of ruling parties, as this makes it easier to distribute privileges and enforce internal discipline and control,[71] Ben Ali's priority was to attract as many people as possible to the RCD. For the new President, a large RCD membership base was a way to claim legitimacy, which was especially important given his lack of a party background.

Self-critique

The Central Committee also engaged in a 'self-critique' to better understand why the party had become weak towards the end of Bourguiba's rule and to devise strategies to strengthen it, a practice borrowed from communist regimes. Indeed, communist officials first introduced 'self-critique' as a form of political redemption for people's 'mistakes', but it also came to be used to correct wider political 'wrongs'.[72] After decades of Bourguiba's personal

---

[68] Interview with Mohamed Ghariani, Tunis, 20 July 2017.

[69] Ibid.

[70] 'Tunisie: Changement d'Appellation; Le Parti Socialiste Destourien Devient le Rassemblement Constitutionnel Démocratique', Le Monde, 1 March 1988, http://www.lemonde.fr/archives/article/1988/03/01/tunisie-changement-d-appellation-le-parti-socialiste-destourien-devient-le-rassemblement-constitutionnel-democratique_4071577_1819218.html, last accessed 27 August 2017.

[71] Membership in the CPSU was deliberately restricted to about 10% of the population. See, for details, Bruce Bueno de Mesquita, Alastair Smith, Randolph M. Siverson, and James D. Morrow, The Logic of Political Survival, Cambridge, MA: MIT Press, 2003, pp. 53–54.

[72] Note that leaders of the Arab republics have also promoted the concept of self-criticism within ruling parties. A report of the Syrian Ba'th Party stressed the importance of self-criticism as a way 'to guarantee proper coordination and discipline in dealing with members' (Hizb al-Ba'th al-'Arabi al-Ishtiraki, Hawla al-Dimuqratiyya al-Markaziyya [About Centralized Democracy], Damascus: Cultural Bureau and Party Preparatory Publications, n.d. [1970s], p. 7, quoted in Joseph Sassoon, Anatomy of Authoritarianism in the Arab Republics, Cambridge: Cambridge University Press, 2016, p. 43). In addition, Souhaïl Belhadj found that upon taking power in 2000, Bashar al-Assad promoted 'internal

rule in Tunisia, the practice of internal criticism had the double advantage of giving party members the sense that they were taking back political agency and control; at the same time, it provided a platform for collective agenda-setting and negotiating deep structural transformations—trends that incumbents could try to steer to their advantage. But such intentions were masked by Ben Ali's seductive correctivist rhetoric. He insisted that the process of self-critique was launched to '[re-examine] the organization of the [party] structures and their internal working to evaluate the situation [the party] had experienced' and rectify any past mistakes.[73] A range of interviewees affirmed that the principal conclusion was that the PSD had lost vigour because internal democratic practices had ceased to exist, including at the local level; some also criticized the merger of state and party structures, particularly during the socialist experiment under Bourguiba. They said that this had allowed activists with insufficient qualifications to take control over the party grass roots.[74]

One of the main challenges towards the end of the Bourguiba era was that historic PSD leaders were growing old and some had passed away. Their successors typically hailed from the same family and—though they did not possess the same political legitimacy—made it very difficult for other activists to climb up the party echelons. Whilst party followers typically opposed democracy as a mode of governance, they considered a certain degree of competition within the RCD necessary for the party to regain its strength. Indeed, within the RCD, the notion of 'democratic practices' came to mean free internal competition and unreserved opportunities for upward mobility, which many followers desired. They were attracted to the language of democracy and even sought to copy some of its practices internally to strengthen a ruling party that served distinctly authoritarian ends.

The main conclusion of the Central Committee's self-critique was to establish a road map to 'renew' the RCD local chapters on the basis of democratic internal elections, in preparation for an extraordinary party congress. The congress was scheduled for the summer of 1988 and intended to overhaul the

dialogue' and established 'brainstorming' committees within the Ba'th party to renew its ideological underpinnings and—ultimately—reinforce his power base. See, for details, Souhaïl Belhadj, *La Syrie de Bashar Al-Assad: Anatomie d'un Régime Autoritaire*, Paris: Belin, 2013, pp. 138–140.

[73] 'Ben Ali Trace: Nous Voulons Réaliser le Changement dans le Pays et Nous Voulons que le R.C.D. en Soit l'Auteur', *Le Renouveau*, 30 July 1988, p. 8.

[74] For example, interviews with Abderrahim Zouari, Tunis, 9 February 2017; Ali Chaouch, Tunis, 11 February 2017.

wider party structures, including its relation to the state.[75] However, as the following sections demonstrate, Ben Ali officials certainly did not intend to induce free competition at the local level. Rather, they took advantage of the state of internal party flux and contingency to discard longtime PSD figures and reconstitute the party according to their own interests.

Local restructuring

Ben Ali's team began the RCD's wide-ranging process of local restructuring by appointing new Secretaries General to the Coordination Committees,[76] the highest regional party instance, arguing that the previous leadership 'was not at all qualified to lead the necessary change.'[77] These intermediaries between the party officials in Tunis and its rank and file were tasked with organizing extraordinary congresses of the party cells to install a new local leadership throughout the country—a total overhaul of the party's grassroots representation.[78] Notably, the new local officials were designated, not elected, as previously agreed with Central Committee leaders. Indeed, despite their stated commitment to internal democratic practices, the new political leaders claimed that appointments were initially necessary to ensure political 'renewal'. Chedli Neffati, a close collaborator of Ben Ali who would head the RCD in later years, explained:

> The cell leaders were dignitaries, activists from important families . . . . Some people respected them [and] some didn't because they had been in power for too long. No matter what we had decided, we would have created a controversy and some people would have been disappointed. We agreed to nominate a new local leadership even though this was undemocratic . . . . Some people told us: 'how is it possible that on the one hand you talk about democracy, but on the other you nominate local leaders?!' We said that this time only—once—we will nominate the leaders and dismiss those who have

[75] 'Ben Ali Trace: Nous Voulons Réaliser le Changement dans le Pays et Nous Voulons que le R.C.D. en Soit l'Auteur', *Le Renouveau*, 30 July 1988, p. 8.

[76] Ibid.

[77] Interview with Naziha Zarrouk, Tunis, 30 January 2017.

[78] Note that incoming dictators in other Arab republics have similarly advanced correctivist frames to restructure the ruling party—all the way from the grass roots through mid-level to senior representatives. For example, upon taking power in Syria, Bashar al-Assad promoted new figures to various party ranks and then made alterations to the Ba'th's internal rules and structures to reinforce his grip over the party. See, for details, Souhaïl Belhadj, *La Syrie de Bashar Al-Assad: Anatomie d'un Régime Autoritaire*, Paris: Belin, 2013.

been [in power] for too long in order to give a chance to new people, to the youth.[79]

Chedli Neffati's testimony reveals the clash between the regime's rhetoric of reform and authoritarian practices, including within the inner ranks of the party. It is notable that despite their wish to introduce internal competitive practices, most party activists became persuaded that appointing new grass-roots leadership was initially necessary to inject fresh blood into the party.[80] This illustrates the centrality of correctivist ideas in instigating wide structural change. Indeed, party followers trusted their figureheads that the appointment of leaders would be an exceptional measure and that elections would be the norm during subsequent cell congresses.[81] Otherwise, they would surely have opposed these practices—just as they had blocked Ben Ali's proposed creation of a rival party during the Central Committee meeting in February 1988. In reality, of course, the designations were deeply strategic measures aimed at reconstructing the party's patronage networks and creating a new power base entirely dedicated to Ben Ali.

When asked about the characteristics of the local leaders who were app-ointed, interviewees advanced two main ideas. The first was that Ben Ali and his team were particularly keen to promote wealthy local entrepreneurs to posts as cell leaders.[82] They sought to bolster the RCD's influence on the ground by linking it to local capital. The prominent families that had dominated the local party leadership under Bourguiba were not necessarily wealthy but typically were known for their political leverage, gained by virtue of their roles in the fight for independence. Replacing some of their leaders with accomplished entrepreneurs—sometimes from rival family clans—was presented as a way to overcome the crisis of socialism by rewarding pro-fessional success. In particular, Ben Ali and his team were keen to integrate Tunisia's new business and commercial class, which emerged in the 1970s in the wake of Bourguiba's tentative economic opening and typically focused on private investments in quickly growing urban areas.[83] Thereby Ben Ali offi-cials created a new, powerful support group within the party. The second

---

[79] Interview with Chedli Neffati, Tunis, 2 February 2017.

[80] For example, interviews with Hamza, Ras Jebel, Bizerte governorate, 9 February 2017; Naziha Zarrouk, Tunis, 30 January 2017.

[81] Ibid.

[82] For example, interview with Hedi Baccouche, Tunis, 22 July 2017.

[83] For details about economic developments at the time, see Gregory White, *A Comparative Polit-ical Economy of Tunisia and Morocco: On the Outside of Europe Looking In*, Albany: State University of New York Press, 2001.

characteristic of the new local officials was that they were markedly younger than their predecessors, some of whom had held their posts for decades.

A new generation

Ben Ali and his entourage were keen to build up a new generation of youthful party activists who had never worked with the previous regime and whose loyalties lay entirely with the new president. The incorporation of young followers also had the potential to substantially increase the overall party size and grassroots reach—in 1987, 73.7% of the population was aged thirty-four or younger.[84] A 1988 internal RCD document denounced that the party 'is almost completely alienated from the youth of Tunisia, their university organizations and environment'.[85] Besides promoting younger activists to local party posts, reinforcing the RCD's sway in schools and especially universities became a priority. During the last decade under Bourguiba, the PSD had been almost non-existent on campuses, where leftists and Islamists dominated student activism. The fragility of Bourguiba's rule had in fact become visible first at universities, where anti-regime protests were staged—reaching their apex in the summer of 1987—and security forces clashed repeatedly with students. To minimize potential threats from such bastions of the opposition, Ben Ali officials sought to gain a grip over campuses, not only by strengthening the RCD's infrastructure there but also by trying to co-opt key student figureheads.

Shortly after taking power, Ben Ali officials announced that campuses were once again a space where student activism could take place freely, as long as it was peaceful and respected the law. Consequently, the leftist General Union of Tunisian Students (UGET) could operate again in a relatively free environment, at least initially. Also, the rival General Tunisian Student Union (UGTE)—which had been outlawed under Bourguiba and consisted mainly of Islamist activists—enjoyed unprecedented freedom of action.[86] The new powerbrokers, it seems, were willing to take some real steps towards political liberalization in their attempt to co-opt key opposition groups, if simple

---

[84] See, for details, 'Pyramide des Âges, Perspective Monde: Tunisie', Université de Sherbrooke, n.d., http://perspective.usherbrooke.ca/bilan/servlet/BMPagePyramide?codePays=TUN&annee=1987, last accessed 13 June 2018; author's own calculations.

[85] Quoted in Tawfik al-Madani, *Suqut al-Dawla al-Bulisiyya fi Tunis* [*The Collapse of the Police State in Tunisia*], Beirut: Arab Scientific Publishers, 2011, p. 80.

[86] See, for details, Adel Thabti, *al-Ittihad al-'Am al-Tunisi lil-Talaba* [*The General Tunisian Student Union*], Tunis: MIPE, 2011.

rhetoric was not enough to win them over.[87] However, Samir Abidi, a UGET follower at the time, suggested that many union activists retained reservations about the new authorities, despite their newly gained liberties. He said:

They [the student activists] were not with Ben Ali; it is important to highlight this. [They were] in the opposition, but the unions worked in a much freer environment. The general spirit of students at the time was to work in the opposition.[88]

To gain a grip over the powerful UGET, Ben Ali approached some of their main figureheads, typically via his ideological lobbyists, many of whom were university professors. They tried to win students over by applauding Ben Ali's support for their activities and popular liberties more generally, suggesting that the free space on campuses evinced the sincerity of his intentions. The new powerbrokers were particularly keen to attract UGET students who had family members in the PSD or the RCD, believing that their party connections would make them more amenable to compromise. One such student was the above-quoted Samir Abidi, who had relatives in the PSD.[89] During the Eighteenth UGET Congress, held between 30 April and 2 May 1988, Samir Abidi was elected head of the union; he later became a key Ben Ali regime ally, indicating the extent to which the new authorities eventually succeeded in co-opting some influential student leaders.

In parallel, Ben Ali officials sought to reinforce the RCD's support base on campuses, though this proved initially somewhat more challenging, given the sway of leftists and Islamist activists. However, despite their reservations about the new authorities, many young people were attracted by the wider tenets of the 7 November declaration.[90] The RCD leadership knew how to capitalize on this. Mohamed Ghariani, the first Secretary General of the RCD student movement, explained:

We found a general sympathy for the 7 November principles. We took advantage of this sympathy to reorganize the party, particularly ... at the university, amongst students, and at the level of university professors. In a way we ...

---

[87] However, most UGTE members initially remained sceptical of the new regime, as the Islamists' imprisoned leaders had not yet been released. For details, see ibid.

[88] Interview with Samir Abidi, Tunis, 30 June 2016.

[89] Ibid.

[90] Compare Tawfik al-Madani, *Suqut al-Dawla al-Bulisiyya fi Tunis* [*The Collapse of the Police State in Tunisia*], Beirut: Arab Scientific Publishers, 2011, p. 80.

exploited this state of glory, [their] hope for democracy and human rights. The 7 November, it was easy for people to like. . . . We seduced the youth.[91]

Mohamed Ghariani stated that the student wing rose from around 100 active members just after Ben Ali took power to as many as 20,000 a few years later. Some students did indeed join the RCD because the 7 November principles 'seduced' them—to use Ghariani's term. Amongst sections of the grass roots, there was a genuine willingness to instigate a political opening—in contrast to the party's more senior members, who mostly played on such rhetoric for political gains. This shows how Ben Ali's correctivist rhetoric was interpreted differently by different constituencies, including within the party's inner ranks. Some young activists also joined the party for more opportunistic reasons. In particular, the RCD leadership attracted young people through a scheme of lucrative youth or student member benefits, which had not existed under Bourguiba. Incentives ranged from free printing services and rare student accommodation guarantees to free vacation trips.[92]

The old guard's decline

The Ben Ali team framed the integration of student activists and ideological lobbyists as part of a wider political 'reconciliation'—a notion first introduced in the 7 November declaration that became a key ideological tenet of the new regime. In line with their correctivist frame, the new authorities presented 'reconciliation' as a way to 'rectify' past mistakes, specifically Bourguiba's crackdown on various opposition groups and, more generally, authoritarian politics and deeply entrenched tensions amongst rival political trends. In practice, the promise of 'reconciliation' took the form of ideological outreach, through which the new officials outwardly promoted political pluralism and democratization—all whilst bolstering their own power: the RCD newcomers pushed the old guard to the margin and fostered the rise of a new party class entirely dedicated to Ben Ali.

---

[91] Interview with Mohamed Ghariani, Tunis, 27 May 2016.

[92] Some of these benefits were formalized, whilst others, such as free vacation trips, were—on paper—available to all students, though in practice party activists were almost exclusively selected. Note that interviewees frequently disagreed on the type of benefits that existed and how they were distributed, which suggests that channels were mostly informal; acquiring key perks and benefits depended on personal relations and individual patronage. Interviews with Aymen, a former RCD student activist, Bardo, 6 October 2015; Hamza, Ras Jebel, Bizerte governorate, 9 February 2017; Hedi Baccouche, Tunis, 22 July 2017; Naoufel, Tunis, 24 July 2017.

However, the newcomers did encounter significant adversaries in the RCD, as Sadok Chaabane—a leftist lawyer who became one of Ben Ali's chief propagandists—observed. He elaborated that the rise of new constituencies was deeply controversial amongst the old guard, who feared they would be sidelined.[93] Ben Ali officials sought to delegitimate the old guard's opposition by attributing it to their authoritarian mindset—this stood, they were keen to suggest, in contrast to the new officials, whose liberalization of the party evidenced the sincerity of their broader democratization intentions.[94] In reality, rather than pitting 'autocrats' against 'democrats', these struggles amongst rival RCD currents mapped frictions concerning the fundamental role and identity of the ruling party, as well as the distribution of resources and political influence amongst competing factions. Ultimately, it was a struggle over decision-making power and executive control.

Members of the old guard, for their part, denounced claims to be at once a 'Destourian' and 'leftist' as inherently contradictory, charging that the academics and intellectuals who had joined the party embraced a foreign ideology, imported from France or the Soviet Union, and hence threatened their nationalist cause. They also objected that the integration of leftists devalued the party's function in society, particularly its historically important role in fostering upward mobility and socioeconomic advancement amongst longtime followers. Mohamed Ghariani explained:

> Under Bourguiba ... the party managed everything, it was the party ... with its members that governed and appointed [people]. Under Ben Ali ... the party played a role, but it wasn't the same because he diversified the sources of recruitment. Ben Ali ... recruited from the administration, intellectual circles, the university. So the party just became one source of recruitment. Under Bourguiba, it was the only source![95]

Though in the course of the interview Ghariani acknowledged that Ben Ali's new recruits were formally 'injected' into the RCD, he did not view them as an integral part of the party. Rather, Ghariani argued that their integration into the RCD reflected the emergence of rival sources of political influence and upwards mobility, such as universities, suggesting that this weakened the party.

---

[93] Interview with Sadok Chaabane, Tunis, 20 July 2017.

[94] Salem Cheikh, 'Parti du Bon Pied', *Le Renouveau*, 29 July 1998, p. 12.

[95] Interview with Mohamed Ghariani, Tunis, 20 July 2017. Note that Ghariani idealized the PSD. In fact, the economic crisis under Bourguiba had limited its role as a social elevator. Further, its structures overlapped to a large extent with those of the state and its administration, making it often difficult to determine which were paramount in matters such as promotions and recruitment.

In reality, however, the opening up of the RCD structures initially only reduced the leverage of the old guard. Indeed, in the immediate aftermath of Ben Ali's assumption of power, it strengthened the party as it bolstered its membership base, grassroots reach, and activism.

Ghariani's testimony illustrates the extent to which the opening up of the RCD remained contested amongst the old guard. Most RCD adherents defended a narrow view of the 'Destourian' and rejected the newcomers. They never came to embrace Ben Ali's declared political 'reconciliation' and denied the newcomers a Destourian identity. The old guard was particularly dismayed because, after decades of personalized politics, the immediate aftermath of Bourguiba's ousting had actually seen a real strengthening of their influence— as evidenced by the Central Committee blocking Ben Ali's plan to create a rival party. But only months later, the opening up of the party structures again reduced the old guard's sway, and they found they were dismissed as blowhards, left with little leverage to contest their decline on moral or political grounds.

Co-opting the opposition

Ben Ali and his team further widened their support base by legalizing key opposition parties and co-opting some of their figureheads. They sought to display the sincerity of their liberalizing intentions by taking the opposition's key concerns into account, such as the abolition of the constitution's presidency-for-life provision and the gradual release of political prisoners incarcerated under Bourguiba. Ben Ali also met with key opposition representatives, including from the Islamist party—a central opponent which Bourguiba had fervently repressed. As the self-assumed 'reconciliator', Ben Ali was keen to portray himself as politically responsive and consensus-seeking. Well aware of the sway of religious forces, he even revived some Islamic institutions and practices.[96] Most religious activists remained wary of the new authorities, but a small minority decided to integrate into the regime. This 'Islamo-Destourian' trend constituted only a small fraction of RCD newcomers, but it did include some prominent figures: importantly, Cheikh Abderrahman Kheli—the Imam of the Great Mosque of Kairouan, who had fallen out with Bourguiba— publicly sided with the new authorities and reminded people that 'the Destour

---

[96] Amongst other actions, Ben Ali restored the status of Tunisia's historic Zaytouna University— which Bourguiba had reduced to a simple Faculty of Islamic Law and Theology—as a university and established a Ministry of Religious Affairs and a Supreme Islamic Council. See, for details, Anne Wolf, *Political Islam in Tunisia: The History of Ennahda*, New York: Oxford University Press, 2017, pp. 68–69.

was founded by a Sheikh, the Sheikh Abdelaziz Thaalbi'.[97] He encouraged his followers to join the 'change' and, during the first parliamentary elections under Ben Ali in 1989, headed the RCD's electoral list in Kairouan.[98]

Whilst courting the more religious portions of society, the authorities also sought to gain a grip over the leftist Tunisian General Labour Union (UGTT)—another key actor with networks throughout the country. Tunisian academic Tawfik al-Madani argues that 'the divorce between the party and the syndicate' had been a key reason behind the PSD's failure 'to hegemonize its ideology among the different social classes'.[99] The union had been substantially weakened in the last years of Bourguiba, who had fiercely cracked down on it. Some UGTT members even wished to reconcile with the new powerbrokers to guarantee at least a minimal level of union activities. They were relieved that Bourguiba had been ousted and believed that henceforth the union's relations with central authorities could only improve. The RCD leftist recruits led discussions between the union and the regime—another illustration of how the ideological lobbyists served to promote the new regime in front of key constituencies. One such central figure was Moncer Rouissi, a leftist recruit who had a background in the UGTT. Rouissi recalled:

[We] sought to . . . normalize relations with the union. We met with Habib Achour, who was a very strong historical figure in the UGTT. . . . I persuaded him to withdraw from the UGTT leadership, to retire. . . . I said, a new page is turning in Tunisia. . . . I also convinced Abdelaziz Boraoui, another union leader, to step down [and] . . . to establish a [UGTT] Committee of Syndicalist Reconciliation.[100]

It is improbable that negotiations between the union and the RCD were as smooth as Rouissi describes, and longtime figureheads such as Habib Achour and Abdelaziz Boraoui are unlikely to have given up their posts voluntarily. However, they ultimately had little choice, given how vulnerable the union had become after years of repression and in the face of a massive popular influx into the RCD, including from their own constituency. This left the UGTT with little bargaining power and more susceptible to co-optation, at least at the leadership level—a striking development, given that the union had once

---

[97] 'Entretien avec le Cheikh Abderrahman Khelif, Tête de Liste R.C.D. Pour la Circonscription de Kairouan, "La Vérité est Multiple"', *Réalités*, 189, March/April 1989, p. 36.
[98] Ibid.
[99] Tawfik al-Madani, *Suqut al-Dawla al-Bulisiyya fi Tunis* [*The Collapse of the Police State in Tunisia*], Beirut: Arab Scientific Publishers, 2011, p. 70.
[100] Interview with Moncer Rouissi, Tunis, 21 July 2017.

acted as an important opposition force under Bourguiba. The new authorities even managed to establish a Committee of Syndicalist Reconciliation within the UGTT—tasked with smoothing the union's ties to the regime, as well as 'reconciling' members of distinct ideologies. And during the 1989 legislative elections, three figureheads of the socialist-leaning UGTT were elected lawmakers for the RCD[101]—quite ironically, given that the party ran on an economically liberal programme and in subsequent years worked hard to weaken the union.

The new authorities' most prominent attempt at co-opting opposition groups was the National Pact, a political roadmap signed on 7 November 1988—the one-year anniversary of Ben Ali's takeover—by sixteen parties and associations, including the UGTT, the influential employers' federation, and the Islamists.[102] The pact enshrined their support for the basic tenets of the regime: popular freedoms, human rights, and the Code of Personal Status, all whilst specifying that this was subject to 'the context of the law'—a qualification to which most observers paid little attention at the time.[103] The key role political pacts had played in democratic transformations in Europe and South America led many to uncritically infer a similar trend in Tunisia.[104] Indeed, the new authorities exploited the authoritarian potential of practices closely associated with democratic consolidation to bolster their own power.

It is notable that the text of the National Pact was discussed and signed at the Presidential Palace, rather than in the framework of an elected body, such as the Parliament. The initiators of the pact—most importantly, Hedi Baccouche—justified this choice by stating that the parliamentary deputies hailed from the Bourguiba era and were therefore not apt to lead the 'change'.[105] However, they could have waited until the first elections under Ben Ali, which took place only five months later, to sign the pact. Clearly, the priority of the new officials was to entice major actors to form a wide support coalition around the person of Ben Ali and boost the legitimacy of the new regime rather than that of its governing organs—let alone to establish democratic

---

[101] They were Amara Abassi, Mohsen Dridi, and Mohamed Sghaier Saidane, representing the governorates of Gafsa, Bizerte, and Kairouan, respectively.

[102] Note that the Islamist party had not been legalized, so its members supported the pact through a representative who signed the final agreement.

[103] For example, US Embassy in Tunis, 'Tunisia Celebrates 7 November; Elections Next April; National Pact Signed', Wikileaks, 8 November 1988, 88TUNIS11598_a, confidential; Lisa Anderson, 'Political Pacts, Liberalism, and Democracy: The Tunisian National Pact of 1988', *Government and Opposition*, 1991, 26, pp. 244–260. Note that Anderson suggests that the National Pact '[devotes attention]. . . to the political rights and responsibilities associated with classical liberalism' (p. 247).

[104] Lisa Anderson, 'Political Pacts, Liberalism, and Democracy: The Tunisian National Pact of 1988', *Government and Opposition*, 1991, 26, pp. 244–260.

[105] Interview with Hedi Baccouche, Tunis, 22 July 2017.

accountability. What the new powerbrokers sold as an avant-garde pact was, however, first and foremost another attempt to co-opt the opposition and control the nature of the demands emanating from it. Indeed, by establishing a pact around the President, the signatories were brought into the regime itself and thereby stripped of their capacity to effectively act in the opposition. They came to share 'the *responsibility* for power' without holding 'power itself'[106]—which remained with the new authorities—and, hence, now had a stake in supporting the new regime and facilitating its survival.

Be with us, or against us

The Ben Ali team framed consensus politics and pact-making as the best ways to achieve the regime's overarching goals of 'progress', 'modernization', and 'democracy', which they placed at the centre of their declared new political era but left deliberately vague and indeterminate. Dictators commonly advance a teleological legitimation of their regime—that is, they justify their rule through some overarching objective or mission. These included Bourguiba himself, who had claimed to be the founder and guarantor of 'modern Tunisia',[107] a stipulation he regularly evoked to pursue his authoritarian politics. To differentiate himself from his predecessor, Ben Ali redefined the boundaries of the 'modern' and 'nationalist'—all whilst drawing from Bourguiba's ruling strategies and ideological frames.

In particular, Ben Ali and his associates spread the narrative that modernization initiatives had, in fact, preceded Tunisia's first president. They revived the image of several nineteenth-century figures who had instigated pioneering reforms—'mythological heroes' of a type commonly evoked by authoritarian leaders as the supposed 'founders of the political community'.[108] They included Kheireddine Pasha al-Tunisi, a former prime minister who, in 1875, founded Sadiki College, which taught modern sciences and was popular in elite circles.[109] Ben Ali also rehabilitated the image of Destourian figureheads who had fallen out with Bourguiba, such as Abdelaziz

---

[106] Philip Selznick, 'Foundations of the Theory of Organization', *American Sociological Review*, 1948, 13, 1, p. 34.

[107] Many commentators have internalized this narrative; see, for example, 'Habib Bourguiba (1903–2000): Fondateur de la Tunisie Moderne', *Manière de Voir*, 2006, 86, 4, https://www.monde-diplomatique.fr/mav/86/A/52521, last accessed 3 September 2018.

[108] Compare Andrew F. March, 'From Leninism to Karimovism: Hegemony, Ideology, and Authoritarian Legitimation', *Post-Soviet Affairs*, 2003, 19, 4, p. 318.

[109] Ben Ali even had Kheireddine Pasha al-Tunisi's picture printed on 20 TND notes, which had previously displayed Bourguiba.

Thaalbi and Salah Ben Youssef, the founder of the Destour and Bourguiba's rival for the Neo-Destour leadership, whom he posthumously awarded the Grand Cordon of Independence.[110] This was presented as a rectification process to establish the Destour's 'real' historical legacy and recognize its 'true' heroes.

However, just like his predecessor, Ben Ali demanded exclusive claim to Tunisia's identity, which he equated with the ideological project of the party. One coursebook published and used by the RCD Centre for Studies and Training—the party's ideological education wing, which, in 1989, was launched on a budget of 250,000 TND[111]—detailed:

> The year 1987 marked the great transition, not only of the state but also the party. The ideology changed and the course of action changed. Today our political battles are internal. . . . The previous battles . . . were against the other [France]. Today's battles . . . compete, within a wide-scale national reconciliation framework . . . . It is true that some movements are connected until today to the other. They did not break their external ties and did not nationalize their affairs . . . . Such movements . . . are not inside our democratic system.[112]

Whilst proclaiming 'the great transition', RCD officials affirmed that some parties still embraced external agendas—though the foreign enemy, France, had been defeated. They applied the same reasoning Bourguiba used to justify the PSD's political dominance to legitimate their own management of political 'pluralism'. They simply redefined which parties were outside the political 'consensus' and threatened the unity of the state. The new authorities enlarged the number of legal opposition parties but were careful to license only those who had come to accept Ben Ali's leadership unconditionally. They criminalized all others. These creeping authoritarian practices proceeded with little critical attention, masked by the seductive rhetoric of 'national reconciliation'.

---

[110] 'Le Chef de l'État Décore des Martyrs et des Résistants', *Le Temps*, 21 March 1989, p. 2.

[111] Interview with Zouhair Mdhafer, Tunis, 10 February 2017.

[112] Sadok Chaabane, 'Tahawwul al-Sabi' min November wa-l-Tajdid al-Fikri li-l-Tajammu' al-Dusturi al-Dimuqrati' ['The 7 November Transition and the Intellectual Renewal of the Constitutional Democratic Rally'], in *Markaz al-Dirasat wa-l-Takwin, Muntadayat al-Fikr al-Siyasi 2008–2009* [*RCD Centre for Studies and Training, Political Thought Forums 2008–2009*], Tunis: RCD Publications, 2009, p. 47.

Establishing executive control

Ben Ali's undeniable—if tactical—political opening clouded another trend that would bestow him with vast powers in the years to come. Having appointed a new local RCD leadership through nationwide cell congresses, Ben Ali and his team next took it upon themselves to replace the party's representatives at the national level and co-opt the ways in which its institutions there were constituted. This was, of course, again legitimated through a correctivist frame promising to address and rectify Bourguiba's many errors and transgressions. The occasion was the first RCD Congress, convened from 29 to 31 July 1988 under the banner of 'salvation', a topic chosen in an attempt to 'prolong' the supposed 'countrywide enthusiasm . . . [for] 7 November'.[113] The conference logo—a hand rescuing someone from drowning—served to remind participants that Ben Ali had managed to 'stop the damage' of the Bourguiba regime, and this without any bloodshed.[114]

The conference brought together both the PSD old guard and RCD newcomers, including its leftist recruits, youth activists, and the local leaders that had been designated earlier in the year. The day of the conference opening, *Le Renouveau* announced that disputes were likely to erupt between these opposing party wings. It remarked:

> At first glance, the democratic current . . . seems to outweigh by far the reactionaries and conservatives. . . . The two RCD trends risk . . . [turning into] a struggle for influence between the supporters of renewal and the PSD old guard, protected through their historic legitimacy, which . . . is no longer suited to influence the course of events or to infuse the Rally with the energy it needs to meet challenges and change mentalities. Congress participants should therefore expect major conflicts between conservatives and reformers.[115]

In less than a year, the confidence of the Ben Ali team had grown to the extent that new officials now dared to denounce the PSD old guard openly as 'reactionaries' and 'conservatives', contrasting them with the RCD's supposedly new 'democratic trend' and 'reformers'; at the Central Committee meeting

---

[113] 'TUNISIE: le "Congrès du Salut"; Le Parti Gouvernemental est Invité à se Rénover en Vue des Futures Échéances Électorales', *Le Monde*, 30 July 1988, http://www.lemonde.fr/archives/article/1988/07/30/tunisie-le-congres-du-salut-le-parti-gouvernemental-est-invite-a-se-renover-en-vue-des-futures-echeances-electorales_4086493_1819218.html, last accessed 25 October 2017.
[114] Ibid.
[115] Salem Cheikh, 'Parti du Bon Pied', *Le Renouveau*, 29 July 1998, p. 12.

just five months earlier, Ben Ali officials had still advanced a much more accommodating discourse. This illustrates how quickly the new powerbrokers had managed to strengthen their leverage within the party and that they had no intention of pursuing conciliatory and responsive politics towards Bourguiba-era figures once they believed they had gained the upper hand.[116] The denunciation of the old guard was also a display of strength, signalling to longtime activists that the Ben Ali team now controlled the official discourse and could easily delegitimate them—inside the party and in the eyes of the wider population.

The key point of disagreement between the old guard and Ben Ali associates was the composition of the National Conference—the body formally charged with electing the RCD president. Specifically, the new powerbrokers sought to establish executive control. The National Conference was composed of the party President, Ben Ali, representatives of the student and youth organizations and of the federations, the Coordination Committee, and all Central Committee members. Whoever controlled the majority of its seats effectively controlled the presidency.

The new officials reinforced their grip over party structures that held substantial sway within the National Conference. Importantly, they changed the composition of the Central Committee and how its mandates were allocated. Under Bourguiba, the Central Committee had consisted of ninety members who were officially elected—though a list of names was typically prepared in advance and voting was more of a formality. Ben Ali enlarged the Central Committee to 200 seats, of which 122 were appointed by the President. The authorities claimed that designations were necessary to open up the party structures to new political faces—the same correctivist rhetoric they had already advanced during the RCD cell congress a few months earlier, when they decided to appoint local party figureheads. Abderrahim Zouari, the ideological lobbyist responsible for the RCD's restructuring, explained:

Two-thirds of the Central Committee was nominated and one-third was elected, to allow the youth, women and academics to become members. They did not have a social base to become elected and we wanted to give them a chance.[117]

---

[116] However, they were still keen to project an overall compromising stance to the outside. At the end of the congress, *Le Renouveau* declared that the expected 'fight between the old guard and the modernists had not taken place' as 'everybody agreed on the 7 November principles'. See, for details, 'Dans le Vif du Salut', *Le Renouveau*, 31 July 1998, p. 1.

[117] Interview with Abderrahim Zouari, Tunis, 9 February 2017.

Zouari suggested that the appointments served solely to integrate RCD new-comers into the Central Committee. Alongside leftists, academics, and youth activists, they included some wealthy entrepreneurs who had come to side with the new powerbrokers.[118] These nominations pushed the old guard to the mar-gins and allowed Ben Ali supporters to gain a majority—that is, to control the Central Committee.

In parallel, the new authorities reinforced their grip over the Coordination Committee—the party's highest regional instance and another key body within the National Conference, whose members they had already appointed anew following the February 1988 Central Committee meeting. Under Bour-guiba, Coordination Committee members were elected, so influential regional figureheads emerged by virtue of their activism and social base in their local-ities. At the Congress of Salvation, Ben Ali reaffirmed that all Coordination Committee members were henceforth to be appointed, not elected. This enabled him to promote his own people to regionally representative posts.

Ben Ali's grip over both the Central Committee and the Coordination Committee meant that his supporters constituted a majority in the National Conference: in other words, he had established executive control. Prior to the congress, some opposition figures had suggested Ben Ali relinquish his position as RCD President to break once and for all with the personality cult of his predecessor and to separate party structures more clearly from those of the state—a necessity if other political voices were to compete with the RCD. Yet, far from following this proposition, at the congress Ben Ali had himself formally elected RCD President—his first official mandate as head of the rul-ing party.[119] Importantly, he was elected by acclamation—that is, clapping by the National Conference members. This public manner of election was sig-nificant as it made any opposition more costly. Refusing to clap would have likely led to one's political marginalization, public delegitimization, and even humiliation. This, however, is not to suggest that resistance to Ben Ali was impossible: an interesting precedent from the Bourguiba era had seen the 1971 party congress transform into a site of internecine struggles when several

[118] Interview with Selim, Regueb, Sidi Bouzid governorate, 27 June 2016. Note that contrary to Zouari's statement, almost no women joined the Central Committee at the time.

[119] Asma Larif-Beatrix, 'Chronique Tunisienne (1988)', *Annuaire de l'Afrique du Nord*, 1990, 27, Paris: CNRS, p. 745. Note that in later years, prominent RCD officials suggested that opposition figures who asked for 'separating the party's presidency from the state's presidency' had 'either ill intentions or hostile attitudes'. See, for details, Ahmed Iyadh Ouederni, 'al-'Alaqa bayn al-Tajammu' wa-l-Dawla fi Zil al-Ta'addudiyya al-Siyasiyya' [The Relationship between the Rally and the State in Light of Political Pluralism], in *Markaz al-Dirasat wa-l-Takwin, Muntadayat al-Fikr al-Siyasi 2008–2009* [*RCD Centre for Studies and Training, Political Thought Forums 2008–2009*], Tunis: RCD Publications, 2009, p. 4.

senior party members openly challenged Bourguiba's increasingly personalist rule and called for reforms to the ruling party.

As soon as Ben Ali was elected, he strengthened his position as President of the party. He abolished the post of RCD Director, until then occupied by Hamed Karoui. Ben Ali preserved only the position of Secretary General, to which he appointed his longtime loyalist Abderrahim Zouari. Mohamed Ghariani elaborated that 'the director was the one who commanded, who led, . . . [but] the Secretary General was a position . . . mainly related to the internal management of the RCD'.[120] The Secretary General was limited to administrative duties and the execution of presidential directives.[121] Ben Ali said he abrogated the position of RCD director to respond to the opposition's demand that party structures be separated from the state, given that the director was also a minister in government;[122] during the RCD Central Committee's 'internal critique', members had voiced a similar demand, believing that a dissociation from the state would strengthen the party. However, Ben Ali could alternatively have changed the RCD's internal statute and limited the director's duties to those pertaining to the party. Moreover, the prime minister remained simultaneously RCD Vice-President—a largely symbolic post, but an illustration that Ben Ali did not genuinely seek to disentangle party institutions from the state. Rather, he abolished the position of RCD director because he did not wish to deal with a strong party figure who could pursue agendas and priorities that might contradict his own interests as President.

Ben Ali officials took other steps that appeared responsive to the demands of party followers—making the RCD look more detached from the state—but ultimately served to bolster their own power base. On the regional level, they stipulated that the position of governor, who under Bourguiba had headed the PSD's regional chapters, was henceforth independent from the RCD. This was not only in the opposition's interests but also served many RCD activists who believed that public servants loyal to Bourguiba had taken over too many party prerogatives. From then on, regional RCD Secretaries General directed the party in their localities.[123] Yet Ben Ali handpicked these Secretaries General

---

[120] Interview with Mohamed Ghariani, Tunis, 20 July 2017.
[121] The RCD's rules of procedure vaguely stated that the Secretary General was 'to help [the President] perform his duties, manage the Rally's bodies, activate its structures [and] enhance its choices'. See, for details, *al-Nizam al-Dakhili li-l-Tajammu' al-Dusturi al-Dimuqrati*, al-Fasl 4, al-Madda 25 [*Statute of the Constitutional Democratic Rally*, chapter 4, article 25], copy received from private archives in Tunis.
[122] 'Conférence de Presse du Dr Karoui: Le Président Ben Ali Restera le Président du R.C.D.', *Le Renouveau*, 30 July 1988, p. 4.
[123] Interview with Mohamed Ghariani, Tunis, 20 July 2017.

personally—establishing vertical party control in the regions to an extent never achieved under Bourguiba.

At the national level, Ben Ali officials promised to give the RCD 'a say in deciding on their government representatives', who had previously been selected by Bourguiba.[124] Sadok Chaabane—the Ben Ali propagandist— opined that 'the most important thing for a party is its capacity to choose, to nominate . . . to present its candidates in Parliament, during municipal elections'.[125] He affirmed that party activists sincerely believed that Ben Ali wanted to strengthen the role of the RCD, given the range of innovations he had brought to its structure and ideological outlook. Many 1988 congress participants indeed testified that they were attracted by the very notion of political reform—after decades of stagnation under Bourguiba—and realized only in subsequent years that many of the changes primarily served the interest of Ben Ali, rather than party followers. Amongst other points, interviewees typically said that they initially supported the practice of designations within the Central and Coordination Committees because it injected new blood into the party, but they came to regret it in later years.[126]

Ben Ali's strategic promotion of what he framed as desirable party change explains why followers did not rebel against his rapid accumulation of personal power: many believed that the wide-ranging changes to the party's internal working were in their interests. The only RCD faction that actually had grounds to contest the new powerbrokers was the old guard, who were increasingly pushed to the margins. However, their weakened position meant that they now faced a collective action problem: staging a rebellion against the new incumbent was risky, with a real chance of failure and losing the little influence they still held.[127] The fact that they were also internally divided between competing figureheads, and the widespread belief that Ben Ali enjoyed real popularity, further undermined their potential to mobilize against the new incumbent. The old guard preferred being at the mercy of the new officials to challenging them.

---

[124] Interview with Sadok Chaabane, Tunis, 20 July 2017.

[125] Ibid.

[126] Though many interviewees were RCD newcomers, who directly profited from the appointments, even some members of the old guard—though a minority—were taken by the wave of new party adherents and initially supported designating some of these to leading posts. Interviews with Naziha Zarrouk, Tunis, 30 January 2017; Hedi Baccouche, Tunis, 22 July 2017.

[127] Compare Barbara Geddes, Joseph Wright, and Erica Frantz, *How Dictatorships Work*, Cambridge: Cambridge University Press, 2018, p. 77; Milan Svolik, *The Politics of Authoritarian Rule*, Cambridge: Cambridge University Press, 2012, p. 6.

Thus, within a year, Ben Ali—who had no background in the PSD—found himself at the forefront of Destourian party politics. He became the RCD's self-proclaimed consensus figurehead—the only person apt to unite its different currents, to instigate innovation into the Destour, all whilst framing this as part of realizing the party's historic legacy and mission. Ben Ali became the very personification of what new Destourian politics was about—and with the reforms at the congress, he controlled the RCD institutions to an extent Bourguiba never did. Not only had Ben Ali managed to gain a political edge, but at the congress he also institutionalized this advantage: he formally changed the party rules and procedures to establish executive control and strengthen his position as the RCD President—wide-ranging transformations that paved the way for future domination. As such, the July 1988 congress demarcated the transition from oligarchic power—previously held by party leaders and the 7 November seizure group—to one-man rule.

The man above all

Whilst establishing control over the RCD, Ben Ali also shielded himself against potential leadership challenges from within the seizure group. In particular, echoing a frequent practice amongst newly minted authoritarian leaders seeking to bolster their power,[128] he dismissed Habib Ammar and Hedi Baccouche—his coup comrades and longtime friends from Hammam Sousse. Following Ben Ali's takeover, Ammar—a military man—had been assigned the influential position of Interior Minister. News soon began circulating that he had played an important role in the deposal of Bourguiba. Indeed, it was Ammar's troops that surrounded the Presidential Palace on the night of 7 November, whereas Ben Ali was mainly in charge of the logistics of the coup.[129]

In July 1988, Ammar was demoted to Minister of State for the Interior, which he described as a position without any real responsibilities.[130] Three months later, he was placed under house arrest and then assigned an ambassadorial post in Austria—that is, he was stripped of any domestic political influence. It is notable that his falling out with the President received very little media coverage. This owed to Ben Ali's control of the flow of information and in

---

[128] Barbara Geddes, 'Minimum-Winning Coalitions and Personalization in Authoritarian Regimes', paper prepared for presentation at the annual meetings of the American Political Science Association, Chicago, 2–5 September 2004.

[129] Interview with Habib Ammar, Gammarth, 27 July 2017; Habib Ammar, *Parcours d'un Soldat: Entre le Devoir et l'Espoir*, Tunis: Simpact, 2016.

[130] Internview with Habib Ammar, Gammarth, 27 July 2017; Habib Ammar, *Parcours d'un Soldat: Entre le Devoir et l'Espoir*, Tunis: Simpact, 2016.

particular his grip over key media outlets.[131] Ammar's sidelining did, however, have wide-ranging implications: with Ammar outside the country, Ben Ali controlled not only the RCD's countrywide networks but also the defence and security apparatus.

Ben Ali would wait a few more months to conclude the dismissal of Baccouche, the Prime Minister and RCD Vice-President. In contrast to Ammar, Baccouche was a prominent political figurehead who had participated in the Neo-Destour's struggle against the French. Ben Ali relied on his historic legacy during the April 1989 general elections, when Baccouche was central in mobilizing the RCD grass roots, including its PSD old guard. However, even before the elections, frictions had emerged between Ben Ali and Baccouche, who wanted the President to acknowledge his contributions to 7 November. These frictions burst out into the open in March 1989, when the weekly *Jeune Afrique* published an interview with Baccouche, quoting him in the title saying 'The Change—I did it!'[132] Through the course of this interview, Baccouche largely qualified this statement, elaborating that: 'on 7 November, I was there and in a strong position' and 'I realize the Change with the President day-to-day.'[133] However, the title was enough for Ben Ali to seethe with anger—it constituted an upfront challenge to his sole leadership.[134] One of Ben Ali's close collaborators at the time recalled:

> With this unfortunate title ... it was over [for Baccouche]. Ben Ali was furious, he was full of rage! He sent Mohamed Jeri, the Director of his Presidential Cabinet, to see Mister Baccouche and ask him to deny the article.[135]

However, Baccouche refused to refute the article, affirming 'there was a lot of good information in it.'[136] Shortly afterwards, Ben Ali launched a propaganda campaign against his Prime Minister—Baccouche's legitimacy was of such a calibre that he could not have dismissed him without providing any official explanation. Ben Ali charged that Baccouche was trying to boycott his political 'change', a discourse many commentators uncritically assumed. When, in September 1989, Baccouche was finally dismissed as Prime Minister,

---

[131] For more information on the media under Ben Ali, see Rachid Khechana, 'Les Médias Tunisiens Face à la prépondérance de l'État Partisan', *Confluences Méditerranée*, 2009, 2, 69, pp. 99–105; Rikke Hostrup Haugbølle and Francesco Cavatorta, '"Vive La Grande Famille des Médias Tunisiens": Media Reform, Authoritarian Resilience and Societal Responses in Tunisia', *Journal of North African Studies*, 2012, 17, 1, pp. 97–112.

[132] 'Hedi Baccouche: "Le Changement, Je l'ai Fait!"', *Jeune Afrique*, 1472, March 1989, p. 28.

[133] Ibid., p. 30.

[134] Interview with Hedi Baccouche, Tunis, 22 July 2017.

[135] Interview with Abbes Mohsen, Tunis, 22 July 2017.

[136] Interview with Hedi Baccouche, Tunis, 22 July 2017.

Le Monde wrote that this was because he had 'blocked [Ben Ali's] politics of modernization'. The article assessed that Ben Ali had 'no other choice' than to dismiss Baccouche if he wanted to pursue his reform project, thus bestowing Ben Ali's decision to fire his Prime Minister with external legitimacy.[137] Blinded by the regime's seductive correctivist rhetoric, most commentators failed to see that Baccouche's replacement, Hamed Karoui—another longtime Ben Ali loyalist from Sousse—was certainly not more reform-minded but less of a political heavyweight and therefore easier to control.

The discrepancy between the regime's democratization rhetoric and its actual ruling strategies and goals became most apparent during the April 1989 general elections. Propagated as the first occasion for 'the popular will . . . to express itself'[138] in Tunisia, the elections strikingly exposed the authoritarian underpinnings of the new regime. Prior to the elections, Ben Ali officials had created a parliamentary commission to reform the electoral code, but it retained the winner-takes-all majority list system that had been used under Bourguiba. It also stipulated that every candidate needed to obtain the support of seventy-five eligible voters prior to the elections, then register them with the municipal authorities, who often belonged to the RCD and could use their administrative discretion to create additional procedural hurdles. This made it very difficult for opposition voices—especially small parties with a limited support base—to present electoral lists.

To divert attention from the code's blatant shortcomings, Ben Ali officials suggested that opposition parties who signed the National Pact establish common lists with the RCD. The new officials sought to promote over and over again cross-ideological pacts that ostensibly fostered political pluralism, but which proved largely useless in this respect and ultimately reinforced their own power base. The establishment of common lists was deeply contentious within the RCD's own ranks as many activists believed they were the only truly nationalist force, some going as far as to label other political trends as 'treasonous'.[139] However, the RCD leadership was quick to convey to its activists

---

[137] 'TUNISIE: La Destitution du Premier Ministre, M. Baccouche; Le Président Ben Ali Charge M. Karoui de Relancer les Réformes', *Le Monde*, 29 September 1989, https://www.lemonde.fr/archives/article/1989/09/29/tunisie-la-destitution-du-premier-ministre-m-baccouche-le-president-ben-ali-charge-m-karoui-de-relancer-les-reformes_4126643_1819218.html, last accessed 1 November 2017.

[138] 'Un Entretien avec le Président Tunisien Ben Ali; La Volonté Populaire Pourra s'Exprimer le 7 Novembre 1989 à l'Occasion d'Élections Présidentielle et Législatives Anticipées', *Le Monde*, 10 September 1988, https://www.lemonde.fr/archives/article/1988/09/10/un-entretien-avec-le-president-tunisien-ben-ali-la-volonte-populaire-pourra-s-exprimer-le-7-novembre-1989-a-l-occasion-d-elections-presidentielle-et-legislatives-anticipees_4090788_1819218.html, last accessed 3 November 2017.

[139] Note that Zakya Daoud affirmed that Belhadj Amor, the Secretary General of the Popular Unity Party, first proposed to establish common lists (Zakya Daoud, 'Chronique Tunisienne (1989)', *Annuaire de l'Afrique du Nord*, 1991, 28, Paris: CNRS, p. 681). However, interviewees denied this account (interviews with Chedli Neffati, Tunis, 2 February 2017; Moncer Rouissi, Tunis, 21 July 2017).

that they would keep the upper hand and could determine the composition of the common lists.[140] It is notable that all major opposition forces initially accepted the proposition, believing this was the only way for them to gain any parliamentary seats. The influential opposition Movement of Socialist Democrats (MDS), a splinter of the PSD, soon backtracked and other parties followed, so the entire initiative collapsed. Subsequently, Ahmed Mestiri, the MDS Secretary General, published a statement demanding 'free competitive elections' and denouncing an 'increase in harassment of opposition activists'.[141]

The Ben Ali officials used the opposition's refusal to present common lists to hold them responsible for the RCD's subsequent political dominance; they were publicly discredited as opponents of their declared 'consensus democracy'.[142] Indeed, it is even possible that the authorities proposed the initiative with exactly this goal in mind and that they never expected the opposition to come on board. In an interview days before the elections, the Prime Minister insinuated that Ben Ali's proposal to create common lists evinced that 'there has been a real internal revolution [within the RCD]', which, he stressed, 'is not true for other political voices'.[143] He portrayed the RCD as the true vanguard of political 'change', in contrast to other parties, which were denounced as inherently conservative and prone to undermining the democratization process. In what sounded like an attempt to prepare the public for the RCD's imminent victory, the Prime Minister declared:

> We are willing to fight and why not to win. Will we have the totality or the majority of seats? 80% or 60% of the votes? We will see this [on election day] and nobody in a democracy is allowed to prejudice the results .... President Ben Ali unblocked the [ruling party], which has been entirely renewed. This gives us a lot of credit ... and leads us to believe that our position on the eve of the elections is strong.[144]

[140] Interview with Moncer Rouissi, Tunis, 21 July 2017.

[141] Zakya Daoud, 'Chronique Tunisienne (1989)', *Annuaire de l'Afrique du Nord*, 1991, 28, Paris: CNRS, p. 680.

[142] In a 2017 statement, many formerly high-ranking RCD officials charged that it wasn't the electoral code but the opposition's rejection of the common lists that reflected an 'abortion of the foundations of the national democratic path'. The only 'criticism' they voiced about the electoral code was that it should 'perhaps' have granted a 'certain degree' of representation to the opposition, possibly via a quota, in order to 'lend more credibility to the democratic process'—an implicit rejection of free, competitive elections. See, for details, 'Istintajat al-Qira'a al-Naqdiyya li-Masarat al-Hukm min Sanat 1955 ila Sanat 2010' ['Conclusions from the Critical Reading of the Trajectories of Governance from 1955 until 2010'], Association of Former Tunisian Parliamentarians, July 2017, private archives in Tunis.

[143] 'Hedi Baccouche: "Le Changement, Je l'ai Fait!"', *Jeune Afrique*, 1472, March 1989, p. 29.

[144] Ibid.

The results of the 2 April 1989 elections offered no surprises: the RCD claimed 80.6% of the votes and won all 141 parliamentary seats. Opposition forces— even those who performed comparatively well—stood no chance of gaining even a limited number of seats. Ben Ali, the only presidential candidate, was elected with 99.27% of the votes to his first official mandate as President of the Republic. Once Ben Ali had established executive control in the RCD, in addition to the grip he had already gained over the state apparatus, his election as President appeared almost a technicality.

Creeping internal dissent

Ben Ali's election to the President and the RCD's domination in the legislatures occurred despite the fact that party followers' enthusiasm for the new regime was beginning to fade. The RCD also faced a relatively vibrant opposition: in particular, representatives of the Islamist Ennahda participated on independent lists and scored up to 30% in several electoral districts.[145] Former RCD activists said they were baffled by the dedication with which Ennahda followers participated in the elections, which contrasted with the behaviour of many members of the ruling party, who were demotivated and largely passive. Hamza, then an RCD cell leader in Bizerte's town of Ras Jebel, recounted that on election day:

> RCD observers came to my office complaining that they did not receive free coffee [as promised]. . . . They were upset and [left] the polling station. . . . I found myself in tears. I said an [RCD] member who believes in the party . . . stays in the polling station all day long—fasting [if necessary]! . . . That's when I realized [the RCD] was in decline . . . . The Islamists . . . arrived [at the polling station] at 7am in the morning, before everybody else. They stayed the entire day . . . . We tried to make them leave for a bit, to falsify [the results] . . . but they never left![146]

Despite the vigilance of Ennahda followers, many polling station officials still ended up manipulating the results by reporting that the Islamists received fewer votes than they did. Hamza explained that ballot station directors feared

---

[145] Michael Willis, *Politics and Power in the Maghreb: Algeria, Tunisia and Morocco from Independence to the Arab Spring*, New York: Oxford University Press, 2014, p. 167.
[146] Interview with Hamza, Ras Jebel, Bizerte governorate, 9 February 2017.

they would be sanctioned if the RCD did not do well enough in their districts, so they tended to inflate the number of people who had voted for the party.[147] Naturally, the election results were also rigged at higher levels. The fact that officials sought to falsify the election results even though they produced a landslide victory for the RCD reveals that they never intended to even tolerate a limited political opposition. Authoritarian practices and habits remained deeply entrenched at all levels of the ruling party.

Hamza's coffee anecdote is particularly revealing as it lays bare the lack of dedication some rank-and-file member displayed on election day—in stark distinction to the enthusiasm on display when Ben Ali assumed power and new activists flocked to the party. Hamza elaborated that party followers in his town of Ras Jebel had been disillusioned by the way in which the RCD's electoral list there had been drawn up. Months before the elections, party cell leaders had been asked to consult their base and together propose a series of names for the list, but ultimately every single candidate was imposed from above.[148] This left many activists—some of whom had spent weeks trying to find suitable front-runners—alienated from the party leaders.

In protest, some party members did not even vote for the RCD—a deeply contentious action that reveals the extent to which Ben Ali's deviation from the correctivist path and increasingly blatant authoritarian practices within the ruling party heightened internecine struggles. Hamza recalled that several party members were startled when the polling station staff requested to see their completed ballot papers in order to determine where they had put their cross. They had not expected that voting in the first elections under Ben Ali would be manipulated as blatantly as it had been under Bourguiba. Some were humiliated in front of other voters when it became apparent they had not cast a ballot for the RCD. Hamza confided that he himself had not supported the RCD in the elections. He stated:

> When I entered the polling station, I only took the paper with the red list [from the RCD]. But I crossed out the name of the head of the list from Ras Jebel, so my vote could not be counted. That's what I did and you are the first person I told about it![149]

Hamza's account is probably truthful given that—despite all of his criticism—he still takes a lot of pride in his previous RCD activism. Hamza explained

---

[147] Ibid.
[148] Ibid.
[149] Ibid.

that his ballot spoiling occurred out of opposition to the RCD's selection as Ras Jebel head of list of a figure, whose name, he said, had not even featured amongst the recommendations his cell had submitted to the leadership.[150]

The fact that Hamza, a cell leader, did not even vote for the RCD exposes the way in which Ben Ali's support base was crumbling amongst some sections of the party—to the extent some followers even disobeyed their superiors and withdrew their support from their own party, even if they acted secretly. They had trusted that their new officials would enact important reforms within the RCD—in particular, that they would open it up to internal competition—and when they realized that the newcomers had no intention of delivering on their promises, these party members felt they had been played for fools.

Now that Ben Ali had established the RCD's political dominance and his correctivist rhetoric had largely been exposed as self-serving, he no longer needed to uphold the pretence of political reconciliation—either amongst the RCD's different wings or towards other parties. Shortly after the elections, authorities began a crackdown on Ennahda, their biggest political opponent. Between 1989 and 1992, they imprisoned up to 8,000 of its followers.[151] They also took tough actions against other political opponents, including even some RCD members, typically from the PSD old guard, who were considered too critical of the regime—though their numbers were, in comparison, very minor. Mohamed, the self-described Destourian activist from Monastir, recounted that when he publicly disapproved of aspects of Ben Ali's foreign policy in 1990, he found himself in prison.[152] Alongside dozens of other Destourian activists at odds with the new powerbrokers, Hamza was charged for pursuing a 'plot against the head of state'. He was tortured and released only after several months in jail.[153] Evidently, as soon as Ben Ali had cemented his grip over the state and party his strategy of domination changed: he now defended his power base through coercion and by reinforcing vertical political control.

---

[150] Ibid.

[151] 'Tunisia: Prolonged Incommunicado Detention and Torture', *Amnesty International*, 4 March 1992, https://www.amnesty.org/en/documents/mde30/004/1992/en/, last accessed 5 November 2017.

[152] Interview with Mohamed, Monastir, 27 July 2017. Note that his account was corroborated through other interviews.

[153] Ibid.

3

Fortifying Carthage

There were jobs, prosperity, stability . . . the economy took off. We did
not have any security issues. The 1990s were Ben Ali's golden era.
Habib, RCD mid-level official, Gafsa, June 2017

When Ben Ali visited France in 1997, Prime Minister Lionel Jospin lauded the
'security' and 'economic performance' established during the first ten years of
his rule.[1] He was not alone in praising the Tunisian President. Several leaders in
the West applauded Ben Ali for seemingly cultivating prosperity and stability.
Some even began to talk about a 'Tunisian miracle'[2] and labelled the country a 'Mediterranean Singapore'—echoing claims made by Tunisian officials.[3]
Until today, indeed, regime figures commonly remember the 1990s as Ben Ali's
'golden era'—be they grassroots, mid-level, or senior followers. They recount
that they had jobs, they could pay their bills, and that Tunisia did not face any
security challenges—unlike after the uprising, they are keen to stress. Even
some opposition figures testified they were grateful for the economic growth
and stability Ben Ali fostered at the time.

This chapter investigates how, in the 1990s, Ben Ali drew substantial domestic and international support, despite the fact that he discontinued his political
liberalization—his main source of legitimacy immediately after assuming
power. Chapter 2 demonstrated that two years after assuming the presidency
Ben Ali's support had declined and some RCD followers began to engage in
contentious activities once they realized that he did not intend to deliver on his
promises. So it is striking that soon afterwards Ben Ali again enjoyed a wide
support coalition—not only including regime figures but also some opposition actors and Western allies. I uncover that Ben Ali regenerated authoritarian

---

[1] 'M. Jospin Confiant dans les Progrès de la Tunisie vers la Démocratie', *Le Monde*, 23 October
1997, https://www.lemonde.fr/archives/article/1997/10/23/m-jospin-confiant-dans-les-progres-de-la
-tunisie-vers-la-democratie_3776732_1819218.html, last accessed 18 June 2018.
[2] Lénaïg Bredoux and Mathieu Magnaudeix, *Tunis Connection: Enquête sur les Réseaux Franco-
Tunisiens Sous Ben Ali*, Paris: Éditions du Seuil, 2012, p. 45.
[3] Zakya Daoued, 'Tunisie: Chronique Intérieure (1994)', *Annuaire de l'Afrique du Nord*, 1996, 33,
Paris: CNRS, p. 722.

Ben Ali's Tunisia. Anne Wolf, Oxford University Press. © Anne Wolf (2023).
DOI: 10.1093/oso/9780192868503.003.0004

legitimacy by creating new normative priorities—most importantly, national security and economic growth, as opposed to democratic politics. When in a position of strength, dictators can indeed promote new values and ideas to justify wide structural transformations, which they launch—top down—to fortify their own power base.[4]

This chapter shows how—once he had established one-man rule—Ben Ali promoted a security paradigm to legitimate a wider redistribution of resources. In particular, he strengthened presidential prerogatives to thwart any challenges to his power. His associates also appointed 'lumpen activists' to the regime's grassroots and mid-level echelons: ostensibly to ensure stability, these figures—who were typically lowly educated and involved in petty corruption—did not shy away from intimidating and coercing any potential opponents. In parallel, Ben Ali nominated officials with a technocratic profile to senior party and state posts. He propagated that these figures were to heighten the regime's efficiency and revive the economy, but they were, in fact, close presidential associates loyally implementing his orders. Although these political transformations weakened the RCD's policy-making capacities (indeed, to a certain extent they hobbled the party), most followers did not object: they supported the regime's new economic and security objectives. In fact, these twin goals became widely internalized—not only amongst ruling party figures but also in the public administration, key associations, and national unions. As a result, internal opposition remained limited.

Stoking fear, evoking chaos

As soon as Ben Ali established one-man rule, he promoted the notion of an internal enemy—Ennahda—to put stability and security at the top of the political agenda in Tunis. The securitization of important opposition forces is a common way through which dictators seek to legitimate their tight control of the political sphere.[5] In the late 1980s and early 1990s, Tunisian officials

---

[4] Some scholars of authoritarian resilience in the Arab world have noted that incumbents bolstered their regimes' security and economic prerogatives at the time. However, they had paid little attention to the questions as to how incumbents create and promote these new prerogatives and to what extent they need to be credible and become embedded in the regime to foster political stability. See, for example, Eva Bellin, 'The Robustness of Authoritarianism in the Middle East: Exceptionalism in Comparative Perspective', *Comparative Politics*, 2004, 36, 2, pp. 139–157; Oliver Schlumberger, *Debating Arab Authoritarianism: Dynamics and Durability in Nondemocratic Regimes*, Stanford, CA: Stanford University Press, 2007.

[5] In particular, many incumbents in the Middle East and North Africa have securitized the Muslim Brotherhood and affiliated Islamist movements, often repressing them fiercely, though some bestowed them a limited political voice, including in legislatures, to better control them. Amongst other

cracked down violently on the Islamists, torturing and imprisoning thousands of them. Eventually, a small subsection of the otherwise peaceful movement decided to choose force to counter the brutal authoritarian regime. On 17 February 1991, grassroots followers set fire to the RCD's Coordination Committee in the district of Bab Souika, central Tunis, where two guards had been spending the night; one of them was so severely burned that he later died from his wounds. Most Ennahda officials claimed that the perpetrators had decided without the leadership's knowledge to set fire to the RCD building—a carefully chosen target symbolizing Ben Ali's authoritarian rule and repressive policies. They also affirmed that the assailants did not intend to harm anyone and were unaware that two guards were inside the building.[6]

By contrast, RCD officials claimed that the attack—which became known as the 'Bab Souika affair'—was carefully planned by the wider Ennahda movement; they subsequently rounded up and convicted twenty-eight people in a trial Amnesty International described as non-transparent and unfair.[7] Five of the perpetrators were sentenced to death by hanging, a verdict carried out on 9 October 1991.[8] Crucially, authorities claimed that the assailants purposely burned the guards in the building.[9] RCD officials, their extended networks in associations, and the media worked hard to spread this account, affirming that the Bab Souika affair laid bare Ennahda's violent and malicious intentions. They even published brochures about the attack in English in an attempt to promote their version of events amongst Western allies.[10] This came as part of an RCD propaganda effort to discredit Ennahda. Titled 'Nipping the evil in the bud', party followers were supposed to convey 'that the Islamists were not

---

examples, in Jordan, candidates of the Islamic Action Front have run for Parliament beginning in 1993; Morocco's Justice and Development Party has participated in legislative elections ever since 1997; and under Hosni Mubarak in Egypt, Muslim Brotherhood candidates contested parliamentary elections beginning in 2000.

[6] Anne Wolf, *Political Islam in Tunisia: The History of Ennahda*, New York: Oxford University Press, 2017, pp. 73–74.

[7] 'Tunisia: Heavy Sentences after Unfair Trials (MDE 30/023/1992)', *Amnesty International*, 19 October 1992, https://www.amnesty.org/en/documents/mde30/023/1992/en/, last accessed 13 February 2018.

[8] 'Further Information on UA 219/91 (MDE 30/20/91, 28 June 1991)—Tunisia: Death Penalty', *Amnesty International*, 10 October 1991, https://www.amnesty.org/en/documents/mde30/024/1991/en/, last accessed 13 February 2018.

[9] Note that Chedli Neffati, who was appointed Interior Minister following the Bab Souika affair, recounted the events as follows: 'They [Ennahda activists] committed this severe mistake . . . in [Bab Souika] . . . on the night of 17 February. . . . There were two guards who watched the [RCD building]. . . . Four or five young [Ennahda] activists entered the house, they tied them to their chairs, dispersed petrol, started a fire, and left. One of the guards died from his burns.' Interview with Chedli Neffati, Tunis, 2 February 2017.

[10] One such brochure concerning the Bab Souika affair is available at the Centre d'Études Maghrébines à Tunis.

only the adversaries of the regime but the enemy of the entire society'.[11] Party followers sought to demonstrate that Ennahda constituted an 'alien ideological threat . . . preventing the expression of an "authentic . . . national ideology"'.[12] Infiltrating Ennahda's associations, spreading lies and rumours—everything was permitted in order to eradicate this 'evil'.[13] This shows how far some RCD activists were willing to go to undermine their biggest political opponent.

In a rare interview, Mohamed Ghannouchi, Prime Minister between 1999 and 2011, admitted that the regime 'exploited [Bab Souika] to imprison the Islamists . . . and to pursue radical policies'. He elaborated that the Bab Souika affair was used to 'demonstrate that Tunisia was right to resort to force to counter this danger [Ennahda]'.[14] Authorities took advantage of the public outrage over the death of the guard to announce the discovery of an even larger plot, only two months after Bab Souika. They said that Ennahda activists, together with a group of sympathizers in the military, were conspiring to topple the regime, even planning to assassinate the President.[15] Whilst some Ennahda supporters indeed plotted against the regime at the time (though it is unlikely that they had any concrete plans to kill Ben Ali), the involvement of army officers was entirely made up. Afraid of the military, Ben Ali officials sought to weaken it by imprisoning influential officers.[16]

The civil war in neighbouring Algeria—which erupted in January 1992 when the army there decided to cancel legislative elections in anticipation of an Islamist victory—provided the Tunisian authorities with further ammunition to counter Ennahda. The violence across the border served as welcome 'proof' that bloodshed was inevitable when Islamists gain too much power, a narrative widely promoted by the state-controlled media. Such efforts at discrediting Ennahda were quite successful in so far as most international observers did not question the regime's accounts of Islamist violence and believed that Tunisian officials had managed to prevent the eruption of Algerian-type turmoil at home. In March 1992, the French weekly *Paris Match* published an article titled 'How Tunisia Subdued Its Religious Extremists—an Example Algeria Should Try to Follow', reflecting the fact that Tunisia appeared quite stable

---

[11] Jean-Pierre Tuquoi and Nicolas Beau, *Notre Ami Ben Ali: L'Envers du 'Miracle Tunisien'*, Paris: La Découverte, 1999, p. 70.

[12] Quoted in ibid.

[13] Ibid., p. 70

[14] Interview with Mohamed Ghannouchi, Tunis, 2 August 2015.

[15] This scheme became known as the 'Barraket Essahel affair', the name referring to the location where officers supposedly met to plot against the regime. See, for details, Sami Kourda, *Le 'Complot' de Barraket Essahel: Chronique d'un Calvaire*, Tunis: Sud Éditions, 2012.

[16] Interview with Mohamed Ghannouchi, Tunis, 2 August 2015.

after the arrests and seeing this as validation for Ben Ali's repressive poli-cies.[17] Also inside Tunisia, an increasing number of opposition figures—afraid of a repetition of the Algerian scenario—came to back Ben Ali. One of them, Tarek Chaabouni, a former leader of the leftist Ettajdid party, said that 'every-body [feared] . . . that if things turn bad in Tunisia we will be like Algeria.'[18] Such perceptions temporarily widened Ben Ali's support base to almost pre-1989 elections levels. They also facilitated a range of institutional innovations strengthening the presidency and its security apparatus.

Expanding the palace

Soon after establishing executive control, Ben Ali decided to expand the phys-ical structure of the palace—the supposedly fragile security environment[19] being a welcome justification for fortifying Carthage. When Ben Ali first assumed office, the palace premises in Carthage were too small and with too little workspace to accommodate his large cabinet, many advisers, and sup-porting staff. Abbes Mohsen—who in 1988 joined the palace as Director of Protocol to the President—recalled that:

> Ben Ali built a gigantic annexe to the Palace, an outbuilding of quality . . . [with] around eighty offices. . . . He must have started [constructing it] in 1989 and it took him around two years. You know these things are very quick with military men like Ben Ali! He instructed all of his close collaborators to work from there.[20]

Once Ben Ali had established one-man rule, such strategic alterations to powerful state institutions occurred relatively swiftly: he could simply order them without first consulting the party. And given the 'distinctive, dismal con-ditions' in which incumbents operate, particularly their 'shroud of secrecy',[21] some party activists may initially not even have been aware of this gradual but highly significant process of power redistribution to the presidency.

---

[17] Quoted in Jean-Pierre Tuquoi and Nicolas Beau, *Notre Ami Ben Ali: L'Envers du 'Miracle Tunisien'*, Paris: La Découverte, 1999, p. 72.

[18] Interview with Tarek Chaabouni, Tunis, 1 October 2015.

[19] Note that alongside the civil war in neighbouring Algeria, the 1990–1991 Gulf War added to regional instability at the time.

[20] Interview with Abbes Mohsen, Tunis, 22 July 2017.

[21] Milan Svolik, *The Politics of Authoritarian Rule*, Cambridge: Cambridge University Press, 2012, p. 81.

The rising importance of Carthage can be illustrated clearly by the growing budget allocated to the presidency. Whilst in 1986, under Bourguiba, the presidency had received a relatively modest sum of 1 million TND, the amount was augmented to 7 million in 1990 and 29 million in 1998; this multiplication of financial resources continued throughout Ben Ali's reign and reached as much as 311 million TND in 2010.[22] Aside from expanding the budget and size of the palace, Ben Ali altered its internal organization to reinforce oversight and control. Interviewees suggested that Ben Ali modelled the Carthage palace's structure on that of an *état-major*, a military command centre, with its various priority areas and units.[23] Mohsen said that:

> since 1987 Ben Ali had been thinking about [creating] an *état-major*.... Do you know how an *état-major* is organized? . . . You have four main offices: logistics, intelligence, operations, and psychological activities.... Ben Ali was a brilliant officer and highly organized. He organized the Palace like an *état-major*.[24]

Carthage's new annex provided the necessary physical space for the complex military-like reorganization of the palace. Mohsen's assessment that Carthage was structured around the four broad poles of logistics, intelligence, operations, and 'psychological activities'—likely referring to strategies to intimidate and terrorize dissidents—is plausible, given that his position as Director of Protocol to the President gave him unique access to internal palace affairs. Others have provided even more details about Ben Ali's *état-major*, including information about its repressive components. In April 1990, an anonymous group of Ben Ali opponents, calling themselves the Tunisian National Salvation Front, published a statement in which they claimed that the palace included a 'disinformation unit' tasked with disseminating news favourable to Ben Ali and silencing critical journalists in Tunisia, as well as an 'external communication unit', which extended this regime propaganda to foreign countries and diplomatic circles. The statement further stipulated that Ben Ali personally headed an intelligence division in the palace, which was linked to a 'unit of ghost brigades', charged with intimidating dissidents,

---

[22] Derek Lutterbeck, 'Tool of Rule: The Tunisian Police under Ben Ali', *Journal of North African Studies*, 2015, 20, 5, p. 816.

[23] Interviews with Abbes Mohsen, Tunis, 22 July 2017; Fouad Mebazaa, Tunis, 30 May 2016; Adel Kaaniche, Tunis, 26 July 2017; Mohamed Ghariani, Tunis, 22 July 2017.

[24] Interview with Abbes Mohsen, Tunis, 22 July 2017.

including through violence.[25] Indeed, whilst coercion and repression had played little role immediately after Ben Ali's assumption of power, they became key tools through which he sought to maintain his grip over the country once he had established one-man rule.

It is notable that some palace insiders have acknowledged the existence of some of the units, though they typically affirm that they became aware of them only after they had left Carthage. Asked about the palace's role in manipulating domestic and, to some extent, international media outlets, Mohamed Jegham—between 1997 and 1999 the Director of the Presidential Cabinet—said:

> I was shocked when I discovered how the media had been treated. . . . There was a structure [at the palace] tasked with dealing with foreign media. . . . [Ben Ali officials] bought off the media . . . especially domestic media. For example, if [journalists] printed the picture of the President [they] received money.[26]

Given that the authorities' clampdown on the media following the 1989 elections was well documented,[27] it is nearly impossible that officials such as Jegham became aware of it only in later years. In 1990, authorities even created the Tunisian Agency for External Communication (ATCE), a public institution with a budget comparable to that of a ministry, whose official task was promoting Tunisia's image abroad through positive media coverage.[28] Therefore Jegham's claim to ignorance is not credible; rather, he sought 'to obfuscate motivations which [he] may not want to acknowledge',[29] that is, that he stood with Ben Ali despite his increasingly authoritarian politics. However, whilst figures such as Jegham must have been aware that the palace had a hand in manipulating the media, they may not have been party to much further detail. Indeed, interviewees suggested that the President was

---

[25] Statement published in Zakya Daoud, 'Chronique Tunisienne (1990)—Annexes Documentaires', *Annuaire de l'Afrique du Nord*, 1992, 29, Paris: CNRS, pp. 804–809. Note that it is unclear how the members of the Tunisian National Salvation Front received their information about the palace's internal organization. Their descriptions are very detailed and include the units' budget and respective leaders, a fact which suggests they are not based on rumours and could have been provided by palace insiders. It is possible that they were members of the four poles Abbes Mohsen evoked. Mohsen himself avoided giving details of Carthage's security structures; likely he wanted to protect his own image by suggesting that he knew no more about them.

[26] Interview with Mohamed Jegham, Tunis, 19 July 2017.

[27] For example, 'Silence, On Réprime', *Reporters Sans Frontières*, 1 June 1999, https://rsf.org/fr/rapports/silence-reprime, last accessed 1 February 2018.

[28] Vincent Geisser, 'Le Président Ben Ali en Campagne Contre les "Médias Sataniques"', *Annuaire de l'Afrique du Nord*, 2002, 38, Paris: CNRS, p. 381.

[29] This wording has been borrowed from Ivan Ermakoff, *Ruling Oneself Out: A Theory of Collective Abdications*, Durham, NC: Duke University Press, 2008, p. 290.

the only one with access to Carthage's full organizational structure, as well as the prerogatives and strategies of its various units and sub-units, including its repressive divisions. Information about the Palace's inner working was provided on a 'need-to-know' basis, and Ben Ali typically left officials in the dark about their colleagues' activities.[30] He deliberately induced information asymmetries to enforce top-down control.

Ben Ali was particularly careful to limit information exchange within key political institutions outside the palace, such as the government. Fouad Mebazaa—a minister and parliamentary head under Ben Ali—said that 'we were not supposed to know what other ministers were working on, there was no flow of information'.[31] Kamel Morjane—a distant relative of the President, who has occupied various ministries, including key portfolios such as foreign affairs—further explained that:

> if you were Foreign Affairs Minister, Ben Ali [did] not discuss with you any other issues [than] foreign affairs.... It was very rare that he [discussed topics] out of your field of responsibility. It was very rare that there were general issues that [were] put on the table and which everybody could discuss. [Ben Ali] was very specific. This [offered] most control.[32]

To effectively implement government strategies and to avoid duplicated effort, ministers need to know about one others' work and prerogatives, but Ben Ali minimized contact between them. Key ministers—such as those responsible for defence, the interior, and foreign affairs—rarely met without the presence of Ben Ali to reduce the risk that they might conspire against him.[33]

Ben Ali further undermined the work of the government by duplicating key ministries in Carthage. This effectively created a shadow cabinet in the palace—a common way through which personalist leaders reinforce top-down control.[34] By the mid-1990s, almost every minister in government had a counterpart in the palace—an adviser who had a specific area of expertise and

---

[30] For example, interviews with Mohamed Jegham, Tunis, 19 July 2017; Abbes Mohsen, Tunis, 22 July 2017.
[31] Interview with Fouad Mebazaa, Tunis, 30 May 2016.
[32] Interview with Kamel Morjane, Tunis, 26 May 2016.
[33] Ibid. Note that Kamel Morjane was also a Defence Minister under Ben Ali.
[34] Amongst other examples, in Morocco, ministers have long been controlled by royal counsellors who effectively constitute a shadow cabinet. See, for details, Michael Willis, *Politics and Power in the Maghreb: Algeria, Tunisia and Morocco from Independence to the Arab Spring*, New York: Oxford University Press, 2014, p. 143; Miguel Hernandode Larramendi and Irene Fernández Molina, 'The Evolving Foreign Policies of North African States (2011–2014): New Trends in Constraints, Political Processes and Behavior', in Yahia Zoubir and Gregory White (eds.), *North African Politics: Change and Continuity*, Abingdon: Routledge, 2016, p. 258.

presided over a large supporting staff.[35] Day to day, the government ministers were in touch with their counterparts in Carthage. This reduced considerably the decision-making and agenda-setting capacities of the actual cabinet and its prime minister. Hamed Karoui, Prime Minister between 1989 and 1999, recalled that:

> the advisers [in Carthage] became more important than the ministers ... they became so important that the ministers were always in touch with them and not with [me], their Prime Minister, for example, when they had to decide about a specific law. . . . It became totally abnormal![36]

Though Karoui seeks to portray himself as critical of the Ben Ali regime, he of course participated in it at the highest levels—even once the government had become little more than the executor of decisions taken in Carthage. To further reinforce their grip over the government, palace officials closely monitored the daily activities of ministers. Adel Kaaniche—a lawyer and close collaborator of Abdelaziz Ben Dhia, one of Ben Ali's most important advisers—affirmed that the shadow ministers in Carthage spied and reported on their opposite numbers in the government. He stated:

> [Carthage was] a ... spying institution. . . . [Ben Ali's] adviser of health policies, who did he spy on? He spied on the Health Minister. . . . The government ministers feared their counterparts in the palace. . . . The advisers and their staff knew everything about the ministers: who they met, which relations they entertained, . . . and about their private lives.[37]

The advisers in Carthage briefed Ben Ali about the activities of ministers, so when the President met with them he appeared to be 'aware of everything'.[38] In addition, Ben Ali personally monitored the whereabouts and movements of key associates, which suggests that he did not fully trust even his closest

---

[35] Some of these shadow ministers were well known, such as Mohamed Ghenima, head of the Tunisian Central Bank under Bourguiba, who was charged with economic and financial affairs, or Mohamed Gueddiche, Ben Ali's personal doctor, who was responsible for health and environmental policies.

[36] Interview with Hamed Karoui, Tunis, 1 February 2017.

[37] Interview with Adel Kaaniche, Tunis, 26 July 2017.

[38] Ibid.

advisers.[39] This tight control allowed 'preemptive strikes against anyone suspected of disloyalty or too much ambition'.[40]

Ben Ali was particularly wary about the Defence Ministry, afraid of possible military coups. Tunisian academic Noureddine Jebnoun has rightly argued that Ben Ali invented the previously discussed 1991 military 'plot' with the sole aim of 'decapitating the army'.[41] Following the officers' arrest, the Defence Ministry lost much of the independence it had until then managed to retain. Instead, Ben Ali elevated the role of the Interior Ministry, which took a central role in Carthage's security establishment. Many Interior Ministry employees came to work inside the palace. In addition, Ben Ali strengthened his influence over the ministry by appointing loyal associates to head it. Interior ministers typically possessed limited political capital of their own and were rotated on a regular basis so that they could not acquire too much influence. In the 1990s, they included Mohamed Jegham, who subsequently became head of Ben Ali's cabinet, and Chedli Neffati, who afterwards served as RCD Secretary General—an indication of the extent to which officials switched between senior posts in the state, Carthage, and the party. Ben Ali further reinforced his grip over the ministry by personally appointing all representatives of its different divisions and instructing them to report to the palace. As a result, 'nearly every directorate within the Interior Ministry had its own connection with the Carthage Palace and [Ben Ali's] inner circle'[42]—in other words, the Interior Ministry became an extension of the palace's security apparatus.

The centralization of intelligence was key to Ben Ali's endeavour to create a security state that could serve as a bulwark against dissent. It was both an attempt to coup-proof against any rivals in the elite and uncover and—if need be—crush any wider popular opposition. Once Ben Ali had gained a monopoly over the state's security establishment, he bolstered its capacities and resources significantly, a tendency illustrated by the rise in the number of wiretaps under his rule. In the mid-1980s, only around twenty wiretaps were recorded and most of them concerned foreign missions, whilst the amount

---

[39] French analysts Jean-Pierre Tuquoi and Nicolas Beau cynically noted that Ben Ali had 'a real passion for information technology' because 'computers can't lie'. They maintained that the President gathered confidential information about all of his close collaborators on his laptop and personally monitored the travel movements of ministers onscreen. See, for details, Jean-Pierre Tuquoi and Nicolas Beau, *Notre Ami Ben Ali: L'Envers du 'Miracle Tunisien'*, Paris: La Découverte, 1999, p. 103.

[40] This wording has been borrowed from Barbara Geddes, Joseph Wright, and Erica Frantz, *How Dictatorships Work*, Cambridge: Cambridge University Press, 2018, p. 160.

[41] Noureddine Jebnoun, *Tunisia's National Intelligence: Why 'Rogue Elephants' Fail to Reform*, Washington, DC: New Academia Publishing, 2017, p. 34.

[42] Ibid., p. 32.

rose to as many as 5,000 in 2004,[43] most of which targeted ordinary citizens—a development underpinned by a roughly eightfold increase in the Interior Ministry's budget during that period.[44]

The securitization of Ennahda alongside elements of the army furnished the ideological justification for the establishment of a massive system of surveillance.[45] Its implementation on the ground was facilitated by the Interior Ministry's vast control over provincial and local state structures. In particular, Interior Ministry officials—in consultation with the President—were responsible for appointing all key state representatives: the governors and the *délégués*. Ministry staff even handpicked the *omda*, the officials representing the lowest state echelons, the 2,073 geographical sectors. On paper, the *omda* served a variety of functions—social, economic, and cultural—but many interviewees insisted that they were primarily the arms of the Interior Ministry. For example, when asked about the profile of these representatives, Chedli Neffati said that 'they are very well informed . . . they are the Interior Ministry.'[46] When he headed that ministry, Neffati considered them part of its apparatus.

Though the governors, *délégues*, and *omda* were charged with security, they were generally not the ones gathering information about potential 'threats'. Analysts commonly suggested that the police were the central actors behind the collection of intelligence, alongside the key role they played in the physical repression and torture of dissidents.[47] Their numbers under Ben Ali were typically estimated at 130,000–140,000,[48] a ratio of about 1:80 officers to inhabitants. However, after the 2010–2011 uprising it came to light that this was an overestimation and that under Ben Ali the internal security forces[49] amounted to about 49,000, a figure which does not stand out by regional standards.

---

[43] Ibid.

[44] In 1984, the Interior Ministry's budget was 92 million TND; it was expanded to 127 million in 1988 and to 549 million in 1998; this multiplication continued throughout the years and in 2010 the budget climbed to as much as 1.106 billion TND. See, for details, Derek Lutterbeck, 'Tool of Rule: The Tunisian Police under Ben Ali', *Journal of North African Studies*, 2015, 20, 5, p. 816.

[45] Note that it is in this context that Tunisian academic Olfa Lamloum affirmed that 'the ideology of policing became an essential part of the dominant state ideology'. See, for details, Olfa Lamloum, 'Le Zaim et l'Artisan ou de Bourguiba à Ben Ali', *Annuaire de l'Afrique du Nord*, 1998, 37, Paris: CNRS, p. 394.

[46] Interview with Chedli Neffati, Tunis, 2 February 2017. Note that Neffati's testimony contrasts with how former *omda* themselves portrayed their duties. They typically stressed their social and economic responsibilities, tasks that governors and *délégues* also highlighted during interviews, a trend indicating that state representatives under Ben Ali still downplay their intelligence and policing functions. For example, interview with Souheil, *omda* under Ben Ali, Tunis-Bab Souika, September 2015.

[47] For example, Jean-Pierre Tuquoi and Nicolas Beau, *Notre Ami Ben Ali: L'Envers du 'Miracle Tunisien'*, Paris: La Découverte, 1999, p. 96; Steffen Erdle, *Ben Ali's 'New Tunisia' (1987–2009): A Case Study of Authoritarian Modernization in the Arab World*, Berlin: Klaus Schwarz, 2010, p. 144.

[48] Steffen Erdle, *Ben Ali's 'New Tunisia' (1987–2009): A Case Study of Authoritarian Modernization in the Modern World*, Berlin: Klaus Schwarz, 2010, p. 144.

[49] The internal security forces include the police, the National Guard, and the civil defence.

Indeed, the police were even enlarged after Ben Ali's ousting because the force was considered too small.[50] Far from the police primarily, the diffuse and decentralized nature of spying provided tight control. The regime's new security paradigm became deeply embedded on the ground, giving rise to new actors, party identities, and prerogatives.

The rise of the lumpen activist

The emergence of a new regime constituency whom I call 'lumpen activists' reinforced the regime's security priorities. Lumpen activists were poorly educated followers of Ben Ali—in terms of the formal education they received, as well as their party-political training—from socioeconomically disenfranchised backgrounds, and they were typically engaged in petty corruption or other illegal undertakings. Aside from intelligence-gathering, which various regime actors carried out, lumpen activists were especially infamous for their coercion and intimidation of suspected opponents, sometimes including physical assault. Comparative studies sometimes refer to this type of regime actor as 'thugs'.[51] However, most scholars fail to conceptualize them in more detail or to thoroughly investigate the role they play, though they are critical to understanding trends of authoritarian reproduction and change.

Lumpen activists are amongst a regime's least ideologically committed actors in that they work for it purely for material objectives rather than a sense of political or ideational affinity or belonging. Their involvement in petty crime makes them easy to control: authorities are aware of their illegal businesses and tolerate them in exchange for costly services; indeed, their criminal activities are even perceived as useful in that they make lumpen activists susceptible to blackmail and bribery.[52] Because they can be mobilized at any moment and are civilians, as opposed to officers in uniforms, they play a central role in the

---

[50] Lea Lavut, 'Building Partnerships towards a Democratic Police Force in the Post-Revolutionary Tunisia Context', *Journal for Deradicalization*, 2016, 8, p. 109. See also Derek Lutterbeck, 'Tool of Rule: The Tunisian Police under Ben Ali', *Journal of North African Studies*, 2015, 20, 5, pp. 813–831.

[51] See, for example, Issandr El Amrani, 'Controlled Reform in Egypt: Neither Reformist nor Controlled', in Jeannie Sowers and Chris Toensing (eds.), *The Journey to Tahrir: Revolution, Protest, and Social Change in Egypt*, London: Verso, 2012, p. 150.

[52] Tunisian academic Tawfik al-Madani has argued that in Tunisia, 'the role of the police [was] primarily to be a guardian and the nourishment of corruption', elaborating that 'when someone from the political class [was] implicated in drug trafficking, embezzlement, or the carrying of unlicensed weapons, the police [made] sure not to allow any investigation of these crimes'. Whilst al-Madani rightly highlights the role of corruption in the perpetuation of political privilege, he does not analyse how it also served as a means of political control—including within the regime's own ranks. See, for details, Tawfik al-Madani, *Suqut al-Dawla al-Bulisiyya fi Tunis [The Collapse of the Police State in Tunisia]*, Beirut: Arab Scientific Publishers, 2011, p. 145.

spread of everyday fear, violence, and terror. At the same time, their civilian nature helps authorities deny any claims that they employ a 'political police' to crush the opposition.[53] It also guards them against the moral hazard associated with empowering, for example, the military: Lumpen activists do not carry guns that can be turned against the authorities. This makes them highly useful to authoritarian regimes, especially during relatively stable times. But they do constitute a risk factor during periods of rapid political change and turmoil: Lumpen activists have no fixed loyalties and are therefore unlikely to defend a regime in crisis.

It is notable that Ben Ali's practice of nominating the leaders of RCD federations and provinces—which he introduced shortly after assuming power[54]—facilitated the rise of lumpen activists. Indeed, if local officials were elected by their party constituents to leadership positions, as was previously more commonplace, this would likely have given rise to much more efficient and honest representatives, who also cared about the party and doing good in their communities. This shows the great extent to which changes to the RCD's rules and procedures that were introduced immediately after Ben Ali's assumption of power became self-reinforcing over time. Indeed, the local and regional nominations initially appeared to be temporary practices and inconsequential; in later years, however, they became key ways through which Ben Ali fortified his power base on the ground. It was the new local and regional officials who appointed the lumpen activists.

Importantly, whilst lumpen activists only represented one constituency, their ascent facilitated a larger shift in party values, practices, and prerogatives. In particular, lumpen *activities*—broadly understood as followers spying and coercing opponents, illegal undertakings, and profit maximization—became increasingly commonplace amongst various groups. Indeed, not only did the new normative priorities of security and stability give rise to lumpen activists, but these actors themselves subsequently also promoted their values and activities within the party and protractedly. In a rare interview, Foued, a former RCD student member, provided some insights into how an increasing number of party cell members pursued surveillance and reporting activities. He said:

---

[53] Béatrice Hibou suggests that Tunisian authorities systematically denied any charges of institutionalized repression by highlighting that 'there is no political police in Tunisia'. See, for details, Béatrice Hibou, *The Force of Obedience: The Political Economy of Repression in Tunisia*, Cambridge: Polity, 2011, p. 82.

[54] See chapter 2 for more details on how Ben Ali discontinued the practice of elections at the local and regional levels of the ruling party.

> Imagine I work for the party in a neighbourhood and I see a stranger [...]
> What do I do? I write a report. I say who I saw, what the person did and give
> [this information] to the head of the party. . . . We also did this with political
> opponents. We reported who prayed, who made a mistake. We denounced
> them. That's how it was under Ben Ali.[55]

Foued's comments suggest that RCD cell activists closely tracked the activities
of political opponents—likely shadowing their every move—in the hope they
would make a 'mistake', which could subsequently be used to pressure, coerce,
or even blackmail them. People who were regularly seen praying at mosques
were suspected of being Ennahda followers and were reported to the RCD
figureheads. Whilst Foued affirmed that monitoring and reporting activities
were 'generally spontaneous', he similarly stated that 'indicators' for this kind
of work existed 'in the framework of the party'.[56] This suggests that spying on
political opponents became an institutionalized practice within RCD cells and
played an important part in what party activism was all about. RCD followers
were trained in recognizing 'indicators' of suspicious activities and reported
on them to their superiors. Further, in the event that a local crisis emerged,
RCD cells were held accountable.[57]

Naturally, even under Bourguiba party activists pursued some security
functions—indeed, during the fight for independence they were paramount.
This legacy explains, in part, why RCD followers were so willing to reassume
them, especially in a context in which many believed the country was facing
a severe security threat. But during Bourguiba, the party never ceased to also
be a maker of politics, including at the regional and local levels. By contrast,
Ben Ali—a military man with little formal education—was keen to sideline
followers seeking to construct an independent political role for the party.[58]

As Carthage increasingly became the centre of power, some RCD activists,
who longed for the party to have political agency and decision-making
capacity of its own, decided to speak out. Indeed, the RCD still provided a
forum for internal opposition and criticism, even if voiced indirectly, including to such sensitive matters as Ben Ali's increasingly personalist rule and grip

[55] Interview with Foued, Tunis, 30 September 2015.
[56] Ibid.
[57] Béatrice Hibou, *The Force of Obedience: The Political Economy of Repression in Tunisia*, Cambridge: Polity, 2011, p. 86.
[58] Tawfik al-Madani suggests that Ben Ali suffered from an inferiority complex owing to his limited
education, which led him to resent highly cultured and educated officials—some of whom presumably
sought to carve an independent role for the ruling party. See, for details, Tawfik al-Madani, *Suqut
al-Dawla al-Bulisiyya fi Tunis* [*The Collapse of the Police State in Tunisia*], Beirut: Arab Scientific
Publishers, 2011, p. 145.

over the party. Specifically, some followers, though a minority, reiterated their demand to dissociate the RCD from 'the state', by which they generally referred to Carthage, the government, or the public administration—institutions with resources rivalling those of the ruling party. In response to their request, Ben Ali reflected, in a November 1990 speech:

> What can we expect of the separation between the state and the party, which some demand? Would this mean that the government would have to implement the political programme of a party other than the party which won the elections, or should we implement the programme of the RCD by a government that does not emerge from this party? If this was the case, it would be a political heresy without precedent![59]

Ben Ali's remarks sound almost like a mockery of those requesting a separation between the party and the state. In his speech, Ben Ali did nothing to address the state's influence over the party, or state–party relations more generally. Instead, he dove into a discussion of how a separation would supposedly undermine the government's representativeness. Ben Ali suggested that it would mean that a minority party could dominate the government—not only a false inference but also not at all the issue at stake. His statement lays bare the extent to which he did not take the demands of party activists seriously— indeed, he did not even bother pretending he did. Instead, Ben Ali now projected an image of strength and superiority towards party followers, in sharp contrast to his responsive demeanour in his first two years of rule.

In the 1990s, the RCD's security work came to take pre-eminence and to some extent replaced its political functions, and lumpen activists were crucial to this shift. To many RCD members, intelligence-gathering and reporting became part of being a good citizen. Some previous RCD activists still affirm that such intelligence activities were carried out only to guarantee security and stability and that the repression and marginalization of political opponents was never an end in itself. In interviews, former party followers sometimes even lamented that such practices ceased to exist after 2011. One cell activist sullenly said that 'denunciation was common under Ben Ali because he wanted to guarantee security—now we have neither [denunciation nor security]!'[60] He suggested that the post-2011 instability was due to the disintegration of Ben Ali's security apparatus, including the RCD's monitoring and reporting

---

[59] 'Séparation État-Parti', *La Presse*, 8 November 1990, p. 1.
[60] Interview with Alaa, Bardo, September 2015.

functions. This shows how deeply security prerogatives became embedded within the ruling party.

A grid of spies

The rise of lumpen activists facilitated the shift towards security norms and practices within the regime. But, as Steven Levitsky and Lucan Way have observed, '[systematic] surveillance, harassment, and intimidation require an infrastructure capable of directing, coordinating, and supplying agents across the national territory'.[61] The following sections reveal how actors within various regime institutions—centred but not limited to the ruling party—focused on security work, which was often tied to lucrative benefits.[62] They included followers in the public administration, university campuses, associations, neighbourhood committees, all the way to the RCD's representation abroad. This grid of spies—who monitored not only the opposition but increasingly also each other—fostered tight control.

The public administration

Data from 1993 reveal that about one-third of RCD activists were public servants—the largest professional contingent.[63] Indeed, party membership was often a precondition for working in the public administration, even on a local level. As part of their securitization of political opponents, Ben Ali officials came to use RCD membership as a way to distinguish between 'good' and 'bad' citizens: if you did not have a membership card, you risked being considered a dissident.[64] Employment depended not only on the jobseeker's political loyalties but also on those of their relatives. If you had a cousin or uncle who was a member of Ennahda, a connection that could relatively easily

[61] Steven Levitsky and Lucan A. Way, *Competitive Authoritarianism: Hybrid Regimes after the Cold War*, Cambridge: Cambridge University Press, 2010, p. 59.
[62] Note that unlike the RCD, some ruling parties in the region had formal security branches or held institutionalized ties to the security sector, including the Ba'th parties of Syria and Iraq. See, for details, Souhaïl Belhadj, *La Syrie de Bashar Al-Assad: Anatomie d'un Régime Autoritaire*, Paris: Belin, 2013; Joseph Sassoon, *Saddam Hussein's Ba'th Party: Inside an Authoritarian Regime*, Cambridge: Cambridge University Press, 2012.
[63] Note that this data refers to the participants at the RCD's second congress in 1993, but there is no reason to believe that it does not reflect wider trends within the party, especially given the large number of grassroots congress attendees. See, for details, 'Faites Connaissance avec les Congressistes', *La Presse*, 22 July 1993, p. 4.
[64] Jean-Pierre Tuquoi and Nicolas Beau, *Notre Ami Ben Ali: L'Envers du 'Miracle Tunisien'*, Paris: La Découverte, 1999, p. 79.

be determined with the help of the Interior Ministry, this could put an end to your career. Through such measures, RCD officials directly participated in the creation and perpetuation of a vast system of economic exclusion of regime opponents and their relatives—in the public service and beyond.[65]

Importantly, the RCD had approximately 2,000 representations—called 'professional cells'—in public-sector companies. The professional branches originated at the time of Bourguiba, who had created them to counter the sway of the UGTT.[66] But—given the union's relative amenability under Ben Ali— in the 1990s, professional cell representatives came to focus almost entirely on bolstering the party's leverage in the public administration, tying upward mobility there to loyal party service. Naturally, after Ben Ali's fall in 2011, many former professional cell leaders maintained that their job was merely to oversee public-sector companies and promote the quality of work. As Imed, a former head of the RCD's thirty professional cells in Gafsa, which gathered around 4,500 members, affirmed:

> The RCD's existence in all state institutions . . . was a force for the RCD. The RCD . . . offered services and monitored all abuses in the public sector administration—all abuses! The Rally was there and demanded to stop all abuses![67]

Clearly, Imed is in denial that professional cell members were themselves the engineers of many 'abuses', which were often institutionalized. The heads of professional cells were similar in rank to the chief managers of companies, and they were typically feared by employees. One former professional cell leader at the post office in Bab Souika told me, full of pride, that he used to 'wear a tie' at work and was well respected.[68] Whilst he perceived his position as a sign of status, to many of his colleagues it likely signalled impunity and vast influence. Indeed, it was the professional cell leaders who typically pushed for hiring practices based on patronage rather than qualifications. They also gathered information about suspected opposition activists—hence acting like a sort of internal company police—and, in cooperation with state representatives such

---

[65] For an example of how political opponents and their families were marginalized, see the memoir of Ennahda official Moncef Ben Salem, *Mudhakkarat 'Alim Jami'i wa-Sajin Siyasi: Sanawat al-Jamr* [*Memoirs of an Academic Scholar and Political Prisoner: The Years of Fire*], n.p. [Tunisia]: self-published, 2013.

[66] For more details, see Clement Henry Moore, *Tunisia since Independence: The Dynamics of One-Party Government*, Berkeley: University of California Press, 1965; Lars Rudebeck, *Party and People: A Study of Political Change in Tunisia*, New York: Praeger, 1969.

[67] Interview with Imed, Gafsa, 22 June 2016.

[68] Interview with Habib, Tunis-Bab Souika, September 2015.

as the *délégués* or *omda*, made sure that employees who were exposed as such promptly lost their jobs.

The RCD on campuses

On university campuses, RCD students took a key role in the surveillance of dissidents. Dictators are keen to draw students into their ruling parties and gain control of universities—typically bastions of the opposition.[69] In fact, being a renowned 'RCD spy' was almost a guarantee of a successful career in later years. The case of Sofien Toubel—a well-known official under Ben Ali—is revealing in this respect. Many interviewees—including from the RCD's own ranks—testified that in the mid-1990s at the University of Tunis El Manar, Sofien Toubel became infamous for filing reports for the RCD on political opponents, typically those belonging to the UGET[70]—a tendency showing that after the massive repression of Ennahda, party activists sought to counter leftist contenders.[71] Aziz, a former RCD activist from Monastir, suggested that Toubel's later promotion to governor was a 'reward' for his policing activities on campuses,[72] an analysis with which other interviewees concurred.[73] Though it is impossible to know for sure if Toubel's appointment as governor was indeed due to his earlier spying activities, Aziz's account is still instructive as it illustrates how closely monitoring and intelligence-gathering was associated with the prospect of a successful career—including within the RCD's inner ranks.[74]

The RCD's spying activities on campus were particularly important because historically, the political opposition there was particularly strong, especially towards the end of Bourguiba's rule. Though in the late 1980s and early 1990s authorities had cracked down on Ennahda and the closely affiliated UGTE student union, leftist opposition activism still prevailed. The UGET was very

[69] For comparative insights, see Saeid Golkar, 'The Reign of Hard-Line Students in Iran's Universities', *Middle East Quarterly*, 2010, 17, 3, pp. 21–29; Guihua Xie and Yangyang Zhang, 'Seeking Out the Party: A Study of the Communist Party of China's Membership Recruitment among Chinese College Students', *Chinese Journal of Sociology*, 3, 1, 2017, pp. 98–134.

[70] For example, interviews with Mohamed, Monastir, 25 July 2017; Amine from Gafsa, Skype, 3 June 2016.

[71] For more information on the Tunisian opposition, see Tawfik al-Madani, *al-Mu'arada al-Tunisiyya, Nash'atuha wa-Tatawuruha* [*The Tunisian Opposition, Its Birth and Evolution*], Damascus: Ittihad al-Kuttab al-Arab, 2001.

[72] Interview with Aziz, Monastir, 25 July 2017.

[73] Interview with Amine from Gafsa, Skype, 3 June 2016.

[74] Milan Svolik has termed the process by which benefits for party members are subject to 'prior costly service' 'sunk investment'. See, for details, Milan W. Svolik, *The Politics of Authoritarian Rule*, Cambridge: Cambridge University Press, 2012, p. 164.

active, especially at the Faculty of Law and Arts in Tunis. One of its former activists affirmed that 'the youth of the UGET was highly visible at almost all faculties throughout the 1990s'.[75] However, in the late 1990s, UGET activism actually decreased, at least on some campuses, owing to a carefully designed strategy to weaken the union. Some of the ways in which Ben Ali sought to gain a grip over universities—such as his recruitment of influential professors and co-optation of certain UGET figures—were discussed in chapter 2. Naturally, the RCD students' spying activities also reduced the sway of the UGET. Amongst the RCD students' tasks was to identify the UGET's most influential activists and to report anything that could be used to threaten, harass, or even expel them.

However, it was only when Ben Ali officials decided to undertake deep changes in the spatial location and distribution of universities that the bastion of the UGET gradually came under threat. In the 1990s, indeed, authorities devised a strategy to 'diversify' the opportunities for higher education by establishing universities throughout the country.[76] The objective was to have one campus per governorate, a plan portrayed as a way to support marginalized regions and enhance their infrastructure.[77] It is unclear whether this was a deliberate strategy to weaken the UGET or if this outcome was merely one of its by-products, but the new campuses came to be dominated by RCD students. One former UGET leader explained that:

> historically the UGET was active in big faculties . . . but with the diversification of universities, we began to have campuses throughout the country . . . and that's where the Destourian students came to dominate.[78]

The new campuses did not have a history of opposition activism, so it was easier for RCD activists there to gain influence and create a power base entirely dedicated to Ben Ali. They not only kept a watch and reported on suspected opponents but were also institutionally represented through their student wing and affiliated associations. The RCD's growing force on campuses is illustrated well in its representation on faculty research councils, through which university professors and students advised on key educational matters.

---

[75] Interview with Youssef from Gafsa, Skype, 3 June 2016.
[76] The number of university establishments increased sharply from 86 during the academic year 1992/1993, to 107 in 2000/2001, reaching as many as 193 in 2010/2011. See, for more details, Dhaher Najem, 'L'Université, un Outil de Développement Local? Le Cas de Jendouba en Tunisie', *Journal of Higher Education in Africa*, 10, 2, 2012, p. 65.
[77] Interview with RCD student leader Amine, Tunis, 24 July 2017.
[78] Interview with Samir Abidi, Tunis, 30 June 2016.

Every year, students organized research council elections to determine their representatives. Whilst in the early 1990s, UGET activists gained the majority of seats nationwide, RCD followers soon began to dominate. Hassouna Nasfi, an RCD student leader at the time, estimated that the party's vote share at the research council elections was '25% in 1994, 55% in 1995 and 1996. Then starting from 1997 we arrived at 90% of seats'.[79] Whilst Nasfi insisted that the elections for student representatives were 'free', opposition activists typically reported that the results were rigged or that they were physically prevented from casting a vote.[80] The RCD students' growing sway on campuses endowed them with new confidence, and by the late 1990s they not only surveilled and reported on opponents but also harassed them and participated in the falsification of election results to deny them any institutional representation. Lumpen activities became deeply engrained within the RCD's wider grassroots structures.

Associations

The creation of many associations and non-governmental organizations (NGOs)—often with the active help of RCD activists—further widened the regime's oversight of society. Whilst in 1987, when Ben Ali assumed power, there were only 1,807 officially recognized associations, by 2003 this number had risen to as many as 8,386.[81] This expansion of NGOs—or, more accurately, 'government controlled non-governmental organizations'[82]—was also seen in other parts of the Arab world at the time.[83] The Tunisian associations were typically linked to the ruling party or relied on its facilities and financial resources for events. Moreover, many influential 'national organizations'

---

[79] Interview with Hassouna Nasfi, Bardo, 24 May 2016.

[80] For example, interview with Amine from Gafsa, Skype, 3 June 2016. Note that legislation no. 97-1070, dated 2 June 1997, stipulates that decisions within the university council are to be made by a majority of present members, thus denying those who were prevented from physically participating in the meeting any voice. A copy of the legislation is available online: https://www.pist.tn/collection/JORT, last accessed 10 February 2022.

[81] Béatrice Hibou, *The Force of Obedience: The Political Economy of Repression in Tunisia*, Cambridge: Polity, 2011, p. 95.

[82] For comparative insights, see Halim Salleh, 'Development and the Politics of Social Stability in Malaysia', *Southeast Asian Affairs*, 1999, 1, pp. 185–203.

[83] Amongst other examples, in his study of authoritarian upgrading in the Arab world, Steven Heydemann found that beginning in the 1990s, 'Arab regimes blended repression, regulation, co-optation and the appropriation of NGO functions by the state to contain the deepening of civil societies and to erode their capacity to challenge political authority'. See, for details, Steven Heydemann, 'Upgrading Authoritarianism in the Arab World', Brookings Institution Saban Center Analysis Paper No. 13, 2007, p. 6.

came to display openly their loyalty to Ben Ali and his RCD, including UTICA and the National Union of the Tunisian Woman (UNFT). In November 2006, an American diplomat attended a UNFT event about Tunisian values, which, he said, 'turned out to be more of a political rally . . . in support of Ben Ali and his policies'. Amongst other activities, UNFT activists 'hung red and purple banners (the colours of the . . . RCD . . .) in the streets' to display their support of the ruling party.[84] Also, UNFT charitable aid was limited to RCD members, and men were additionally required to evince a minimum of three years of party cell activism.[85] The UNFT—just like many other associations—essentially became an auxiliary of the ruling party.

Up until the 1990s, the only truly independent association with any leverage was the Tunisian Human Rights League (LTDH), which had a membership base of about 4,000 stretching throughout the country.[86] Upon taking power, Ben Ali officials had sought to co-opt the LTDH leadership, but without success. The authorities consequently decided, in 1992, to pursue legal channels to gain a grip over the association. In March 1992, a new law was passed that denied associations the right to reject candidates. This paved the way for RCD activists to infiltrate the LTDH. Moncef Marzouki, the LTDH leader at the time, initially sought to defy the law and refused to admit the new RCD adherents; however, in February 1994 Marzouki was forced to cede the leadership owing to what he described as a 'real coup' within the LTDH.[87]

Marzouki's successor, Taoufik Bouderbala, pursued a conciliatory approach towards the Ben Ali authorities and allowed RCD figures to integrate into the league's leading ranks. Abbes Mohsen, an RCD official who worked with the LTDH, explained how under Bouderbala the composition of the association's various offices was determined:

> In [the office of] Belvédère, for example, we put three RCD members, two communists, and five MDS activists. In the Tunis office we put five RCD members, four communists and only one activist from the MDS. The composition of the offices was negotiated intelligently.[88]

[84] US Embassy in Tunis, 'Womens' "NGO": Less Hijab, More Ben Ali', Wikileaks, 1 November 2006, 06TUNIS2679_a, confidential.
[85] Béatrice Hibou, *The Force of Obedience: The Political Economy of Repression in Tunisia*, Cambridge: Polity, 2011, p. 106.
[86] Noureddine Sraieb, 'Tunisie: Chronique Intérieure (1992)', *Annuaire de l'Afrique du Nord*, 1994, 31, Paris: CNRS, p. 956.
[87] Interview with Moncef Marzouki, former LTDH head and Tunisia's first democratically elected president, Tunis, May 2015.
[88] Interview with Abbes Mohsen, Tunis, 22 July 2017.

The key takeaway from Mohsen's statement is that LTDH representatives were selected by authorities in an attempt to infiltrate the league's leading ranks and to establish top-down control, and he probably overstated the weight of the political opposition in its local chapters. Mohsen acknowledged, however, that despite Bouderbala's accommodating stance and the RCD's sway over the LTDH, the authorities sought to further 'strangle the league . . . to make it [even] more compliant'.[89] Whilst this substantially weakened the LTDH, it is noteworthy that some activists continued to defy the RCD members. For example, in 2005, league members closed several offices that were controlled by the ruling party, a decision that led the Tunis Court of First Instance to suspend all LTDH activities.[90] Ben Ali was determined to gain control of the LTDH—by all means possible.

Neighbourhood Committees

Authorities implemented further oversight of citizens in 1991 by creating about 5,000 'Neighbourhood Committees', which enjoyed associational status but were formally linked to the Interior Ministry. The prerogatives of the Neighbourhood Committees were defined broadly: law number 1753 on the structural organization of the Interior Ministry, which created the committees, stipulated that they were tasked to 'look after the events of the neighbourhoods, follow up on its activities, and organize . . . internal, national, regional, and local forums'.[91] Ben Ali associates also stressed that they promoted the development of neighbourhoods, ensured their cleanliness, and organized cultural events.[92] In reality, however, the committees primarily served to bring local communities under the direct control of the Interior Ministry, and their composition and tasks closely resembled those of the RCD cells. One interviewee, reflecting a typical account, explained that:

Everybody [in the committees] was a member of the ruling party. . . . It was important for committee members to belong to the RCD otherwise they couldn't be trusted. . . . There were a few exceptions [but] generally

---

[89] Ibid.

[90] 'Tunisia: Intimidation of the Tunisian League for Human Rights Must Stop (MDE 30/015/2005)', Amnesty International, 7 September 2005, https://www.amnesty.org/en/documents/MDE30/015/2005/fr/, last accessed 27 February 2018.

[91] Legislation no. 1763 from 23 November 1991 on the amendment of legislation no. 453 from 1 April 1991 on the structural organization of the Interior Ministry. A copy of the legislation is available online: https://www.pist.tn/collection/JORT, last accessed 10 February 2022.

[92] For example, interview with Sadok Chaabane, Tunis, 20 July 2017.

you found almost the same people [in the RCD cells and Neighbourhood Committees].[93]

Moreover, just like the RCD cells, the Neighbourhood Committees performed monitoring and surveillance functions in their districts, and it was also within these structures that many lumpen activists rose to leading ranks. Though some committees pursued social and cultural activities, these were clearly not their priority. Adel Kaaniche, the lawyer who worked for the Ben Ali regime, maintained that the Neighbourhood Committees:

> used Tunisians as spies! Its members were willing to play the game of espionage, to follow indicators [drawn up for spying activities], to shadow people. . . . Instead of doing politics we [Tunisians] became spies![94]

Naturally, Kaaniche's statement is an exaggeration and not all Tunisians conducted espionage. His account is, however, revealing as it highlights the extent to which some party followers became frustrated as they increasingly performed security functions instead of proposing and discussing policies. Given that the Neighbourhood Committees pursued the same surveillance tasks as the RCD grass roots, the question arises as to why they were created in the first place. It is likely that Ben Ali sought to strengthen the sway of the Interior Ministry and further subdue the party, which he never fully trusted. Though the RCD cells also coordinated with the Interior Ministry, the committees went a step further because they structurally belonged to it. One interviewee deplored that the committees were 'competing' with the party and 'existed in parallel'.[95] The committees also monitored the RCD cells—and vice versa. This suggests that officials were increasingly paranoid about 'subversive' activities. They '[lived] in perpetual irrational fear of its citizens, seeing any sign of discontent as an existential threat'[96]—including within the regime's own ranks. Ben Ali officials artificially introduced competition amongst various political institutions, in order to play activists off against each other, instigate fear amongst followers, and project an image of omnipresent control. Everybody was a potential suspect, and RCD members were not exempt from this.

---

[93] Interview with RCD grassroots member Naoufel, Tunis, 24 July 2017.
[94] Interview with Adel Kaaniche, Tunis, 26 July 2017.
[95] Interview with Abbes Mohsen, Tunis, 22 July 2017.
[96] Tawfik al-Madani, *Suqut al-Dawla al-Bulisiyya fi Tunis* [*The Collapse of the Police State in Tunisia*], Beirut: Arab Scientific Publishers, 2011, p. 137.

The RCD abroad

Ben Ali officials were particularly anxious about the activities of Tunisians living abroad. Consonant with their counterparts in other dictatorships, their concern was essentially twofold: (1) gaining a grip of opposition forces, specifically in democracies, where they are free to organize, all whilst (2) bolstering the image of their authoritarian regime abroad.[97] Many European countries, especially France, Germany, and Italy, were home to large Tunisian communities. In the 1990s, these migrants were joined by hundreds of exiles from Ennahda and other opposition parties. Their presence threatened to tarnish the image of the regime, especially once some exiles spoke out about their experience of repression and torture at home. The 1990 creation of ATCE—the media organization tasked with promoting Tunisia's image abroad—must be understood in this context. In addition, officials established hundreds of associations throughout Europe that served as a propaganda tool of the regime.

Most famously, the Rally of the Tunisians in France (RTF), located on Rue Botzaris in Paris, was officially charged with all sorts of cultural and social activities. Like many Tunisian associations, it openly displayed its loyalty to Ben Ali and his RCD, for instance, through pictures of the President and banners with the ruling party's colours.[98] Following Ben Ali's ousting in January 2011, some of the association's documents were seized and published online. They reveal that the RTF was none other than the RCD headquarters in France, convening around 60,000–70,000 party members based in the country.[99] Headers on some of the seized documents displayed the name 'Rally of the Tunisians in France', but next to it is detailed in Arabic 'Constitutional Democratic Rally, Central Committee in France' with the official logo of the RCD.[100]

Tunisian officials outwardly concealed the fact that Botzaris was the RCD's France headquarters in order to comply with French law, which banned the

---

[97] For comparative insights, see Irene Fernández Molina, *Moroccan Foreign Policy under Mohamed VI, 1999–2014*, London: Routledge, 2015; Madawi Al-Rasheed, *The Son King: Reform and Repression in Saudi Arabia*, London: Hurst, 2020.

[98] '"Botzarileaks": Les Archives du RCD à Paris Révèlent les Malversations du Parti de Ben Ali,' *Les Observateurs*, 21 September 2011, http://observers.france24.com/fr/20110921-botzarileaks-archives-rcd-paris-revelent-malversations-parti-ben-ali-tunisie-revolution, last accessed 1 March 2018.

[99] See, for details, Mathilde Zederman, 'Contrôle Social et Politique de la Diaspora Tunisienne: Un Autoritarisme à Distance?', in Amin Allal and Vincent Geisser (eds.), *Tunisie: Une Démocratisation au-dessus de Tout Soupçon?*, Paris: CNRS Editions, 2018, p. 403.

[100] '"Botzarileaks": Les Archives du RCD à Paris Révèlent les Malversations du Parti de Ben Ali,' *Les Observateurs*, 21 September 2011, http://observers.france24.com/fr/20110921-botzarileaks-archives-rcd-paris-revelent-malversations-parti-ben-ali-tunisie-revolution, last accessed 1 March 2018.

existence of foreign political parties on national territory. It is difficult to believe, however, that French authorities were not aware that Botzaris was the RCD's France headquarters. They likely decided to turn a blind eye on the matter to protect their relations with the Ben Ali regime, and thence facilitated the perpetuation of authoritarian structures abroad.[101] Tunisian officials took advantage of the RFT's associational status to reap financial benefits from the French state.[102] The Botzaris leaks also reveal that RCD officials asked Tunisian public-sector companies based in France to pay the salaries of party activists. Such 'shadow jobs', in which party members were fictively employed by the state, were common and bolstered the RCD's financial muscle. In several letters, the RCD head in France explicitly asked that Tunisair, the Tourism Office, and the Tunisian Shipping Company pay the salaries of some 'employees and civil servants' who worked either for the RTF or an affiliated association.[103]

Alongside the RTF, 'around a hundred partner associations were created, which gathered the disabled, poets, writers, as well as boxers or taxi drivers'.[104] Some of these associations were formally linked to the RCD, whilst others kept a neutral facade but de facto worked for the ruling party. For example, the Rally of the Tunisian Students in Paris (RETAP) officially sought to 'help students from Tunisia . . . in their everyday life; and to play a bridge between France and Tunisia through diverse activities, in order to foster intercultural dialogue and mutual understanding'.[105] However, in internal documents, the RETAP presented itself as the 'student cell of the RCD in Paris'.[106] Ben Ali officials were particularly keen to regulate the activities of politicized students—a

---

[101] For more information on how Western countries have, at times, contributed to the perpetuation of authoritarian practices in the Arab world, see Mustapha K. Sayyid, 'International Dimension of Middle Eastern Authoritarianism: The G8 and External Efforts at Political Reform', in Oliver Schlumberger (ed.), *Debating Arab Authoritarianism: Dynamics and Durability in Nondemocratic Regimes*, Stanford, CA: Stanford University Press, 2007, pp. 215–230.

[102] Amongst other details, the Botzaris documents reveal that in 1994 the RTF received 110,000 French francs—around 17,000 euros (EUR)—in public money from the Social Action Fund for Immigrant Workers and Their Families, as well as 80,000 FF—about 11,500 EUR—from the city hall in Marseille for social and urban development projects. See, for details, '"Botzarileaks": Des Organismes Publics Français ont Versé des Subventions au Parti de Ben Ali', 23 September 2011, *Les Observateurs*, http://observers.france24.com/fr/20110923-botzarileaks-suite-organismes-publics-francais-ont-verse-subventions-parti-ben-ali-rcd-tunisie-botzaris, last accessed 1 March 2018.

[103] '"Botzarileaks": Les Archives du RCD à Paris Révèlent les Malversations du Parti de Ben Ali', *Les Observateurs*, 21 September 2011, http://observers.france24.com/fr/20110921-botzarileaks-archives-rcd-paris-revelent-malversations-parti-ben-ali-tunisie-revolution, last accessed 1 March 2018.

[104] Jean-Pierre Tuquoi and Nicolas Beau, *Notre Ami Ben Ali: L'Envers du 'Miracle Tunisien'*, Paris: La Découverte, 1999, p. 192.

[105] Quoted in Mathilde Zederman, 'Contrôle Social et Politique de la Diaspora Tunisienne: Un Autoritarisme à Distance?', in Amin Allal and Vincent Geisser (eds.), *Tunisie: Une Démocratisation au-dessus de Tout Soupçon?*, Paris: CNRS Editions, 2018, p. 404.

[106] Ibid.

common concern of authoritarian leaders seeking to fend off anti-regime resistance abroad.[107] The RCD's informal, sometimes covered and decentralized approach to regrouping the Tunisian community in France had a 'double advantage': it made it easier to attract financial support from the French state and strengthened the RCD's 'capacity to infiltrate hostile milieus'.[108]

Indeed, consonant with their local chapters, one of the key functions of the RCD abroad was to monitor opposition activists. Seifeddine Ferjani, who was exiled in London with his father, an Ennahda leader, told me that regime figures used to shadow his family. 'At the beginning [they] were even searching our rubbish to collect information about us,' he said.[109] One high-ranking security official under Ben Ali estimated that around seventy 'police officers'—likely referring to a range of actors performing monitoring and policing functions—were employed throughout France,[110] in illustration that 'the authoritarian state has ample opportunities to extend its coercive power beyond borders'.[111] It is unclear whether these figures operated primarily via the Tunisian embassy or the RCD headquarters—probably both were involved. Relations between the party and embassy staff were close, and the vast majority of senior diplomats had a background in the RCD.[112]

In fact, the Botzaris leaks reveal that embassy staff used party members for a range of surveillance functions, including during such sensitive times as the Tunisian elections. They show inter alia that it was the RCD—and not the embassy, as stipulated by the law—that scrutinized the voting results of Tunisians in France. They also selected election observers, whose job it was to identify and report on people who did not cast a ballot for the ruling party—a relatively easy task, given that votes could be identified through a system of coloured cards that were slipped into transparent envelopes. In a typical example of such monitoring and denunciation activity, one observer handed in an election report in which she detailed 'all the information about

[107] Amongst other examples, see Adele Del Sordi, 'Sponsoring Student Mobility for Development and Authoritarian Stability: Kazakhstan's Bolashak Programme', *Globalizations*, 2018, 15, 2, pp. 215–231.

[108] Jean-Pierre Tuquoi and Nicolas Beau, *Notre Ami Ben Ali: L'Envers du 'Miracle Tunisien'*, Paris: La Découverte, 1999, p. 192.

[109] Interview with Seifeddine Ferjani quoted in Anne Wolf, *Political Islam in Tunisia: The History of Ennahda*, New York: Oxford University Press, 2017, p. 88.

[110] Mathilde Zederman, 'Contrôle Social et Politique de la Diaspora Tunisienne: Un Autoritarisme à Distance?', in Amin Allal and Vincent Geisser (eds.), *Tunisie: Une Démocratisation au-dessus de Tout Soupçon?*, Paris: CNRS Editions, 2018, p. 408.

[111] Marlies Glasius, 'Extraterritorial Authoritarian Practices: A Framework', *Globalizations*, 2018, 15, 2, p. 186.

[112] Mathilde Zederman, 'Contrôle Social et Politique de la Diaspora Tunisienne: Un Autoritarisme à Distance?', in Amin Allal and Vincent Geisser (eds.), *Tunisie: Une Démocratisation au-dessus de Tout Soupçon?*, Paris: CNRS Editions, 2018, p. 399.

the people [she] saw who voted for the "blue card" or "golden card" [of the opposition]'.[113] Authoritarian practices was an important way to identify and stifle contentious voices abroad.

Silencing the opposition

Naturally, the illegal monitoring of votes cast in France was only a reflection of much wider electoral interference at home. During general elections in 1994, Ben Ali—who ran unopposed—claimed 99.9% of the votes, and the RCD received 144 out of 163 parliamentary seats. Following a change in the electoral law, nineteen parliamentary mandates had been reserved for the opposition: these were allocated to parties that were relatively loyal to the Ben Ali regime. The introduction of quotas to grant the opposition a limited parliamentary presentation was a wider trend in the Arab world at the time. Rather than a step towards democratic politics, it served to co-opt and divide political opponents, weakening their contentious potential.[114] The MDS, which gained ten seats, was headed by Mohamed Moada at the time, who followed a reconciliatory line with the regime. In an interview in *La Presse* in 1992, he stressed the need 'to revise the concept of the political opposition' because 'a switch of power of 100% has become outdated'[115] and, in reference to the presidential elections, pronounced the 'immutable confidence' of MDS activists in Ben Ali.[116] Some leaders of the legal opposition were indeed willing to back Ben Ali publicly. They supported his new economic and security prerogatives and hoped he would elevate their political standing.[117]

Other parties that gained seats included the Unionist Democratic Union (UDU) with two mandates. The UDU was founded in 1988 by Abderrahmane Tlili, an RCD member at the time. Mohamed Jegham explained that shortly after taking power, Ben Ali 'pushed some people he knew to create . . . so-called opposition parties', but these parties 'were of course not at all from the

---

[113] '"Botzarileaks": Les Archives du RCD à Paris Révèlent les Malversations du Parti de Ben Ali', *Les Observateurs*, 21 September 2011, http://observers.france24.com/fr/20110921-botzarileaks-archives-rcd-paris-revelent-malversations-parti-ben-ali-tunisie-revolution, last accessed 1 March 2018.

[114] See, for more details, Ellen Lust-Okar, *Structuring Conflict in the Arab World: Incumbents, Opponents, and Institutions*, Cambridge: Cambridge University Press, 2005.

[115] Mohamed Moada, quoted in Noureddine Sraieb, 'Tunisie: Chronique Intérieure (1992)', *Annuaire de l'Afrique du Nord*, 1994, 31, Paris: CNRS, p. 977.

[116] Jean-Pierre Tuquoi and Nicolas Beau, *Notre Ami Ben Ali: L'Envers du 'Miracle Tunisien'*, Paris: La Découverte, 1999, p. 73.

[117] Ellen Lust has noted that elections in dictatorships are an important arena to compete over state resources. See, for details, Ellen Lust-Okar, *Structuring Conflict in the Arab World: Incumbents, Opponents, and Institutions*, Cambridge: Cambridge University Press, 2005; Ellen Lust, 'Elections under Authoritarianism: Preliminary Lessons from Jordan', *Democratization*, 2006, 13, 3, pp. 456–471.

opposition'.[118] The UDU was part of the RCD's network and its sole purpose was to bolster Ben Ali and the ruling party by conveying an image of ostensible political pluralism and liberalization. Loyal opposition forces indeed constitute an important source of authoritarian legitimation.[119] However, despite these parties' public backing of the Tunisian regime, the authorities were not willing to extend the favour of limited representation to the May 1995 municipal elections: the RCD claimed 99.86% of the votes.

To some leaders, including from the more accommodating opposition, the municipal election result was just too difficult to accept. Mohamed Moada wrote an open letter to Ben Ali denouncing the lack of political freedoms. Together with several other prominent opposition activists, he was sentenced to jail on trumped-up charges. One scholar remarked on the situation that 'the government was cracking down on outspoken secular political opponents and human rights advocates, who now joined al-Nahda militants as political prisoners'.[120] Alongside Mohamed Moada, these included Khemais Chammari, a LTDH activist, and Moncef Marzouki, the former league President who had set up the Congress of the Republic (CPR) party, which remained illegal. This shows that the authorities' prior crackdown on Ennahda was never about Islamism as such but about the maintenance of their power, and other dissidents soon followed suit.[121]

Whilst authorities widened the scope of repression to a range of opposition forces, they also decided to change their strategy for the 1999 elections and bestowed legal parties with a greater voice in Parliament. Officials employed over and again a carrot-and-stick approach towards the opposition, a practice common in many dictatorships.[122] In November 1997, Ben Ali announced that opposition parties would be granted a share of 20% of seats in Parliament and local assemblies; presidential associates henceforth praised this 'pluralism' and 'reforms of the electoral law, which . . . ensure the credibility of the votes'—at least so they claimed.[123] For the first time, Ben Ali also opened up the

---

[118] Interview with Mohamed Jegham, Tunis, 19 July 2017.

[119] For comparative insights, see Holger Albrecht, 'How Can Opposition Support Authoritarianism? Lessons from Egypt', Democratization, 2005, 12, 3, pp. 378–397; Francesco Cavatorta, '"Divided They Stand, Divided They Fail": Opposition Politics in Morocco', Democratization, 2009, 16, 1, pp. 137–156.

[120] Kenneth J. Perkins, A History of Modern Tunisia, Cambridge: Cambridge University Press, 2008, p. 197.

[121] For more details, see Tawfik al-Madani, al-Mu'arada al-Tunisiyya, Nash'atuha wa-Tatawuruha [The Tunisian Opposition, Its Birth and Evolution], Damascus: Ittihad al-Kuttab al-Arab, 2001.

[122] For comparative insights, see Jason Brownlee, Tarek Masoud, and Andrew Reynolds, 'Why the Modest Harvest?', in Larry Diamond and Marc F. Plattner (eds.), Democratization and Authoritarianism in the Arab World, Baltimore, MD: Johns Hopkins University Press, 2014, p. 131.

[123] Zouhair Mdhafer, 'Al-Tahawwul al-Dimuqrati wa-Khususiyyat al-Nizam al-Intikhabi fi Tunis' ['Democratic Transition and the Electoral System Specificities in Tunisia'], in Markaz al-Dirasat wa-l-Takwin, Muntadayat al-Fikr al-Siyasi 2008–2009 [RCD Centre for Studies and Training, Political Thought Forums 2008–2009], Tunis: RCD Publications, 2009, p. 14.

presidential elections to other candidates, though a variety of 'safety' clauses ensured that only two figures were qualified to run besides himself: Abderrahmane Tlili and Mohamed Belhaj Amor, another loyal opposition leader who openly expressed his support for Ben Ali during the campaign. The election results did not offer any surprises: in 1999, Ben Ali officially scored 99.45% of the vote and the RCD received all seats other than the 20% that had been reserved for the opposition.

In parallel, Ben Ali reinforced coercion and control inside the ruling party. The RCD's leftist members and ideological lobbyists were the first victims. Amongst other figures, Moncer Rouissi—the former Ben Ali adviser who joined his cabinet shortly after he took power—testified that he was marginalized, beginning in the mid-1990s.[124] One of his colleagues, Khemais Ksila, a former UGTT activist and LTDH leader who had joined the RCD's leading ranks following Ben Ali's assumption of power, was even imprisoned in 1998 after he denounced the repressive practices of the regime. These ideologically committed individuals, who had sincerely believed that Ben Ali intended to open up the political sphere—even if many did not support 'full' democracy owing to their anti-Islamist sentiments—now constituted an internal hazard: they were critically minded and had important ties to the West—all of which risked destabilizing the regime's power base from within. Ben Ali's fierce crackdown on individual challengers, however, ensured that most decided not to publicly voice their discontent. The more asymmetric the power relations between an incumbent and ruling party, the less likely it is that internal opponents will, in fact, embark upon contentious actions—especially if their leader enjoys substantial legitimacy within wider regime circles, as was the case with Ben Ali at the time.

The tiger of the Mediterranean

Officials sought to mitigate and mask their blatant authoritarian practices by continuously refining and adjusting the ideational underpinnings of the RCD. Though, in the 1990s, Ben Ali officials kept advancing the promise of democracy, they increasingly stressed that—owing to the supposedly volatile domestic and regional security environment—this was now 'a complex and difficult process'.[125] Such discourse intended to suggest that free multiparty

---

[124] Interview with Moncer Rouissi, Tunis, 21 July 2017.
[125] Sadok Chaabane, *Ben Ali, Bâtir une Démocratie: De la Lutte des Croyances à la Compétition des Programmes*, Tunis: Maison Arabe du Livre, 2005, p. 68. Note that Chaabane was one of the principal ideologues of the Ben Ali regime.

politics would not occur at any point soon but would prove a long-term project, essentially postponing it indefinitely. In addition, by the mid-1990s, authorities came to equate the party with a wider 'civilizational project'[126] or 'enterprise'[127]—one which was threatened by opposition forces that worked 'against the system',[128] that is, by those who did not endorse Ben Ali or the RCD. In a 21 March 1990 speech, Ben Ali elaborated that:

> today the significance of Independence has become a synonym of economic strength, presence on the international scene, attachment to our values and achievements, the mastery of science, industry, technology.[129]

This statement is important in so far as it illustrates Ben Ali's effort to reinterpret the meaning of independence, the main ideological referent of the Destour, which he emphasized was no longer about 'the evacuation of foreigners from our territory' but about wider socio-economic, technological, and cultural achievements.[130] Realizing this end became a new foundation of the regime's raison d'être. Such performance-based strategies of legitimation are common across a variety of dictatorships.[131] Scholars of authoritarian upgrading in the Arab world have found that beginning in the 1990s, a range of incumbents stressed their regimes' supposedly great efficiency and achievements.[132] However, the literature has paid less attention to the questions as to whether authoritarian stability was, in fact, contingent on their performance and, if so, on *which* performance, when, why, and how—key concerns of this book.

One of the main *acquis* Ben Ali officials sought to highlight was their promotion of women's rights, which has been a common legitimation strategy in the Middle East and North Africa.[133] Bourguiba himself had already supported the

---

[126] 'La Motion du Règlement Intérieur: Garantir la Cohésion et l'Unité des Rangs pour Préserver les Acquis', *Le Renouveau*, 1 August 1993, p. 7.

[127] 'Solidaires dans l'Excellence', *Le Renouveau*, 1 August 1998, p. 9.

[128] Sadok Chaabane, *Ben Ali, Bâtir une Démocratie: De la Lutte des Croyances à la Compétition des Programmes*, Tunis: Maison Arabe du Livre, 2005, p. 13.

[129] 'Ben Ali à l'Occasion de la Fête de l'Indépendance: La Démocratie est la Responsabilité de Tous', *La Presse*, 21 March 1990, p. 4.

[130] Ibid.

[131] Christian Von Soest and Julia Grauvogel, 'Identity, Procedures and Performance: How Authoritarian Regimes Legitimize Their Rule', *Contemporary Politics*, 2017, 23, 3, pp. 287–305.

[132] Volker Perthes, *Arab Elites: Negotiating the Politics of Change*, London: Lynne Rienner, 2004; Steven Heydemann, 'Upgrading Authoritarianism in the Arab World', Brookings Institution Saban Center Analysis Paper No. 13, 2007; Oliver Schlumberger, *Debating Arab Authoritarianism: Dynamics and Durability in Nondemocratic Regimes*, Stanford, CA: Stanford University Press, 2007.

[133] Aili Mari Tripp, *Seeking Legitimacy: Why Arab Autocracies Adopt Women's Rights*, Cambridge: Cambridge University Press, 2019; Dörthe Engelcke, *Reforming Family Law: Social and Political Change in Jordan and Morocco*, Cambridge: Cambridge University Press, 2020.

creation of some influential women's associations and propounded pioneering legislation to promote gender equality, most importantly the Personal Status Code, which was further developed under Ben Ali. However, Ben Ali sought to take matters a step further and also bolster women's standing in politics. Naziha Zarrouk, one of the first women to join the RCD leadership ranks, explained that 'we [RCD leaders] very much enhanced the representation of women within the party institutions and in policy-making instances, such as in ministries or the cabinets of ministers'.[134] During the RCD's 1993 congress, the proportion of women in party leadership positions rose from 1.5% to 3%.[135]

The 1998 party congress, which took place under the slogan of 'Excellence', further increased the number of female figureheads as a new stipulation required 20% of Central Committee members to be women. At the event, Ben Ali declared that 'we refuse [to accept] that the woman is lagging behind compared to the man . . . because we cannot succeed in the path of excellence without the woman'.[136] The number of female leaders indeed increased markedly under Ben Ali, including in government (see Figure 3.1). Whilst some regime officials may have genuinely wanted to champion women's rights, these prerogatives were also highly strategic in that they served to co-opt leftist and Francophile portions of society and promote a 'modern' image of Tunisia for the benefit of its Western partners. Even Ben Ali's fiercest critiques could hardly deny that in certain areas there was, indeed, progress—the figures spoke for themselves. However, it was only RCD women who had a chance to be promoted (female opposition candidates were repressed), and then only those from the political elite as women remained starkly underrepresented in the lower echelons of the party.[137]

Importantly, the 1998 congress slogan 'Excellence' refers to another central premise of the Ben Ali regime, namely, that of 'economic strength'. In interviews, many RCD activists insisted that in this respect '[Tunisia] was a success'[138] and that the 1990s constituted a 'golden era' owing to the supposedly 'economic and social growth' then under way.[139] Data from the International

---

[134] Interview with Naziha Zarrouk, Tunis, 30 January 2017.
[135] 'Déclarations de M Chédli Neffati, Secrétaire Général du RCD, aux Journalistes', published in Noureddine Sraieb, 'Tunisie: Chronique Intérieure (1993)', *Annuaire de l'Afrique du Nord*, 1995, 32, Paris: CNRS, p. 626.
[136] 'La Vitesse Supérieure', *Le Renouveau*, 1 August 1998, p. 8.
[137] Doris Gray and Terry Coonan, 'Notes from the Field: Silence Kills! Women and the Transitional Justice Process in Post-Revolutionary Tunisia', *International Journal of Transitional Justice*, 2013, 7, 2, pp. 348–357; Anne Wolf, *Political Islam in Tunisia: The History of Ennahda*, New York: Oxford University Press, 2017, pp. 83–86, 113–114.
[138] For example, interviews with Abbes Mohsen, Tunis, 22 July 2017; Afif Chelbi, Tunis, 22 September 2015.
[139] For example, interview with Selim, Regueb, Sidi Bouzid governorate, 27 June 2016.

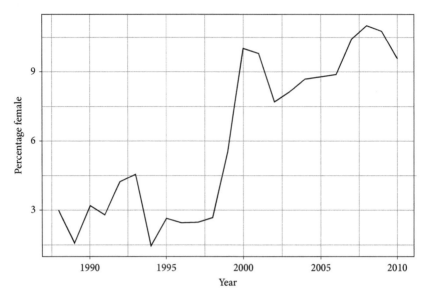

Figure 3.1 Gender composition of the cabinet

Source: author's own calculations. The calculations are based on the data set used in Clionadh Raleigh and Daniel Wigmore Shepherd, 'Elite Coalitions and Power Balance across African Regimes: Introducing the African Cabinet and Political Elite Data Project (ACPED)', *Ethnopolitics*, 2022, 21, 1, pp. 22–47; additional data was provided by Dr Andrea Carboni, University of Sussex.

Monetary Fund suggest that in the 1990s, growth rates were peaking at about 5% annually.[140] Many interviewees cited praise from international donor institutions as 'evidence' of their exemplary performance at the time, illustrating the great importance of external sources of regime legitimation.[141] Succeeding economically and making Tunisia a '"tiger" of the Mediterranean'[142] became a key concern of the RCD leadership. They pronounced growth as one of the preconditions for solving other challenges. For example, party figureheads affirmed that socioeconomic strain made people more prone to join 'extreme' groups; addressing the causes of this strain would reduce their salience, which would allow authorities to embark upon a wider political opening[143]—a clever attempt at tying democratization to economic success. Of course, even in times

[140] 'Tunisia: Selected Issues', *International Monetary Fund*, Country Report No. 16/47, International Monetary Fund, 2016, p. 3.

[141] For example, interviews with Mohamed Ghariani, Tunis, 22 July 2017; Afif Chelbi, Tunis, 22 September 2015. In a 1995 report, World Bank officials noted approvingly that 'the government plays an enormous role in creating an environment that promotes entrepreneurial agility, strong human resources, and labor force flexibility'. See, for details, 'Republic of Tunisia towards the 21st Century, Country Economic Memorandum', World Bank, Report No. 14375-TUN, October 1995, p. 62.

[142] Robert J. King, 'The Political Logic of Economic Reform in Tunisia', in Azzedine Layachi (ed.), *Economic Crisis and Political Change in North Africa*, Westport, CT: Praeger, 1998, p. 107.

[143] Interviews with Mohamed Ghariani, Tunis, 22 July 2017; Afif Chelbi, Tunis, 22 September 2015.

of growth, the political system remained closed. The incumbent's emphasis on socioeconomic performance also encouraged people to focus on their daily achievements and work—rather than, say, big revolutionary objectives—and hence contributed to the routinization of Ben Ali's rule and authoritarian stability more generally.

The RCD's mission did not stop at promoting prosperity, however. 'Solidarity' became one of the catchphrases the RCD used to suggest—at least outwardly—that everybody should be able to benefit from growth; nobody should be left behind.[144] Ben Ali was portrayed as standing at the core of this solidarity: the 'father of the nation' cared about his children and was empathetic and benevolent. Joseph Sassoon has highlighted that leaders in the Middle East and North Africa try to 'project images of loyalty ... and affection ... in order to show that they [are] compassionate'.[145] Similar is true for ruling party officials, who were keen to stress that RCD cells and affiliated associations organize charity work to support the poor. For some RCD members, this solidarity was a reality: amongst other examples, a former grassroots member told me, full of pride and gratitude, that he had never had to pay for his children's notebooks and pens for school because they were provided by the party.[146]

There were other ways Ben Ali officials sought to make 'solidarity' one of the guiding principles of the state and party. Importantly, this new normative priority was accompanied by the creation of prominent development institutions, which outwardly bestowed some credibility on the regime's claim to boost people's well-being—including at the lowest echelons of society. In 1994, the National Solidarity Fund (FNS)—often referred to as the 26–26 Fund after its postal account number—was launched to enhance infrastructure in marginalized areas and help some particularly deprived people. The same year, the Local Council for Development was created to identify socioeconomic, cultural, and educational priorities in specific districts. In 1996, the National Employment Fund (FNE) was additionally set up, most importantly to provide training opportunities for the jobless. A year later, the Tunisian Bank of Solidarity (BTS) was created to help the disadvantaged access finances and microcredit.

---

[144] Sadok Rebah, former Social Affairs Minister, quoted in Noureddine Sraieb, 'Tunisie: Chronique Intérieure (1995)', *Annuaire de l'Afrique du Nord*, 1997, 34, Paris: CNRS, p. 802.
[145] Joseph Sassoon, *Anatomy of Authoritarianism in the Arab Republics*, Cambridge: Cambridge University Press, 2016, p. 187
[146] Interview with Sadok, Bardo, September 2015.

Naturally, things were not as glorious as the authorities tried to suggest. Béatrice Hibou observed that 'access to BTS microcredit is made all the easier if the candidate for the loan is a member of one of the various associations linked to the party'.[147] Moreover, the members of the Local Council for Development included the municipal president, party activists, and the *omda*. The new development institutions were, indeed, deeply embedded in the state's security structures, and its representatives tightly controlled who received access to resources. RCD officials also commonly pressured people to contribute to the FNS and FNE, which relied on public and private donations, sometimes employing 'intimidation, or even repressive practices'.[148] Not all people who ended up giving money actually had the means to do so comfortably. The new development prerogatives were instrumental in promoting authoritarian stability as they served to co-opt key constituencies who profited, all whilst acting as a tool of exclusion and extortion of wide sections of society to whom the regime's premise of solidarity was not extended.

All the President's 'technocrats'

To lend further credibility to his claim to improve the regime's efficiency and economic performance, Ben Ali promoted the rise of a new constituency of ministers with a markedly technocratic profile—a wider trend in the region at the time.[149] He argued that Bourguiba-era figures were not at all qualified to lead Tunisia to wealth and stability. These new officials also took a key role in the RCD, replacing most of the remaining historic party leaders. However, despite their technocratic profile, they were, first and foremost, trusted Ben Ali associates, loyally implementing his orders. As Houchang Chehabi and Juan Linz have rightly pointed out, 'a certain rationalization' of the state bureaucracy or the government does not stand in contradiction to neopatrimonial rule—'as long as this rationalization enhances the ability of the ruler and his cronies to extract resources from society'.[150]

---

[147] Béatrice Hibou, *The Force of Obedience: The Political Economy of Repression in Tunisia*, Cambridge: Polity, 2011, p. 190.

[148] Ibid., p. 190.

[149] For comparative examples, see Abdeslam Maghraoui, 'Depoliticization in Morocco', *Journal of Democracy*, 2002, 13, 4, pp. 24–32; Holger Albrecht and Oliver Schlumberger, '"Waiting for Godot": Regime Change without Democratization in the Middle East', *International Political Science Review*, 2004, 25, 4, pp. 371–392.

[150] H. E. Chehabi and Juan J. Linz, 'A Theory of Sultanism', in H. E. Chehabi and Juan J. Linz (eds.), *Sultanistic Regimes*, Baltimore, MD: Johns Hopkins University Press, 1998, p. 12. Famously, during

A new ministerial class

Many RCD figures came to support the government's technocratization—
especially following years of economic stagnation under Bourguiba. They
assumed Ben Ali's critique of Bourguiba-era ministers who—Ben Ali was keen
to stress—promoted many historic party figures but few technical experts
and specialists.[151] In reality, though, Bourguiba had himself also appointed a
mounting number of technical ministers, beginning in the 1970s.[152] Still, the
ministers in the cabinets following Ben Ali's assumption of power held, on
average, greater technical expertise. Amongst other examples, this can be seen
by the increasing number of engineers appointed to key positions: whereas
the last two governments under Bourguiba only featured one engineer each,
in the first cabinet under Ben Ali seven engineers received posts, representing
one in three government officials.[153] Many held positions critical to boosting
the economy and employment, including the Tourism, Agriculture, and Infrastructure and Housing Ministries. Ben Ali also charged an important number
of economists with key prerogatives. He tripled the number of ministers with
degrees in economics, and they came to head central ministries, such as those
of Finance and National Economy.[154]

Technocratization processes can be an important source of authoritarian
legitimation, especially if the new officials succeed in bringing about economic
growth and structural innovations.[155] However, technical expertise does not
make a minister apolitical or independent, as is often assumed.[156] Officials
have multifaceted identities, and their actions are shaped by diverse factors
and interests, and their technical expertise often just represents one source of
influence, even if it is an important one. And under Ben Ali, the increasingly

the military rule of Augusto Pinochet, a group of technocrats who had studied at the University of
Chicago—the so-called Chicago boys—took a central role in shaping the regime's policies and prerogatives and bolstering its legitimacy both domestically and abroad. Patricio Silva, 'Technocrats and
Politics in Chile: From the Chicago Boys to the CIEPLAN Monks', *Journal of Latin American Studies*,
1991, 23, 2, pp. 385–410.

[151] Interview with Mohamed Ghariani, Tunis, 27 May 2016.

[152] Éric Gobe and Michaël Bechir Ayari, 'Les Cadres Supérieurs de la Fonction Publique Tunisienne: Réalités d'une Condition Socioprofessionnelle', *Cahiers du Gdr Cadres*, 2004, 8, p. 90. Note that
towards the end of his rule, Bourguiba nominated some technically oriented ministers, partially to
marginalize some rivals in the party but, importantly, also to revive the economy, especially after the
socialist experiment had failed.

[153] Author's own calculations and unpublished data set of Andrea Carboni, University of Sussex, on
ministers under Ben Ali.

[154] Ibid.

[155] H. E. Chehabi and Juan J. Linz (eds.), *Sultanistic Regimes*, Baltimore, MD: Johns Hopkins
University Press, 1998.

[156] Duncan McDonnell, 'Defining and Classifying Technocrat-Led and Technocratic Governments',
European Journal of Political Research, 2014, 153, p. 657.

technical profile was certainly not the central feature of the ministerial change that was under way in the 1990s. Indeed, what defined the ministers even more so than their professional background was their total allegiance to Ben Ali. They were, first and foremost, Ben Ali's men and—more rarely—women. Though the 1987 government of Hedi Baccouche had still included some critical voices, most of them were eliminated within two years. The establishment of the shadow cabinet in Carthage—previously discussed—further underpinned Ben Ali's sway over the ministers.

Alongside technocrats, Ben Ali promoted a new bureaucratic elite, which came to replace the remaining historic party leaders. Indeed, the 1989 government of Hamed Karoui—which lasted for ten years, though in various shapes—no longer included any prominent party officials. Though Karoui himself hailed from the generation of Tunisian independence fighters and therefore possessed significant political capital, he never occupied any leading party posts under Bourguiba;[157] in any case, he was the last party figure from that era in government. Instead of party leaders, Ben Ali appointed many high-ranking bureaucrats and civil servants to ministerial posts, lauding their supposedly superior work discipline and efficiency. Many of them had no party experience or ambition at all. Tunisia's prominent National School of Administration (ENA) became a key supplier of such ministerial personnel. Under Bourguiba, the school had played little role in furnishing cabinet officials, likely because it was created in 1949 under the French protectorate to train a new elite of public servants and was therefore perceived as politically compromised. By contrast, Ben Ali came to rely on the ENA to fill many government posts: one in four ministers in Karoui's 1989 cabinet had passed through the ENA, a figure that remained relatively constant throughout the 1990s.[158] One scholar—though recognizing the partially instrumental nature of the cabinet reforms—praised that they 'considerably smoothed the work of the government';[159] such external performance validations were common and bolstered the legitimacy of Ben Ali at the time.

It is notable that many of the new officials were markedly younger than their predecessors. Ministers in the 1989 cabinet were, on average, under fifty

---

[157] Hamed Karoui did, however, hold regionally representative positions in his province of origin, Sousse.

[158] Author's own calculations.

[159] Steffen Erdle elaborated that 'The "de-politicization" of the administration . . . has allowed for a certain "normalization" of its daily work, and taken officials out of the "line of fire"—meaning that they can increasingly work to their own rules again, without being over-laden with "hidden agendas."' Steffen Erdle, *Ben Ali's 'New Tunisia' (1987–2009): A Case Study of Authoritarian Modernization in the Arab World*, Berlin: Klaus Schwarz, 2010, pp. 150–151.

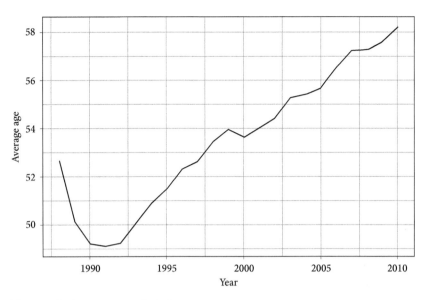

Figure 3.2 Average age of ministers

Source: author's own calculations. The calculations are based on the data set used in Clionadh Raleigh and Daniel Wigmore Shepherd, 'Elite Coalitions and Power Balance across African Regimes: Introducing the African Cabinet and Political Elite Data Project (ACPED)', *Ethnopolitics*, 2022, 21, 1, pp. 22–47; additional data was provided by Dr Andrea Carboni, University of Sussex.

years old (see Figure 3.2).[160] They still had much of their career ahead and could rise with the new president, and their political success depended entirely on the goodwill of Ben Ali, given that they held little political leverage of their own. Some ENA graduates were appointed to the most sensitive government positions, including the Interior and Defence Ministries. This was part of Ben Ali's strategy to coup-proof against any rivals as internal competitors often hail from these ministries. However, placing bureaucrats to these sensitive posts was comparatively safe: they were political lightweights or, more accurately, in most cases 'no-weights', at the total mercy of Ben Ali, and had to please him and execute his demands in order to retain their posts.

Importantly, the ministers were injected into the ruling party, though they had no prior party experience or ambition per se. This was because the internal RCD statute automatically bestowed upon ministers 'affiliated with the party' Central Committee membership.[161] Their insertion into the RCD

---

[160] Author's own calculations.
[161] See, for details, al-Nizam al-Dakhili li-l-Tajammu' al-Dusturi al-Dimuqrati [Statute of the Constitutional Democratic Rally], copy received from private archives in Tunis.

further marginalized historic activists, and political visionaries and thinkers amongst the party's leading ranks. It contributed to the depoliticization of the RCD's leadership and the bureaucratization of party politics more generally. Thus, the new ministerial class in the 1990s not only reduced the role of the RCD in government, it also served to replace many historic party cadres—a process reinforced by the rise of a new type of Secretary General.

The new Secretaries General

Chapter 2 showed that the RCD's early leadership was marked by figures who possessed significant political capital of their own: Hedi Baccouche, by virtue of his role in the fight for independence, which bestowed him with ample political legitimacy; and, to a somewhat lesser extent, Abderrahim Zouari, his successor. Baccouche cared deeply about the RCD, given its historic roots in the nationalist movement. Unlike Baccouche, Zouari was not a pure product of the party: he was a lawyer and made most of his career in the state—he had served as the governor of various provinces and eventually even became head governor, a post which oversees all other governors. Zouari also sought to strengthen the RCD for it to become an independent pole of power, though he never advocated for a complete separation of the RCD from the state.

In February 1990, Ben Ali appointed Chedli Neffati as RCD Secretary General. Unlike Baccouche and Zouari, Neffati was primarily a product of the administration: he was an ENA graduate. Like Zouari, Neffati also made a career as governor and then head governor. In an interview, Neffati said— without being prompted on the topic—that despite his background in the state, he felt very strongly about the RCD and had participated in Destourian politics since his childhood. He affirmed that his mission as Secretary General was to bolster the party and dissociate it from the state's structures. He elaborated:

> I tried to strengthen the party. Why? Because I really thought that Tunisia would embark upon a democratic opening. . . . If you want to have democracy . . . it is necessary that the party counts on itself. . . . I told everybody who worked with me: now [the party] needs to rely on itself, not on the support of the government, the governors, [or] *délégués*. We began to work [on this], we began to become independent, to separate ourselves from the state. . . .

We began to [count] on our own competencies, our own means, our own activists.[162]

Neffati suggests that under his leadership, the RCD acquired independent political leverage. Yet other RCD officials contradicted this account: Mohamed Ghariani said that Neffati was first and foremost an 'administrator';[163] Adel Kaaniche affirmed that he was just following the orders of Ben Ali and his Interior Minister and strongman, Abdallah Kallal.[164] This suggests that Ben Ali chose Neffati as RCD Secretary General mainly because he was a trusted civil servant with limited political ambitions of his own and hence did not pose a threat to his own power base; however, on a personal level, Neffati may still have supported bolstering the party.[165]

Whilst Neffati resembled more a high-ranking bureaucrat than a party figurehead with political capital of his own, he was still more invested in Destourian politics than Abdelaziz Ben Dhia, a lawyer who succeeded him as RCD Secretary General in June 1996. Regime insiders frequently described Ben Dhia as 'Ben Ali's man', affirming that he worked only to reinforce the power of the President.[166] According to Neffati, Ben Dhia's 'sole mission [as RCD Secretary General] was to . . . reduce the party',[167] an analysis other interviewees shared.[168] To illustrate how Ben Dhia's RCD leadership vision differed from his, Neffati described an encounter he had with him in later years, when Ben Dhia was appointed head of the Presidential Cabinet. He said:

I was in the office of Ben Dhia . . . with a few other people. Ben Dhia—perhaps he did this on purpose in front of me to [provoke] me—he said to one of our colleagues: 'I was RCD Secretary General for three years, but I never phoned my representative in the regions, never! I only knew the governors who represented the state and the government. I always called the governors,

---

[162] Interview with Chedli Neffati, Tunis, 2 February 2017.

[163] For example, interview with Mohamed Ghariani, Tunis, 8 February 2017.

[164] Interview with Adel Kaaniche, Tunis, 26 July 2017.

[165] Note that there are other indications that Neffati was not the political reformer he claims to have been, such as his fierce anti-Islamist rhetoric, which was spread by regime officials in the late 1980s and 1990s to justify their political dominance. As Interior Minister between 1988 and 1990, Neffati must also have played a key role in repressing Ennahda. In the 2000s, some officials believed that the Islamist 'threat' was under control and that Tunisia was ripe for further political reforms. So Neffati may have supported a political opening in these later years, after he ceded the RCD leadership, but it is unlikely that he ever wanted to fully dissociate the state from the party to install a competitive democracy.

[166] Interview with Mohamed Ghariani, Tunis, 8 February 2017.

[167] Interview with Chedli Neffati, Tunis, 2 February 2017.

[168] For example, interview with Mohamed Ghariani, Tunis, 8 February 2017.

who then instructed the [regional] Secretaries General [to do something]'.
This was a conception totally opposed to mine and I replied: 'I was Secretary
General for five years and four months . . . but I never called a governor!'[169]

Neffati probably exaggerated his disagreement with Ben Dhia—who was one
of the most disliked former Ben Ali officials—and it is highly unlikely that he
'never' called a governor, especially because—as previous Head Governor and
interior minister—he must have known most of them personally. However,
Neffati's anecdote still suggests that he and Ben Dhia differed in their visions
for the RCD; the fact that Neffati wonders whether Ben Dhia was deliberately
trying to provoke him at the meeting only underscores this. Whilst as a trusted
civil servant, Neffati mostly followed the orders of the palace, he still possessed
some agency of his own. Liaising with the regional RCD Secretaries General
instead of the governors may have been one of the ways in which he sought
to bolster the party.[170] By contrast, Ben Dhia deliberately marginalized RCD
representatives in the regions to subdue the party.[171]

Thus, during the first decade under Ben Ali, the profile of RCD Secretaries
General changed from independence activists immediately after his assumption of power—when he still needed the support of party followers to remain
in office—to bureaucrats with little personal investment in the ruling party;
and last, to the presidential loyalist of Ben Dhia (see Figure 3.3). This shift
in party leadership profiles reflects the regime's wider transformation from
oligarchic to personalist rule at the time. It is notable that Bourguiba himself
also picked close associates as party leaders. But the key difference is that—
despite their loyalty to Bourguiba—they held ample political capital of their
own, typically having figured prominently in the fight for independence.[172]
The few times that Bourguiba did not appoint an independence fighter to the
position of party director or Secretary General was towards the very end of his
rule, when he feared internal party rivals. By contrast, Ben Ali—who lacked the
revolutionary legitimacy of Bourguiba—marginalized prominent figures from
the very beginning to reinforce his grip over the party and fortify his rule. This
shows that dictators can use processes of technocratization to subdue their
ruling parties by stripping them of prominent figureheads.

---

[169] Interview with Chedli Neffati, Tunis, 2 February 2017.
[170] Note that I was unable to independently confirm that Chedli Neffati was primarily in touch with
the RCD's regional representatives and not the governors.
[171] Other interviewees also suggested that Ben Dhia greatly strengthened the state.
[172] For example, Mohamed Sayah, a longtime director of the PSD, held ample political leverage.

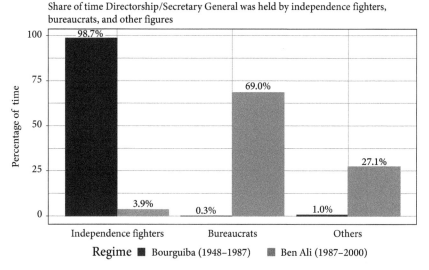

Figure 3.3 Party leadership profiles
Source: author's own calculations.

Limited internal opposition

Many RCD followers supported the promotion of more technical and bureau-cratic personnel in government, believing it would enhance the regime's efficiency, though they opposed their rise within the ruling party. Some of them, though a minority, sought to counter the party's political marginalization—however, not by openly challenging Ben Ali's policies. This would have been a highly risky undertaking and branded them as regime opponents, which they were not. Instead, they tried to bolster RCD figures' own training and skills to raise their profile and compete with the new officials. One notable initiative in this respect was the 1997 creation of a 'Political Academy', through which these RCD followers sought to cultivate a new party elite. Ryadh Saada, former head of the academy, explained: 'we wanted to train people so that they could take on leading positions in politics as well as the state'.[173] In contrast to the RCD's other ideological training schemes, which were inherited from the PSD and mainly targeted the grass roots and youth branches, the Political Academy explicitly focused on the elite. Admission to the academy was extremely competitive: annually only one RCD member was selected per governorate; candidates needed to be at least forty years of age and hold a

---

[173] Interview with Ryadh Saada, Tunis, 24 July 2017.

university degree. For a year, Political Academy members came together once a week to enhance their ideological training, develop leadership skills, and participate in networking events. They were introduced to senior political representatives, in part to learn from their experience but also to promote their profiles in Carthage. Saada explained:

> We wanted the President to get to know [RCD activists] he [could] nominate.... The Political Academy was meant to be a pool of skills and competence [with which] the President could surround [himself]. He could get to know their level of education, their political training. [Political Academy members] were people who had proven themselves![174]

Naturally, it wasn't the President who met academy members, but Saada hoped that Ben Ali could learn about them via his associates who had participated in one of their networking events. The idea was that the Political Academy would become recognized as a leading source for recruitment, something which would have significantly bolstered the RCD's capacity to propose appointments and affect policies. The inceptors of the academy believed Ben Ali's new normative priorities were sincere and wanted to promote them within the ruling party to heighten RCD figures' standing and political voice.[175] However, Saada conceded that 'this did not work well' as only a few Political Academy members ended up being appointed to high-ranking positions.[176] This underscores yet again that the rise of ostensibly technocratic officials was primarily not about bolstering governmental expertise but personalist control, and Ben Ali sought to keep the RCD's political leverage in check.

This raises the question as to why Ben Ali allowed—indeed, even supported—the creation of the Political Academy, given that its members sought to reinvigorate a party he tried to subdue. There are several likely reasons. Most obviously, the academy provided an effective tool for ideological indoctrination, including of highly educated portions of society who joined the academy and subsequently could promote the regime's new normative priorities—security, stability, and prosperity—in front of their constituencies. In addition, ideological work kept people busy. The academy's large number of events and training sessions—alongside the production and diffusion

---

[174] Ibid. Information corroborated through other author interviews.
[175] Ibid.
[176] Ibid.

of ideology—were ways 'through which [party] organization [could] be perpetuated'.[177]

For these reasons, the Political Academy, in fact, facilitated what its inceptors sought to counter: the separation between party activism and high politics. Though some RCD followers despised the subjugation of their party, overall, internal resistance remained limited. This chapter showed that in the 1990s, large sections of the RCD came to endorse Ben Ali's economic and security prerogatives. These twin objectives were, indeed, widely internalized in Tunisia—even beyond the regime's traditional constituency. Many RCD figures thought Ben Ali was the man of the moment, protecting the country and delivering on his key promises—including regional development and the promotion of women's rights. And those party figures who had cause to challenge the central powerbrokers—such as the intellectual lobbyists, who were discarded—faced a collective action problem: they were in the minority and faced tight control and the ever-looming prospect of repression.

---

[177] Compare Clement H. Moore, 'The Single Party as Source of Legitimacy', in Samuel P. Huntington and Clement H. Moore (eds.), *Authoritarian Politics in Modern Society: The Dynamics of Established One-Party Systems*, New York: Basic Books, 1970, p. 66.

4

All in the Family

> The party became a machine . . . to control the country . . . and Ben
> Ali became completely adrift, it was his family who ruled. It was his
> family who destroyed the wealth of the country. This was the end of
> the regime.
>
> Abada Kefi, Bardo, 26 May 2016

In an interview, Nejib, a former RCD grassroots activist and truck driver
from Tunis, recounted that each year on 7 November, he and his friends
used to await with great impatience Ben Ali's annual speech, delivered in
commemoration of the day he took power in 1987. 'It was a speech that made
us dream, in which salary rises and financial benefits were announced, as well
as infrastructure projects and [other plans] to improve the living conditions of
Tunisians', he said. Nejib emphasized, however, that 'in the last five to ten years,
the speech no longer made us dream', elaborating that he and his friends had
'lost faith in the regime'.[1] His testimony reflects a mounting sense of frustration
with Ben Ali, not only in the wider population but also amongst RCD activists.

This chapter investigates why, in the 2000s, Ben Ali's support base began to
crumble, including within inner regime ranks—even though he propagated
the same economic and security prerogatives and, on top of that, continued
his liberalization reforms. I argue that these premises exhausted themselves
because they were no longer credible: Ennahda—deemed the main security
threat—had been defeated, and instead of launching a genuine political opening, Ben Ali further centralized and personalized power. In particular, an
important number of his family members and their associates became major
economic and political stakeholders. They also took key positions in the RCD,
marginalizing long-standing figures. The family's interest in the ruling party
became most pronounced in the late 2000s, when the presidential succession
became a critical topic, and any future president was expected to emerge out
of the RCD.

---

[1] Interview with Nejib, Tunis, 29 June 2016.

Ben Ali's Tunisia. Anne Wolf, Oxford University Press. © Anne Wolf (2023).
DOI: 10.1093/oso/9780192868503.003.0005

The increasing visibility of the presidential family led many Tunisians, such as the above-quoted Abada Kefi—a parliamentary deputy[2] and lawyer who defended Ben Ali–era officials after the uprising—to suspect that they were actually the ones ruling the country and that the President was no longer in charge. He believed that the RCD had become a 'machine', the sole objective of which was to reinforce the family's muscle.[3] This chapter investigates how presidential relatives accumulated vast power, the party-political transformations their rise entailed, and the effects on regime stability. Many long-standing RCD followers were dismayed when Ben Ali's kin came to exert real political influence. As a result, internecine tensions began to mount. Some marginalized followers contested the growing role of presidential relatives and their stooges. However, they were a minority, were regional and local party followers, and acted mostly in inconspicuous ways. This chapter reveals that Ben Ali officials responded by further reinforcing their grip on power. This culminated in 2008, when presidential relatives and their cronies usurped the RCD party leadership, a process that has not been investigated so far.

A looming succession crisis

The President's family developed a keen interest in integrating into the RCD at a time when Ben Ali's succession was becoming a topic of heated discussion and speculation. Scholars have shown that leadership successions pose a key challenge to authoritarian stability, especially when dictators have personalized power.[4] In the 2000s, several leaders of the Arab republics were trying to groom a relative to succeed them.[5] In Tunisia, Ben Ali pushed through a constitutional referendum, held on 26 May 2002, which abolished the three-term limit for presidents and raised the age restriction for any incumbent president from seventy to seventy-five, thus allowing Ben Ali to remain in power

---

[2] In October 2014, Abada Kefi was elected lawmaker for Nidaa Tounes, but he left the party shortly thereafter.

[3] Note that similar suspicions were voiced by many other interviewees. For example, interview with Nejib, Tunis, 29 June 2016.

[4] Erica Frantz and Elizabeth Stein, 'Countering Coups: Leadership Succession Rules in Dictatorships', *Comparative Political Studies*, 2017, 50, 7, pp. 1–29; Anne Meng, 'Winning the Game of Thrones: Leadership Succession in Modern Autocracies', *Journal of Conflict Resolution*, 2021, 65, 5, pp. 950–981.

[5] Mohamed Tharwat, 'Asr al-Jumhuryat al-Malakiyya [*The Era of Monarchical Republics*], Cairo, Egypt: Al-Dar al-Thaqafiyya lil-Nashr, 2002; Larbi Sadiki, '"Wither Arab 'Republicanism"'? The Rise of Family Rule and the "End of Democratization" in Egypt, Libya and Yemen', *Mediterranean Politics*, 2010, 15, 1, pp. 99–107; Roger Owen, *The Rise and Fall of Arab Presidents for Life*, Cambridge, MA: Harvard University Press, 2012, pp. 139–142; Joseph Sassoon, *Anatomy of Authoritarianism in the Arab Republics*, Cambridge: Cambridge University Press, 2016.

until 2014. The RCD became the main tool to ensure prompt advertisement and adoption of the constitutional changes, which were prepared by the Presidential Cabinet and rubber-stamped by Parliament prior to the plebiscite. Ali Chaouch, RCD Secretary General at the time, recalled:

> The party did not participate in the preparation of the constitutional amendment, which was launched by the Presidential Cabinet. Only the [RCD] Political Bureau was asked to discuss the basic features of the project, but that's it.... However, parliamentary committee leaders are Destourians, that is, those who took part in discussing the project in Parliament were party activists.... So the party did not participate directly in the choice [of the referendum] ... but the party is disciplined ... and must of course support the project that was presented by its president and adopted by Parliament; hence we organized a conventional electoral campaign.[6]

Chaouch's comments highlight the high degree to which the RCD managed to enforce unity and discipline. This was despite the referendum being 'very controversial', as Chaouch acknowledged, 'not only amongst the political opposition but also amongst some people who were with the regime'.[7] Indeed, many former RCD activists, such as Hamza, the previous mid-level party leader in Bizerte, said they were far from convinced by the referendum but decided not to voice any criticism, at least in public, because they believed 'they couldn't do anything about it'[8]—a testimony that is credible, given his otherwise marked devotion to the regime. This illustrates that well into the 2000s, Ben Ali could rely on the RCD's full institutional support irrespective of mounting internecine disagreement with his policies.

Whilst the constitutional changes gave Ben Ali ten more years in power, some provisions were introduced that suggest the President had also begun to think about the era after his rule ended. Specifically, legal channels were included for the transfer of power in cases of presidential incapacity, illness, or death. These allowed the president to delegate his powers to the prime minister if he was temporarily incapable of ruling the country—a provision replacing the clause Ben Ali had used to oust Bourguiba, which stipulated that the prime minister could determine the president's incapacity himself. The constitutional reform also enshrined legal immunity for the president, specifying that this

---

[6] Interview with Ali Chaouch, Tunis, 11 February 2017.
[7] Ibid.
[8] Interview with Hamza, Ras Jebel, Bizerte governorate, 9 February 2017. Information corroborated through other interviews.

included the period after his rule. A law passed in 2005 further elaborated the benefits any former president and his family would enjoy. Amongst other entitlements, it granted a past president a life annuity equivalent to what he earned in office, in Ben Ali's case, reportedly 21,000 TND per month (9,200 USD),[9] a striking amount compared to Tunisia's average income of 795 TND (348 USD) per capita.[10] The law also stipulated that when a president died, his wife would continue to enjoy benefits such as housing, health care, and security and support staff, as well as 80% of his life annuity.[11]

Partially because of these provisions, rumours began circulating—including within the RCD—about the President being ill, possibly terminally, and no longer able to rule the country. In particular, Ben Ali was alleged to suffer from prostate cancer, a suspicion uttered even by foreign diplomats.[12] The ubiquitous spread of gossip about the ruling clique is common in long-standing dictatorships, often indicating an atmosphere of stagnation or crisis—especially in the context of uncertainty about the ruler's successor.[13] Many people close to Ben Ali asserted that in addition to his advancing age and alleged illness, the 2005 birth of his son Mohamed had led him to spend more time at home and less at his office.[14] They said that after five daughters, Ben Ali was overjoyed finally to have a son, and that playing with Mohamed on a regular basis had become a priority for him. When I asked Ben Ali's daughter Nesrine whether the birth of her brother changed her father, she affirmed that this was 'true'. Later in the interview, she tried to qualify her response somewhat, saying:

When you accumulate, accumulate, and accumulate [mandates], you get tired at the end, and he was getting old. I don't think it was . . . my brother who

[9] 'Zine El Abidine Ben Ali: Un Salaire de 21.000 DT et un Retrait de 500.000 DT une Semaine avant Son Départ', *Business News*, 30 January 2011, http://www.businessnews.com.tn/zine-el-abidine-ben-ali-un-salaire-de-21000-dt-et-un-retrait-de-500000-dt-une-semaine-avant-son-depart,520,23307,1, last accessed 23 September 2018.

[10] Author calculations, based on World Bank data for 2010: 'World Development Indicators', World Bank, n.d., http://databank.worldbank.org/data/reports.aspx?source=2&country=TUN, last accessed 20 March 2017.

[11] See, for details, law no. 2005–88 of 27 September 2005, *Journal Officiel de la République Tunisienne*, 78, 30 September 2005, http://www.cnudst.rnrt.tn/jortsrc/2005/2005f/jo0782005.pdf, last accessed 27 March 2017.

[12] US Embassy in Tunis, 'Succession in Tunisia: Finding a Successor or Feet First?', Wikileaks, 9 January 2006, 06TUNIS55_a, secret.

[13] Roger Owen, *The Rise and Fall of Arab Presidents for Life*, Cambridge, MA: Harvard University Press, 2012, pp. 139–142.

[14] Interviews with Mohamed Ghariani, Tunis, 27 May 2016; Mahmoud Cheikhrouhou, personal pilot of Ben Ali, Tunis, 1 July 2016; Mohamed Ghannouchi, Tunis, 2 October 2015.

changed a lot, . . . but he took the time to play with him, to see him. However, I don't think this changed the hours he spent in office.[15]

The amount of time Ben Ali spent with his son remains unclear. However, it is improbable that as Nesrine suggested, his schedule and presidential commitments were mostly unaffected—particularly as prior to Mohamed's birth he was known for working solidly all day without breaks. This shows the importance of scrutinizing incumbents' personal and emotional ties and their effects on authoritarian stability, specifically in personalist regimes— dynamics that rationalist models of analysis fail to capture.[16] One former official said that Ben Ali's work discipline had once been so strong that he always picked up his phone or called him back personally—except during his last years in office, when he was sometimes unreachable.[17] Nesrine recognized that in the 2000s, her father was not as vigorous and energetic as he had once been. Some people close to the President, such as Afif Chiboub, whose sister- in-law Dorsaf is Ben Ali's second daughter with his first wife, went so far as to claim that Ben Ali became 'completely cut off from the rest of the world'. Afif Chiboub said that even some presidential relatives did not see him 'as much as they used to', reproaching the President's second wife and entourage for 'isolating' him.[18]

Afif Chiboub's statements are exaggerated, as Ben Ali certainly possessed agency. However, they reflect the extent to which frictions had begun to grow between rival family clans and that family members were aware that an end to Ben Ali's rule was approaching. Indeed, Nesrine admitted that she and other relatives repeatedly asked Ben Ali about a succession plan, trying to push for someone younger who would not pose a threat to the family's inter- ests.[19] In the Arab republics of Yemen, Egypt, and Libya, rulers were grooming their sons to succeed them,[20] but this was certainly not feasible in Tunisia, given Mohamed's young age. Even foreign diplomats seemed clueless when it

---

[15] Interview with Nesrine Ben Ali, Viber, 13 February 2017.

[16] For comparative insights on the role of the families and specifically the wives of Romania's Nicolae Ceaușescu and Zimbabwe's Robert Mugabe, see Vladimir Tismaneanu, *Stalinism for all Seasons: A Political History of Romanian Communism*, Los Angeles: University of California Press, 2003; Geoffrey Nyarota, *The Graceless Fall of Robert Mugabe: The End of a Dictator's Reign*, Cape Town: Penguin Books, 2018.

[17] Interview with Adel, a former official of the Ben Ali regime, Tunis, 2 February 2017.

[18] Interview with Afif Chiboub, Tunis, 13 February 2017.

[19] Interview with Nesrine Ben Ali, Viber, 13 February 2017.

[20] Alongside the works cited earlier, see, for more details, Louis J. Cantori, Tim Jacoby, Sheila Cara- pico, Samer Shehata, Ellen Lust-Okar, Banu Bargu-Hasturk, Glenn E. Robinson, and Ebtesam Al-Kitbi, 'Political Succession in the Middle East', *Middle East Policy*, 2002, 9, 3, pp. 105–123.

came to possible succession scenarios.[21] This was extremely worrying for the President's relatives. By the mid-2000s, most of Ben Ali's daughters had come of age and married, and their husbands had established themselves as wealthy and influential public figures. The next section introduces the main family clans, their leading figures and assets, information that is key to understanding internal regime dynamics at the time.

High stakes, many clans

The key players within Ben Ali's family emanate from two lineages: (1) the three children and in-laws from the President's first marriage, to Naima Ben Ali, born in Kefi; and (2) the relatives of his second wife, Leila Ben Ali, formerly Trabelsi. Ben Ali's family of origin—particularly his seven siblings and their relatives—was also influential, especially in his hometown Hammam Sousse.[22] Naturally, many more people were linked to the Presidential Palace through more distant relatives. Steffen Erdle speaks about 'a tightly knit web of altogether about 60 "ruling families" whose inner core involved a three-digit number of individuals'.[23] This section will focus on the relatives of Naima and Leila, given their particular weight in the Ben Ali galaxy of power. Ben Ali's divorce from Naima and marriage to Leila, and the wider economic and political transformations both induced, are crucial for understanding the decay and eventual collapse of his regime. As her maiden name indicates, Naima's family hails from the rural mountainous Kef region in northwest Tunisia. Yet upon marrying Ben Ali, Naima managed to integrate into and forge close ties with the Tunisois elite. This owed in part to the high status of her father, Mohamed Kefi, who rose to fame during the struggle for independence.[24] Naima's success owed also to the clever alliances she and Ben Ali forged with

---

[21] US Embassy in Tunis, 'Tunisia: What Succession Scenario?', Wikileaks, 9 May 2008, 08TUNIS493_a, secret.

[22] Tawfik al-Madani details how Ben Ali's family of origin, specifically his brother Moncef, was involved in smuggling various goods, including 'cigarettes, luxury alcoholic beverages, bananas, [and] electronic devices'. See, for more details Tawfik al-Madani, *Suqut al-Dawla al-Bulisiyya fi Tunis* [*The Collapse of the Police State in Tunisia*], Beirut: Arab Scientific Publishers, 2011, p. 230.

[23] Steffen Erdle, *Ben Ali's 'New Tunisia' (1987–2009): A Case Study of Authoritarian Modernization in the Arab World*, Berlin: Klaus Schwarz, 2010, p. 146.

[24] Sharan Grewal, 'A Quiet Revolution: The Tunisian Military after Ben Ali', Carnegie Endowment for International Peace, 24 February 2016, p. 14. Note that General Kefi had once been Ben Ali's superior and had been behind his quick ascent within the military hierarchy. Indeed, in 1964 (the same year Ben Ali married Naima), Kefi tasked Ben Ali, back then a simple staff officer, with creating a military security department, which he would head for ten years. See also 'President Ben Ali: Ben Ali's Biography', *Changement* [archived], https://web.archive.org/web/20101021083832/http://www.changement.tn/english/president-ben-ali/ben-ali-s-biography-zine-el-abidine-ben-ali-president-of-the-tunisian-republic–2.html, last accessed 21 March 2017.

prominent Tunisian family clans, most obviously by marrying their children into them.

Ben Ali and Naima have three daughters: Ghazoua, the oldest, married Slim Zarrouk, his name suggesting a descent from the old Zarrouk family of Tunisois notables. Following the marriage, Zarrouk obtained important economic holdings, such as the company Tunisie Plastiques Systemes. The middle daughter, Dorsaf, wed Slim Chiboub, a former volleyball champion, whose ties to the palace facilitated his presiding over Tunisia's National Olympics Committee and the prominent football club Esperance. His business holdings—also developed through his marriage to Dorsaf—focused on sports franchises, advertising, and retail. The youngest of the three, Cyrine, wed Marouane Mabrouk, who hailed from a prominent Tunisois family. The Mabrouks already had a foot in the economy prior to Marouane's marriage, specifically in food and real estate, but his kinship to the President helped him diversify his assets. Mabrouk gained shares in a wide range of sectors, including banking, retail, tourism, and telecommunications.[25]

Despite the quick—some might consider undeserved—economic ascent of Ben Ali's sons-in-law, it is important to highlight that elite circles did not view their success too negatively. This was most obviously because Zarrouk and Mabrouk themselves hailed from prominent families, which subsequently also profited from their ties to the President, whereas Chiboub was recognized as related to an important businessman, Taoufik Chaibi, and as a sports champion. Indeed, to many elite figures, their marriages into the palace were part of an ongoing reinforcement and balancing of alliances, which for centuries had allowed prominent families to impose themselves on the country's political and economic arenas—a common tendency in the Arab world and elsewhere.[26] Members of Ben Ali's ruling clique of the late 1980s and early 1990s frequently emphasized their close ties to Naima and her relatives. For example, Chedli Neffati, the previous RCD Secretary General, said his wife was close friends with Naima and that his family was honoured to have been invited to the wedding of Cyrine[27]—naturally, a unique opportunity to forge even deeper personal and professional ties to the presidential family.

---

[25] Together, Cyrine Ben Ali and Marouane Mabrouk also launched Tunisia's first private internet provider, Planet Tunisie. See, for more details, US Embassy in Tunis, 'Corruption in Tunisia Part IV: The Family's Holdings', Wikileaks, 5 July 2006, 06TUNIS1672_a, confidential.

[26] For comparative insights in the Arab world, see Robert Springborg, *Family, Power, and Politics in Egypt: Sayed Bey Marei—His Clan, Clients, and Cohorts*, Philadelphia: University of Pennsylvania Press, 1982; Daniel Corstange, 'Kinship, Partisanship, and Patronage in Arab Elections', *Electoral Studies*, 2018, 52, pp. 58–72; Lisa Blaydes, 'Rebuilding the Ba'thist State: Party, Tribe, and Administrative Control in Authoritarian Iraq, 1991–1996', *Comparative Politics*, 2020, 53, 1, pp. 93–115.

[27] Interview with Chedli Neffati, Tunis, 2 February 2017.

There were other reasons elite circles were relatively accepting of the fast-growing wealth of Ben Ali's sons-in-law. Importantly, Zarrouk, Chiboub, and Mabrouk were cautious not to appear too aggressive in their economic endeavours, meaning that many elite figures considered them no threat to their own interests. Their business deals typically focused on commerce and they did not seek to take a leading role in lucrative sectors dominated by old elites, such as real estate, tourism, the automotive sector, and aviation—very much unlike the relatives of Ben Ali's second wife, Leila.

The Trabelsis

Leila's background has been the subject of many rumours and heated discussions. Many people suggest she was a hairdresser, alluding to the possibility that she got to know Ben Ali whilst cutting his hair.[28] Yet regime insiders revealed that Leila was not a hairdresser but Ben Ali's longtime mistress.[29] They elaborated that it was not unusual for senior officials to have extramarital relationships, although they naturally sought to keep them confidential out of fear of a public outcry and possible demotion. In the case of Ben Ali, senior figures who worked with him typically stated that they had become aware of his affair with Leila by 1986. That year, their private liaison attracted attention within some regime circles when Leila became pregnant and decided to keep her child. Chedli Neffati, who worked for several months in 1987 at the Interior Ministry—when Ben Ali was Interior Minister—stated:

> One day [Leila] told Ben Ali he would become the father of an illegitimate daughter. This was very serious . . . an extramarital, illegitimate child in the Muslim world, in addition he was Interior Minister! Ben Ali was very lucky because Bourguiba didn't know. Nobody told Bourguiba, because people were afraid of Ben Ali, who was a very tough interior minister. . . . If Bourguiba had known, he would have fired him immediately![30]

---

[28] Many academics have internalized this account. They include Christopher Alexander, *Tunisia: From Stability to Revolution in the Maghreb*, Abingdon: Routledge, 2016, p. 72; Jeremy Bowen, *The Arab Uprisings: The People Want the Fall of the Regime*, London: Simon & Schuster, 2012; James L. Gelvin, *The Arab Uprisings: What Everyone Needs to Know*, New York: Oxford University Press, 2012, p. 45.

[29] Interviews with Hamed Karoui, Tunis, 1 February 2017; Chedli Neffati, Tunis, 2 February 2017. These key informants explained that pundits confused Leila Ben Ali with a person of the same name who was, indeed, a hairdresser in Tunis. Note that in her memoirs, Leila Ben Ali insisted that she had never been a hairdresser. See, for details, Leila Ben Ali, *Ma Vérité*, Paris: Éditions du Moment, 2012, pp. 105–106.

[30] Interview with Chedli Neffati, Tunis, 2 February 2017.

On 16 January 1987, Leila gave birth to a girl, Nesrine, in secrecy.[31] Given how delicate Ben Ali's situation was and that he risked losing not only his reputation but also his job, Kamel Eltaief—an influential businessman and longtime aide of Ben Ali, from his hometown Hammam Sousse—tried to convince him to buy a house for Leila and the child in Europe. Eltaief hoped their resettlement would allow Ben Ali to dissociate himself from them.[32] Far from this, however, in 1988, Ben Ali made the decision to divorce Naima and a few years later, in 1992, he married Leila. Still visibly agitated by Ben Ali's choice, Chedli Neffati stated:

> Some people might think [marrying Leila] was personal. No, it is no longer personal if you are President of the Republic! . . . [Naima and Ben Ali] were fighting all the time, they disagreed a lot. But Ben Ali's big mistake was to divorce her and to officially marry this woman [Leila]. . . . She had been with a very large number of men and was not suited to become [first lady]![33]

Chedli Neffati's comments highlight how from the very beginning, elite circles refused to accept Leila. Her profile was considered too controversial—her father was a simple merchant in the medina of Tunis and some interviewees alleged Leila had once been a prostitute, a claim likely driven by misogynist sentiments. Many figures contrasted her background with Naima's respectable family history. Thus, Ben Ali's divorce from Naima was taken also as a 'divorce' from her friends in the elite, and tensions between them and Leila quickly heightened.

As Naima had done before her, Leila took advantage of her status as first lady to promote her relatives to key economic posts. In contrast to Naima's family, however, Leila's relatives sought to gain a stake in all key branches of the economy. They included highly visible sectors traditionally dominated by elite actors, who had profited from Ben Ali's early economic reforms.[34] Commenting on the business interests of Leila's family, an American diplomat said in the mid-2000s that they 'extend to virtually every corner of the economy from information and communication technology, to manufacturing, retail, transportation, tourism, banking, and agriculture and food processing'.[35]

---

[31] Interview with Hamdi, a trusted friend of the Ben Ali family, Tunis, 5 February 2017. Information corroborated through other interviews.

[32] Ibid.

[33] Interview with Chedli Neffati, Tunis, 2 February 2017.

[34] See, for more details, Stephen J. King. *Liberalization against Democracy: The Local Politics of Economic Reform in Tunisia*, Bloomington: Indiana University Press, 2003.

[35] US Embassy in Tunis, 'Corruption in Tunisia Part II: The Anatomy of Exploitation', Wikileaks, 29 June 2006, 06TUNIS1630_a, confidential.

Only offshore activities were relatively immune from the family's influence, with Tunisian businessmen established abroad reporting little interference by presidential relatives[36]—arguably because a good external image was a key concern of Ben Ali.

But inside Tunisia, possible competitors in sectors where the family operated were systematically and ruthlessly sidelined, including through blackmail and extortion[37]—a kleptocratic reality hitherto unseen in independent Tunisia.[38] Whilst all of Leila's close relatives developed a key economic interest, some of them emerged as particularly aggressive and monopolizing actors. These included Leila's youngest brother, Belhassen Trabelsi. His niece Nesrine characterized him as 'a 100% capitalist', thus suggesting a keen appetite for profit.[39] Belhassen launched Karthago Airlines, the first private airline in Tunisia, and became a leading figure in sectors as diverse as tourism, retail, telecommunications, and manufacturing. Many formerly high-ranking figures said that Belhassen came to dine with Ben Ali on a regular basis. Reportedly, the President valued the information his new brother-in-law relayed through his wide network of employees, many of whom acted as informants on future business deals and opposition figures.[40]

Naturally, the quick ascent of Belhassen to a position of economic heavyweight and trusted aide of the President deeply upset many longtime Ben Ali officials and the more traditional elite, some of whom had suffered massive economic losses because Belhassen had forced them out of business. Chedli Neffati disdainfully recalled: 'I knew Belhassen in 1989. He had nothing, not even a moped.' He elaborated: 'It is not a crime to come from a very poor family and become wealthy—as long as you respect the law!'[41] In reality, of course, many elite figures particularly despised Leila's relatives for the supposedly low educational level that came with their modest family background, denouncing them as primitive *nouveaux riches*.

Aside from Belhassen, another key figure within the Trabelsi family was Leila's nephew Imed. In 2006, Imed attracted international attention when he stole a yacht from a well-known French businessman with his cousin Moaz. Their theft became known when the yacht appeared, freshly repainted, in

---

[36] Interview with various Tunisian business figures who were established abroad at the time, including Faouzi Elloumi, CEO of Elloumi Group, Tunis, 28 September 2015.
[37] Interviews with victims of extortion by the Trabelsi family, including Dhamir Mannai, Tunis, January 2014, and Khayem Turki, Tunis, February 2014.
[38] Note that Bourguiba placed a lot of importance on living modestly.
[39] Interview with Nesrine Ben Ali, Viber, 16 February 2017.
[40] Interviews with various former government officials, including Hamed Karoui, Tunis, 1 February 2017; Chedli Neffati, Tunis, 2 February 2017; Ali Chaouch, Tunis, 11 February 2017.
[41] Interview with Chedli Neffati, Tunis, 2 February 2017.

the harbour of Sidi Bou Said, an upper-class coastal town north of Tunis.[42] Imed's lawyer explained that 'Imed began his first steps in the business world in 1999 [when] he asked his aunt [Leila] to help him make a career'.[43] Subsequently, Imed rose to become a key figure in the economy with interests allegedly including the illegal trafficking of goods such as drugs. The lawyer's account that Leila personally intervened to help Imed is credible, given that many interviewees suggested he was her favourite nephew.[44] Leila allegedly even helped her mother, Hajja Nana, become self-sufficient, which the latter did by facilitating business deals, sometimes in exchange for a commission.[45] The family's role as an economic intermediary, of course, came at the expense of the Tunisois elite and regional notables who traditionally held this function.

The fact that Leila helped her favourite relatives, Belhassen and Imed, attain so much wealth underscores yet again that the specific political dynamics in the 2000s can only be grasped by analysing internal family affairs. Personal relations are particularly crucial to scrutinizing the strategy Leila and her relatives pursued towards elite figures. Whilst sidelining actors perceived to be in conflict with their economic interests, the family engaged in a strategy of revenge against figures who had tried so hard in the mid-1980s to convince Ben Ali to rid himself of Leila and Nesrine. Kamel Eltaief—who had wanted Leila and Nesrine resettled in Italy—became a target. Following a series of attacks on his businesses, Kamel Eltaief granted an interview to *Le Monde* in October 2001 in which he denounced Leila's family's corruption and what he claimed to be a regime-initiated intimidation campaign against him—a rare instance of public opposition against the Trabelsis. One month later, he was arrested and sentenced to a year in prison.[46]

In parallel, Leila fostered close ties to select Tunisois notables to better anchor her family in the capital. In 2004, Nesrine wed Sakher el-Materi, who hailed from an important political family: his father had plotted a coup against Bourguiba in 1962. Moreover, Belhassen married Zohra Djilani, whose family was part of the Tunisois aristocracy. Zohra's father, Hedi Djilani, was the head

---

[42] See, for details, Jacques Follorou, 'Une Affaire de Vol de Yachts Trouble la Relation Paris-Tunis', *Le Monde*, 20 August 2009, https://www.lemonde.fr/afrique/article/2009/08/20/une-affaire-de-vol-de-yachts-trouble-la-relation-paris-tunis_1230218_3212.html, last accessed 25 June 2018.

[43] Interview with Anis Boughattas, Tunis, 4 February 2017.

[44] For example, interviews with Sadok and Hamza, Ras Jebel, Bizerte governorate, 9 February 2017.

[45] Ibid.

[46] 'Tunisie: Reprise du Procès de Kamel Eltaief', *Le Monde*, 22 November 2001, http://www.lemonde.fr/archives/article/2001/11/22/tunisie-reprise-du-proces-de-kamel-eltaief_4151370_1819218.html, last accessed 26 March 2017.

of Tunisia's powerful UTICA employers' union.[47] Evidently, the Trabelsis built alliances according to an 'either-with-or-against' logic—people who became part of their inner circle were protected, and the rest were denounced as opponents. They were much less cautious than the Kefis to safeguard the interests of the Tunisois elite and would go so far as to marginalize anyone challenging their thirst for profits and influence.

The party and the family

Alongside the Trabelsis' forging of ties to certain influential elite actors, they developed a keen interest in the ruling party. In their early years, when the Trabelsis were still building up their power base, the RCD was a useful tool to amass and protect their wealth, especially as they did not themselves hail from an established family with long-standing business ties of their own. The party, indeed, served as a ready-made network to promote their economic interests and to strike business deals, even bestowing a certain degree of legitimacy on these affairs. Close Trabelsi associates benefited as well. Hedi Djilani observed:

> In a small country like Tunisia, you cannot live without politics. [How can] . . . an idea pass or a choice be accepted if you are not a political actor? I was a major economic actor and a major political actor. I was a member of the [RCD] Central Committee. The Central Committee actually did not have a lot of power, but the fact that I was President of UTICA gave me a certain influence.[48]

Djilani stressed that whilst he was both economically and politically highly influential, presiding over UTICA was what made him a notable figure in politics, not his RCD Central Committee membership per se. Indeed, his economic leverage allowed him to initiate policy proposals, which presumably often served his own interests or those of his family and cronies, whilst his RCD post helped validate any decisions taken.[49] Once Ben Ali family members

---

[47] Following Zohra's marriage, Hedi Djilani acquired Financière Tunisienne, Immobilière Echarifa, Hannibal Lease, and Manufacture Tunisienne d'Exploitation Industrielle, amongst other companies. See also US Embassy in Tunis, 'Corruption in Tunisia Part IV: The Family's Holdings', Wikileaks, 5 July 2006, 06TUNIS1672_a, confidential.

[48] Interview with Hedi Djilani, Tunis, 6 February 2017.

[49] Hedi Djilani elaborated that he also pursued 'the politics of football' by heading the club Espérance Sportive de Tunis for several years, a position that helped him become a central public figure. 'When Espèrance wins, you have two million people who are happy', he said. Heading football clubs was indeed an important way for senior figures of the Ben Ali regime to establish themselves without being

became established officials, a key function of the RCD was to bestow legitimacy on their economic and political affairs, at least outwardly. When asked more directly what kind of advantages he enjoyed as a presidential relative, Hedi Djilani stated they centred on administrative facilitations. Taking the example of real estate, he said: 'If you are a normal citizen and ask for an authorization to build something, it will take you two years [until you receive it]. If you are from the Ben Ali family, it takes two hours.'[50]

The extended delays and frequent *de facto* denial of authorizations excluded many citizens from large swaths of Tunisia's economy. In contrast, the RCD's omnipresence in the public sector allowed the family and their associates to obtain permits promptly, including in remote areas. Such bureaucratic control is common in authoritarian regimes.[51] As the Trabelsis rose in prominence, Ben Ali and his associates increasingly adopted a rational-legal legitimation discourse, stressing the importance of due respect to formal procedures and the law—such as the obtaining of permits.[52] There were, indeed, few other ways through which the rising profile of the Trabelsis could be justified.

In addition, the RCD's monitoring and coercive functions suggest that family members also used the party to 'muzzle' rivals, and multiple reports exist about figures such as Belhassen and Imed eliminating competitors, sometimes forcibly.[53] Illustrating the close association between the presidential family, business affairs and the ruling party, one American diplomat wrote in 2006:

---

perceived as stepping on the toes of the President. It allowed them to garner an independent support base, at least to a certain extent, whereas figures within the RCD were doomed to remain in the shadow of its president (interview with Hedi Djilani, Tunis, 6 February 2017).

[50] Interview with Hedi Djilani, Tunis, 6 February 2017.

[51] Scholars have long highlighted the importance of bureaucratic control, though initially in a context of bureaucratic-military regimes. See, for more details, Guillermo O'Donnell, *Bureaucratic Authoritarianism: Argentina, 1966–1973, in Comparative Perspective*, Berkeley: University of California Press, 1988; Nazih Ayubi, 'Arab Bureaucracies: Expanding Size, Changing Roles', in Giacomo Luciani (ed.), *The Arab State*, London: Routledge, 1990, pp. 129–149.

[52] Various dictators have adopted such legitimation discourse, including to justify authoritarian elections or hereditary power transfers. See, for details, Christian Von Soest and Julia Grauvogel, 'Identity, Procedures and Performance: How Authoritarian Regimes Legitimize Their Rule', *Contemporary Politics*, 2017, 23, 3, pp. 287–305.

[53] See, for example, US Embassy in Tunis, 'Corruption in Tunisia Part IV: The Family's Holdings', Wikileaks, 5 July 2006, 06TUNIS1672_a, confidential. Note that in other personalist dictatorships with a pronounced family dimension, presidential relatives have used ruling parties to silence rivals and further their own interests. For comparative examples in Egypt, North Korea, and Zimbabwe, see Jason Brownlee, 'A New Generation of Autocracy in Egypt', *Brown Journal of World Affairs*, 2007, 14, 1, pp. 73–85; Paul French, *Our Supreme Leader: The Making of Kim Jong-un*, London: Zed Books, 2016; Geoffrey Nyarota, *The Graceless Fall of Robert Mugabe: The End of a Dictator's Reign*, Cape Town: Penguin Books, 2018.

President Ben Ali attended the opening session of [the] 14th UTICA congress on November 21 and was introduced by current UTICA Chairman Hedi Djilani. . . . Djilani's introduction was predictably laudatory, stressing that UTICA's members had responded to all of Ben Ali's directives. . . . The only thing UTICA wanted in return, said Djilani, was for Ben Ali to remain in power.[54]

The 'directives' given to UTICA at that time revolved around a massive privatization programme, which Ben Ali had commenced in the 1990s with the support of international financial institutions and which was intensified in the 2000s. Though publicly promoted as 'liberalizing' the economy, this drive led to the concentration of a very large volume of private assets with the presidential family—a reality of crony capitalism that resulted in a real distortion of economic activity, as representatives of the International Monetary Fund retrospectively acknowledged.[55] Mohamed Ghannouchi, Prime Minister between 1999 and 2011, elaborated that the Trabelsis frequently acquired businesses through lesser-known individuals who presented themselves for privatized projects that ultimately benefited the presidential family.[56] I will elaborate in more detail below.

Elite restructuring

An extensive process of elite restructuring facilitated the family's political and economic ascent in the 2000s. This consisted mainly of marginalizing long-standing, high-profile RCD figures—especially those who had risen with Ben Ali immediately after his assumption of power—and simultaneously promoting family associates to key posts. Whilst the objective of this process was partially financial, in that many of these associates were promoted to influential economic positions, the intention was also to protect the regime from senior figures who might eventually seek to challenge Ben Ali, given that he was no longer as vigorous as in his early years in power. In particular, Ben Ali's close

[54] US Embassy in Tunis, 'Ben Ali Announces New Policies to Facilitate Business', Wikileaks, 24 November 2006, 06TUNIS2798_a, unclassified.

[55] Bob Rijkers, Caroline Freund, and Antonio Nucifora, 'All in the Family: State Capture in Tunisia', World Bank, Policy Research Working Paper No. 6810, March 2014; 'The Unfinished Revolution: Bringing Opportunity, Good Jobs and Greater Wealth to All Tunisians', World Bank, Development Policy Review, Report No. 86179-TN, May 2014.

[56] Interview with Mohamed Ghannouchi, Tunis, 2 August 2015. Information corroborated through other interviews.

associates increasingly limited access to the President, a regime preservation strategy used in other long-standing dictatorships.[57] Chedli Neffati explained:

> They [Ben Ali's entourage] said the President is a bit tired, we need to protect him, especially he should never lose his temper, get angry, because that's not good for his health. So we need to establish filters, . . . everything needs to go through [Abdelaziz] Ben Dhia. All reports that come from ministers, all problems [they raise]. And Ben Dhia together with Belhassen and Leila decided which topics to pass on to the President.[58]

Several important deductions can be drawn from Chedli Neffati's statement. First, the establishment of 'filters' reinforced the sway of the Trabelsis as they began to control, in part, the flow of information between ministries and the palace. At the same time, the above statement highlights that the regime's 'number two' was not a family relative but Ben Dhia, who in his previous role as RCD Secretary General had worked hard to subdue the party. This is significant in so far as many interviewees affirmed that Ben Dhia worked first and foremost for the President, not for the Trabelsis.[59] This illustrates that the Trabelsis did not gain full control over palace affairs. Ultimately, Ben Ali remained in charge of filling the most important posts. Former RCD Secretary General Mohamed Ghariani rationalized Ben Dhia's promotion as follows:

> Ben Ali wanted [an adviser] only for himself. Ben Dhia worked for him, not for his family. . . . The President is intelligent, he does not like when people hurt his family, but he also does not want someone who is totally dependent on his family. Ben Dhia played the game of being only dependent on the President. He was loyal to Ben Ali, but did not have a problem with his family.[60]

---

[57] An extreme example of this preservation strategy is Algeria, where President Abdelaziz Bouteflika was barely seen after suffering a stroke in 2013, his younger brother Said allegedly limiting access to him and running the presidency. The President was cut off to such an extent that a group of officials even publicly requested to meet him in 2015 after they had not seen him in over a year. See, for details, Carlotta Gall, 'Who Runs Algeria? Many Doubt It's Ailing President Abdelaziz Bouteflika', *New York Times*, 23 December 2015, https://www.nytimes.com/2015/12/24/world/africa/suspicions-mount-that-ailing-president-abdelaziz-bouteflika-is-no-longer-running-algeria.html, last accessed 25 June 2018; George Joffé, 'Shame-Faced No Longer?', *Journal of North African Studies*, 2020, 25, 2, pp. 159–166.

[58] Interview with Chedli Neffati, Tunis, 2 February 2017.

[59] The Trabelsis were closer to Abdelwahab Abdallah—another palace associate who was hierarchically below Abdelaziz Ben Dhia. Interview with Mohamed Ghariani, Tunis, 8 February 2017. Information corroborated through other interviews.

[60] Interview with Mohamed Ghariani, Tunis, 8 February 2017. Information corroborated through other interviews.

Ben Dhia's rise came as part of a wider reshuffling of cabinet and RCD posts, which the President ordered in 1999 and again—in consultation with Ben Dhia—in 2001, 2003, and 2004. As part of this restructuring, many long-standing RCD figures were at best demoted and in most cases sacked. This was, naturally, not a measure to inject fresh life into politics, as Ben Ali and his advisers claimed, but one aimed at tightening the President's inner circle in the face of a looming succession crisis. Indeed, dictators frequently reshuffle governments to display strength and '[ensure] that no one individual or faction is able to accumulate too much power'.[61] During the 1999 cabinet change, the most prominent dismissal was that of longtime Prime Minister Hamed Karoui, who was replaced by Mohamed Ghannouchi, a previous economy and finance minister from Sousse. Hamed Karoui told me:

[My dismissal] was normal; I had been Prime Minister for ten years. In addition, it occurred the day [Ben Ali] had to make an oath following the [1999] elections. . . . He was so embarrassed he didn't dare to tell me [about the dismissal] himself. The information was delivered to me by Mohamed Jegham, who was the Director of the Presidential Cabinet at the time.[62]

Though dismissed as Prime Minister, Hamed Karoui retained his appointment as RCD Vice-President, mainly an honorary post. He elaborated:

The prime minister is automatically [RCD] vice-president, but even when I was no longer Prime Minister, Ben Ali kept me as Vice-President. My successor [Ghannouchi] became second Vice-President. My role [as Vice-President]? It was to follow affairs, to discuss with the President and, mostly, to preside over the Political Bureau or the Central Committee in the absence of the President.[63]

What is striking about Hamed Karoui's discourse is that it is markedly defensive of the regime, despite his sidelining. Whilst his position as RCD Vice-President was clearly a demotion, Hamed Karoui tried to suggest that he was satisfied with it as it allowed new faces to enter politics and instigate 'renewal'. However, many of his close allies, who were also marginalized at that time, somewhat qualified this response, affirming that nobody would have left their

---

[61] Thomas Ambrosio, 'Leadership Succession in Kazakhstan and Uzbekistan: Regime Survival after Nazarbayev and Karimov', *Journal of Balkan and Near Eastern Studies*, 2015, 17, 1, p. 56.
[62] Interview with Hamed Karoui, Tunis, 1 February 2017.
[63] Ibid.

post voluntarily.[64] By stressing that Ben Ali did not dare to tell him person-ally about his demotion, Hamed Karoui further sought to convey that the President held him in high esteem. The vast majority of figures discarded by Ben Ali in the 2000s expressed a similar discourse, which highlights how, despite their dismissals, they remained deeply respectful of and faithful to the President.[65]

Scholars Amin Allal and Vincent Geisser affirmed that RCD activists who were 'relatively detached from the business and mafia circles of the Palace fam-ilies . . . generally belonged to the liberal wing of the RCD'.[66] Yet the deep admiration many of them harbour for Ben Ali to this day suggests tensions with the party were not about issues of 'liberalism'; in conversations with American diplomats and with me, figures such as Hamed Karoui appeared anything but liberal.[67] The divisions that arose and led to their removals can be attributed to the conflicting interests of different regime clans, pitting family members and their associates against longtime officials.

According to some regime insiders, Hamed Karoui was sidelined because Ben Ali thought he 'interfered a lot' in government affairs.[68] Yet given his participation in the struggle for independence, his status within the party was of such a calibre that he retained the honorary post of RCD Vice-President—at least for the time being. Legitimacy perceptions still mattered to the powerbrokers. Most other long-standing RCD figures were completely cast aside, especially those with experience in offices considered 'sensitive' for the presidential succession line. These included the Interior and Defence Minis-ters, whose support was crucial for any future president, as well as high-profile officials such as the Prime Minister, Foreign Minister, and the RCD Secretary General, who were well known and could acquire both domestic and foreign support.

The President's close associates felt particularly threatened by figures who had direct access to the President, typically those who had already worked with him under Bourguiba or during the early years of the 'change'. These

---

[64] For example, interview with Chedli Neffati, Tunis, 2 February 2017.

[65] For example, ibid.; interview with Abderrahim Zouari, Tunis, 9 February 2017.

[66] Amin Allal and Vincent Geisser, 'La Tunisie de l'Après-Ben Ali', *Cultures & Conflits*, 2011, 83, p. 123.

[67] Notably, Hamed Karoui said that opposing the regime in the name of human rights 'doesn't mean anything' and that 'human rights activists were paid by foreign countries' (interview with Hamed Karoui, Tunis, 1 February 2017). Moreover, in 2007, he affirmed that 'Tunisia was pursuing political reform at an appropriate pace and [blamed] weak opposition parties for not being more active'. See, for details, US Embassy in Tunis, 'RCD VP Lauds Party Influence, Bemoans Opposition Weakness', Wikileaks, 26 June 2007, 07TUNIS841_a, confidential.

[68] Interview with Mohamed Ghariani, Tunis, 8 February 2017. Information corroborated through other interviews.

included Abderrahim Zouari, the previous RCD Secretary General, who had been renominated to that post in November 1999, replacing Ben Dhia. Under Ben Dhia's recommendation, Zouari was dismissed only a year later as part of the adviser's efforts to establish 'filters' between high officials and the President. Zouari explained:

> For them [Ben Ali's entourage] I was a danger, the Secretary General of the RCD is known at the national and even international level. . . . Ben Dhia controlled everything and all issues passed through him. . . . I was not used to that and was in direct contact with the President. [Ben Dhia] was not pleased. He said I was 'undisciplined'.[69]

Alongside his Secretary General position, Zouari had held a range of important RCD and cabinet posts. Some regime insiders said that he had become a 'political animal' with his 'own interests' and 'plots': in other words, a potential threat to the presidency.[70] His wide experience and high profile even led some American diplomats to place him on a list of potential presidential successors.[71] But Zouari's dismissal must also be understood through the lens of the palace's regional and intra-family rivalries. Indeed, Mohamed Ghariani said Zouari's origin in the region of Kef had helped him become close to Naima Kefi and her son-in-law Marouan Mabrouk, whose mother also hailed from Kef.[72] This underscores yet again the importance of family alliances and regional cleavages in national politics.[73] Zouari could have constituted a future presidential candidate of Naima's family, a scenario the increasing sway of the Trabelsis undermined. At the same time, Zouari's ties to Naima's side of the family ensured he did not completely disappear from the political scene following his dismissal as Secretary General[74]—an attempt of Ben Ali to manage intra-family feuds.[75]

---

[69] Interview with Abderrahim Zouari, Tunis, 9 February 2017.

[70] Interview with Mohamed Ghariani, Tunis, 8 February 2017.

[71] US Embassy in Tunis, 'Tunisia: What Succession Scenario?', Wikileaks, 9 May 2008, 08TUNIS493_a, secret.

[72] Interview with Mohamed Ghariani, Tunis, 8 February 2017.

[73] For a discussion of the role of patrimonial politics following the end of colonial rule in Tunisia, Morocco, and Iraq, see Mounira M. Charrad, 'Central and Local Patrimonialism: State-Building in Kin-Based Societies', *Annals of the American Academy of Political and Social Science*, 2011, 636, 1, pp. 49–68. For comparative insights on Palestine, see Abdalhadi Alijla, 'Politics of Tribe and Kinship: Political Parties and Informal Institutions in Palestine', *ISPI Analysis* 173, May 2013.

[74] In September 2002, Abderrahim Zouari was nominated Youth and Sports Minister; however, his portfolio was very limited. His continuing political presence again reflects the fact that the Trabelsis lacked full control over political affairs, although they could certainly initiate and accelerate specific trends.

[75] Ben Ali continued to bestow limited influence on relatives and aides of his first wife. Some of the President's former allies said this was to 'calm' and 'manage' the disputes between the two sides of his

Whilst some key figures such as Zouari and Karoui remained present in politics, albeit with much-reduced visibility, most senior figures of Ben Ali's early years as President were completely shut out of public office.[76] The RCD's July 2003 congress accelerated and, indeed, formalized the marginalization of many high-profile officials. This occurred under the usual rubric of 'change', alongside the congress theme of 'ambition'. At the closure of the four-day event, articles in *Le Renouveau* announced that 'the level of renewal of Central Committee positions had reached 48.4%'; in other words, almost half of its members had been dismissed.[77] Amongst other people, Beji Caid Essebsi, a foreign minister under Bourguiba and Speaker of the Chamber of Deputies in the 1990s, lost his Central Committee membership—supposedly because he had once been close to Bourguiba's wife, Wassila, and accordingly could not be fully trusted.[78] Significantly, the congress extended the sidelining of prominent RCD figures to middle-ranking and regional party posts. One of those targeted was the RCD student leader at the time, Hassouna Nasfi. From a family of rural notables in Gabes, Nasfi stated that he 'left' political life in 2003 and his father, a *délégué*, 'retired' the same year—allusions many people use to gloss over the fact they were actually dismissed.[79]

Those RCD figures who hailed from influential families but remained present in political life were typically designated to honorary posts. Hamza, who is well known in his governorate of Bizerte and hails from a family with a long history of Destourian party activism, said that without prior consultation, authorities informed him one day he was now Bizerte's RCD Vice-President.[80] Respected party figures like him were often nominated to RCD vice-presidency posts in their governorates, where they served to bestow a degree of legitimacy on the RCD without actually holding any power to affect specific policies. The real powerbrokers were associates of the presidential

family, but he was, of course, at the very heart of their conflict. Interview with Mohamed Ghariani, Tunis, 8 February 2017.

[76] Chedli Neffati said that upon his dismissal as Social Affairs and Solidarity Minister in 2004, his former colleagues broke off contact with him. Even figures who had once worked for Neffati and owed much of their careers to his support were implicated. Citing the case of Rafik Belhaj Kacem, who became Interior Minister in 2004, Neffati exclaimed, still visibly indignant about the extent of his isolation: 'He used to be my head of cabinet at the Interior Ministry. I was responsible for his promotion. But then he stopped talking to me . . . he didn't call me once to ask how I was doing!' Clearly, nobody wanted to be associated with figures who no longer enjoyed the trust of the palace. Interview with Chedli Neffati, Tunis, 2 February 2017.

[77] Abdelkrim Dermech, 'Le Rassemblement Gagnera sous la Conduite de Ben Ali le Pari de l'"Ambition"', *Le Renouveau*, 1 August 2003.

[78] Interview with Chedli Neffati, Tunis, 2 February 2017. Information corroborated through other interviews.

[79] Interview with Hassouna Nasfi, Bardo, 24 May 2016.

[80] Interview with Hamza, Ras Jebel, Bizerte governorate, 9 February 2017.

Figure 4.1 An RCD membership card
Source: private collection.

family, who restructured local and regional patronage networks to their own advantage.[81]

The rise of family associates

Many interviewees affirmed that the new political class that rose in the 2000s consisted of marionette-like figures who strictly followed orders but had few obvious competencies; they were 'nobodies' who '[owed] everything to the leader'.[82] Brahim, a pharmacist and RCD grassroots follower from the governorate of Bizerte, stated that authorities 'chose officials who were totally dedicated to the party, who were active in the party . . . yes-men . . . who agreed with everything they were being asked'.[83] One of Tunisia's most infamous 'yes-men'—denounced as such by numerous interviewees—was Mohamed Ghannouchi, who succeeded Hamed Karoui as Prime Minister in 1999. Subservient figures like him, who answered to Carthage, also rose at the regional level. Brahim said they came to dominate party structure in Bizerte. One of his friends, Mohamed, further elaborated that the old RCD elite had joined the party out of 'passion' and 'commitment'. He contrasted their motivations

---

[81] For a discussion about the early links between local, regional, and national patrimonial politics and strategies in Tunisia, see Mounira M. Charrad, 'Central and Local Patrimonialism: State-Building in Kin-Based Societies', *Annals of the American Academy of Political and Social Science*, 2011, 636, 1, pp. 49–68.

[82] This wording was borrowed from Jeroen Van den Bosch, 'Personalism: A Type or Characteristic of Authoritarian Regimes?', *Politologická Revue*, 2015, 21, 1, p. 15.

[83] Interview with Brahim, Bardo, 7 February 2017.

with those of the new followers, whom he called 'arrivistes' and 'mercenaries' and accused of adhering to the party only in order to make money.[84]

Mohamed's testimony reflects the degree of bitterness and jealousy the old elite harboured towards those who took their positions. Yet it also reveals a struggle for Destourian legitimacy, in that the old guard claimed they alone were committed and 'true' party activists. Whilst certainly not all of the 'arrivistes' joined the party solely out of self-serving and materialistic objectives, some certainly enriched themselves through their newly acquired locally and regionally representative posts. Abdelaziz, a longtime RCD activist in Gafsa, observed:

> The corruption came from the Ben Ali family, the Trabelsis and from some specific lobbies. The Trabelsis created lobbies and with them dirty money began to circulate everywhere. . . . The lobbies worked for the family, they were active in all regions.[85]

It is striking that as early as the mid-1990s, some influential Trabelsi associates—members of Abdelaziz's so-called lobbies—could be identified at both the national and regional level. At first, they primarily served the family's economic interests. Amongst other examples, Bourguiba-era figure Slaheddine Ben Mbarek was dismissed as Commerce Minister in 1995. His successor, Mondher Zenaidi, who later became Tourism Minister, was a key stooge of the Trabelsis, particularly Leila and Belhassen. Mohamed Ghariani said 'he facilitated the family's business interests in commerce [and] tourism', specifying that 'it was with Mondher Zenaidi that Belhassen built his hotels, other family members received import and export authorisations because of him'.[86] Reportedly the Trabelsis were particularly interested in Zenaidi's services because he was from a prominent Tunisois family and eager to help counter the economic sway of the Sousse clan.[87]

Only when Ben Ali's succession became a topic of concern did his family seek to promote their associates to posts that were more overtly political. Naturally, even then Ben Dhia remained highly influential and responsible for filling many party positions. Indeed, all RCD Secretaries General after Zouari were trusted aides of Ben Dhia. Some of them also had close ties with Ben Ali relatives. Steffen Erdle described Ali Chaouch, who succeeded Zouari in

---

[84] Interview with Hamza, Ras Jebel, Bizerte governorate, 9 February 2017.
[85] Interview with Abdelaziz, Gafsa, 23 June 2016.
[86] Interview with Mohamed Ghariani, Tunis, 8 February 2017.
[87] Ibid.

December 2000, as someone who conformed to the general profile of past RCD Secretaries General because, as many previous party strongmen had done, he served briefly as Interior Minister between 1997 and 1999.[88] Yet whilst a super-ficial analysis might lead to such conclusion, deeper investigation shows that many features clearly set Chaouch apart from his predecessors.

According to Mohamed Ghariani, Chaouch was 'someone loyal, who respected his position in the hierarchy, not someone who made plots, such as Zouari'.[89] Thus, in contrast to Zouari, he abided strictly by Ben Dhia's enforce-ment of 'filters' between the palace and party. Chaouch told me that he 'didn't disturb Ben Ali for issues he could solve with his Vice-President'[90]—a state-ment that suggests his access to the President was quite limited. Moreover, in terms of regional affiliation, Chaouch hails from a small, deprived town in the interior region of Siliana, not from the Sahel—the coastal belt to the east— or Tunis like so many of his predecessors. Even more importantly, Chaouch never acquired a university degree[91]—a stark irregularity for a senior official in a country that prides itself on its high number of doctors, engineers, and lawyers. He was one of the RCD's new officials who rose due to their total dedication and strict observance of rules, irrespective of their professional qualifications.

Chaouch's successor Hedi Mhenni, a medical doctor, was appointed in 2005 to the post of RCD Secretary General likewise primarily because of his strict execution of orders from Carthage, specifically from Ben Dhia. Mhenni and Ben Dhia hailed from neighbouring towns in the Sahel—Sayada and Moknine, about four kilometres apart—and had been friends for a long time. Regime insiders told me that Mhenni 'followed whatever Ben Dhia asked him'[92] and that he was 'the guy who couldn't say no'.[93] In addition to his ties to Ben Dhia, Mhenni was friends with Mohamed Gueddich, another palace adviser and a doctor, who was personally in charge of the President's health.[94] Between 2002 and 2004, Mhenni was Defence Minister; he then briefly served as Interior Minister before being nominated RCD Secretary General. Neffati commented on Mhenni's career that 'nobody expected him to become a political leader, a

---

[88] Steffen Erdle, *Ben Ali's 'New Tunisia' (1987–2009): A Case Study of Authoritarian Modernization in the Arab World*, Berlin: Klaus Schwarz, 2010, p. 163.

[89] Interview with Mohamed Ghariani, Tunis, 8 February 2017.

[90] Interview with Ali Chaouch, Tunis, 11 February 2017.

[91] Ibid. Note that Chaouch said he began a degree in economics, but at the age of twenty-two had to stop his studies and earn money for 'family reasons'; official biographies state that he acquired the degree.

[92] Interview with Zouhair Mdhafer, Tunis, 10 February 2017.

[93] Interview with Chedli Neffati, Tunis, 2 February 2017.

[94] Mohamed Ghariani speculated that Mhenni's daughter was married to a son of Gueddich. Interview with Mohamed Ghariani, Tunis, 8 February 2017.

minister, and especially not the RCD Secretary General!',[95] an illustration that few of the old guard really appreciated the new officials. Mhenni presents a key example of how Ben Ali's entourage placed their most trusted stooges in sensitive posts in the 2000s, at a time when Ben Ali's health was deteriorating and his succession had become a matter of concern.

It is worth mentioning that many Tunisians have never heard of either Ali Chaouch or Hedi Mhenni—a striking phenomenon, given that they were the RCD Secretaries General—which exemplifies the extent to which they were essentially shadows following the real powerbrokers in Carthage.[96] Hedi Mhenni's successor, Mohamed Ghariani, is well known in Tunisia, but this is because he was the last Secretary General and therefore very much in the spotlight during the 2010–2011 uprising. Indeed, prior to his appointment, Ghariani had been an ambassador, but he had never held any government portfolio. Born into an impoverished family in Kairouan, central Tunisia, Ghariani joined the RCD at a young age, and as a student rose to the position of RCD youth leader. Similarly to Chaouch, Ghariani was a pure product of the party. And just like his two predecessors, he was promoted to Secretary General because he had developed strong ties to Ben Dhia, a reality Ghariani himself acknowledged.[97]

Some long-standing party figures affirmed that Ghariani was not very well qualified as Secretary General because he had earned a degree only in sociology, not in a more respected discipline such as medicine, engineering, or law.[98] Such statements reflect a certain educational elitism, common amongst the old guard, which devalues most subjects in the humanities and social sciences. They also highlight that earlier and later RCD figureheads hailed from distinct educational and socioeconomic backgrounds. Steeped in French education, the old guard typically preferred to converse with me in French. In contrast, the French of the new party officials was anything but flawless, and they preferred talking in Tunisian Arabic. Though many of them had received a university education, Ghariani's case highlights how their degrees were not as highly regarded as those of their predecessors, and the entrance requirements for their studies were more flexible.

The somewhat lower professional status of party newcomers is linked to their backgrounds. They often hailed from deprived families in rural areas with

[95] Interview with Chedli Neffati, Tunis, 2 February 2017.
[96] In comparison, the same people would typically know about Abderrahim Zouari and Abdelaziz Ben Dhia—real political heavyweights (interviews and informal conversations in Tunis, Sidi Bouzid, and Gafsa, June 2016 and February 2017).
[97] Interview with Mohamed Ghariani, Tunis, 8 February 2017.
[98] Interviews with several former government officials, Tunis, 1 and 2 February 2017.

limited access to higher education, in contrast to the notables, technocrats, and high-ranking civil servants who had dominated the political elite during Ben Ali's earlier years. This weakened Ben Ali's claim to promote the country's most qualified professionals and technocrats, an important way through which he generated authoritarian legitimacy in the 1990s. Many RCD figures who made their careers in the 2000s told me their families were 'very poor'.[99] For them, RCD activism constituted the only way to climb up the socioeconomic ladder and acquire a certain status in society, a standing many representatives of the old guard enjoyed simply by virtue of an important family name. One figure elaborated:

> In the regions, the RCD is an etiquette . . . the RCD is important, RCD leaders are important. When ministers visit a region, they invite RCD leaders. When regional meetings and events take place, RCD leaders take part in them . . . . As an RCD leader you are considered a notable in your region. In Tunis, RCD membership is a bit less important, given the range of influential figures there. But [for example] in Siliana or Beja, a member of the RCD Central Committee is a personality, a deputy is a personality![100]

This statement highlights that in the regions, senior RCD membership constituted a key source of social capital, to the extent that party officials were even considered part of the nobility. Naturally, this was very attractive to the new generation of RCD leaders, who were typically born into an environment with limited financial means and societal standing. Their rise was conditional on the Trabelsis, who hailed from a very similar socioeconomic background, or one of their associates, and thence ensured their loyalty to the presidential family. The Ben Ali family tried to 'exploit the opportunism and career incentives among the population'—specifically amongst deprived sections—'in order to create a stake in the perpetuation of the regime'.[101] This makes ruling parties highly useful for leaders seeking to regenerate authoritarian stability, especially in the context of succession preparations. Nowadays, of course, few people want to admit they served Ben Ali's family. However, many were willing to provide examples of how the family gained a foothold in their regions. Hamza, the mid-level RCD official from Bizerte, remembered:

---

[99] For example, interview with Akram Sebri, Tunis, 26 May 2016. Note that Akram Sebri was an activist in his thirties from a small town in central Kairouan. He said that he integrated into the RCD grass roots at an early age and climbed up the party ladder. In 2004, Sebri became a member of the RCD National Council, an advisory body, and in 2007 he was promoted to Secretary General of the RCD youth organization.

[100] Interview with Hedi Djilani, Tunis, 6 February 2017.

[101] Milan Svolik, 'The Regime Party as an Instrument of Authoritarian Co-optation and Control', paper presented at IPSA–ECPR Joint Conference, 2011, 16, 19, p. 3.

One time in the municipality of Ras Jebel, a person came to me saying that Belhassen had sent him because he had a problem with a construction project. . . . I welcomed him and we had a small discussion of five minutes. He talked politely to me and I said we would . . . accelerate the procedures so [Belhassen] would obtain the authorisation to build as soon as possible.[102]

When I enquired as to whether Belhassen's project hurt Bizerte, Hamza said it didn't. Indeed, he insisted that his construction was legal and even assisted the region's development somewhat because it came with infrastructure obligations such as a working sanitary system and electricity supply.[103] This underscores yet again the great extent to which perceptions of legality mattered and that regional party officials took a key role in the prompt furnishing of business permits for the presidential family. Hamza's statements also suggests that the Trabelsis' business stakes per se were not always subject to popular disapproval. Rather, people were concerned by the multiple—and sometimes indirect—trickle-down effects of their projects; for example, in terms of how jobs and social services were distributed and patronage exercised.

The Trabelsis' holdings provided new economic opportunities for inter-mediaries in the regions. Hamza said that the person he encountered was middle-ranking at most, but high-profile figures with ties to the family profited as well, sometimes substantially. Khalil, a former head of an RCD cell in Jendouba, explained that one day Mouldi Ayari, a close friend of Hedi Dji-lani and former Vice-President of UTICA, was promoted to the governorate's RCD Secretary General. Chorfi charged that Ayari became 'very influential' in the 2000s but did little to help with Jendouba's unemployment crisis and marginalization, instead directing profits towards his cronies.[104] Clearly, the family's business interests affected much wider patterns of economic resource distribution, which touched all social echelons.

The case of Rafaa Dkhil

A key example is that of Rafaa Dkhil. Born into a humble family in the Biz-erte town of Ras Jebel, Dkhil acquired high-ranking posts in government, the party, and business 'simply for the "benefits"' he offered to the family—as one

---

[102] Interview with Hamza, Ras Jebel, Bizerte governorate, 9 February 2017.
[103] Ibid.
[104] Interview with Khalil, Jendouba, 29 May 2016.

American diplomat observed in 2008.[105] Dkhil was not only close to Belhassen but also befriended other influential family members. RCD grassroots member Brahim, who went to school with Dkhil in Ras Jebel, alleged that he became the 'darling of Leila and her mother', asserting that he 'kneeled down before the powerbrokers, just so he could become close to them'.[106] Owing to the trust the presidential family came to place in him, in 1991 Dkhil was appointed head of the Gafsa Phosphate Company, one of Tunisia's most important enterprises. Many interviewees suggested that in this post Dkhil enabled presidential relatives to profit directly from the lucrative phosphate industry, for example, by using the transportation and manufacturing equipment of firms owned by the Trabelsis.[107] It is noteworthy that almost everyone in Bizerte seems to be able to recount examples of Dkhil's corrupt business deals with the presidential family, some of which were later officially confirmed to have been true.[108] This illustrates the great influence and visibility he acquired in his governorate but also the acute awareness people there had of his transgressions—to the extent that many of them seem to have become part of the region's collective memory.

In 2001, Dkhil received two further promotions: in January, he was nominated Secretary of State to the Minister of Industry and in October he became CEO of Tunisair, the prestigious national airline. The same year, Dkhil integrated the government as Minister of Industry. In 2005 he became Minister of Communication. The promotion of the Trabelsis' regional intermediaries to cabinet positions was a more general trend at the time. Indeed, under Ben Ali the number of ministers from the regions increased steadily between the late 1980s and the early 2000s—by which time their number had doubled (see Figure 4.2). Subsequently, a substantial number of ministers from Tunis were additionally appointed—the hometown and, increasingly, a stronghold of the Trabelsis.

By virtue of his government positions, Dkhil also became a member of the RCD Central Committee, which gave him considerable sway over local nominations, the distribution of social services, and other economic favours the party had to offer. Trabelsi associates integrated into the party's leading

---

[105] US Embassy in Tunis, 'Tunisia: What Succession Scenario?', Wikileaks, 9 May 2008, 08TUNIS493_a, secret.

[106] Interview with Brahim, Bardo, 7 February 2017.

[107] For example, interview with Hamza, Ras Jebel, Bizerte governorate, 9 February 2017. Note that I was unable to confirm such allegations.

[108] In February 2016, the Tunis Court of First Instance found Dkhil guilty of financial wrongdoing and abuse of power, amongst other reasons because he created fictitious jobs at Tunisair. The case was dismissed shortly thereafter owing to procedural inconsistencies. See, for details, Rabaa H., 'Tunisie: Rafâa Dkhil Condamné à Deux Ans de Prison', Tunisie Numérique, 2 February 2016, https://www.tunisienumerique.com/tunisie-rafaa-dkhil-condamne-a-deux-ans-de-prison/, last accessed 28 June 2018.

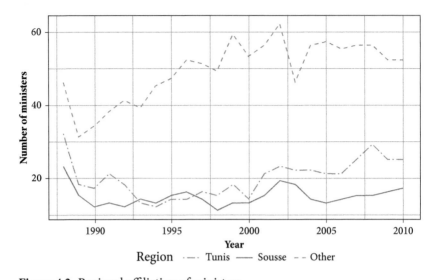

Figure 4.2 Regional affiliation of ministers

Source: author's own calculations. The calculations are based on the dataset used in Clionadh Raleigh and Daniel Wigmore Shepherd, 'Elite Coalitions and Power Balance across African Regimes: Introducing the African Cabinet and Political Elite Data Project (ACPED)', *Ethnopolitics*, 2022, 21, 1, pp. 22–47; additional data was provided by Dr Andrea Carboni, University of Sussex.

ranks and came to dominate its patronage networks. It is important to highlight that it was not because of Dkhil's relations with the Trabelsis or his senior RCD post that people in Bizerte started despising him and rumours about his corrupt deals began to circulate. Rather, it was because his connections and influence did not spill over and commute into economic benefit for his region—quite the contrary. Brahim recalled:

> There was an extraordinary hostility against Dkhil in Bizerte, in his hometown and in the entire region . . . [because] despite all the influence he had, he didn't do anything for . . . the people of Bizerte . . . nothing at all! Even when some went to see him to ask for a job, for example at Tunisair, he said no. He closed all doors. Because what interested him were his people and his political future, not what happened to the children of Bizerte![109]

Brahim's comments highlight that as Dkhil moved up the social ladder, he sought to dissociate himself from the environment he grew up in, which had little to offer for his career aspirations. Moreover, investing in Bizerte would likely have conflicted with his complete allegiance to the Trabelsis, which did

---

[109] Interview with Brahim, Bardo, 7 February 2017.

not allow for any competing loyalties, regional or otherwise. Brahim further elaborated that Dkhil was interested in hiring people who worked only for him, not for the general good of the region.[110] The RCD's function of socioeconomic redistribution became starkly reduced, and mostly people who had connections to the presidential family or their associates benefitted—including at the local and regional level. Hamza, Bizerte's RCD Vice-President in the early 2000s, corroborated his account. He stated:

> During the 2004 election campaign, Rafaa [Dkhil] called me. He was a minister at that point. . . . I told him about the problem we had with the youth, . . . I said [in Ras Jebel] we created some committees [to help them] but that they have little financial means. . . . I asked him if he could help. He replied: 'I don't give a damn about Ras Jebel'. Imagine! He said this to me! I was so exasperated I swore all kinds of things and then hung up. Given how I behaved, you know what he did? He fired me![111]

Hamza's account is probably accurate, given that he was generally quite loyal to the regime. His anecdote highlights, on the one hand, that only full obedience mattered to regional strongmen like Dkhil and that anyone voicing discontent risked losing their job. On the other hand, it also shows that despite the repressive system some people still dared to voice opposition, at least occasionally. Khallifa's rebuke of Dkhil can be considered an instance of resistance against his indifference to the plight of the people and the wider regional marginalization it fostered. It illustrates the rise of contention within the RCD following the sidelining of longtime leaders and activists. The next section discusses further forms of resistance and civil disobedience that occurred in response to the rise of Ben Ali relatives and their associates.

Forms of resistance

Until the mid-1990s, the Islamist Ennahda movement constituted Tunisia's principal opposition force, but in the 2000s, a range of political actors sought to challenge Ben Ali. One of the opposition's most important initiatives was the 18 October movement, a cross-ideological coalition demanding greater rights

---

[110] Ibid.
[111] Interview with Hamza, Ras Jebel, Bizerte governorate, 9 February 2017.

and freedoms.[112] In addition, for many people the internet became a medium through which to voice their discontent. The dissident site Tunisnews.net was launched in 2000, followed by TUNeZINE.tn in 2001 and Naawat.org in 2004. Despite the great dangers of opposition activism, in the mid-2000s an increasing number of people became active on these websites. It is notable that they hailed from a range of backgrounds, and some identified as Destourians.

An illustrative example is that of Neila Hachicha-Charchour.[113] In 2003, she created the Liberal Mediterranean Party, which, according to Vincent Geisser and Éric Gobe, had no base at all and until 2004 served solely to offer public support for Ben Ali, including advocating for his re-election as president that year.[114] Then suddenly, in 2005, Hachicha-Charchour completely changed her political stance and launched an online campaign against the regime, targeting particularly the Trabelsis. Amongst other initiatives, Hachicha-Charchour created a blog named *yezzi fock* ('That's enough'), which called upon the people to 'organise a virtual protest campaign against the autocratic Tunisian regime'.[115]

When asked what prompted her change of heart, Hachicha-Charchour affirmed that she started the *yezzi fock* initiative out of indignation over the fact that in 2005, merely a year after the presidential elections, in which Ben Ali was re-elected with an obviously fraudulent 94.48% of the vote, and the RCD received 87.59% of the total vote share,[116] some party activists had already started discussing Ben Ali's next candidacy for 2009. She was also increasingly appalled by the business practices of Ben Ali's new son-in-law, Sakher el-Materi, who married Nesrine in 2004.[117] Indeed, in 2005, el-Materi made a fortune with the privatization of the Banque du Sud through practices French journalists denounced as insider deals.[118] He subsequently bought the company Ennakl, an automobile dealership, which shortly thereafter became

---

[112] For more details on the Tunisian opposition, see Tawfik al-Madani, *al-Mu'arada al-Tunisiyya, Nash'atuha wa-Tatawuruha* [*The Tunisian Opposition, Its Birth and Evolution*], Damascus: Ittihad al-Kuttab al-Arab, 2001; Rikke Haugbølle and Francesco Cavatorta, 'Will the Real Tunisian Opposition Please Stand Up? Opposition Coordination Failures under Authoritarian Constraints', *British Journal of Middle Eastern Studies*, 2011, 38, 3, pp. 323–341.

[113] Note that Neila Hachicha-Charchour is the daughter of Mahmoud Charchour, a senior official of the Bourguiba regime, who had been an ambassador to Lebanon and was an RCD figure until his death in 2001.

[114] Vincent Geisser and Éric Gobe, 'Des Fissures dans la "Maison Tunisie"? Le Régime de Ben Ali Face aux Mobilisations Protestataires', *L'Année du Maghreb*, 2007, 2, Paris, CNRS, p. 85.

[115] Neila Charchour Hachicha, 'Yezzi ... Fock', *Nawaat*, 3 October 2005, https://nawaat.org/portail/2005/10/03/yezzi-fock-nch/, last accessed 29 April 2017.

[116] 'Consécration de la Transparence, du Respect de la Loi et de la Neutralité de l'Administration', *Le Renouveau*, 26 October 2004.

[117] Email interview with Naila Hachicha-Charchour, 15 April 2017.

[118] Florence Beaugé, 'Le Parcours Fulgurant de Sakhr El-Materi, Gendre du Président Tunisien Ben Ali', *Le Monde*, 24 October 2009, http://www.lemonde.fr/afrique/article/2009/10/24/le-parcours-fulgurant-de-sakhr-el-materi-gendre-du-president-tunisien-ben-ali_1258326_3212.html, last accessed 29 April 2017.

the official car supplier of the public administration. Also in 2005, he formed the industrial group Princesse El Materi Holding, which, amongst other activities, came to manage lucrative cruise activities at the Tunis port of La Goulette. It is unclear why el-Materi decided to add 'Princesse' to his surname and whether it refers to Nesrine. In any case, this choice stoked fears amongst many people, who interpreted it as yet another sign that the mode of domination in Tunisia increasingly came to resemble that of a family dictatorship. One RCD leader commented that '[the presidential family] wanted to reign over Tunisia as if they were kings!'[119]—echoing claims made by the political opposition.[120]

Hachicha-Charchour was alarmed not only by the quickly rising profile of el-Materi but also by the increasing number of public appearances made by Leila Ben Ali. Indeed, starting in the mid-2000s Leila began to be seen regularly on television delivering speeches, particularly in support of vulnerable groups such as women, children, the elderly, and disabled people. She also came to head the prominent state-run Centre for Research, Studies, Documentation, and Information on Woman (CREDIF) and created the BASMA Association for the Promotion of Employment of the Disabled (*basma* meaning 'smile' in Arabic). Hachicha-Charchour believed that the first lady's supposedly 'charitable activities' were purely self-serving, alleging that she sought thus to enhance her image to pave the way for a political career. Like many interviewees, Hachicha-Charchour suspected that Leila was aspiring to succeed Ben Ali as President, which would have allowed her to protect her own leverage and that of her family once her husband was no longer able to do so.[121]

The creation of the Destourian Democrats

Hachicha-Charchour's political turnaround is reflective of more widespread frustration with the regime, which in the mid-2000s became apparent not only amongst putative opposition parties traditionally loyal to the regime but also within the inner ranks of the ruling party. Most illustrative of this trend was the creation of a clandestine group of RCD challengers who called themselves 'Destourian Democrats' and, in 2005, published a set of dissident

---

[119] Interview with Chedli Neffati, Tunis, 2 February 2017.

[120] For a discussion on the role of Ben Ali's family by a representative of the opposition Progressive Democratic Party (PDP), see Tarik al-Qayzani, *al-Hizb al-Dimuqrati al-Taqaddumi* [*The Progressive Democratic Party*], Tunisia: Dar Muhammad for Publishing, 2011.

[121] Leila herself has rejected such accusations. See, for details, Leila Ben Ali, *Ma Vérité*, Paris: Éditions du Moment, 2012, p. 125.

communiqués.[122] In their statements, the group suggested their members were 'neither numerous nor few',[123] claiming they reflected the 'silent majority of RCD activists who no longer recognize themselves in the mediocre practices of the government'.[124] To this day, the identities of the Destourian Democrats remain a mystery, and I was unable to identify their members.

Given the broad range of party leaders interviewed for this book and that nowadays it is no longer controversial to talk about dissident activism under Ben Ali, it is improbable that the Destourian Democrats included senior RCD figures. Rather, they were likely middle-ranking members who were marginalized in the mid-2000s, alongside certain party chiefs. In their statements, they wrote in elegant French, appeared politically connected, and had insider knowledge of the political establishment. Moreover, Hachicha-Charchour said she had been in contact with one of the group's members via a dissident blog. Though he remained anonymous to protect himself, Hachicha-Charchour learned that he knew her father, a Bourguiba-era official, which suggests that at least some members might have belonged to the generation of PSD activists that subsequently integrated into the RCD. This could also explain the detailed knowledge some communiqués provided about political developments in the Sahel,[125] a region overrepresented in politics under Bourguiba and particularly during Ben Ali's early reign but whose sway the Trabelsis sought to counter.

One statement, published on 28 February 2005, further underpins the Destourian Democrats' likely connection to the party's old guard. In this statement, the Destourian Democrats refer to a set of well-known public figures as their model. They includes Ahmed Mestiri (who split from the PSD to found the MDS in 1978), Mustapha Ben Jaafar (an ex-MDS figure who, in 1994, created the rival Ettakatol), Beji Caid Essebsi (a Bourguiba-era official who was marginalized in the 2000s), and Mohamed Jegham (a long-standing Ben Ali ally from Sousse who was also cast aside at that time).[126] This suggests that the primary root of the Destourian Democrats' frustration lay in the structural changes induced within the RCD in the 2000s—that is, the sidelining of figureheads who were highly regarded within inner party circles, not the lack of democratic politics per se. Their statements focused on denouncing

---

[122] US Embassy in Tunis, 'Anonymous Communiqués Allege RCD Discontent with Ben Ali', Wikileaks, 18 May 2005, 05TUNIS1047_a, confidential.

[123] Destourian Democrats Communiqué of 8 April 2008, cited in ibid.

[124] 'Des Destouriens Démocrates Révèlent et Dénoncent les Dérives et les Crimes de Ben Ali et de Son Système', TUNeZINE, 28 February 2005, http://www.tunezine.tn/read.php?1,148167, last accessed 14 April 2017.

[125] Ibid.

[126] Ibid.

the corrupt practices of the Trabelsis, charging that they were 'stealing the wealth, resources, and the means of production of the country'.[127] In particular, they attacked Belhassen and el-Materi as the most unscrupulous of the president's relatives, and provided details about some of their controversial business deals.[128]

The Destourian Democrats and their dissident statements constituted an important form of resistance from within the RCD. The group's members took great personal risk to make their grievances public, and they succeeded in gaining attention from civil society representatives, political opponents, and fellow RCD activists, some of whom discussed their statements with foreign diplomats.[129] Arguably, this was already an important achievement at the time, given that the palace did not tolerate any sort of criticism, least of all when it targeted the President and his relatives. Though the Destourian Democrats remained the sole instance of concerted opposition from within the RCD, individual cases of resistance also increased in the mid-2000s at the regional and local level. Such contentious actions—even if a minority phenomenon—point at much wider internal disapproval of the regime. Indeed, the more asymmetric the distribution of political power, the less likely it is the weaker actors will contest the stronger ones[130]—especially in authoritarian contexts. Most party followers chose not to act on the grievances they harboured, given the great costs associated with dissident activities. This was in particular the case at the national level, where figures were more exposed. Chedli Neffati elaborated that the elites in Tunis refrained from defying the President and his family, even those who were cast aside:

> Nobody dared to [resist the changes]. . . . The presidential family was too strong and acted without soul and mercy. . . . Anyone saying a word [against] the family . . . would have been crushed, destroyed.[131]

To underscore the extent to which party leaders were afraid of the palace, Neffati told me that he and his friends sometimes shared stories about the

---

[127] Ibid.

[128] One of the goals of the Destourian Democrats was to raise public awareness of the presidential family's dubious acquisitions. Their decision to publish in French, as opposed to Arabic, made their statements easily accessible to many foreigners and embassy staff in Tunis.

[129] US Embassy in Tunis, 'Anonymous Communiqués Allege RCD Discontent with Ben Ali', Wikileaks, 18 May 2005, 05TUNIS1047_a, confidential.

[130] Paul Pierson, 'Power and Path Dependence', in James Mahoney and Kathleen Thelen (eds.), *Advances in Comparative-Historical Analysis*, Cambridge: Cambridge University Press, 2015, p. 126.

[131] Interview with Chedli Neffati, Tunis, 2 February 2017. His account was corroborated by other interviews with RCD leaders on the national level.

harsh treatment of political dissidents in jail, an experience they surely did not want to risk going through themselves. Other party officials concurred that contention from within the RCD was nonexistent at the national level.[132] However, in the regions, some party followers—though a small minority— decided to stand up against the injustices and transgressions they witnessed. This became most evident during a major uprising in Gafsa in 2008.

The Gafsa protests

In January 2008, protests erupted in the governorate of Gafsa against unemployment and preferential hiring practices at the local phosphate company. The demonstrations, geographically clustered around the mining basin area, lasted for several months. They were the most important revolts since the 1984 Bread Riots under Bourguiba, and—just as back then—security forces cracked down violently on the protesters, killing several. Outside Gafsa, the events received little coverage. State media did not report on them, and only limited video footage and articles about the protests made it onto social media. Naturally, though, in Gafsa it was impossible for the authorities to pretend everything was in order, so the RCD leaders of the region sought to discredit the protesters by portraying them as violent 'terrorists' who wanted to instigate instability and chaos in Tunisia, possibly with the help of foreign states. Yet such propaganda had only limited impact, as many local RCD members, especially amongst the rank and file, knew people at the phosphate company— the largest employer in the region—and some even worked there themselves. Several former RCD members testified that they understood and sympathized with the grievances of the local demonstrators, many of whom were young and held university degrees. Ezzeddine, an RCD student leader at the time, for instance recalled:

> The RCD [leadership] declared that these demonstrations were linked to terrorism, that they were organized by foreign countries . . . by Islamist extremists. . . . However, I didn't [see] Islamists or terrorists [protesting in Gafsa]. I saw young people looking for jobs. I saw people in very difficult economic situations.[133]

---

[132] For example, interviews with Mohamed Ghariani, Tunis, 8 February 2017; Brahim, Bardo, 7 February 2017. Note that some RCD leaders in Tunis claimed they became dissidents in the years before Ben Ali's ousting; however, their accounts were not judged credible because they were unable to elaborate much on their supposed opposition activism.

[133] Interview with Ezzeddine, Skype, 12 June 2016.

Ezzeddine affirmed that he talked with the RCD leadership in Gafsa and even contacted members of the National Bureau in Tunis to inform them about the roots of the uproar in the mining basin, initially believing they might have sincerely misunderstood the nature of the protests. However, instead of responding to his assessment of the situation, they advised him to move to Tunis and enrol at university there—according to Ezzeddine, presumably in the hope that studying in the capital would make him 'forget' about the Gafsa events.[134]

Ezzeddine was not the only RCD activist affected by the turmoil in the mining basin. After moving to Tunis, Ezzeddine started following social media sites that provided sporadic updates about the situation back home. There, he noticed that some RCD activists he knew also expressed sympathy for the protesters. 'Some [RCD members] wrote [on Facebook] that [the demonstrators] are poor workers [and] incapable of the violence they are accused of', he remembered, elaborating that 'their posts were subsequently deleted and [authorities] prohibited them from talking again [about Gafsa]'.[135] Whilst such online support for the protesters was typically limited to the RCD grass roots, interviews revealed that even some regional leaders sided with them, even if not publicly.

Fawzi, a local student activist of the leftist UGET, told me that due to the Gafsa events, his father's support for the regime crumbled, even though he had been a longtime RCD leader in the governorate.[136] Fawzi said that up until 2008 he had frequent political quarrels with his father, who disapproved of his leftist activism and did not believe his stories about the mounting scale of regime repression, including on campuses. However, his father's stance changed completely with the unrest in Gafsa. 'When he saw with his own eyes what was happening, he became totally against Ben Ali', Fawzi said.[137] When asked how this manifested, Fawzi explained that his father did not renew his RCD membership card and tried to stay away from party events—a quiet but presumably already risky form of contestation for a senior official, particularly given the charged political atmosphere in the governorate at the time.

Some RCD individuals even appear to have gone as far as offering support to the protesters. Sami Amroussia, a leader in the demonstrations who today represents the leftist Popular Front alliance in Gafsa, said that most RCD

[134] Ibid.
[135] Ibid.
[136] Interview with Fawzi, Skype, 3 June 2016.
[137] Ibid.

officials acted as informants and conducted monitoring and policing services during the unrest. Yet a small minority also provided help to the protesters, sometimes unexpectedly. Amongst other incidents, Amroussia remembered that one night he and his friends were in the middle of distributing articles about the violence the protesters endured when the police caught them by surprise. The next thing he recalled was the door of a nearby house opening and the owner inviting them to come inside and hide. The homeowner later even refused to give them up to the police—a brave act of resistance that caught Amroussia completely by surprise because it came from a well-known RCD figure in the neighbourhood.[138] This highlights the importance of 'focal events' in the rise of internal regime opposition in that party activists who witnessed the regime's injustice firsthand were more likely to side with the Gafsa protesters.

Naturally, acts of resistance were still very rare, especially amongst RCD representatives. Most party members who sympathized with the protesters' plight simply decided to withdraw from political activism, typically gradually and quietly, in the hope that regime figures would not notice. Ezzeddine suggested that the RCD in the governorate split in two: 'One group continued to support Ben Ali and wanted to solve the problem of demonstrations using the security services', he said. 'But others understood that these young protesters were only looking for jobs.'[139] During interviews, senior RCD leaders tended to belong to the first group, especially those who could be identified as allies of regional strongmen. However, as the accounts of Fawzi and Sami Amroussia illustrated, important exceptions existed even amongst the party's higher echelons. In contrast, more youthful activists were mostly sympathetic to the protesters—a generational divide that is of little surprise, given that the demonstraters themselves were predominantly young.

The Soliman Group

The Gafsa events reflect how high-level corruption and nepotism, which were notorious at the phosphate company, trickled down gradually to lower echelons of society and the party. This is not to say that the RCD ceased completely to provide any benefits to its rank and file in the 2000s, but the distribution of such benefits became more unequal, exclusive, and generally more limited.

---

[138] Interview with Sami Amroussia, Gafsa, 23 June 2016.
[139] Interview with Ezzeddine, Skype, 12 June 2016.

One grassroots activist stated that until the ousting of Ben Ali he continued to receive items such as notebooks and pens for free and that local party chapters provided gifts during national holidays and Ramadan. However, he noted that in the last years of Ben Ali, such presents became rarer, and he alleged that party representatives kept at least half of them for themselves.[140] Even more importantly, party activism no longer guaranteed a job—not even a minor post somewhere in the public administration—and many RCD members testified that they were struggling to make ends meet.[141]

Aside from the socioeconomic uproar which this dynamic caused in Gafsa, other channels emerged through which people manifested their discontent with the regime. In particular, Tunisia experienced a religious resurgence in the 2000s. This entailed a sharp increase in the numbers of women wearing the Islamic headscarf, not only out of religious conviction but also to display symbolic disagreement with a regime in which figures such as Leila Ben Ali pretended to champion Western-style women's rights but fiercely persecuted dissidents, including many female activists.[142] This chapter will not explore this religious revival in much detail, as it owed not only to internal developments in Tunisia but also to ideological factors and international developments. However, it is notable that in the 2000s a range of people became attracted to religion, usually peacefully, with some inevitably, however, espousing violence. This development was significant to the extent it affected even a limited number of people with links to the RCD—in itself a striking trend.

One example is illustrative in this regard: it concerns the 2006 Soliman Group, a militant Islamist group whose members plotted to attack state and security institutions to bring down the regime by force.[143] The Soliman Group existed only for six weeks, but it is noteworthy that it managed to quickly expand its membership, numbering forty at its peak.[144] Whilst its members came from a range of social backgrounds, they 'all . . . harboured grievances against the Tunisian state and its repressive security regime', as one of their

---

[140] Interview with Larbi, a former RCD grassroots activist, Tunis-Bab Souika, 1 October 2015.
[141] For example, interview with Ezzeddine, Skype, 12 June 2016.
[142] Anne Wolf, 'An Islamist "Renaissance"? Religion and Politics in Post-Revolutionary Tunisia', *Journal of North African Studies*, 2013, 18, 4, pp. 560–573; Anne Wolf, *Political Islam in Tunisia: The History of Ennahda*, New York: Oxford University Press, 2017, p. 108; Doris Gray and Terry Coonan, 'Notes from the Field: Silence Kills! Women and the Transitional Justice Process in Post-Revolutionary Tunisia', *International Journal of Transitional Justice*, 2013, 7, 2, pp. 348–357.
[143] The name Soliman Group refers to the town, southeast of Tunis, where the entity was later raided and dismantled by security forces.
[144] Anne Wolf, *Political Islam in Tunisia: The History of Ennahda*, New York: Oxford University Press, 2017, pp. 125–126.

defence lawyers stated at the time.[145] This included figures with links to the ruling party. One diplomat, who in February 2008 attended the Soliman trial, recalled:

> An observer at the trial told [me] ... she had attended law school with defendant Mohamed Amine Jaziri. Whilst he was a 'rebel' at the time, she pointed to his mother in the crowd and [said] ... the elegantly dressed woman was President of the ruling RCD party office in [Sidi Bouzid]. ... If educated and privileged Tunisians inside the regime cannot prevent their children from supporting extremism, one has to wonder about the less fortunate.[146]

One of the Soliman militants was the son of the RCD President in Sidi Bouzid. Whilst one cannot generalize from one case, it is entirely possible that more sons and daughters of prominent RCD families were implicated, along with others, though authorities were keen to keep any internal regime opposition quiet. Indeed, by the late 2000s popular grievances had reached such a level that some people openly began to defy the regime, including from within its inner circles, though—as the previous examples indicate—their channels and methods often differed considerably. However, rather than addressing their plight, presidential kin further reinforced their grip on power, going as far as usurping the very leadership of the RCD. Internecine contestation, in fact, triggered authoritarian reinforcement, at least in the short term, as family members sought to immunize themselves against their challengers.

Usurping the party leadership

The rapidly mounting struggles within the RCD deeply unsettled the presidential family. By the late 2000s, Ben Ali's relatives had managed to acquire at least 273 companies, often in the most lucrative sectors.[147] Many more businesses were owned by more distant kin and cronies. A 2014 World Bank report revealed that 220 of these firms accounted for a striking 21% of all

---

[145] US Embassy in Tunis, '2006/2007 Terror Cell in Tunisia: What Happened and Why', Wikileaks, 24 January 2008, 08TUNIS75_a, secret.

[146] US Embassy in Tunis, 'Appeal Court Reduces Sentences of Some "Soliman" Terrorists', Wikileaks, 22 February 2008, 08TUNIS168_a, confidential.

[147] 'Al-Yawm al-I'lami hawla al-Tasarruf fi al-Amwal wa-l-Mumtalakat al-Musadara: Min al-Musadara ila al-Tasarruf' ['Media Day on Disposal of Confiscated Funds and Property: From Confiscation to Disposal'], al-Lajna al-Wataniyya li-l-Tasarruf fi al-Amwal wa-l-Mumtalakat al-Ma'niyya bi-l-Musadara aw al-Istirja' li-Fa'idat al-Dawla [The National Committee for the Disposal of Funds and Property Designated for Confiscation or Disposal for the Benefit of the State], Ministry of Finance Publications, November 2013.

private-sector profits, totalling 233 million USD in 2010 alone.[148] To protect these assets in an increasingly volatile political environment, the family tightened its grip on the party. Mohamed Ghariani explained:

> You can be economically influential, but if you aren't politically influential, you won't be left with anything. So [family relatives] integrated into the party to protect their interests.... They believed that all political matters post–Ben Ali would be managed by the party.[149]

Therefore, in the late 2000s, some presidential kin integrated into the RCD's decision-making structures. As Mohamed Ghariani described, initially this was mainly to defend their economic stakes. However, this section demonstrates that certain family members also harboured a keen interest in politics as such. The family's integration into the RCD upper echelons was facilitated by the new subservient party elite who owed their posts entirely to the palace. Alongside creeping internecine resistance, presidential relatives were worried about the nearing prospect of a post–Ben Ali era. By the late 2000s, the presidential succession had become a critically pressing issue. The constitution allowed Ben Ali to remain in power only until 2014, though he might have attempted to change the constitution yet again to prolong his time in office. However, this would have been a risky undertaking in an environment marked by mounting disapproval of his rule, including amongst his own ranks.[150] The RCD was central to the succession preparations—just as ruling parties in Yemen and Egypt were at the time.[151]

The family's anxiety about 'the day after' rose to such an extent that its leading figures began to compete amongst themselves for the presidential succession line. This occurred indirectly, in the form of rival family clans struggling for economic and political dominance. Nesrine Ben Ali explained: 'there was a race for everything [in the family]: bigger houses, bigger companies... [because of] competition', joking that 'it was like a real telenovela'.[152] The

---

[148] Bob Rijkers, Caroline Freund, and Antonio Nucifora, 'All in the Family: State Capture in Tunisia', World Bank, Policy Research Working Paper No. 6810, March 2014, p. 3.

[149] Interview with Mohamed Ghariani, Tunis, 8 February 2017.

[150] Ben Ali's former allies suggested he would never have dared to alter the constitution once more, though it is worth acknowledging that such discourse might have been crafted in retrospect, to bolster the President's image by suggesting his rule was not as misguided and unrelenting as commonly understood. For example, interviews with Kamel Morjane, Tunis, 26 May 2016; Mohamed Ghariani, Tunis, 27 May 2016.

[151] For comparative insights see Jason Brownlee, 'The Heir Apparency of Gamal Mubarak', *Arab Studies Journal* 2007, 25/16, 2/1, pp. 36–56; April Longley Alley, 'The Rules of the Game: Unpacking Patronage Politics in Yemen', *Middle East Journal*, 2010, 64, 3, pp. 385-409.

[152] Interview with Nesrine Ben Ali, Viber, 13 February 2017.

prevailing belief was that the most influential and powerful relative would eventually determine the successor to Ben Ali, either taking the presidency himself or controlling it less conspicuously through a trusted stooge. The internal frictions in the presidential family became so pronounced they gradually trickled down to the RCD's wider structures. Naziha Zarrouk, a former ambassador to Lebanon and deputy RCD Secretary General, recounted that the party itself became divided along the lines of family clans, with members prioritizing their allegiances to specific presidential relatives over competing affiliations and interests. Zarrouk specified that she was part of Leila Ben Ali's clan, elaborating:

> I became close to Leila Ben Ali. . . . The Trabelsis had their own ambitions, they wanted to enrich themselves, but [Leila] was very human. Some say I cannot [judge] because I was close to her. . . . However, I witnessed many of Leila's actions in support of women—abused women, young mothers. . . . I saw this myself and . . . I am not afraid to testify about it![153]

Zarrouk, alongside other female RCD leaders, praised Leila's advocacy for women and more generally her supposedly 'modernist' outlook, typically affirming that her activities and vision were paramount and much more significant compared to the economic transgressions committed by her family. It is notable that the first lady's female associates mostly hailed from the Francophone elite and feared that the Islamic revival of the mid- and late 2000s would strengthen religious actors, whom they accused of promoting 'backward' policies.[154] In addition to Zarrouk, a key associate of Leila was Saïda Agrebi, a member of the RCD Central Committee, founder of the Tunisian Organisation of Mothers in 1992, and commonly known as the right hand of the first lady.[155] This is not to say that Leila had only female cronies, but they were particularly common within her clan, and the party was otherwise dominated by male figures.

Leila's work for women illustrates that some presidential relatives publicly defended certain convictions and ideas. The propagation of specific norms and ideas was an attempt to regenerate authoritarian legitimacy. It also allowed different family members to distinguish themselves from one another. Beyond

---

[153] Interview with Naziha Zarrouk, Tunis, 30 January 2017.
[154] For a detailed discussion on the regime's claim to promote women's rights, see Tarik al-Qayzani, *al-Hizb al-Dimuqrati al-Taqaddumi* [*The Progressive Democratic Party*], Tunisia: Dar Muhammad for Publishing, 2011.
[155] Tounssihor, 'Saida Agrebi Bras Droit de Leila Ben Ali', YouTube, 16 April 2011, https://www.youtube.com/watch?v=BjGyXL69v2Y, last accessed 3 May 2017.

Leila, the main contenders for the presidential succession were Belhassen Trabelsi, who was driven purely by materialistic objectives and did not propose any particular political vision, and Sakher el-Materi, the husband of Nesrine, who—contrary to Leila—portrayed himself as a practising Muslim to capture more traditional portions of society. However, it is noteworthy that the different ideas propagated by presidential relatives were often only of secondary importance to those senior party officials with substantial financial interests. Indeed, interviews suggested that in the 2000s some business executives even switched their alliances to specific relatives depending on who benefitted them more.[156] This shows that most associates of the presidential relatives were not drawn in by the latter's normative priorities—in fact, many judged them not credible—but driven by materialistic objectives, which are a comparatively weak source of political loyalty.[157]

Partially because of the business elite's somewhat pragmatic forging of alliances, in the last years of Ben Ali's reign the balance of power constantly shifted between the three presidential contenders. Whilst many Tunisians affirm that Leila was a key candidate for the succession, evidence suggests that in the last two years of Ben Ali's time in office, Sakher el-Materi and Belhassen Trabelsi were the two figures leading the race for the presidency. This was because even though Leila harboured political ambitions, she herself never integrated into the RCD—unlike her two rivals, as will be shown shortly. Arguably, by the mid-2000s, Leila had become such a conspicuous public figure that many people would have equated her integration into the RCD with her *de facto* succession of the President. Naturally, Ben Ali and his advisers wanted to avoid generating such a perception, so as not to appear weak— and because Leila remained a deeply controversial figure amongst the RCD's old guard and many other Tunisians, who denounced her charitable activities as purely self-serving or rejected her ascent on religious or misogynistic grounds.[158]

The RCD was such an important structure for the presidential succession because of its persistent mobilization function, high degree of internal party

---

[156] This reveals that the process of elite restructuring was, at least occasionally, a two-way street, and some figures only answered to specific family members if they were the best placed to serve their interests. Interview with Chedli Neffati, Tunis, 2 February 2017.

[157] For a general discussion on the role of opportunists in political institutions, including their 'ambiguous preferences about institutional continuity', see James Mahoney and Kathleen Thelen, 'A Theory of Gradual Institutional Change', in James Mahoney and Kathleen Thelen (eds.), *Explaining Institutional Change: Ambiguity, Agency, and Power*, Cambridge: Cambridge University Press, 2010, p. 26.

[158] Amongst other criticisms, many interviewees sneered that Leila was an 'easy woman', suggesting that she had had sexual relations with many men. For example, Chedli Neffati, Tunis, 2 February 2017.

discipline, countrywide networks, and ability to provide a source of political legitimation, even at times of mounting regime crisis. Moreover, any presidential successor needed the support of powerful RCD ministers, particularly the Prime Minister, Interior, and Defence Ministers—and it was possible that the successor might emerge out of one of these posts directly. Equally importantly, article 57 of the constitution stipulated that if the president died or could no longer exercise his functions, the Head of Parliament—traditionally a leading RCD cadre—would temporarily take over his duties and organize upcoming elections. Though this figure was not allowed to run as a candidate in the ensuing presidential ballot, he still held a lot of power and could influence the succession scenario. Thus, any contender would need him as an ally.

It is in this light that Belhassen Trabelsi and Sakher el-Materi developed a key interest in the party. Belhassen Trabelsi was better connected within both the business world and the RCD, having been influential for a much longer period of time—essentially since Leila married Ben Ali. However, he had no political credentials or ambitions per se and considered politics solely as a means to further enrich himself. It is for this reason that he sought to groom for the presidency his most trusted associate—that is, Mondher Zenaidi,[159] who, as Transport, Tourism, and Commerce Minister, had assisted him in acquiring so much wealth in the first place. A member of both the RCD Central Committee and the Political Bureau, Mondher Zenaidi left the Commerce Ministry in 2007 to become Public Health Minister. Arguably, his ministerial reshuffle was part of the succession preparations at that time and meant to boost his political standing and capital amongst the public, especially because he was expected to launch major health reforms. In 2008, an American diplomat listed Zenaidi amongst the most likely successors to Ben Ali:

With a wealth of economic experience . . . and a long history of RCD activism, Zenaidi is increasingly rumoured to be a candidate for the Prime Ministry. However, he is largely unknown among Tunisians and needs to demonstrate success in the troubled health sector before he will gain public support.[160]

---

[159] Mohamed Ghariani repeatedly affirmed that Mondher Zenaidi was the presidential candidate of Belhassen Trabelsi. Interviews with Mohamed Ghariani, Tunis, 27 May 2016 and 8 February 2017. Information corroborated through an interview with a trusted friend of the Ben Ali family, Tunis, 10 February 2017.

[160] US Embassy in Tunis, 'Tunisia: What Succession Scenario?', Wikileaks, 9 May 2008, 08TUNIS493_a, secret.

As Prime Minister, Zenaidi would have held a key position to contest the succession of Ben Ali—not least because the 2002 constitutional changes stipulated that the President could delegate his powers to the Prime Minister if he was temporarily incapable of governing. Moreover, in contrast to the Head of Parliament, the Prime Minister was allowed to run for office immediately after the President died or became unable to carry out his duties.

In contrast to Belhassen Trabelsi, Sakher el-Materi was a relatively new arrival on the public scene, becoming an important economic actor only after his marriage to Nesrine in 2004. However, el-Materi possessed a certain claim to political capital—or, at least, this perception was one that his allies in the party sought to cultivate. He hailed from an important Tunisois political family and was associated with his father's history of opposition activism against Bourguiba.[161] In addition, his wife, Nesrine, was Ben Ali's favourite daughter,[162] and they both exercised considerable leverage within the palace. Indeed, in the late 2000s, even Ben Dhia and RCD Secretary General Mohamed Ghariani came to support el-Materi's candidacy.[163] The fact that Ben Dhia—who had previously never entered into family machinations and answered only to the President—decided to back el-Materi illustrates the extent to which the succession had become a pressing issue. Everyone in the palace began to worry about the day after, even Ben Ali's most trusted advisers.

However, el-Materi was only in his late twenties at the time and constitutionally still too young to contest the presidency, the minimum age for which was set at forty. He therefore decided to cultivate an association with Kamel Morjane, a distant relative of Ben Ali who had once represented Tunisia at the United Nations and who in the 2000s headed the Defence and then Foreign Affairs Ministries. Many Westerners hoped Kamel Morjane might emerge as Ben Ali's successor, describing him as 'outgoing and friendly' and part of the 'liberal' wing of the regime.[164] El-Materi supported his candidacy and sought to cultivate him as a mentor with whom he might maintain a relationship until he reached the age to contest the presidency himself. As part of this

---

[161] For more details about Moncef el-Materi, see his memoir, Moncef el-Materi, *De Saint-Cyr au peloton d'exécution de Bourguiba*, Tunis: Arabesques, 2014.

[162] A range of interviewees affirmed that Nesrine is Ben Ali's favourite daughter, elaborating that he felt guilty that she was born out of wedlock (e.g. interview with Mohamed Ghariani, Tunis, 8 February 2017; interview with a trusted friend of the Ben Ali family, Tunis, 10 February 2017). Nesrine repeatedly stressed how close she is to her father. Interviews with Nesrine Ben Ali, Viber, 10, 13, and 23 February 2017.

[163] Interview with Mohamed Ghariani, Tunis, 27 May 2016. Information corroborated through other interviews.

[164] See, for example, US Embassy in Tunis, 'Tunisia: What Succession Scenario?', Wikileaks, 9 May 2008, 08TUNIS493_a, secret; US Embassy in Tunis, 'Ambassador's Courtesy Call with Minister of Defense', Wikileaks, 4 January 2007, 07TUNIS29_a, secret.

strategy, he came to portray himself as a liberal and reformist figure along the lines of Morjane. He did this by acquiring the media group Dar Assabah in 2009, which gave a certain voice to political opponents—naturally, only as long as they did not challenge the foundations of the regime. In addition, el-Materi positioned himself as a conciliatory political figure who allowed some space for the repressed religious opposition, even seeking dialogue with the exiled Ennahda movement.[165] To prop up his religious credentials, in 2007 he launched the religious Zitouna FM radio station, and two years later created the Zitouna Bank, which specialized in Islamic banking. Ghariani elaborated:

> With Radio Zitouna, we played the card of the Islamists, and with Dar Assabah, we played the card of the modernists, the progressives. Sakher [el-Materi] was not a thinker, but we wanted him to learn how to manage political life ... by proposing reforms and a political opening. ... One year before the revolution, Dar Assabah had almost become an opposition newspaper![166]

It is noteworthy that Ghariani's reference to el-Materi not being 'a thinker' likely alludes to his limited education—he repeated at least two years in high school and never went to university, allegedly owing to drug consumption, amongst other issues. It is in part for these reasons that many figures in the RCD believed he was unfit to run the country, denouncing Ghariani and Ben Dhia's efforts to groom him for the highest office.[167] El-Materi's wife, Nesrine, suggested that senior political figures pushed him into taking a more prominent role, as did his politicized father, Moncef el-Materi.[168] However, el-Materi would certainly not have let himself be pressured too much had the prospect of becoming Tunisia's next President not appealed to him at least somewhat.

The congress of succession

Competition between Sakher el-Materi and Belhassen Trabelsi, the two front-runners for the succession, increased in the summer of 2008, peaking during

---

[165] Anne Wolf, '"Dégage RCD!" The Rise of Internal Dissent in Ben Ali's Constitutional Democratic Rally and the Tunisian Uprisings', *Mediterranean Politics*, 2018, 23, 2, p. 257.

[166] Interview with Mohamed Ghariani, Tunis, 27 May 2016.

[167] It is notable that Mohamed Ghariani's account of Sakher el-Materi's political strategy, using the personal pronoun 'we' rather than 'he', raises the questions of whether el-Materi was actually in charge of it and the extent to which senior figures such as Ghariani and Ben Dhia exploited his inexperience and comparative youth in the hope of forging roles for themselves in the post–Ben Ali era. When asked about these issues, Ghariani suggested it was a 'two-way street'. Sometimes el-Materi 'manipulated' him and Ben Dhia and sometimes it was the other way around. Interview with Mohamed Ghariani, Tunis, 27 May 2016.

[168] Interview with Nesrine Ben Ali, Viber, 13 February 2017.

the RCD's fifth congress, a four-day event that kicked off on 30 July. Organized around the theme 'challenge', the congress promised to focus on strategies to tackle mounting unemployment and poverty in Tunisia. This theme was certainly chosen to calm the protests in Gafsa, which at that time were still ongoing, and to prevent them from spreading to other regions. However, far from representing an opportunity to discuss and address the growing socioeconomic challenges, in reality the congress served to pave the way for one of the two presidential front-runners to succeed Ben Ali. Crucially, both el-Materi and Belhassen integrated into the RCD Central Committee. Reportedly, el-Materi first announced his intention to become a member of the committee and, upon hearing this plan, Belhassen followed suit so as not to be outflanked by his younger rival.[169] Ali Chaouch commented on their integration into the party's highest echelons:

> Sakher [el-Materi] presented himself at the elections, he was elected at the local level and then to the Central Committee, it is important to recognize this.... Of course, everyone knew that the President wanted him to be elected and party activists were disciplined [so] he was elected.... By contrast, Belhassen Trabelsi was part of the list of Central Committee members who were [appointed] by the President.[170]

Chaouch here underscored how the ways in which el-Materi and Belhassen joined the Central Committee differed. In his eyes, el-Materi's election to the Central Committee bestowed his membership with greater legitimacy than Belhassen's appointment. This illustrates once again the growing importance of internal party procedures and regulations, in particular to justify the presidential family's political ascent, even if they were a simple masquerade. El-Materi's election was certainly staged. However, on their own, rational-legal legitimation bases are limited, as they rarely draw in a support base of committed followers. Indeed, apart from Chaouch and some other family cronies, most congress participants were deeply distrustful of the family's ascent within the party, if they did not outright reject it, even those who considered it lawful. Their scepticism was fuelled by el-Materi's attitude at the congress. Hamza recalled:

> What upset me so much during the congress was that Sakher [el-Materi] showed up with his bodyguards . . . four to five people who protected him.

---

[169] Interviews with Naziha Zarrouk, Tunis, 30 January 2017; Mohamed Ghariani, Tunis, 8 February 2017.
[170] Interview with Ali Chaouch, Tunis, 11 February 2017.

It was very badly perceived and hurt me a lot. . . . Did he really believe that we Destourians would harm him? . . . He wanted to show off . . . to show that he was above everybody else![171]

Hamza suggested that el-Materi appeared presumptuous and arrogant at the event, a perception many other attendees shared.[172] Though Hamza reflected that el-Materi came with bodyguards mainly to show off, it is also possible that he genuinely did not feel safe, and el-Materi was probably well aware that his Central Committee membership was deeply controversial amongst party activists of all ranks. This was particularly the case because major structural changes were initiated during the congress that allowed el-Materi and Belhassen not only to integrate into but also to gain a hold over the party's leading structures.

Specifically, the Central Committee was enlarged from 250 to 343 posts, and 83% of its seats were replaced.[173] The new members hailed from two principal groups: businesspeople and young party activists. The party leadership justified the integration of the former by suggesting their economic expertise was needed to tackle rising unemployment and poverty.[174] Over 13% of the population was jobless throughout the 2000s, with many more people struggling to make ends meet.[175] Yet in reality, the business figures were associates of Belhassen and, to a lesser extent, of el-Materi, and their ascent in the party reinforced the family's control of its central institutions. Moreover, the promotion of young party activists was sold as part of the RCD's efforts to promote a younger generation of members to leading party posts.[176] However, sources within the party's leadership at the time suggested that their integration into the Central Committee served solely to pave the way for el-Materi's political future. Ben Dhia and Ghariani sought to groom a new generation of party leaders on which el-Materi could rely once he was old enough to compete for the highest office.[177]

[171] Interview with Hamza, Ras Jebel, Bizerte governorate, 9 February 2017.

[172] One congress participant from Gafsa called Sakher el-Materi a 'brat' and 'big baby'. Interview with Abderrazek, Gafsa, 23 June 2016.

[173] 'Le RCD par les Chiffres', Le Renouveau, 30 July 2008, p. 7.

[174] Interview with Ali Chaouch, Tunis, 11 February 2017. Information corroborated through other author interviews.

[175] Diego F. Angel-Urdinola, Antonio Nucifora, and David Robalino, 'Labor Policy to Promote Good Jobs in Tunisia', World Bank, 2015, p. 13.

[176] For example, 'La Jeunesse Tunisienne: Détermination Renouvelée à Relever le Défi', Le Renouveau, 30 July 2008, p. 7; interview with Mohamed Ghariani, Tunis, 8 February 2017.

[177] Interview with Chedli Neffati, Tunis, 2 February 2017. Note that Mohamed Ghariani denied this account. Interview with Mohamed Ghariani, Tunis, 8 February 2017.

As part of el-Materi and Belhassen's quests for party leadership, most of the remaining longtime party officials were discarded, especially vocal figures who could have posed a challenge to their presidential ambitions. These included highly popular leaders who had featured during the fight for independence, such as Hamed Karoui, who was dismissed as RCD Vice-President. Given these wide-ranging changes, most party activists quickly realized the only 'challenge' the congress sought to tackle was that of the presidential succession. Many interviewees maintained it was the 'worst congress ever'.[178] One said 'it marked the end' of the party.[179] Even Tunisians who were not part of the RCD said they were alarmed by the congress because it 'meant that the family [had] got the party'.[180] Indeed, el-Materi and Belhassen now exerted key control within the RCD's central organ, in addition to the sway they already held over many ministers, party leaders, and advisers in the palace.

Aside from preparing el-Materi and Belhassen for the presidential succession, the congress also arranged for Ben Ali to remain in power for another term—officially his last. Again, everything was done to convey the image that Ben Ali was merely responding to the people's 'call to run again'.[181] During the subsequent general election held on 25 October 2009, Ben Ali was confirmed with an obviously rigged 89.62% of votes cast, and the RCD gained a clear majority in Parliament. It is notable that el-Materi used the occasion to become a lawmaker in Parliament alongside Afif Chiboub—the brother-in-law of Dorsaf, Ben Ali's middle daughter. After the ballots, popular celebrations were staged at the 7 November Sports Hall of Rades, nine kilometres south east of Tunis, which has a 60,000-strong capacity and appeared to be full in pictures subsequently circulated by the state media (such as that in Figure 4.3).[182] This shows that party officials still managed to enforce internal discipline—with the help of material rewards if needed—and mobilization was allegedly achieved by paying activists to participate in the celebrations.[183]

Whilst it was still feasible to feign a certain degree of stability and support for the regime at the national level, this was much more challenging locally. Indeed, municipal elections held on 9 May 2010—just months before

---

[178] For example, interview with Khalil, Jendouba, 29 May 2016.

[179] Interview with Hamza, Ras Jebel, Bizerte governorate, 9 February 2017.

[180] Author conversation with Bochra, a Tunisian political observer and economist, Tunis, 24 February 2017.

[181] For example, 'Ben Ali Dit Oui à l'Appel du Devoir', *Le Renouveau*, 30 July 2008, pp. 2–6.

[182] Note that the 7 November Sports Hall of Rades was renamed 'Sports Hall of Rades' after the fall of the Ben Ali regime.

[183] Note that Mohamed Ghariani denied such allegations but conceded that participants received free food and beverages, arguably already an important incentive for many grassroots activists, who struggled to make ends meet. Interview with Mohamed Ghariani, Tunis, 27 May 2016.

Figure 4.3 RCD followers celebrating Ben Ali's 'victory' in the 2009 elections
Source: Tunisian News Agency.

the uprising—laid bare the extent of the RCD's internal crumbling. Some party followers recounted that they decided not to vote, amongst other reasons because they no longer recognized the names of those running on local RCD lists.[184] The decision of some RCD followers not to cast a vote was an important instance of internecine contention. Authorities closely monitored who voted, and refusing to do so was considered an act of dissent. One RCD student leader held that in some localities party representatives even struggled to come up with a list, as many longtime activists did not want to present themselves in the ballots.[185] Those who ended up running were often complete political newcomers, regime cronies, or family members who sought to gain relevance at the local level. Amongst others, Imed Trabelsi—Leila's favourite nephew—was elected mayor of La Goulette, which hosts the port of Tunis, a strategically important location for his illegal trading business.

The municipal elections illustrate the deep gulf that emerged between the RCD grass roots and a leadership they believed was serving only the President's family and associates. Essentially, the RCD had come to resemble a family party, its internal cleavages and patronage structures increasingly mirroring the various clans of the President's kin—all the way from the central leadership to regional representatives and down to local officials. This chapter has shown that some of the marginalized RCD activists began to engage in contentious activities against their superiors. Many of these party 'losers' affirmed that they would 'never' have accepted presidential relatives to take over the RCD, let alone to succeed Ben Ali as President.[186] But the evidence

[184] Interview with Ezzeddine, Skype, 12 June 2016. Note that the official participation rate was 84%, though this figure may have been inflated and many people were coerced and intimidated into casting a vote.
[185] Interview with Hassouna Nasfi, Bardo, 24 May 2016.
[186] For example, interview with Chedli Neffati, Tunis, 2 February 2017.

presented suggests that by the late 2000s, the Ben Ali family had already gained control over the RCD's key decision-making organs and was well advanced on the path towards a dynastic-like succession, and that there were no apparent threats to the unfolding of this scenario. Indeed, the rise of internecine contention even prompted the presidential family to reinforce their grip on power. However, the growing discontent within the regime paved the way for wider transformative change when countrywide protests erupted in December 2010, a topic which chapter 5 explores in more detail.

5

The Rebellion

The Destourian family was at the very heart of the regime's weakness.
It killed the regime and thereby it got itself killed.

Mohamed Anour Adhar, Bardo, 26 May 2016

Tarek al-Tayeb Mohamed Bouazizi's self-immolation on 17 December 2010 in the marginalized region of Sidi Bouzid sparked mass protests that soon engulfed the entire country and even swept to neighbouring states. On 14 January 2011, Ben Ali left Tunisia amidst the turmoil. He would never return. Whilst scholars have investigated the uprising in much depth, specifically the protesters' demands and dynamics of mobilization,[1] inner regime factors and the response of the RCD to the upheaval have received little attention. When I broached this topic, many interviewees were quick to affirm that the demonstrations occurred largely out of a sense of indignation at the RCD machinery—along with police violence and economic downturn. Yet when inquiring more deeply about specific people and events linked to the former regime, interviewees came to reveal that the RCD's role in the protests was much more complex than is commonly understood and key to understanding the breakdown of the regime.

This chapter shows that during the uprising, tensions burst out into the open between the RCD's different wings, pitting associates of the Ben Ali family—who sought to defend the regime—against the many party 'losers' who had been sidelined in the 2000s. The marginalized followers became dissenters in the uprising—although their grievances, contentious activities, and demands varied: regional party representatives typically performed acts of passive resistance with the goal of propping up their own standing within the regime. But contention also evinced a generational dimension as many young RCD

---

[1] Important works include Ridha Zouaoui, *al-Thawra al-Tunisiyya, Thawrat al-Hamish 'ala al-Markaz* [*The Tunisian Revolution: The Power of the Marginalized*], 'Ala' al-Din: Sfax, 2012; Nouri Gana (ed.), *The Making of the Tunisian Revolution: Contexts, Architects, Prospects*, Edinburgh: Edinburgh University Press, 2013; Alcinde Honwana, *Youth and Revolution in Tunisia*, London: Zed Books, 2013; Lahmar Mouldi (ed.), *al-Thawra al-Tunisiyya* [*The Tunisian Revolution*], Doha: Arab Center for Research and Policy Studies, 2014.

Ben Ali's Tunisia. Anne Wolf, Oxford University Press. © Anne Wolf (2023).
DOI: 10.1093/oso/9780192868503.003.0006

activists joined the protest movement, especially in marginalized governorates and the ones with a particularly high number of deaths during the uprising. Many of them eventually came to call for the fall of the regime. Importantly, through interviews with key actors, this chapter reveals that the absence of countermobilization supportive of Ben Ali provided a political opportunity for figures within the elite to move against the President. Indeed, the breakdown of the Ben Ali regime and his departure to Saudi Arabia was not an immediate consequence of the mass protests but owed to a secret coup d'état, which occurred amidst the demonstrations.

This is not to suggest that the collapse of the Ben Ali regime was inevitable, however. Ben Ali's ousting was highly contingent on a series of decisions made by influential actors, whose agency was critical at this period of political turmoil and uncertainty.[2] This chapter uncovers how 'individual actors . . . [exercised] substantial power to channel the direction of subsequent events'[3]—sometimes in unintended ways, such as Ben Ali deciding to leave for Saudi Arabia. Indeed, the tumultuous events were beyond the control of either the party or the elite, who underestimated the people's broader discontent and their own capacity to restore order once Ben Ali left. Pressure from the streets gradually forced them to dissolve the RCD.[4] It is this very process that Mohamed Anour Adhar, a Member of Parliament who hails from a Destourian family, refers to in the epigraph of this chapter when stating that the Destourians 'killed the regime' and, by doing so, unwillingly 'killed' themselves.

A Destourian revolt?

At the time of the uprising, Sidi Bouzid was home to about 650 active RCD cells, each consisting of 200–300 members.[5] In total, the 415,900-strong[6]

---

[2] For more information on the role of individual agency during moments of collective uncertainty, see Ivan Ermakoff, *Ruling Oneself Out: A Theory of Collective Abdications*, Durham, NC: Duke University Press, 2008; Ivan Ermakoff, 'The Structure of Contingency', *American Journal of Sociology*, 2015, 121, 1, pp. 64–125.

[3] Ronald Aminzade, 'Historical Sociology and Time', *Sociological Methods and Research*, 1992, 20, 4, p. 463.

[4] Scholars of contentious politics and social movements have long emphasized the importance of scrutinizing 'both intended and unintended consequences of movement activity, though typically limiting their analysis to the intentions of anti-regime actors'. Marco Giugni, Doug McAdam, and Charles Tilly, *How Social Movements Matter: Social Movements, Protest, and Contention*, Minneapolis: University of Minnesota Press, 1999, p. xi.

[5] Interviews with Mohamed Ghariani, Tunis, 27 May 2016; Abir Moussi, Tunis, 31 May 2016.

[6] The data is for 2011 and was retrieved from *al-Nashra al-Shahriyya li-l-Ihsa'iyyat [Monthly Bulletin of Statistics]*, al-Ma'had al-Watani li-l-Ihsa' [National Institute for Statistics], September 2012, p. 9.

governorate included about 162,500 card-carrying RCD members, that is, 39.1% of its population.[7] As a matter of fact, Sidi Bouzid was the governorate where RCD membership rates amongst the population were the highest nationally.[8] To find so many RCD activists in the very cradle of the Arab Uprisings and where people from diverse backgrounds still fervently defend their legacy may seem contradictory. After all, the protests are generally perceived as having occurred against the regime and its institutions. But far from this, interviews and group discussions revealed that many of Sidi Bouzid's party followers had been understanding of, or even actively supporting, the protests—though their rationales for doing so differed. Senior officials who hailed from the old guard—who had been sidelined in the 2000s—hoped that the protests would pressure the government into improving the economic situation in Sidi Bouzid and enhance the standing of party activists within the wider RCD structure—an objective many younger activists initially shared. However, whilst the old guard sought to reestablish the party's leadership role and did not actively participate in the demonstrations, many youthful followers came to call for a complete overhaul of the regime once the protests turned more violent.

The old guard's early embrace of the demonstrations was underpinned by the fact that even many of Sidi Bouzid's prominent party leaders were deeply affected by the city's poverty and high levels of unemployment. Abderrazek Daly—a lawyer in his sixties from one of the most important families in Sidi Bouzid and the governorate's RCD Vice-Secretary General at the time of the uprising—is a case in point. Daly's much-frequented law office in the centre of Sidi Bouzid is still decorated with an RCD flag, a rare public demonstration of persistent loyalty to the former ruling party. Still, when the demonstrations erupted in December 2010, Daly considered them to be legitimate. He explained:

Within the [RCD] we were convinced that we must have these demonstrations because we are an impoverished region, we are a ruined region. Our children have no work. For my part, I am from the RCD but I have four [family members] with law degrees who are jobless: my wife, my sister, as well as my two brothers![9]

[7] These calculations are based on an estimated average of 250 members per RCD cell.
[8] Interviews with Mohamed Ghariani, Tunis, 27 May 2016; Abir Moussi, Tunis, 31 May 2016.
[9] Interview with Abderrazek Daly, Sidi Bouzid, 25 June 2016.

Like many long-standing party officials, Daly defended the protests, which initially focused on socioeconomic concerns—even if it certainly did not cross his mind to participate in them—as unemployment affected people close to him. By quietly supporting the demonstrations, Daly claimed that his main hope was 'that the region of Sidi Bouzid can have its share in the political system, that's all'.[10] For many officials from the old guard such as Daly, strengthening Sidi Bouzid's anchorage in the political system was closely associated with socioeconomic advancement. Daly positioned himself within a group of RCD followers whose rationale for supporting the protests was purely economic and who were 'convinced that the political system must exist and has to resist'. He elaborated about this camp:

> Some RCD followers said that we . . . need to defend the RCD because that's our political system. . . . They did not say that they wanted to overthrow Ben Ali. They were against the Trabelsis and other thieves, but they did not say they were against Ben Ali.[11]

Whilst Daly was critical of the most prominent beneficiaries of the political system (i.e., the Trabelsis), he clearly supported Ben Ali. Loyal regime followers commonly blame people close to the President for any political and economic mistakes whilst protecting their leader.[12] Daly harboured deep disdain for RCD members who gradually came to ask for regime change, particularly party cell activists. The party's Secretary General at the time, Mohamed Ghariani, who visited the southern governorate during the protests, confirmed the active participation of RCD cell members in the protest movement in Sidi Bouzid and their call for political change. Ghariani said that some cell leaders even encouraged their members to take to the streets because they were very close to their constituents, who pressured them into supporting the protests.[13] In an attempt to discredit party activists who came to call for the overthrow of the regime, Daly said that 'at the level of the local and regional cells [in Sidi Bouzid], [RCD followers] were profiteers'. He reflected that 'they were not activists with well-defined objectives . . . and were not interested in their [party] and Destourian political solutions'. Visibly

---

[10] Ibid.

[11] Ibid.

[12] A focus of their criticism has been the wives of the dictators and their supposedly malicious influence. See, for example, Sadri Khiari, 'De Wassila à Leïla, Premières Dames et Pouvoir en Tunisie', *Politique Africaine*, 2004, 3, pp. 55–70; Geoffrey Nyarota, *The Graceless Fall of Robert Mugabe: The End of a Dictator's Reign*, Cape Town: Penguin Books, 2018.

[13] Interview with Mohamed Ghariani, Tunis, 27 May 2016.

agitated, Daly went as far as to claim that for party cell activists who called for the fall of Ben Ali, 'being Destourian were a facade'.[14] Such attempts at denying RCD protesters a Destourian identity was echoed by other senior officials.[15]

To further discredit RCD followers who had called for regime change, Daly claimed that they were pursuing foreign agendas. Daly also insisted that Bouazizi's self-immolation was exaggerated, even suggesting that Bouazizi did not actually want to burn himself but did so accidentally after drinking a small quantity of petrol and subsequently smoking a cigarette.[16] Daly's degrading portrayal of Bouazizi, who was well known in central Sidi Bouzid, as sufficiently foolish to kill himself 'by mistake' somewhat calls into question his previous claim that he cared for Sidi Bouzid's many young residents who struggled to make ends meet. Rather, Daly and many other members of the old guard supported the economic demands of the protesters primarily out of self-serving motives. They hoped that pressure on the regime would bolster their own socioeconomic sway and that of their close associates. These officials now blame those RCD activists who demanded the overthrow of the regime for the economic downturn, which has only deepened in Sidi Bouzid since Ben Ali was ousted.[17] They charge that the many development projects promised to the city during the protests—in which they had hoped to become key stakeholders—were not implemented because of the fall of his regime.[18] The RCD became deeply divided during the uprising—divisions that have persisted ever since amongst ex-party followers.

The RCD activists who asked for regime change did not believe the authorities' promises of jobs and development were sincere. In contrast to senior party members such as Daly, young activists have developed a deeply ambiguous relationship towards the former regime. Many are ashamed and wish to hide their previous political affiliation, particularly at the level of the rank and file, which makes research into RCD grassroots activism during the uprising challenging. In one case, former RCD officials helped organize a group

[14] Interview with Abderrazek Daly, Sidi Bouzid, 25 June 2016.

[15] For example, interview with Abir Moussi, Tunis, 31 May 2016.

[16] Interview with Abderrazek Daly, Sidi Bouzid, 25 June 2016. Note that his account is contradicted by eyewitnesses who talked to me and by video footage of Bouazizi's self-immolation.

[17] Sidi Bouzid's unemployment rate roughly doubled between 2010 and mid-2012, when almost 30% of its residents were jobless. See, for details, Tunisian National Institute of Statistics, http://www.ins.tn, last accessed 10 February 2022.

[18] For example, Abderrazek Daly maintained that 'Sidi Bouzid lost a very big possibility [as] starting from 25 December 2010 . . . President Ben Ali ordered big [business] heads to establish themselves in Sidi Bouzid. They were about to create 5,000 to 6,000 jobs.' Interview with Abderrazek Daly, Sidi Bouzid, 25 June 2016.

discussion with people who they said were young former party members in Sidi Bouzid.[19] Yet when I first broached the topic of the RCD during the uprising, one participant, Salma, hastily stated: 'we [group discussants] were all revolutionaries and everything that happened before January 14 was against the former Rally party'. Visibly nervous and affronted by the research topic, Salma added, 'I can personally confirm that before January 14 nobody in this group was a member of a political party!'—a confirmation she made despite not knowing two of the other participants.

Rather than talk about the RCD, these young people were keen to narrate their revolutionary activism and individual contributions to the protest movement in Sidi Bouzid. Questioned more closely about the role of the RCD during the protests, the participants initially affirmed that all members of the former ruling party were in their homes at the time of the uprising because they feared the protesters. 'They were afraid of the youth [because] some young people burned their cars and their houses!', one stated.[20] Yet even whilst fiercely criticizing RCD officials, all discussants regularly spoke highly of the senior party members who had organized the group discussion, such as Daly, the governor's RCD Vice-President at the time of the uprising, who hails from an important family in the city.

Their criticism of ruling party officials was not directed against longtime figureheads such as Daly, who themselves no longer profited substantially from the party. It was directed towards the region's central authorities—the corrupt associates of the Ben Ali family, discussed at great length in chapter 4. Indeed, regional RCD vice-presidency positions were mostly honorific nominations and typically filled by people who possessed significant political legitimacy by virtue of their activism in the independence movement or their family history—as was the case with Daly. But Ben Ali family associates were the real powerbrokers of governorates and headed the RCD's regional structures, and these were the figures towards whom the group directed its disdain.

The group discussants' praise for figureheads such as Daly also shows that party membership is only one amongst a range of important affiliations in Sidi

---

[19] I conducted the group discussion with Salma, Houda, Tayeb, and Anis in Sidi Bouzid, 25 June 2016.

[20] Interview with Houda, Sidi Bouzid, 25 June 2016. Note that this contradicts the statements of RCD senior members, who typically claim they were present during the protests and tried to reason with those demonstrators who went as far as to demand the overthrow of the regime and the dissolution of the RCD. In doing so, these former officials wish to convey that they were not part of the RCD's networks of corruption but were sufficiently respected by the people that they did not have to hide during the unrest.

Bouzid; ties to a specific family clan are also important. It is probable that group participants initially overstated their dislike of the RCD and the extent to which its officials were the target of the protests out of fear of exposing themselves as former party activists or sympathizers, particularly in front of people they did not know well. In fact, after more than an hour of discussion, one of the participants, Anis—a local businessman—had had enough of the others attacking the RCD. In the middle of a heated argument about RCD corruption in Sidi Bouzid, Anis suddenly proclaimed: 'My family was in the RCD and I am proud of it!' He went on to explain that his agriculture business had suffered tremendously in the years before the uprising because his produce did not sell well. Beyond these socioeconomic concerns, Anis was deeply affected by the self-immolation of Bouazizi. Anis said he had known Bouazizi personally because the two of them frequented the same café—the last time the night before Bouazizi's self-immolation. 'I was the first one [in my family] to participate in the protests', he stated, visibly full of pride, affirming that his relatives supported his revolutionary endeavours.[21]

Apologetic in the face of Anis's unexpected revelation, Salma, who had been so critical of the RCD, conceded that 'not all RCD activists were wrongdoers'.[22] Salma even admitted that there were RCD members in her own family, who, she said, 'are not wrongdoers, they are not thieves, they are good people'. For Anis, however, Salma's proclamation did not go far enough. He insisted:

All RCD activists who were part of big RCD families [in Sidi Bouzid] protested and encouraged the protests to turn into a revolution.... RCD followers were revolutionaries.... The RCD no longer wanted Ben Ali, because the four years prior to the uprising we experienced real economic problems.... Who do you think was behind Ben Ali's fall? The [RCD activists] of Sidi Bouzid![23]

Anis's allegation that the participation of RCD followers in the protest movement in Sidi Bouzid forced Ben Ali out of power illustrates that former party membership is not only a source of shame amongst its youth. Some grassroots activists, such as Anis, are still proud of having belonged to the RCD and participated in the protests. They framed contention inside the ruling party as a rational response to the mounting injustice perpetuated by some regime

---

[21] Interview with Anis, Sidi Bouzid, 25 June 2016.
[22] Interview with Salma, Sidi Bouzid, 25 June 2016.
[23] Interview with Anis, Sidi Bouzid, 25 June 2016.

actors. It is noteworthy that Anis stresses that the RCD protesters were from 'big . . . families', that is, influential families of rural notables.[24] The conflict in Sidi Bouzid wasn't primarily about the 'regime versus protesters' but about the marginalization of longtime activists, rural notables, and the region as a whole. Sidi Bouzid is one of Tunisia's most disenfranchised governorates and even prominent families were increasingly cut out of economic development projects, which were disproportionally directed towards the Sahel area and Tunis[25]—strongholds of the Ben Ali family.

The group's sometimes divergent and contradictory statements about the party and its role reveals that party activists' responses to the protests were deeply heterogeneous. The key divide was threefold: between Ben Ali family associates, who supported the regime until the very end; rural notables of important families, who demanded reforms to elevate their own standing within the party hierarchy; and a protesting party base that called for the overthrow of the regime once the demonstrations grew in magnitude and were violently repressed.

In many cases, the protesters' increasingly anti-regime stance was reinforced by personal relationships with victims of the uprising, their deaths constituting focal points revealing the repressive nature of the regime.[26] Aside from Anis's ties to Bouazizi, RCD followers in Sidi Bouzid were deeply affected by the death of Chaouki Ben Lakhdhar Ben Houssine Hidri, the first person killed by a bullet during the uprising. He was the son of a prominent Destourian activist, Houssine Ben Lakhdher.[27] His death sent shockwaves throughout the city and lay bare that anyone participating in the demonstrations, or simply happening to be outside at the time of the unrest, risked their life.[28]

Once the police used live bullets against protesters and snipers began to target random people walking in the streets, even some mid-level and senior party officials came to sharply denounce Ben Ali's handling of the situation.

---

[24] Ibid.

[25] By 2010, 95% of foreign direct investment was absorbed by Tunis, Nabeul, Sousse, Monastir, Sfax, and Bizerte—coastal towns where the Trabelsis dominated economic affairs. See, for details, Mongi Boughzala and Mohamed Tlili Hamdi, 'Promoting Inclusive Growth in Arab Countries: Regional and Rural Development and Inequality in Tunisia', Brookings Institution, Working Paper, February 2014, p. 6.

[26] For comparative insights, see Susanne Lohmann, 'The Dynamics of Informational Cascades: The Monday Demonstration in Leipzig, East Germany, 1989–91', World Politics, 1994, 47, pp. 42–101.

[27] Houssine Ben Lakhdher passed away shortly after the uprising. I was unable to confirm whether he was an active member of the RCD.

[28] One of Chaouki's brothers, Alaa Hidri, was also severely wounded in the course of the uprising. For details, see Henda Chennaoui, 'Retour de Manivelle: Quand la Police et la Justice s'Acharnent contre les Jeunes de la Révolution Tunisienne!', Nawaat, 1 June 2014, http://nawaat.org/portail/2014/06/01/retour-de-manivelle-quand-la-police-et-la-justice-sacharnent-contre-les-jeunes-de-la-revolution-tunisienne/, last accessed 19 July 2016.

Selim, who at the time was a member of the Executive Bureau of RCD students and hails from Regueb, a rural village in Sidi Bouzid, is a case in point.[29] Regueb, where Selim founded the party's first local office, witnessed a particularly high number of deaths during the uprising.[30] In an interview, Selim recalled painfully that his cousin was shot during the protests, as was his neighbour, a woman who left two children behind. In response to these events, he claims to have written a letter demanding to see RCD Secretary General Mohamed Ghariani to protest the deaths in his village and hoping to receive answers about the violent events, but the latter never responded. Visibly struggling to explain the events, Selim elaborated that the origins of the snipers shooting at the people were never determined and that they may have come from outside Tunisia.[31] Evoking the possibility that the violence may have been enacted, at least in part, by external forces has become a prominent narrative amongst some previous party officials, who deny that Ben Ali ordered it.[32]

Sidi Bouzid's 'traitors'

The high number of victims in Sidi Bouzid, including family members of RCD activists and presumably even party followers themselves, was a key factor driving the protesters' increasing hostility towards Ben Ali. Thus, a mounting number of people came to call for the overthrow of the regime. Even some mid-level officials with links to victims of the uprising, such as Selim, became progressively supportive of the demonstrators. This contrasts with RCD representatives in governorates with few or no victims, who tended to denounce the turmoil. Indeed, even in marginalized governorates such as Jendouba, where unemployment and poverty levels were almost as high as in Sidi Bouzid but nobody died, mid-level officials fiercely rejected calls for the fall of the regime, which threatened to undermine the elevated social status they held. Yet the rank and file—particularly young people and card-carrying RCD members—mostly joined the protests, even in regions with

---

[29] Interview with Selim, Regueb, Sidi Bouzid governorate, 27 June 2016.

[30] In Regueb, a village of roughly 7,800 residents, four young men and one woman were killed during the protests. For details, see Muhammad al-Arabi al-Zuraibi, *al-Regueb min al-Tahrir ila al-Ta'mir* [*al-Regueb: From Liberation to Reconstruction*], Tunis: Dar Al-Qalam Publishing, 2016, pp. 219–220.

[31] Interview with Selim, Regueb, Sidi Bouzid governorate, 27 June 2016.

[32] In another case, Mounir Ben Miled, a former member of the RCD Executive Committee and a fervent conspiracy theory adherent, insisted that 'the head of the national guard wrote three times to the entire national guard that they are not allowed to use real live bullets'. He elaborated that therefore 'nobody knows' who really shot at the protesters or 'whether they actually were from Tunisia'. Interview with Mounir Ben Miled, Tunis, 24 May 2016.

no civilian deaths; their superiors continued to support Ben Ali until the very end.

Many RCD representatives from locations with few or no victims charged their counterparts in Sidi Bouzid and neighbouring Kasserine—where major protests also erupted promptly after the self-immolation of Bouazizi and which had the highest death toll of all regions—of not having been 'true' Destourians. Some even denounced them as traitors. One of them, Zakaria, asserted that in Sidi Bouzid and Kasserine, 'the RCD is something entirely different'.[33] Zakaria, who hails from Gafsa, explained that following the regime's harsh crackdown on the 2008 Gafsa protest movement, people from the phosphate city learned their lesson, which is why only a few took to the streets in 2010–2011.[34] Zakaria sharply denounced the revolutionary endeavours of RCD activists in Sidi Bouzid and Kasserine, arguing that in these governorates:

> There are no real RCD activists. [People there] are anti-patriots, they are not Tunisians. In Sidi Bouzid and Kasserine they are not Tunisian, they can't be! They have remained Berbers. . . . They have no clue about what is happening in the world, they do nothing except eating and sleeping!

He elaborated:

> There is a real difference between the people from Gafsa and the *khorbech* [local saying close to 'uncultured' or 'uncivilized'] from Sidi Bouzid. In Gafsa our big family clans are at the borders of the city, they protect our city from [illegal people]. But in Sidi Bouzid they are all . . . Bedouins![35]

Clearly, Zakaria tried hard to portray the citizens of Sidi Bouzid as ignorant and uncivilized. He attributed Sidi Bouzid's supposed backwardness to the 'Berber' roots of some people there. In doing so, he asserted the supposed superiority of Tunisians of Arab origin, completely disregarding the fact that some citizens in Gafsa are also not 'pure' Arabs but have Amazigh ancestors. To further degrade the people of Sidi Bouzid, Zakaria used the Bedouin metaphor to suggest that they are without country allegiance and hence unpatriotic.

---

[33] Interview with Zakaria, Gafsa, 24 June 2016.

[34] Many interviewees in Gafsa confirmed that few people took to the streets in the mining city. Such limited mobilization is likely due to the trauma of the regime's violent crackdown against its 2008 protest movement and fear of repeating similar bloodshed. For example, Sami Amroussia, a leftist opposition activist, affirmed that when the UGTT organized a protest on 12 January 2011, 'not even twenty people participated in it, because [most citizens of Gafsa] were afraid'. Interview with Sami Amroussia, Gafsa, 23 June 2016.

[35] Interview with Zakaria, Gafsa, 24 June 2016.

One of the consequences, he elaborated, is that Sidi Bouzid is full of 'illegals'. Zakaria affirmed that this tendency stands in stark contrast to Gafsa's reliance on old family tribes, who protect the city's borders from unwanted people seeking to enter.[36] By denying Sidi Bouzid's people their Tunisian roots and citizenship, Zakaria sought to undermine the legitimacy of their revolutionary demands.

Zakaria's degrading remarks about his RCD counterparts in Sidi Bouzid and Kasserine illustrate the extent to which frictions burst out in the open during the uprising and have persisted between party members of different governorates, pitting those from regions with a large number of victims—who came to call for regime change—against those from areas with fewer or no deaths, who fervently rejected such demands, specifically at the mid-level and senior level. Zakaria's remarks also encapsulate many RCD activists' persistent denial of the people's plight in marginalized localities such as Sidi Bouzid and Kasserine. During interviews, many of them completely disregarded or downplayed the level of poverty and police violence endured in these regions.[37]

Whereas activists such as Zakaria were not shy in denouncing party followers who protested in Sidi Bouzid and Kasserine, many felt even more strongly about a minority of members who took to the streets in their own regions, where most continued to support the regime until the very end. For many of them, the 'treason' associated with protesting against Ben Ali was much more personal in their own governorates. Abdelaziz, a leader of the RCD's professional cells in Gafsa, is a case in point. Abdelaziz recounted that a few days before the departure of Ben Ali he saw Adil—a well-known local RCD journalist, who worked for the newspaper *Al-Chourouk*—joining the protest movement. Still in disbelief and horror over what he had witnessed that day, Abdelaziz, who, like many other former party officials, still daily frequents the same café in front of the former party headquarters in central Gafsa, stated:

> I was sitting here drinking my coffee when a spontaneous demonstration erupted that passed by the street. [Adil] walked in it [holding] a placard with the slogan 'Tunisia is free, free Tunisia' and 'the Rally needs to leave'. When I saw him I started crying.[38]

---

[36] Interview with Zakaria, Gafsa, 24 June 2016. Aside from calling the citizens of Sidi Bouzid or Kasserine 'Bedouin', 'Berber', and 'khorbech', many interviewees from rival governorates also denounced them as 'barbarian' or as *zebla* [trash].

[37] Zakaria even wrongly alleged that owing to the large number of card-carrying RCD members in Sidi Bouzid and Kasserine, people there used to receive a lot of money from the former President—who, he asserted, went to great lengths to develop Tunisia's interior and southern regions.

[38] Interview with Abdelaziz, Gafsa, 22 June 2016.

Abdelaziz's account of seeing a RCD 'brother'—not from Sidi Bouzid or Kasserine but from his own beloved city—take to the streets, and even challenge the ruling party, reflects the deep feeling of betrayal experienced by many former party members who still harbour a sense of allegiance to the RCD 'family'.[39] It is notable that despite his fierce condemnation of the demonstrations, Abdelaziz—like many other RCD activists who were still dedicated to the regime and the ruling party during the uprising—did not do much to counter them, for example, by talking to the protesters or trying to initiate rallies in favour of the President. Indeed, party followers launched few pro–Ben Ali activities. The following section discusses why their endeavours remained so limited and the RCD's mobilization potential eroded—a factor crucial to understanding the President's departure on 14 January 2011—as well as the ways a minority of activists still sought to counter the demonstration.

Sidelined loyalists

When the revolts erupted in mid-December, some RCD members who were still loyal to the regime initially sought to counter the protesters by reporting their identities to the security forces.[40] Particularly prevalent amongst these were student leaders at universities and lumpen activists of local cells and Neighbourhood Committees, whose tasks included monitoring dissidents and reporting 'suspicious' activities. For example, Foued—a former member of the RCD student Executive Committee—explained that 'we tried at the beginning to control the demonstrations by going to the police and telling them who took part in them'.[41] Former student leader Ezzeddine confirmed such activities, stating that initially 'some youth activists and RCD members of neighbourhood cells [prepared] lists of the protesters [and gave them] to the police'. Thereby they hoped to become closer to the RCD powerbrokers: '[They] wanted to show to the leaders that they are active, that they are servants of Ben Ali and the RCD', Ezzeddine affirmed.[42] However, such endeavours were generally limited to the first week of the protests and became impossible once they grew in magnitude.

---

[39] In an attempt to explain why Adil joined the protests, Abdelaziz suggested that he may not have been a 'real' Destourian but rather an Islamist who infiltrated the RCD.

[40] Note that when the protests first erupted, the confidence of many loyal RCD students was bolstered by the fact that only days before they had scored a landslide victory in the university council elections—even if the results were obviously rigged.

[41] Interview with Foued, Tunis, 30 September 2015.

[42] Interview with Ezzeddine, Skype, 12 June 2016.

Ben Ali, for his part, seemed not to consider that the apparently limited nature of the RCD's pro-regime pursuits posed a problem. Indeed, until the last days of the uprising, Ben Ali never asked the RCD to launch any particular activities, such as rallies in his defence. This may have reflected a fear that this would empower rivals in the party but also illustrates his erroneous belief that he could control the riots through a security response alone, just as he had done in Gafsa in 2008.[43] Ben Ali's decision not to reach out to the RCD early on likely affected the direction of subsequent events: the party's marginalization further divided the RCD and pushed even loyal activists—who were dismayed the President did not see any role for them—into resignation. It was a major miscalculation on the part of Ben Ali and illustrates the extent to which the RCD completely lost its role of ensuring persistent information flow—one of the most important functions of ruling parties in authoritarian regimes[44]—in that it failed to inform the President of the severity of the deteriorating situation on the ground. Indeed, had the President involved RCD activists—possibly even offering concessions to disgruntled officials—this would have kept the party much more united. And this would have signalled that Ben Ali still enjoyed legitimacy within his own ranks, hence likely limiting inner regime defections and attempts to counter him.

Interviewees who were in touch with the President during the uprising typically stated that Ben Ali initially believed he would be able to gain control over the demonstrations in a matter of days.[45] As a consequence, the President, who was in the middle of a family holiday in Dubai when the protests first erupted, returned to Tunis only on 28 December 2010, when protests were fast increasing in magnitude and had even reached the capital city. Even then, the President appeared relatively unconcerned when his plane arrived at the Tunis–Carthage International Airport. Nabil Chettaoui, former Director of Tunisair, the company that provided Ben Ali's presidential plane, whose job included greeting the President upon his arrival at the airport, remembered:

When [Ben Ali] came out of the presidential plane he appeared very relaxed. . . . Together with some colleagues, I stood in front of the plane and we were surprised. Generally, Ben Ali does not like social movements.

[43] Interview with Mohamed Ghariani, Tunis, 27 May 2016.
[44] For an example of how ruling party officials sought to manage the flow of information internally, see Dariusz Magier, 'Political Party Archives: The System of Recording and Conveying Information in Local Structures of the Communist Party in Poland's Biała Podlaska Province, from 1975 to 1989', *Archival Science*, 2018, 18, 4, pp. 279–290.
[45] Interview with Mohamed Ghariani, Tunis, 27 May 2016.

When there is a problem, he is annoyed. So we expected that he would be annoyed when leaving the plane, because of the demonstrations.... We didn't understand.[46]

In the days following his return, Ben Ali mostly coordinated with the defence and security establishment. Ghariani recalled that 'Ben Ali managed the crisis essentially with the Interior Minister, the Defence Minister, and his principal [advisers].' In addition, Ben Ali officials bolstered pro-regime propaganda, which was spread through traditional media outlets as well as the internet in response to the central role social media was playing in the rapid growth of the protest movement.[47] More than ever before, the RCD's official publications praised the President's many achievements, whilst entirely ignoring the fact that demonstrations had erupted in the south—a strategy also pursued by other regime mouthpieces. State propaganda at the time of the uprising appeared particularly cynical, given that 2010 was the United Nations International Year of Youth, an initiative widely publicized in the country because it had been launched by the UN's Tunisian representatives.[48] Thus, on the first anniversary of the adoption of the Tunisian initiative, which happened to be the day after the self-immolation of Bouazizi, events were staged throughout the country to celebrate Ben Ali's supposedly 'avant-gardist approach' vis-à-vis young people.[49] *Le Renouveau* lauded 'the forward-looking vision of the head of state and the particular interest he has in promoting the youth,'[50] and media outlets throughout the country kept reiterating this narrative.

A prime undertaking of some party figureheads was to continue to propagate an overall picture of law and order and widespread support for Ben Ali, even at a time when many political analysts feared the turmoil might eventually lead to a civil war. Throughout the uprising, *Le Renouveau* continued to publish articles on a daily basis detailing the many 'honourable' events supposedly taking place in favour of Ben Ali and his RCD, even in remote and marginalized locations in the south and the interior. However, when asking specific RCD activists about events *Le Renouveau* wrote they had participated in, it was

---

[46] Interview with Nabil Chettaoui, Tunis, 29 June 2016.

[47] See, for more details, Muzammil M. Hussain and Philip N. Howard, 'What Best Explains Successful Protest Cascades? ICTs and the Fuzzy Causes of the Arab Spring', *International Studies Review*, 2013, 15, 1, pp. 48–66; Sherry Lowrance, 'Was the Revolution Tweeted? Social Media and the Jasmine Revolution in Tunisia', *Digest of Middle East Studies*, 2016, 25, 1, pp. 155–176.

[48] 'Tunisia: UN Proclamation of 2010 International Youth Year—President Ben Ali Sends Message of Consideration to General Assembly President', *AllAfrica*, 22 December 2009, https://allafrica.com/stories/200912221137.html, last accessed 5 February 2022.

[49] 'Année Internationale de la Jeunesse: La Consécration d'une Démarche Avant-Gardiste', *Le Renouveau*, 19 December 2010, p. 8.

[50] Ibid.

not uncommon for them to have no recollection of them at all, revealing that the extent of pro–Ben Ali activism was often amplified and sometimes staged. This was even the case at the level of the RCD Political Bureau. Indeed, in several articles *Le Renouveau* mentioned activities and meetings of the Political Bureau, but in interviews its members had often no memory of them whatsoever.[51]

In late December, official media outlets switched from a strategy of ignoring the protests to one of vilifying them whilst celebrating the economic concessions the President announced he would make to some marginalized governorates.[52] Naturally, many high-ranking party officials participated in this regime propaganda, trying very hard to discredit the demonstrations and laud Ben Ali. The office of the Chamber of Deputies, dominated by the RCD, released a statement denouncing 'all forms of violence, anarchy, and irresponsible behaviour' and 'the slander campaign orchestrated against Tunisia'.[53] The statement also affirmed the deputies' 'complete commitment to the reform choices of President Ben Ali and cohesion around his person'.[54] For his part, Ghariani, the only RCD official who visited Sidi Bouzid during the uprising, on 24 December, declared in a speech he held in the governorate that 'Tunisia rejects . . . the attempts of opponents to exploit isolated incidents in order to question the wider achievements in the country'.[55] It is noteworthy that a picture of the Sidi Bouzid visit published in *Le Renouveau* shows that only roughly fifty people attended his speech,[56] illustrating the degree to which the party's support base had eroded in the southern governorate. By contrast, elite figures firmly stood by Ben Ali—at least for the time being.

When asked in more detail about the nature of the activities he pursued at the time of the uprising, Ghariani claimed he had only talked to the demonstrators and tried to calm the situation. Most RCD interviewees delivered a very similar, almost mechanical-sounding response to the same question, suggesting they may have prepared it in advance; their actual activities may have

---

[51] Interviews with Kamel Morjane, Tunis, 26 May 2016; Fouad Mebazaa, Tunis, 30 May 2016.

[52] For example, on 25 December 2010, *Le Renouveau* announced that Sidi Bouzid was awarded three development projects worth 15 million TND and creating 698 jobs. Also, Kasserine was awarded a series of projects, including an industrial park. For details, see 'Sidi Bouzid: Signature de Trois Projets de Développement Intégré pour un Investissement de 15 MD', *Le Renouveau*, 25 December 2010, p. 3; 'Plan de Développement des Gouvernorats de l'Intérieur: Une Première Tranche de Projets au Profit de la Région de Kasserine', *Le Renouveau*, 25 December 2010, p. 2.

[53] 'Le Bureau de la Chambre des Députés Dénonce les Campagnes Calomnieuses Orchestrées Contre la Tunisie', *Le Renouveau*, 28 December 2010, p. 3.

[54] Ibid.

[55] 'M. Mohamed Ghariani Préside un Meeting à Sidi Bouzid', *Le Renouveau*, 25 December 2010, p. 3.

[56] Ibid.

been more extensive. Moreover, it is questionable whether any of them actually talked directly to the protesters as they claim; many probably stayed away from the demonstrations as they feared for their own safety, especially once the protests grew in magnitude. An interview with Akram Sebri, the Secretary General of the RCD youth at the time of the uprising—who was under tremendous pressure, given that many of the party's approximately 350,000 youth members joined the protests—further suggests this.[57] Sebri initially affirmed the only activism he pursued during the uprising was to 'try to calm the demonstrations . . . by peaceful means, [such as] communication, dialogue, and negotiations', stressing that '[RCD activists] were not allowed to do anything against the protesters'. Yet in the course of the interview, he conceded that even during the height of the unrest, all party leaders kept working at the RCD headquarters, situated on Avenue Mohamed V in central Tunis, where they sought to come up with various responses to the upheaval. He stated:

> Every time we had a new situation, we [leaders] met to decide [what to do about it]. Sometimes we met two or three times per day. . . . The atmosphere was characterized by panic, because the situation was entirely new, we never lived a similar experience. As a result, the decisions were characterized by a lot of panic.[58]

Sebri's admission that RCD leaders met several times per day to coordinate possible party responses to new developments in the uprising shows that elite figures continued to support Ben Ali, though they were increasingly distressed. This raises the question as to what they might have decided. Many of their endeavours were likely related to damage control. For example, many RCD followers who joined the protests said that videos and pictures of known party activists in the demonstrations were rapidly taken down from the web, probably because RCD leaders believed they might encourage even more of their own to join the riots.[59] Thus, the party elite in Tunis may have been involved in developing strategies to identify RCD members in videos and pictures to help block them online. Moreover, Sebri's insistence that the party leadership panicked during the unrest reveals the high level of uncertainty during the unrest, which may have led some officials to resort to 'harsher' measures in an attempt to contain the protests. This could have involved identifying and threatening central figures in the demonstrations. Some RCD activists

---

[57] Interview with Akram Sebri, Tunis, 26 May 2016.
[58] Ibid.
[59] Interview with Ezzeddine, Skype, 12 June 2016.

have also been accused of attacking protesters on the streets. But even if some assaults on protesters occurred, they likely constituted isolated instances, as most RCD activists certainly did not dare to confront the far more numerous demonstrators.

The old guard's revenge

Unlike the RCD headquarters in Tunis, many of the party's regional chapters were completely deserted two weeks into the uprising, even in fairly stable governorates with few or no victims and where limited numbers of people took to the streets. In Gafsa, for example, party activists recalled bitterly that, two weeks after the protests erupted, the RCD's main representative there—a Ben Ali family associate—left his office in the regional headquarters. He never returned, so they had nobody to instruct them how to respond to the upheaval. The same happened in Jendouba, where most mid-level officials vehemently denounced the uprising, especially once protesters called for the fall of the regime, which threatened to undermine the elevated social status they held in the city. At the same time, they were frustrated that their party leaders did not even have the courtesy to tell them what to do—if anything—in response to the protests. They felt completely marginalized and made redundant and this at a critical point in the party's history.

This absence of communication owed to the deeper structural fissures within the RCD between the Ben Ali family associates who held positions as regional party chiefs and the historic party leaders who had been cast aside. In defiance of what they perceived to be degrading treatment by their leadership, the old guard did not bother trying to stage pro-regime activities such as local rallies. In fact, many historic figures believed that by remaining passive, they would send a signal conveying that they also wanted things to change.[60] This attitude has become known amongst former RCD ranks as 'a form of silent protest'.[61] This form of contention is similar to the support party officials in marginalized governorates or regions with many victims evinced towards the protesters—a stance driven there by socioeconomic disenfranchisement and the immediacy of the horrors of the repression. In other regions, figures of the old guard engaged in passive resistance more explicitly to protest the enormous sway the Trabelsi family and their associates had come to wield over the party, a dynamic that had strongly diminished their own political

[60] Interview with Khalil, Jendouba, 29 May 2016
[61] Interview with Ezzeddine, Skype, 12 June 2016.

and economic influence. The general turmoil in the country provided them with a rare opportunity to display their discontent without fear of sanctions or reprisal.

The old guard hoped their passive stance would put pressure on the regime, forcing its powerbrokers to rethink the role of the RCD, as well as how nominations within the party were being handled. Khalil, the party cell leader from Jendouba who so fervently denounced the uprising, bitterly recalled that during the protests he and his colleagues 'waited for Ben Ali to make adjustments, for him to do something new for the party, for the country. But he was busy with his family, his son, and tourism [in Dubai]!'[62] Like many RCD activists from prominent Destourian families, Khalil especially denounced the role of Ghariani within the party, who he said 'was worth nothing' and was 'not suited to become Secretary General'. In particular, Khalil criticized Ghariani for being close to the Ben Ali family, especially to Leila and Sakher el-Materi. Many also did not hold Ghariani in high esteem because he came from a simple background, in contrast to figures from influential families and independence fighters who used to dominate the party leadership. They wanted a party leader they considered more respectable.

It is important to emphasize yet again that despite their fierce disapproval of many developments within the Ben Ali regime, figures such as Khalil never questioned the basis of its existence or that of the party. They erred on the conservative side of the protest movement, and the passive resistance in which they engaged was mainly a complaint against the marginalization of key Destourian activists in favour of simple family puppets. Importantly, many thought it appropriate to remain silent because they did not believe their passive stance would pose a threat to Ben Ali's power base or the existence of the RCD. Indeed, after almost twenty-five years under Ben Ali, most Tunisians never seriously believed the President could be forced to give up power, let alone through pressure from the streets. The Tunisian regime was the first one to fall in 2011—there was not yet an Arab Spring precedent. As Hassouna Nasfi, the former RCD student leader who hails from Gabes, elaborated: 'not even 1% [of the people] believed that the President would leave the country'.[63] Indeed, it is doubtful whether the old guard would even have pursued a silent protest had they suspected what might come next, that is, Ben Ali leaving the country and shortly afterwards the RCD being dissolved. Their contentious intentions, in fact, stood in contrast with the actual outcomes of the

[62] Interview with Khalil, Jendouba, 29 May 2016.
[63] Interview with Hassouna Nasfi, Bardo, 24 May 2016.

uprising.[64] The goal of their passive resistance was to boost their own standing and leverage—not to destroy its very basis.

Eroding countermobilization

Just as many RCD officials overestimated the stability of the regime, Ben Ali inaccurately evaluated the extent of his own power base and capacity to mobilize his constituency, if need be. Whilst promising economic concessions, in two speeches the President infamously emphasized that the uprising owed to 'false and unchecked allegations', constituted instances of 'fabrication and defamation',[65] and was engineered by 'a small group of hostile elements who are offended by the success of Tunisia'.[66] Faced with mounting protests, on 13 January 2011, Ben Ali took a slightly more conciliatory stance. He claimed he had 'understood' the people and would establish an 'independent commission . . . to look into corruption, bribery, and the mistakes of officials'. He declared there was 'no presidency for life' and that he had been 'misled' by some people who were 'hiding the truth from [him]'.[67] Yet he refrained from explicitly implicating the Trabelsis, thereby neglecting a key grievance of wide sections of society, including from figures within the regime, who despised the monopolization of resources by Ben Ali's relatives and their cronies. Many RCD followers who engaged in passive resistance or joined the protests said they were waiting for the President to do something about his most corrupt relatives, such as Belhassen.

In an attempt to convey an image of popular support, on 11 January 2011, Ben Ali, for the first time, tasked RCD officials with organizing rallies to counter the anti-regime protests taking place on Avenue Habib Bourguiba, the main street in downtown Tunis, located in front of the Interior Ministry. Buses carried willing activists to the city centre, but most ended up joining

---

[64] For a detailed analysis of the importance of distinguishing revolutionary intentions from outcomes, see Charles Tilly, *From Mobilization to Revolution*, Reading, MA: Addison-Wesley, 1978, pp. 189–222.

[65] English transcript of Ben Ali's speech of 27 December 2010. For details, see 'Tunisia: Speech by President Ben Ali', *al-Bab*, n.d., http://al-bab.com/documents-section/tunisia-speech-president-ben-ali, last accessed 3 August 2016.

[66] English transcript of Ben Ali's speech of 10 January 2011. For details, see 'Tunisia: Speech by President Ben Ali', *al-Bab*, n.d., http://al-bab.com/documents-section/tunisia-speech-president-ben-ali-0, last accessed 3 August 2016.

[67] Amjadrus, 'The Last Speech of Bin Ali', YouTube, 17 January 2011, https://www.youtube.com/watch?v=kANXV_onYhQ, last accessed 23 September 2018.

the protesters when they saw the massive crowd of angry people.[68] They likely feared clashes with the far more numerous anti-regime camp. This 'fragmentation, defection, and loss of confidence' within authoritarian regimes typically occurs alongside 'the increasingly large and frequent demonstrations of the masses'.[69]

The crumbling of the regime's support base was facilitated as few people in the pro-Ben Ali camp were actually fervent supporters of the President. Many were, in fact, lumpen activists, who did not have strong loyalties and likely had initially joined the pro-regime rally because of the incentives provided to them, such as free food and beverages, possibly even money.[70] The pro–Ben Ali crowd on Avenue Habib Bourguiba thus quickly evaporated, showing that the President's capacity to mobilize his own constituency—one of the most important sources of political capital on which dictators rely—had completely eroded. On 12 January 2011, RCD officials in Sousse sought to stage another rally to denounce 'the violent incidents and troubles' in the country, but pictures of the event suggest they managed to gather up to 100 people—at most.[71] Further pro-regime protests were organized on the evening of Ben Ali's 13 January speech. Scholars Abdelaziz Belkhodja and Tarak Cheikhrouhou attested that:

> hundreds of [rented cars] were driven in the streets (which were deserted because of the curfew) honking loudly, [the supposed festivity] underpinned by songs, portraits [of the President], and flags. In order to influence foreign diplomats, groups also drove to neighbourhoods in which ambassadorial residencies of influential countries were located. . . . At the windows, dazed citizens watched them. Some of them joined the staged euphoria. But realising that the scenario was everywhere the same, internet users quickly unveiled the masquerade on social media.[72]

The fact that the protesters drove in rental cars to hide their identities illustrates the extent to which publicly rallying for Ben Ali constituted a key security

---

[68] Interviews with RCD activists who observed the protests, including Selim, Regueb, Sidi Bouzid governorate, 27 June 2016.

[69] Rasma Karklins and Roger Petersen, 'Decision Calculus of Protesters and Regimes: Eastern Europe 1989', Journal of Politics, 1993, 55, 3, p. 589.

[70] Ghariani confirmed that protesters received free food and beverages but denied they were paid. Interview with Mohamed Ghariani, Tunis, 27 May 2016.

[71] 'À Sousse: Marche Populaire Imposante de Dénonciation des Actes de Violence et de Troubles', Le Renouveau, 13 January 2011, p. 5.

[72] Abdelaziz Belkhodja and Tarak Cheikhrouhou, 14 Janvier: L'Enquête, Tunis: Apollonia Editions, 2013, p. 51.

risk, even after the ostensible reforms he had announced. And even this brief moment of staged enthusiasm on 13 January 2011 evaporated later in the evening when the news broke that on that day alone, thirty-nine Tunisians had been killed.[73]

The next day, confrontations between the police and protesters risked culminating in a bloodbath. Particularly worrying was the fact that security forces were running out of tear gas, meaning they would soon have no other option than to resort to live bullets to protect sensitive sites. At around 2 pm on 14 January 2011, protesters stormed an administrative subdivision of the Interior Ministry situated a few hundred metres from its headquarters. Around the same time, the Bouchoucha jail in Tunis city centre, where many political prisoners were held, came under siege. Authorities feared that a great number of arms and explosives stocked at the Bouchoucha zone would fall into the hands of the protesters. Concurrently, an unprecedented mass of several tens of thousands of people came together on Avenue Habib Bourguiba, chanting the famous slogan *Al-sha'b yurid isqat al-nizam!*—'The people want the fall of the regime!' It is worth mentioning that their anger contrasted with the pragmatism of key opposition party leaders, who proclaimed they welcomed the reforms Ben Ali had announced the previous evening.[74] Ghariani said he had been in touch with figures from opposition parties and that many of them had agreed to participate in a live political debate, scheduled to air the evening of 14 January from al-Wataniya—Tunisia's main public television channel—an initiative meant to bestow substance on the reforms announced by the President the previous night.[75]

Most protesters, however, became even more enraged by such political stunts, which did not answer their demands but rather reflected the extent to which the political class was detached from the concerns of the population. Tasked once again with organizing counterdemonstrations that day, Ghariani was afraid the situation on the ground might escalate. If RCD activists were driven to Avenue Habib Bourguiba, he feared, they would be confronted by an unparalleled crowd of furious protesters, and major clashes between them might ensue.[76] Knowing that security forces were running short of tear gas and that live bullets would be the next step, Ghariani panicked. He repeatedly tried

[73] Ibid.
[74] For example, Nejib Chebbi said Ben Ali's speech was 'important politically and corresponds to the expectations of civil society and the opposition'. Mustapha Ben Jaafar declared that the speech 'opens up possibilities'. For details, see 'Tunisian Opposition Welcomes President Ben Ali's Pledge', *BBC*, 14 January 2011, http://www.bbc.co.uk/news/world-africa-12188439, last accessed 3 August 2016.
[75] Interview with Mohamed Ghariani, Tunis, 27 May 2016.
[76] Ibid.

to phone Ben Ali to receive instructions about what to do, but the President never answered his calls.[77] Ghariani consequently decided to coordinate with Ahmed Friaa, the Interior Minister;[78] they reportedly agreed to cancel the rallies.[79] The fact that Ben Ali did not even bother to take Ghariani's calls illustrates the extent to which he clearly did not consider the RCD a priority in his endeavours to gain control over the unfolding chaos—in retrospect, a severe miscalculation. As a consequence, the party's potential for countermobilization completely dissolved. In the midst of the turmoil, some angry protesters sought to take matters into their own hands. The Trabelsis were a major target.

Where are the Trabelsis?

Popular resentment towards the Trabelsis was exacerbated by prominent dissident blogs, such as *Nawaat*, publishing increasing volumes of information about their corruption and nepotism in the weeks and months prior to the uprising, often using Wikileaks as a key source. One article, posted two days before Bouazizi's self-immolation, highlighted that 'of the 22 diplomatic cables about Tunisia that are already available, three talk about Sakher el-Materi alone.'[80] The piece, which features a French translation of one of the US embassy cables about Ben Ali's son-in-law and highlights his life of 'great wealth and excess',[81] was widely shared on social media during the uprising, reinforcing protesters' contempt for the Trabelsi clan. Many Tunisian dissident sites were almost exclusively devoted to sharing incriminating information about Leila's relatives.[82] Some demonstrators marched with placards in protest against the family, sometimes bearing the question: 'Where are the

---

[77] Ibid.

[78] On 12 January 2014, Ben Ali sacked Interior Minister Rafik Haj Kacem and replaced him with Ahmed Friaa, a member of the RCD Central Committee.

[79] RCD activists told me they were informed by text message that the rallies were cancelled (e.g., interview with Hassouna Nasfi, Bardo, 24 May 2016). It is noteworthy that Ghariani sought to take sole credit for having recalled the protesters. He affirmed that he 'took his responsibility' and thereby prevented a bloodbath. Interview with Mohamed Ghariani, Tunis, 27 May 2016.

[80] 'Tunileaks—Tunisie: Un Diner avec Sakhr El Matri [Traduction]', *Nawaat*, 15 December 2010, https://nawaat.org/portail/2010/12/15/tunileaks-tunisie-un-diner-avec-sakhr-el-matri-traduction/, last accessed 9 August 2016.

[81] The US embassy in Tunis cable translated on *Nawaat* is titled 'Tunisia: Dinner with Sakher el-Materi' (09TUNIS516_a, classification: secret) and is available on Wikileaks.

[82] For details, see 'Les Magouilles des Ben Ali, Trabelsi, Materi and Co', 'Tunisie: Comment s'Enrichit le Clan Ben Ali?', and 'Trabelsi Lorgne sur les Casinos', all published on 11 January 2011, *Al Hiwar*, http://www.alhiwar.net/ShowNews.php?Tnd=13204, last accessed 9 August 2016.

Trabelsis?'[83] in illustration of the extent to which finding and punishing key members of Ben Ali's family became a central concern.

Well aware that they constituted a main target of the protesters, the Trabelsis began to panic. One of them—Nejia Jeridi-Trabelsi, the mother of Imed Trabelsi, who was married to Leila's brother Naceur—told me that during the uprising, they 'lived in fear and were in shock'.[84] Their anxiety seems to have been so great they even temporarily forgot about some of their internal frictions and power struggles. Particularly unsettling to many was that Ben Ali tried very hard to avoid contact with the most notoriously corrupt family members, including Belhassen, well aware that being seen with key members of the clan would only enflame further opposition to his rule. Rather, Ben Ali sought rapprochement with family members of his first wife, Naima, who were much more accepted by the people. Ghariani remembered that at the time of the uprising:

[The family] of Naima tried to push Ben Ali to distance himself from Leila and her brothers. . . . It was a conflict between the [former and the current] wife, a conflict between two families. It was . . . presented as a conflict between democrats and non-democrats. However, in reality it was a conflict of interests.[85]

Naima's family, particularly Ben Ali's eldest daughter, Cyrine, and her husband Marouane Mabrouk, sought to save the President by playing the reformist card, a strategy they certainly hoped would also enhance their own standing within the family hierarchy. Mabrouk even charged one of his close friends and business partners, the French Tunisian Hakim el-Karoui—a well-known public figure in both countries—with advising the President directly on how to manage the crisis. El-Karoui sent two letters to the President on 12 and 14 January 2011.[86] In the first letter, he recommends that Ben Ali 'send a clear and strong signal about those who claim themselves to be part of [his] network and are at the origin of the injustice felt by the people', but stops short of referring directly to the Trabelsis. The second letter urges the President to get rid of his infamous adviser Abdelaziz Ben Dhia as well as demonstrate

---

[83] One placard with this slogan was captured in a picture shared by the blog *Nachoua*, 'La Révolution des Braves', http://www.nachoua.com/Jan-2011/Revolution.htm, last accessed 9 August 2016.

[84] Interview with Nejia Jeridi-Trabelsi, Tunis, 4 February 2017.

[85] Interview with Mohamed Ghariani, Tunis, 27 May 2016.

[86] A copy of the letters was published in Mathieu Magnaudeix and Lénaïg Bredoux, 'Hakim El Karoui a Conseillé Ben Ali Jusqu'au Bout', *Nawaat*, 8 February 2011, https://nawaat.org/portail/2011/02/08/hakim-el-karoui-a-conseille-ben-ali-jusquau-bout/, last accessed 9 August 2016.

that he is serious about combatting corruption. El-Karoui also suggests the President announce a government reshuffle to take place in the subsequent days. It is noteworthy that Mabrouk and Cyrine were also in touch with several key figures of the government to widen their influence. For example, Samir Abidi, then Communications Minister, said that Cyrine 'called him often' during the uprising. In one instance, Cyrine phoned him after security forces cracked down on a group of protesting intellectuals and artists on Avenue Habib Bourguiba, downtown Tunis. She reportedly said it was unacceptable that violence had been used against them and asked Abidi to do something about it.[87]

For his part, Mabrouk sought a rapprochement with Kamel Morjane—the distant Ben Ali relative who portrayed himself as a reformist figure and was well liked by Western diplomats. In a conversation with me, Morjane—who was Foreign Minister at the time—maintained that Mabrouk's role 'was very positive . . . he was encouraging [Ben Ali] to open up the government'.[88] Morjane said that Mabrouk 'called [him] many times from the presidency'—correspondence, he stressed, he 'didn't tell anybody [about] before'.[89] In particular, Morjane supported Mabrouk and el-Karoui's plan to reshuffle the government. Morjane's resignation from government on 13 January 2011 and public announcement on the morning of 14 January that a government of national union was 'feasible',[90] must be understood in this light. Indeed, Morjane probably believed that by putting some distance between himself and the unfolding of violent events, he would naturally emerge as one of the key leaders once the turmoil was under control. His resignation was not an instance of internecine contention but an attempt at authoritarian regeneration. A television debate with prominent opposition party figures, scheduled on al-Wataniya on the evening of 14 January 2011, was a sign that under the advice of Cyrine and Mabrouk, the President may indeed have introduced some new faces into government. However, given his poor record on democratization, it is unlikely that he had a genuine government of national unity in mind. Rather, he sought to bestow opposition figures with a limited voice in government in

---

[87] Samir Abidi said he suggested the Minister of Culture, Abderraouf el-Basti, receive the group of intellectuals and artists and apologize to them—a proposition the President supposedly accepted. Abidi affirmed the plan was to film the meeting to convey that the reforms the President had announced were finally bearing fruit. Interview with Samir Abidi, Tunis, 30 June 2016. Note that I was unable to independently confirm his account.

[88] Interview with Kamel Morjane, Tunis, 26 May 2016.

[89] Ibid.

[90] 'Tunisie: Gouvernement d'Union "Faisable"', Europe 1, 14 January 2011, http://www.europe1.fr/international/tunisie-gouvernement-d-union-faisable-e1-371903, last accessed 9 August 2016.

exchange for their support for the regime—authoritarian pacts other incumbents have used to re-establish regime stability, especially in times of crisis.[91]

Whilst relatives of Ben Ali's first wife clearly believed that they could save the President, and even lead the country once the turmoil was under control, the Trabelsis' anxiety grew day by day. Some family members feared the President might eventually be forced to arrest some of their own to calm the protesters. Their distress was exacerbated when some demonstrators decided to take things into their own hands by attacking the property of prominent members of their clan. Hedi Djilani—the head of UTICA, whose daughter was married to Belhassen Trabelsi—testified that 'on 13 January people came to burn my house. I was at home with my children and grandchildren. They wanted to burn all our houses.'[92]

In the midst of the rapidly accelerating hostility towards the Trabelsis, Sakher el-Materi decided to speak out during a parliamentary plenary session on 13 January, which was aired live in an attempt to legitimate Ben Ali's commitment to more transparency.[93] El-Materi took the opportunity to announce his 'joy' about the decisions taken by the President. He tried very hard to convey that he 'understood' the protesters, stressing that the government had failed 'to discuss with the youth'. He also affirmed that officials were to blame for the 'hatred' against them, urging them to welcome international journalists to Tunisia. By calling for these changes, el-Materi attempted to portray himself as a reformist figure along the lines of Cyrine, Mabrouk, and Morjane.[94] At the same time, el-Materi affirmed that Al Jazeera, which had covered the Tunisian uprising in great depth, was in receipt of 'wrong information'.[95] The fact that el-Materi sought to deny Al Jazeera agency reveals the limits of his reform endeavours and that his main reason for speaking out was to protect his own skin and that of his family.

Naturally, the broadcasting of el-Materi's speech on public television was deeply controversial at a time when security forces were cracking down

---

[91] During the Arab Uprisings, a range of incumbents launched liberalization reforms and bestowed a greater voice to the opposition in the hope of calming the protests, in some cases, such as in Algeria and Morocco, successfully. See, for details, Jason Brownlee, Tarek Masoud, and Andrew Reynolds, *The Arab Spring: Pathways of Repression and Reform*, Oxford: Oxford University Press, 2015.

[92] Interview with Hedi Djilani, Tunis, 6 February 2017.

[93] Information about el-Materi's speech was accessed via a video recording of it, which is available on YouTube. For details, see Rideaudur, 'Sakhr El Materi ne Sait pas Parler Arabe—13 Janvier—Tunisie', YouTube, 16 January 2011, https://www.youtube.com/watch?v=dCTJROhdm70, last accessed 9 August 2016.

[94] Mohamed Ghariani confirmed that during the uprising, 'Sakher played the card of being close to the others [Cyrine, Mabrouk, and Morjane], he wanted to play the role of a reformer.' Interview with Mohamed Ghariani, Tunis, 27 May 2016.

[95] Rideaudur, 'Sakhr El Materi ne Sait pas Parler Arabe—13 Janvier—Tunisie', YouTube, 16 January 2011, https://www.youtube.com/watch?v=dCTJROhdm70, last accessed 9 August 2016.

violently on protesters. Many people were quick to ridicule his performance on social media, suggesting that his speaking in Tunisian dialect in Parliament—where classical Arabic is the norm—was an indication of his low educational level.[96] Well aware of the controversy caused by el-Materi's speech, some deputies and ministers retrospectively pretended that it had also filled them with indignation. For example, Afif Chelbi, then Industry and Technology Minister, maintained that it caused 'tremendous tension between the members of the government and the MP [el-Materi]', adding that 'we believed that it was no longer sustainable that Ben Ali had members of his family in Parliament'.[97] However, there is no evidence that on 13 January 2011 anyone in Parliament dared to speak out against el-Materi or that the atmosphere there was tense because of his speech, as Chelbi claims.[98] Indeed, contrary to Chelbi's testimony, then Ettajdid deputy Tarek Chaabouni insisted in reference to el-Materi's discourse that 'nobody dared to say anything publicly about the family of Ben Ali, there was not a word of protest, not even a word!'[99] Moreover, Chaabouni suggested that the only unusual thing about that day was the extent of ministers' and deputies' confusion and distress, mentioning in passing that far from criticizing el-Materi's intervention, 'Afif Chelbi was running in the corridor asking me what was going on.'[100] These officials were increasingly panic-stricken and 'seeking behavioural cues from others', which is typical in moments of collective uncertainty.[101]

Ben Ali's decision not to distance himself from the Trabelsis in his 13 January 2011 speech, combined with the particularly high number of civilian deaths that day and with el-Materi's controversial speech, raised tensions in Tunisia to an unprecedented level. The conflict risked turning into a civil war. Out of fear of being targeted that night, many of Leila's relatives sought refuge in the President's Palace in Sidi Dhrif—even very distant family members who had never met one another.[102] Nejia Jeridi-Trabelsi said:

Cars of the military or the police attacked our houses.... It was organized....
They destroyed the doors of the houses and entered, taking all valuables....

---

[96] The previously referenced title of the YouTube video of el-Materi's speech in Parliament mockingly states: 'Sakhr El Materi does not know how to speak Arabic'. Note that during his speech, el-Materi regularly struggled to finish sentences, a dynamic that underscored his overall nervous appearance.

[97] Interview with Afif Chelbi, Tunis, 22 September 2015.

[98] Whilst videos of el-Materi's eight-minute intervention are widely available on social media, I was unable to find a recording of the entire plenary session of 13 January 2011.

[99] Interview with Tarek Chaabouni, Tunis, 1 October 2015.

[100] Ibid.

[101] Ivan Ermakoff, 'The Structure of Contingency', *American Journal of Sociology*, 2015, 121, 1, p. 100.

[102] Abdelaziz Belkhodja and Tarak Cheikhrouhou, *14 Janvier: L'Enquête*, Tunis: Apollonia Editions, 2013, p. 53.

The [masked men] took everything of value. After that they called upon the people to attack the houses. . . . Many of us sought protection at the palace.[103]

It is impossible to know for sure whether the men attacking the Trabelsi houses were indeed from the security forces; such suggestion was likely crafted to show they were unjustly targeted by powerful actors. It has, however, been established that some police officers turned a blind eye to the ransacking that subsequently occurred in their homes.[104] In distress, many family members fled their properties, sometimes in such a rush they did not even have time to take their passports with them.[105] The Trabelsis thought they had been left on their own and—fearing for their lives—many promptly decided to leave Tunisia the following day. At around noon on 14 January 2011, Belhassen Trabelsi asked an official at the Tunis–Carthage Airport to reserve him and his family seven places on the next flight leaving the country. In parallel, other Trabelsi family members prepared their escape. After those who had arrived empty handed were issued new passports by the palace staff, they left for the airport accompanied by the Intervention and Diplomatic Protection Group, an elite security unit charged with protecting the presidential family.[106]

Ben Ali's ousting

Whilst the Trabelsis were fleeing for their lives, Ben Ali decided to get his wife and children out of the country for a few days, which he believed was sufficient time to get the situation under control. Around noon on 14 January 2011, Director of State Protocol Mohsen Rhim called Nabil Chettaoui, the head of Tunisair, and asked him to prepare the presidential plane for Ben Ali's family, under the pretext they wished to perform the Umrah in Saudi Arabia. Chettaoui immediately phoned Ben Ali's personal pilot, Mahmoud Cheikhrouhou.[107] Cheikhrouhou told me that, although it would have typically taken him several days to prepare for such a trip, he was tasked with

---

[103] Interview with Nejia Jeridi-Trabelsi, Tunis, 4 February 2017.

[104] Florence Beaugé, 'Tunisie: Incertitude sur le Sort des Trabelsi après la Mise à Sac de Leurs Résidences', Le Monde, 14 January 2011, http://www.lemonde.fr/afrique/article/2011/01/14/les-residences-de-la-famille-trabelsi-a-tunis-mises-a-sac_1465757_3212.html, last accessed 10 August 2016.

[105] Abdelaziz Belkhodja and Tarak Cheikhrouhou, 14 Janvier: L'Enquête, Tunis: Apollonia Editions, 2013, p. 57.

[106] Ibid., pp. 57–58.

[107] Interview with Nabil Chettaoui, Tunis, 29 June 2016.

getting everything ready within three hours at most.[108] After Chettaoui's call, Cheikhrouhou left for the airport, where he met Ben Ali and his family. A particular challenge was that Leila—afraid of any attempts at sabotage—wished to keep the flight schedule and destination secret, even to airport control. As a result, Cheikhrouhou decided to pretend to fly to Djerba—an island in southern Tunisia—and, once he arrived there, ask the Libyan officials for authorization to enter their airspace and continue the flight via Egypt to Saudi Arabia.[109]

Whilst Cheikhrouhou prepared the plane for Ben Ali's close family, the Trabelsis were waiting only a few hundred metres away in the VIP lounge of the airport for their departure. Accompanied by the masked forces of the Intervention and Diplomatic Protection Group, their arrival had drawn much attention. Pictures of them at the airport were soon shared on social media, further igniting the spirit of the angry protesters. It is less known that news of the Trabelsis' attempt to leave the country also unnerved many members of an increasingly demoralized security force. For almost a month, police officers had been working relentlessly day and night. In some instances, their relatives had decided to join the protest movement, which the police had been ordered to suppress, putting many security officials in a very difficult position.[110] As a result, even high-ranking security figures were appalled when they learned the Trabelsis were about to escape. Lieutenant Colonel Samir Tarhouni, then Commander of Tunisia's Antiterrorism Brigade, recalled:

I knew that to 80% the revolution took place because of the corruption of this family. I had been convinced of this for a while. Like all Tunisians, I believed the problems [in the country] ran very deep, because I knew numerous things about [the family]. And when one knows these things from close by, one becomes convinced that every day will be worse than the preceding day.[111]

[108] Interview with Mahmoud Cheikhrouhou, Tunis, 1 July 2016.
[109] Ibid.
[110] Email interview with Hedi, the son of a high-ranking police officer in Gafsa who joined the protests, 30 May 2016.
[111] 'Témoignage du Colonel Major M. Samir Tarhouni sur le Déroulement des Événements du 14 Janvier 2011 à l'Aéroport de Tunis Carthage', in Abdeljelil Temimi (ed.), L'Observatoire de la Révolution Tunisienne, Tunis: Fondation Temimi pour la Recherche Scientifique et l'Information, 2015, p. 49.

He elaborated:

> We were about to shoot unarmed people and the entire family wanted to escape. In other words, those who are responsible for our situation wanted to leave the country.[112]

Tarhouni testified that together with a few colleagues he decided to head to the airport with the intention to arrest the Trabelsis. Indeed, video footage shows him looking for Ben Ali's relatives there.[113] Arriving at the airport around 2:20 p.m., the group began searching for the Trabelsis, who no longer appeared to be in the VIP lounge. Tarhouni's wife happened to work as a controller at the airport and informed him that a private plane was about to take off. However, when Tarhouni went to see it he only found Ben Ali's daughter Cyrine and her children, who were apparently also attempting to leave the capital for a few days, so he continued his search. The fact that few people cared about the departure of Cyrine illustrates the extent to which anger was directed almost exclusively towards Leila and her kin—not towards the family of the President's first wife.[114]

It is notable that while Tarhouni insisted that he planned on arresting the Trabelsis, other members of his group testified that they went to the airport merely to provide protection for the Trabelsis, not to arrest them—although it is possible that they later changed their stance. These contradictory testimonies show that many figures of Ben Ali's regime retrospectively sought to boost their revolutionary legitimacy by claiming they played a key role in his ousting, even if they probably didn't. The contradictory testimonies also highlight the increasing atmosphere of chaos and uncertainty at the airport. Many actors no longer knew where they politically stood and what others were up to. Amidst the turmoil, an increasing number of figures decided to act on their own behalf, in part depending on their interpretations of others' actions. The sudden insistence of Ali Seriati, Head of Presidential Security, that Ben Ali join his family on their trip to Saudi Arabia lends some credibility to this theory.

---

[112] Ibid., p. 52.

[113] Ibid., p. 53.

[114] It is noteworthy that some Ben Ali loyalists claim that Tarhouni's lack of interest in arresting Cyrine is evidence that he, in fact, acted on Ben Ali's orders, arguing that it was Ben Ali himself who had decided to arrest the Trabelsis. According to this narrative, Ben Ali was never aware of the great damage the Trabelsis inflicted on Tunisia, but once he realized it he immediately sought to correct his mistake. However, if Ben Ali had truly decided to arrest the Trabelsis to calm the protesters, he surely would have publicized and taken credit for it.

Indeed, Ben Ali's pilot, Cheikhrouhou, said that Seriati convinced the President at the very last minute to take off with his family by claiming he was no longer able to guarantee his security, given the mounting chaos at the airport.[115] Ben Ali—via a statement published by his lawyer—recounted the events as follows:

> On the morning of 14 January 2011, Ali Seriati . . . informed the President that . . . an officer from the Presidential Guard has been tasked with the assassination of the President. He added that the situation in the Tunisian capital is out of control. . . . Ali Seriati recommended to the President that he lets his wife and children board a plane that has been prepared to fly to Jedda. Later however, Seriati insisted that the President flies with his family to Jedda and stays there for a few hours until the security agencies . . . guarantee the security of the President. On the basis of this information, the President boarded the plane with his family members.[116]

Ben Ali agreed to leave, though he intended only to drop his family in Saudi Arabia and return to Tunis the next day. In the meantime, Seriati was tasked with investigating who had given the unauthorized order to arrest the Trabelsis.[117] Cheikhrouhou said that Seriati even had to unload his own luggage from the plane, as he had initially arranged to travel with the family to Djeddah. For his part, Seriati affirmed that he convinced Ben Ali to depart to avoid bloodshed; this statement could be interpreted as an implicit recognition that he was complicit in his ousting, but it may have been crafted retrospectively to protect himself from the revolutionaries.[118] Ben Ali and his family members, for their part, consider Seriati to be a key conspirator against the President.[119]

Around the same time that Ben Ali and his family took off, Rachid Ammar—Chief of Staff of the Tunisian Armed Forces, who had kept a low profile during

---

[115] Interview with Mahmoud Cheikhrouhou, Tunis, 1 July 2016. See also Noureddine Hlaoui, 'En Video, le 14 Janvier, Raconté par Ali Seriati', *Businessnews*, 27 July 2011, http://www.businessnews.com.tn/article,534,25864,1, last accessed 5 July 2018.

[116] 'Tasrih al-Ra'is Bin Ali—20 Huzayran 2011' ['Declaration of President Ben Ali—20 June 2011'], published via his lawyer, Akram 'Azuri, Beirut, 20 June 2011.

[117] Cheikhrouhou's description of the events reflects Ben Ali's own account of the circumstances of his departure. Interview with Nesrine Ben Ali, Viber, 6, 13, and 18 February 2017; 'Tasrih al-Ra'is Bin Ali—20 Huzayran 2011' ['Declaration of President Ben Ali—20 June 2011'], published via his lawyer, Akram 'Azuri, Beirut, 20 June 2011.

[118] Interview with Ahmed, an associate of Ali Seriati, Tunis, 8 February 2017.

[119] Interview with Nesrine Ben Ali, Viber, 13 February 2017.

the unrest—received a call from Defence Minister Ridha Grira, who reportedly asked him to provide protection for the Trabelsis.[120] Grira also ensured that Seriati, whom he probably believed to be behind a plot against the President, was arrested shortly after Ben Ali's departure.[121] Although at first sight, it may appear that Grira's actions were meant to protect the President, it is plausible that the Defence Minister was trying to prepare his own coup d'état, in which he wanted no one to interfere.

The unprecedented uncertainty caused by Ben Ali's departure—even if it was meant to be only temporary—incited a range of key actors to compete for the highest office. It provided figures, such as Grira, who wanted to safe their own skin, with an unprecedented opportunity to move against an increasingly isolated president.[122] Mancur Olsen has highlighted the intrinsic fragility of authoritarian leaders, whose survival very much depends on the perception that they are invincible. 'If the cadre observe a moment of vacillation, an incident of impotence, a division of leadership . . . all the power of an imposing regime can vanish in the night air.'[123] Ben Ali's departure exposed how vulnerable he was—to the extent he had easily been persuaded to leave his country amidst unprecedented political crisis. It is in this light that subsequent events of that evening must be understood. Shortly after the presidential plane took off, several high-ranking officials met at the Interior Ministry, where they collectively plotted to oust Ben Ali. Mohamed Ghannouchi, who attended the meeting, told me:

I was at the Interior Ministry with the Interior Minister, the Defence Minister, the Chief of Staff of the Tunisian Armed Forces, [and some] members of the national security council. We held a meeting [and decided] that we needed to enact constitutional provisions to replace Ben Ali.

[120] For example, 'Témoignage du Colonel Major M. Samir Tarhouni sur le Déroulement des Événements du 14 Janvier 2011 à l'Aéroport de Tunis Carthage', in Abdeljelil Temimi (ed.), L'Observatoire de la Révolution Tunisienne, Tunis: Fondation Temimi pour la Recherche Scientifique et l'Information, 2015, p. 56; Pierre Puchot, La Révolution Confisquée. Enquête sur la Transition Démocratique en Tunisie, Paris: Sindbad, 2012, p. 39.

[121] See, for details, Noureddine Hlaoui, 'En Video, le 14 Janvier, Raconté par Ali Seriati', Businessnews, 27 July 2011, http://www.businessnews.com.tn/article,534,25864,1 last accessed 5 July 2018.

[122] Contacted by me in July 2016, Grira, who was diagnosed with cancer, said that due to his medical treatment he was unfit for interviews.

[123] Mancur Olsen, 'The Logic of Collective Action in Soviet-Type Societies', Journal of Soviet Nationalities, 1990, 1, 2, p. 17.

Ghannouchi stressed that Grira was the person taking the lead in conspiring against Ben Ali:

> The Defence Minister affirmed in the presence of the Chief of Staff of the Tunisian Armed Forces and [the other] officials . . . that the army is not capable of guaranteeing the security of the President if he ever wants to return to the country. If [Ben Ali tried], there would be a bloodbath. That's what he declared.[124]

Under the pretence of being unable to protect the President, Grira pushed Ghannouchi to apply Article 56 of the constitution and announce that as the Prime Minister, he would take over power for a while—another key moment that launched a wider constitutional process that would formally oust Ben Ali.[125] Article 56 states that 'Should the President of the Republic fail, temporarily, to assume his duty, he can delegate, by Degree, his authorities to the Prime Minister but cannot dissolve the parliament.' Grira's decision to enact constitutional provisions to oust Ben Ali, even though they were not formally applicable (Ben Ali had not delegated power to Ghannouchi), recalls Ben Ali's own constitutional coup against Bourguiba in 1987. Everything was done to convey constitutional validity. Grira himself wished to keep a low profile, probably so as not to raise suspicions that he had a hand in Ben Ali's fall; as Defence Minister, he anyway already held the most influential position in the country and likely expected to emerge as a key figure in the aftermath of his ousting.

At 6:45 pm, in a short television statement on Channel Tunis 7, Ghannouchi declared: 'I provisionally take over the function of Interim President', elaborating that 'President Ben Ali was temporarily incapable of exercising power'.[126] Furious when hearing the statement, Ben Ali called Ghannouchi from the plane. He ordered him to take back what he had said on television so that

[124] Interview with Mohamed Ghannouchi, Tunis, 2 October 2015.

[125] Note that Ghannouchi pretended that it was he who had pushed for the application of Article 56; this is unlikely, given that Grira was the main person in charge. Interview with Mohamed Ghannouchi, Tunis, 2 October 2015. Ghannouchi's account has been internalized by most researchers and academics. See Pierre Puchot, '14 Janvier 2011 à Tunis: Le Jour où Ben Ali est Tombé', *Mediapart*, 10 November 2011, https://www.mediapart.fr/journal/international/071111/14-janvier-2011-tunis-le-jour-ou-ben-ali-est-tombe, last accessed 5 July 2018.

[126] For details, see 'Constitutional Debate after Ben Ali', *Al Jazeera*, 14 January 2011, http://www.aljazeera.com/news/africa/2011/01/2011114204942484776.html, last accessed 21 August 2016.

he could return to Tunisia, but Ghannouchi refused.[127] Whilst Ghannouchi now portrays himself as a key figure behind Ben Ali's departure, his refusal to follow Ben Ali's orders and retract his statement may not have been a willing one, given that he was a key associate of the President—his infamous 'yes-man'—with little political capital of his own. However, he had little hope of protecting Ben Ali and helping him return to Tunisia in the face of Grira's fierce determination to overthrow him, alongside the popular opposition against his rule.[128]

Soon after Ben Ali's plane arrived in Djeddah, his pilot, Cheikhrouhou, saw Ghannouchi's declaration on television. Bewildered, he called his boss, Chettaoui, the head of Tunisair. According to Chettaoui, Cheikhrouhou asked him what to do in response to Ghannouchi's unexpected announcement.[129] In contrast, the pilot stated that he explicitly told the head of Tunisair that he wished to return to Tunisia immediately and alone.[130] Chettaoui subsequently called Ghannouchi for instructions. He affirmed that Ghannouchi handed his call over to Defence Minister Grira, who was with him, and ordered Chettaoui to call the pilot back. Ghannouchi, for his part, claimed that he personally instructed Chettaoui that the pilot return to Tunisia without Ben Ali.[131] These contradictory statements illustrate, in part, the extent of chaos and uncertainty caused by Ben Ali's departure, prompting a range of actions by key figures, sometimes in parallel and without full knowledge of others' behaviours. But they also reveal how various figures seek to retrospectively bolster their legitimacy by claiming to have been decisive in Ben Ali's ousting, though most of them were actually just following orders. Of all their accounts, Chettaoui's is one of the most credible as he was only an interlocutor and thus had little at stake. After receiving Grira's orders, Chettaoui phoned Cheikhrouhou and ordered him to fly back to Tunis immediately. It is notable that Ben Ali could easily have prevented his pilot from returning, for example, by placing him under surveillance. The failure to do so cemented his ousting: Ben Ali had not only been tricked into leaving Tunisia but now no longer had his pilot to fly him home.[132]

---

[127] Interviews with Nesrine Ben Ali, Viber, 6 February 2017; Mohamed Ghannouchi, Tunis, 2 October 2015.

[128] Ghannouchi told me that Ben Ali even suggested Ghannouchi become Interim President until he returned to Tunisia.

[129] Interview with Nabil Chettaoui, Tunis, 29 June 2016.

[130] Interview with Mahmoud Cheikhrouhou, Tunis, 1 July 2016.

[131] Interview with Mohamed Ghannouchi, Tunis, 2 October 2015.

[132] Note that Ben Ali subsequently still tried to return to Tunisia. Indeed, in 2012, recorded phone conversations between him and several high officials, such as Mohamed Ghannouchi, were published on several Tunisian websites in which he tried to convince them to support him coming back. It took the

The dissolution of the RCD

Though Ben Ali intended only to drop his family in Saudi Arabia and then return to Tunisia, following his departure news outlets around the world proclaimed the success of Tunisia's 'revolution',[133] propagating the rumour that the President was 'forced to flee as protesters claim victory'.[134] The silence of key figures, such as Grira, behind the President's overthrow and the eruption of major demonstrations in other countries in the region reinforced the perception that it was solely people power that was behind Ben Ali's sudden 'escape'. Grira and Ghannouchi likely remained quiet about the details of the events on 14 January 2011 to protect themselves from accusations of having engineered a coup d'état. They believed they would naturally acquire key posts in the post–Ben Ali era, enabling them to reconfigure state and party to their own advantage.

However, Grira and Ghannouchi soon came to realize they were far from being in control of events. Immediately after Ghannouchi's televised speech on the evening of 14 January 2011, judges began to challenge the decision to evoke article 56 of the constitution to replace Ben Ali. A constitutional committee subsequently convened, deciding that instead article 57[135] applied, bestowing not the Prime Minister but the Head of Parliament, Fouad Mebazaa, with the post of Interim President. More importantly, Ben Ali's departure and the widespread belief in a 'Tunisian revolution' had energized demonstrators with new confidence; they had an epistemic impact in so far as they altered protesters' 'expectations about collective outcomes', which increased the 'likelihood of these outcomes'.[136]

An article published in *The Economist* reported that after the President left for Saudi Arabia, his 'party emerged as a new focus of pressure', with looting

---

international media until 2022 to pick up on this 'breaking' story. See, for details, Emir Nader, 'Secret Audio Sheds Light on Toppled Dictator's Frantic Last Hours', *BBC News*, 14 January 2022, https://www.bbc.co.uk/news/world-africa-59972545, last accessed 28 February 2022.

[133] See 'How a Fruit Seller Caused Revolution in Tunisia', *CNN*, 16 January 2011, http://edition.cnn.com/2011/WORLD/africa/01/16/tunisia.fruit.seller.bouazizi/, last accessed 24 August 2016.

[134] Angelique Chrisafis and Ian Black, 'Zine al-Abidine Ben Ali Forced to Flee Tunisia as Protesters Claim Victory', *The Guardian*, 15 January 2011, https://www.theguardian.com/world/2011/jan/14/tunisian-president-flees-country-protests, last accessed 10 August 2016.

[135] Article 57 of Tunisia's 1959 constitution states: 'should the office of President of the Republic become vacant because of death, resignation, or absolute disability', the Head of Parliament 'shall immediately be vested with the functions of Interim President of the Republic'.

[136] Ivan Ermakoff, 'The Structure of Contingency', *American Journal of Sociology*, 2015, 121, 1, p. 80.

of local RCD offices occurring on a daily basis.[137] One protester on Avenue Habib Bourguiba proclaimed: 'After Ben Ali and his wife, we want to bring down his thieves.'[138] Another deplored that 'The regime's head has been cut off but the beast is still breathing.'[139] Naturally, RCD, activists were panic-stricken when they realized they suddenly constituted the centre of attention for many protesters. Many had remained quiet—or even supported the protests—in the hope they could force Ben Ali to distance himself from the Trabelsis and rethink how nominations were being handled within the party, never imagining that the RCD itself would eventually come under threat. Ezzeddine, the former party activist and self-proclaimed 'silent protester' in the uprising, maintained—still visibly horror-stricken—that after Ben Ali left, everybody from the RCD was 'attacked . . . I believed it was the beginning of a civil war.'[140] Like many other party activists, Ezzeddine decided not to leave his house for a couple of weeks for fear of his safety.

In an attempt to appease the protesters' appetite for even more wide-ranging change, Ghannouchi announced the establishment of independent commissions to investigate corruption and human rights abuses and promised liberalizing political reforms, including abolishing censorship, releasing political prisoners, and organizing free elections within six months. However, when forming a government of national unity on 17 January 2011, his decision to retain RCD officials in key posts and to hand only minor positions to the legal opposition brought into question his commitment to reform and provoked further protests. Notably, he nominated ministers of the RCD leftists and old guard—such as Moncer Rouissi and Mohamed Jegham—who were marginalized in the 1990s and 2000s but now sought to stage a political comeback. Their appointments led four of the ministers from the political opposition to resign from the cabinet just one day after its creation. Ghannouchi sought to defend the inclusion of former regime officials by affirming that their 'great expertise' was 'needed in this phase'; he called on the people to give them 'a chance so that [they] can put in place this ambitious programme of reform'[141]—a discourse echoing Ben Ali's praise of technocrats to

---

[137] 'Ali Baba Gone, But What About the 40 Thieves?', *The Economist*, 20 January 2011, http://www.economist.com/node/17959620, last accessed 24 August 2016.

[138] Quoted in Lin Noueihed and Christian Low, 'Police Fire Shots to Disperse New Tunis Protest', *Reuters*, 20 January 2011, http://in.reuters.com/article/idINIndia-54283420110120, last accessed 24 August 2016.

[139] Quoted in Angelique Chrisafis, 'Tunisia Protest Town Fears for Unfinished Revolution', *The Guardian*, 7 February 2011, https://www.theguardian.com/world/2011/feb/07/tunisia-protest-kasserine-unfinished-revolution, last accessed 24 August 2016.

[140] Interview with Ezzeddine, Skype, 12 June 2016.

[141] Quoted in 'Tunisie: Le RCD Radie Ben Ali de Ses Rangs', *Le Monde*, 18 January 2011, http://www.lemonde.fr/tunisie/article/2011/01/18/tunisie-le-gouvernement-de-transition-de-plus-en-plus-conteste_1467084_1466522.html, last accessed 24 August 2016.

justify his authoritarian policies. In a similar vein, RCD officials evoked their supposedly superior political experience and high profile to justify their decision to join the government. Kamel Morjane explained that shortly after Ben Ali left:

> I went to see the Prime Minister and he told me that he has to have a new government and he asked me to [join it]. . . . He insisted very much and especially he used an argument which I could not contradict. [Ghannouchi said] I cannot have a minister who doesn't know anybody and who isn't known to anybody. You have no choice [but] to stay with me. And I said in this case I accept.[142]

It is important to note that whilst protesters called for a complete overhaul of the regime and the dismantling of the RCD networks, important opposition parties such as the Progressive Democratic Party (PDP) defended the RCD members in government. A member of the PDP Executive Committee even went as far as to denounce the resignation of the four ministers from Ghannouchi's unity government as 'irresponsible'.[143] PDP officials only demanded that the RCD announce a separation between the party and the state—that is, the public administration and the presidency. They did not criticize the RCD filling of all key government posts,[144] thereby implicitly recognizing the Destour's persistent political leadership. Naturally, the perceived complicity of legal opposition forces such as the PDP in perpetuating the RCD's dominance further infuriated many people.

Demonstrators soon targeted the RCD headquarters on Avenue Mohamed V and tried to take it. In an attempt to counter the attacks on their party and discredit the protest movement, some RCD activists are believed to have paid militias to instigate further chaos. Bedma Askri, a lawyer from Kasserine, stated that a group of about 1,000 bandits assaulted public buildings in the rural city. She affirmed that 'The RCD paid criminals and thugs around 15 TND each to do this.'[145] Whilst it is impossible to verify this account independently, it is entirely plausible that some party figures sought to discredit the new authorities and their capacity to

---

[142] Interview with Kamel Morjane, Tunis, 26 May 2016.

[143] Angelique Chrisafis, 'Tunisia's Caretaker Government in Peril as Four Ministers Quit', *The Guardian*, 18 January 2011, https://www.theguardian.com/world/2011/jan/18/tunisia-caretaker-government-ministers-quit, last accessed 24 August 2016.

[144] Ibid.

[145] Quoted in Angelique Chrisafis, 'Tunisia Protest Town Fears for Unfinished Revolution', *The Guardian*, 7 February 2011, https://www.theguardian.com/world/2011/feb/07/tunisia-protest-kasserine-unfinished-revolution, last accessed 24 August 2016.

gain control of the turmoil. Ezzeddine remembered that after hearing of the President's departure, some of the most loyal party followers and family associates, who had defended Ben Ali until the very end, 'switched off their phones . . . and went into [hiding]'. He maintained that even within the RCD nobody was able to reach them.[146] Whilst many just sought to disappear until the situation calmed down, some figures may have tried to take matters into their own hands by organizing attacks on protesters.

However, it is unlikely that they coordinated with the RCD leaders in Tunis, who, as some observers affirmed, were mainly 'confused' and 'didn't understand anything of what was happening'.[147] Amidst the turmoil, Ghariani, for his part, quickly sought to jump on the revolutionary bandwagon to save his skin, bolster his own legitimacy, and protect the RCD. In official statements published in the days after Ben Ali left, party leaders, indeed, tried very hard to position themselves on the side of change, calling on their militants to 'continue to strengthen solidarity between the members of Tunisian society . . . and to work towards the construction of a new democracy, which excludes nobody'.[148] Moreover, an RCD statement declared that Tunisia's former President was henceforth banned from the party, as were six of the most powerful associates of his family. This divorce between Ben Ali's family and the party was a key demand of many of its own members. In addition, Mohamed Ghannouchi and Fouad Mebazaa officially resigned from the RCD in what the party announced was a step towards assuring 'separation between the institutions of the state and political parties'.[149] Subsequently, more RCD ministers and deputies left the party, which triggered the dissolution of its Political Bureau and Central Committee. However, the closure of some party structures was probably intended to be only a temporary measure to appease the protesters and calm the general atmosphere.

Aside from the pressure on the streets, the RCD leadership also came under fire from some of its own activists. In some governorates, particularly those that had seen a high number of victims and where the trauma of repression and violence still loomed large, the party's rank and file started calling for the

---

[146] Interview with Ezzeddine, Skype, 12 June 2016.

[147] Ibid. Note that Ezzeddine affirmed that he talked with Ghariani and other leaders several times in the period immediately following Ben Ali's departure.

[148] Cited in 'Tunisie: Dissolution du Bureau Politique du RCD', L'OBS, 20 January 2011, http://tempsreel.nouvelobs.com/monde/20110120.OBS6606/tunisie-dissolution-du-bureau-politique-du-rcd.html, last accessed 24 August 2016.

[149] Quoted in 'Tunisie: Le RCD Radie Ben Ali de Ses Rangs', Le Monde, 18 January 2011, http://www.lemonde.fr/tunisie/article/2011/01/18/tunisie-le-gouvernement-de-transition-de-plus-en-plus-conteste_1467084_1466522.html, last accessed 24 August 2016.

dissolution of the RCD. Muhammed al-Arabi al-Zuraibi, a Tunisian historian from Regueb, the rural town in Sidi Bouzid that suffered a particularly high number of casualties, observed:

15 January marked the beginning of loud demands for the dissolution of the ruling party in Regueb. . . . To advance and realise this demand, the idea of resignation was brought up for self-dissolution of the RCD. Therefore, a resignation form was drafted by some activists in Regueb. The [RCD] Secretary General of the federation responded to this demand on 19 January 2011, followed by other members, including dozens of heads and members of divisions who arrived at the municipality to sign the document to resign from the party.[150]

The document (shown in Figure 5.1) obliged its signatories to:

Officially resign from the Constitutional Democratic Rally and stand with the people of Regueb and the entire Tunisian population in their choice and demand for the separation between the state and the party in pursuit of a true path to democracy and freedoms.[151]

A Ministry of Interior representative officially validated their resignations by stamp. Without a leader capable of keeping the party united and providing its members with a new vision, the RCD grassroots structures crumbled. The mass resignations in Regueb indicate that some RCD activists indeed believed in popular freedoms and multiparty politics. They sought a new beginning after the bloodshed their town had witnessed. Others may have signed the letter out of a thirst for revenge and frustration with what they perceived to be a useless party that only perpetuated the region's misery. The resignation form appears almost like an act of redemption, enshrining its signatories' rejection of the ruling party and their support for the protesters' demands.

In the face of persistent demonstrations against the RCD and the weakness of the party structures, Farhat Rajhi, who was appointed Interior Minister in Ghannouchi's government of national union, announced, on 6 February, to criminalize all RCD activities and any meetings of its members and to close all

---

[150] Muhammad al-Arabi al-Zuraibi, *al-Regueb min al-Tahrir ila al-Ta'mir* [*al-Regueb: From Liberation to Reconstruction*], Tunis: Dar Al-Qalam Publishing, 2016, p. 225.
[151] A copy of the resignation form is available in ibid., p. 227.

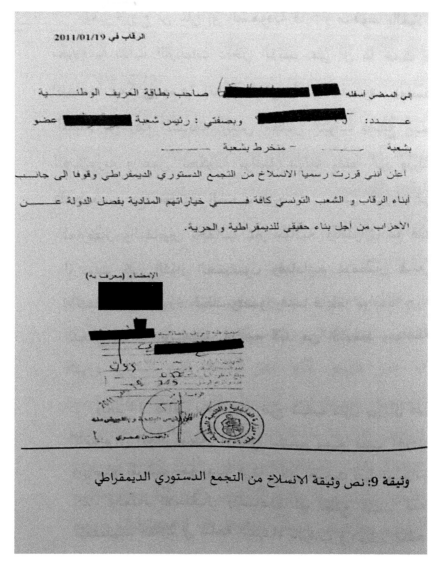

الرقاب في 2011/01/19

إلى المضى أسفله _____ صاحب بطاقة التعريف الوطنية

عـــدد: _____ وبصفتي : رئيس شعبة _____ عضو

شعبة _____ __ منخرط بشعبة _____

أعلن أنني قررت رسميا الانسلاخ من التجمع الدستوري الديمقراطي وقوفا إلى جانـب

أبناء الرقاب و الشعب التونسي كافة فـــــي خياراتهم المنادية بفصل الدولة عـــن

الأحزاب من أجل بناء حقيقي للديمقراطية والحرية.

الإمضاء (معرف به)

وثيقة 9: نص وثيقة الانسلاخ من التجمع الدستوري الديمقراطي

Figure 5.1 RCD resignation form.

Source: Muhammad al-Arabi al-Zuraibi, *al-Regueb min al-Tahrir ila al-Ta'mir* [*al-Regueb: From Liberation to Reconstruction*], Tunis: Dar Al-Qalam Publishing, 2016, p. 227.

of its offices.[152] Protesters, however, continued to call for the official dissolution of the RCD. They also demanded the end of the government, which still

[152] 'Dans l'Attente de sa Dissolution, Suspension du RCD et Fermeture de Ses Locaux', *Tunisie Numérique*, 6 February 2011, http://www.tunisienumerique.com/tunisie-a-lattente-de-sa-dissolution-suspension-du-rcd-et-fermeture-de-ses-locaux/6295, last accessed 24 August 2016.

featured many Ben Ali–era heavyweights such as Grira and Ghannouchi, who had engineered the constitutional coup. Faced with such persistent popular opposition, Ghannouchi was finally forced to resign as Prime Minister on 27 February 2011 and his cabinet was dissolved. This illustrates that despite their critical role in ousting Ben Ali, senior members of his regime failed to gain a grip over the uprising. They never stopped shaping its trajectory, however: following Ghannouchi's departure, Interim President Mebazza made sure that his successor, Beji Caid Essebsi, also came from the ruling party, though Essebsi, who had long been marginalized by the Ben Ali family, was less well known and therefore more easily accepted by the people. Mebazza explained:

> I knew [Essebsi] from before. When he was Interior Minister, I was Director of National Security. When he was Foreign Affairs Minister, I was ambassador in Geneva. . . . He was someone who knew the wheels of the state at a period when it was necessary to secure the wheels of the state![153]

Soon after becoming Prime Minister, Essebsi announced free elections for a Constitutional Assembly, tasked with rewriting the country's constitution. He also paved the way for the dissolution of the RCD by court order—the Destourians' ultimate concession in the face of pressure from the streets. A video taken during the trial shows angry protesters, some dressed as judges and standing on tables in the court room, shouting 'RCD *dégage*' and chanting the national anthem. Abir Moussi, one of the lawyers charged with defending the party, is having her hair pulled and being called a 'slut' by the protesters.[154] On 9 March 2011, the RCD was officially dissolved by court order.

[153] Interview with Fouad Mebazaa, Tunis, 30 May 2016.
[154] TUNISIEINFOS, 'Haqiqat Kull Ma Jara dakhil Qa'at Jalsat Tafasil Ma Jara' ['The Truth of Everything that Happened in the Courtroom, the Details of What Happened'], YouTube, 3 March 2011, https://www.youtube.com/watch?v=B6ylHKlfNm8, last accessed 25 August 2016.

6

Conclusion

This book has examined why members of Ben Ali's ruling party participated in protests against his regime—in some cases going as far as calling for the downfall of the regime—of which they themselves were part. On a broader level, it has investigated the factors influencing the relationship between a dictator and ruling party and the effects of this relationship on authoritarian stability and collapse. Ruling parties are generally perceived to be a source of regime durability, with activists seeking to perpetuate and defend a system from which they benefit. Thus, it does seem puzzling that party followers would, in fact, decide to stage a revolt from inside the regime. This book explained how the politics of ideas is central to understanding trends of internecine contention, as well as authoritarian stability and collapse in hegemonic and dominant party regimes more generally.

Why is this an important topic? Ideas are intrinsic to politics, and this is also true in authoritarian contexts. However, scholarship in the field has not much focused on them, preferring instead to concentrate on factors, such as the role of the security apparatus, economic resources, and nominally democratic institutions, amongst other topics, in fostering authoritarian stability. Moreover, the quantitative turn in political science has put measurable variables to the forefront, typically in the context of large, cross-country comparisons. Whilst these studies have produced important insights, this book has highlighted the parallel importance of ideas, norms, and questions of legitimacy and authority more broadly in authoritarian politics.

The book builds on a nascent scholarship that takes the complexity and variation within authoritarian institutions seriously.[1] More specifically, ruling parties are not static but subject to constant change (mostly incremental, but sometimes rapid and revolutionary), developments that can be driven by both external and endogenous factors. The adaptability and changing nature of authoritarian regimes and ruling parties have been noted, especially in

---

[1] Note that I have used the term 'authoritarian institutions' as a broad category, including various formal political institutions in dictatorships, such as ruling parties, legislatures, and the government.

Ben Ali's Tunisia. Anne Wolf, Oxford University Press. © Anne Wolf (2023).
DOI: 10.1093/oso/9780192868503.003.0007

area studies,[2] but until now these topics have not made it to the forefront of the authoritarian politics literature. Those who have scrutinized variation amongst ruling parties have often focused on those parties' degree of 'credibility', 'strength', or 'institutionalization'.[3] But in the process, they have frequently omitted—either partially, or in full—a core variable of all politics: ideas. There are important exceptions, and some scholars have recognized the autonomous force of ideas,[4] sometimes indirectly, arguing, for example, that revolutionary parties that emerged out of independence struggles are particularly strong, at least initially.[5]

However, many dictators inherit pre-existing ruling parties, and this book shows that the politics of ideas is also central to understanding processes of authoritarian regeneration and why some may exhaust themselves over time. In particular, it is key to investigating how incumbents continuously seek to bolster their own positions within ruling parties, as well as when, why, and how party followers may engage in contention against their leader—possibly even the entire regime—and with what effect. This book makes three claims that address shortcomings in the authoritarian politics literature.

1. The politics of ideas is central to understanding how and why some leaders succeed in personalizing powers, whereas others fail. It is an indispensable component in understanding this success or failure, beyond

[2] Steven Heydemann, 'Upgrading Authoritarianism in the Arab World', Brookings Institution Saban Center Analysis Paper No. 13, 2007; Oliver Schlumberger, *Debating Arab Authoritarianism: Dynamics and Durability in Nondemocratic Regimes*, Stanford, CA: Stanford University Press, 2007.

[3] Steven Levitsky and Lucan A. Way, *Competitive Authoritarianism: Hybrid Regimes after the Cold War*, Cambridge: Cambridge University Press, 2010; Yonatan L. Morse, *How Autocrats Compete: Parties, Patrons, and Unfair Elections in Africa*, Storrs: University of Connecticut Press, 2018; Anne Meng, *From Personalized Rule to Institutionalized Regimes*, Cambridge: Cambridge University Press, 2020.

[4] As stated previously, those scholar investigating dictators' politics of ideas, including their legitimation modes and strategies, tend to focus on how they justify their rule in front of the wider population, rather than amongst regime circles, often in the context of framing and discourse analysis. See Robert Mayer, 'Strategies of Justification in Authoritarian Ideology', *Journal of Political Ideologies*, 2001, 6, 2, pp. 147–168; Holger Albrecht and Oliver Schlumberger, '"Waiting for Godot": Regime Change without Democratization in the Middle East', *International Political Science Review*, 2004, 25, 4, pp. 371–392; Mariya Y. Omelicheva, 'Authoritarian Legitimation: Assessing Discourses of Legitimacy in Kazakhstan and Uzbekistan', *Central Asian Survey*, 2016, 35, 4, pp. 481–500; Yue Hu, 'Refocusing Democracy: The Chinese Government's Framing Strategy in Political Language', *Democratization*, 2020, 27, 2, pp. 302–320; Christian Von Soest and Julia Grauvogel, 'Identity, Procedures and Performance: How Authoritarian Regimes Legitimize Their Rule', *Contemporary Politics*, 2017, 23, 3, pp. 287–305; Johannes Gerschewski, 'Legitimacy in Autocracies: Oxymoron or Essential Feature?', *Perspectives on Politics*, 2018, 16, 3, pp. 652–665.

[5] Samuel P. Huntington and Clement H. Moore (eds.), *Authoritarian Politics in Modern Society: The Dynamics of Established One-Party Systems*, New York: Basic Books, 1970; Benjamin Smith, 'Life of the Party: The Origins of Regime Breakdown and Persistence under Single-Party Rule', *World Politics*, 2005, 57, 3, pp. 421–451; Steven Levitsky and Lucan A. Way, *Competitive Authoritarianism: Hybrid Regimes after the Cold War*, Cambridge: Cambridge University Press, 2010; Steven Levitsky and Lucan A. Way, 'Not Just What But When (and How): Comparative-Historical Approaches to Authoritarian Durability', in James Mahoney and Kathleen Thelen (eds.), *Advances in Comparative-Historical Analysis*, Cambridge: Cambridge University Press, 2015, pp. 97–120.

considerations of the size of the coercive apparatus and collective action problems.

2. Personalist leaders typically promote new normative ideas to regenerate authoritarian legitimacy and bolster their own power. If they don't, or their attempts fail, the regime enters a state of decay and ruling parties cease to be self-reinforcing.

3. Contention amongst various regime ranks played an essential role in the collapse of autocracies during the Arab Uprisings. Scrutinizing such internecine contention helps explain regime trajectories beyond what existing scholarship on protest movements, the political opposition, or elite politics can explain.

Correctivism and the personalization of power

When trying to explain how dictators personalize their rule, scholars of authoritarian politics commonly point to the importance of the security apparatus. They argue that incumbents' threat or use of force discourages others from challenging them.[6] However, the obviousness of the coercion argument has been misleading in that scholars have mostly asserted rather than proven it.[7] Indeed, this book shows that Ben Ali—although he ousted Bourguiba with the help of the security forces—did not rely on coercion primarily to establish personalist rule. The literature has failed to explain how dictators—including those who take power through the security apparatus—manage to remain in office the day after the coup if they depend on the support of pre-existing political institutions, such as ruling parties. The fact that many coup leaders are ousted within their first three years in power[8]—often by regime rivals—suggests that this is an important line of enquiry.

This book uncovers how incumbents promote specific ideational and structural innovations to accumulate greater power and fortify their rule. New dictators—such as Ben Ali was when he took office in 1987—tend to be

---

[6] Milan W. Svolik, *The Politics of Authoritarian Rule*, Cambridge: Cambridge University Press, 2012; Barbara Geddes, Joseph Wright, and Erica Frantz, *How Dictatorships Work*, Cambridge: Cambridge University Press, 2018; H. E. Chehabi and Juan J. Linz (eds.), *Sultanistic Regimes*, Baltimore, MD: Johns Hopkins University Press, 1998.

[7] This point has previously been made in Ivan Ermakoff, *Ruling Oneself Out: A Theory of Collective Abdications*, Durham, NC: Duke University Press, 2008, p. xiii.

[8] See Barbara Geddes, 'What Do We Know about Democratization after Twenty Years?', *Annual Review of Political Science*, 1999, 2, pp. 115–144; Milan Svolik, 'Power Sharing and Leadership Dynamics in Authoritarian Regimes', *American Political Science Review*, 2009, 102, 2, pp. 153–168.

responsive to party followers' concerns and demands. Indeed, the ideational changes they propose often have wider appeal. Typically, they revolve around the promise to correct the 'mistakes' of the previous leadership, realize the regime's 'true path', or return to its 'proper' roots. The book suggests that this 'correctivist strategy' allows incumbents to build up a broad support base beyond the regime's traditional constituency—a critical first step to entrenching their power. Once the new leaders have sufficient backing, they propose to revise some of the regime's formal rules and practices, which—they claim— is necessary to realize their ambitious reform programme. And it is precisely amidst the tearing down of old structures and the contingency of the moment that incumbents try to advance self-serving reforms to establish executive control.

This book has revealed how Ben Ali promoted such a correctivist frame that allowed him—within two years of assuming power—to establish personal rule. Amongst other correctivist strategies, Ben Ali hired 'ideological lobbyists' to refine the regime's ideational foundations and promote it in front of a variety of constituents. He also launched a 'self-critique' within the ruling party to put internal reform centre stage, and he promised to establish internal party democracy—which many followers desired. This ideational work paved the way to launch a complete makeover of the ruling party. Importantly, Ben Ali officials appointed new representatives who were favourable to them: this occurred in a bottom-up process from the grass roots to mid-level officials, all the way up to senior representatives. Once Ben Ali had thus secured sufficient internal party support, he promoted new formal rules and practices in the party, a process through which he secured executive control.

It is notable that even some coup leaders who relied much more heavily on the security apparatus to consolidate their power have used correctivist frames to widen their support base and outflank potential rivals. In 1970, in Syria, Hafez Assad staged a coup d'état by ordering the army to surround a building where the Ba'th Party was holding a congress. Most party followers, in fact, supported rival leader Salah Jadid, but they had little choice but to surrender. In the months that followed, Assad flexed his security muscle by arresting key allies of Jadid—who himself spent the rest of his life in prison.[9] However, Assad's support base was initially much smaller than Jadid's. This led him to launch a 'Corrective Movement', the stated objective of which was to 'restore [the regime] to the true path'.[10] As part of this strategy, he appealed to the legacy

---

[9] Patrick Seale, *Asad: The Struggle for the Middle East*, Berkeley: University of California Press, 1989, pp. 161–164.

[10] Raymond Hinnebusch, *Syria: Revolution from Above*, Abingdon: Routledge, 2001, p. 65.

of Ba'th party founder, Michel Aflaq, and invited his supporters to join the regime's 'revolution'. Assad's correctivist frame allowed him to draw in new constituents, including the ulama and the Damascus bourgeoisie[11]—which gradually resulted in a real shift of power, fortifying his rule.

Correctivist frames are also instructive for understanding how some leaders of ruling parties that have hitherto practised collective decision-making and leadership rotation succeed in discontinuing these practices and establish personal rule, whereas others do not—irrespective of their coercive muscle. For example, when Xi Jinping took over as Secretary General of the Chinese Communist Party (CCP) in 2012, some commentators forecast that his leadership would be particularly 'fragile' owing, amongst other factors, to his 'weak personal networks with other power elites'.[12] But far from this, in 2018, the CCP Central Committee approved a Xi-sponsored law removing the two-mandate limit on the presidency, essentially allowing him to stay in office indefinitely.

Xi's accumulation of vast personal powers followed a textbook correctivist approach. Upon assuming office, he blamed China's mounting political and economic challenges on the decentralized and collective decision-making of the CCP, instead advocating a more hierarchical and 'disciplined' process,[13] which—he claimed—would restore the 'original aspirations' and 'mission' of the ruling party.[14] As part of this strategy, he launched a 'rectification campaign' in the party, a hallmark of which was the fight against corruption—which many followers themselves desired.[15] In the first five years of his tenure, around two million people were disciplined on corruption charges—not only mid-level and grassroots followers but also key Xi rivals in the elite.[16] In fact, only people with a personal connection to the President were largely

---

[11] Patrick Seale, *Asad: The Struggle for the Middle East*, Berkeley: University of California Press, 1989, pp. 171–173.

[12] Sangkuk Lee, 'An Institutional Analysis of Xi Jinping's Centralization of Power', *Journal of Contemporary China*, 2017, 26, 105, p. 326.

[13] Ibid., p. 329.

[14] Willy Wo-Lap Lam, 'Xi Jinping Evokes the "Original Aspirations" of the Communist Party—While Seeking to Further Consolidate His Hold on Power', *Jamestown Foundation*, 2019, July 31, https://jamestown.org/program/xi-jinping-evokes-the-original-aspirations-of-the-communist-party-while-seeking-to-further-consolidate-his-hold-on-power/, last accessed 14 December 2021.

[15] Ibid. Note that previously in China, the Yan'an Rectification movement allowed Mao Zedong to consolidate power. See, for details, Gao Hua, Stacy Mosher, and Cuo Jian, *How the Red Sun Rose: The Origins and Development of the Yan'an Rectification Movement, 1930–1945*, Hong Kong: Chinese University of Hong Kong Press, 2018.

[16] 'Visualizing China's Anti-Corruption Campaign', *ChinaFile*, 15 August, 2018, https://www.chinafile.com/infographics/visualizing-chinas-anti-corruption-campaign, last accessed 14 December 2021.

protected.[17] To further bolster his muscle, Xi created new political institutions in sensitive sectors, such as domestic security, which he personally oversees.[18] Thus, by the time he pushed through a 2018 law scrapping presidential term limits, Xi already held vast influence. Accordingly, there was almost no resistance to his power grab. This book, indeed, shows that elite rivals tend not to challenge an incumbent if they believe their revolt may not succeed, such as when a leader already holds ample powers or is popular amongst wider party ranks—both of which were the case for Xi.

This is not to say that all new leaders pursue correctivist strategies or that their attempts necessarily result in personal rule. This book, in fact, highlights the importance of political context and wider power dynamics in analysing strategies of power fortification and internecine contention. Some incumbents may judge personalist politics undesirable or unachievable, for example, given the great influence of other officials—including in rival political institutions— or leadership legacies. After the personalist rule of Mao Zedong in China, President Deng Xiaoping advanced a correctivist strategy, which took the form of a brief period of political liberalization known as the 'Beijing Spring'. Deng encouraged freer speech and criticism, intended to assess Mao's 'mistakes as well as his merits'.[19] As part of this rectification process, he advocated for the reintroduction of presidential term limits—a strategic move to solidify his own rule without stoking fears he might become yet another unrestrained leader.

Moreover, whilst the above examples pertain to dictators with ruling parties, other leaders have also advanced correctivist frames—including democratically elected presidents seeking to consolidate greater powers and rule unchecked. This book stops with the collapse of the Ben Ali regime in 2011, after which Tunisia saw a decade of democratic politics, but its insights are, in fact, instructive to understand subsequent trends of authoritarian resurgence. Importantly, in 2019, Kais Saied, a political newcomer and populist, was elected President. Two years into his mandate, he staged a coup that at the time of writing looks like it may put an end to the country's decade-long democracy.

[17] Peter Lorentzen and Xi Lu, 'Personal Ties, Meritocracy, and China's Anti-Corruption Campaign', 21 November 2018, https://ssrn.com/abstract=2835841.

[18] Sangkuk Lee, 'An Institutional Analysis of Xi Jinping's Centralization of Power', *Journal of Contemporary China*, 2017, 26, 105, p. 326.

[19] Oriana Fallaci, 'Deng: Cleaning Up Mao's Feudal Mistakes', *Washington Post*, 31 August 1980, https://www.washingtonpost.com/archive/opinions/1980/08/31/deng-cleaning-up-maos-feudal-mistakes/4e684a74-8083-4e43-80e4-c8d519d8b772/, last accessed 20 December 2021.

Saied vowed to '[correct] the path of the revolution and the path of history'[20]—and this without any support party. Indeed, he denounced all political parties as 'corrupt', instead advocating for a strong presidency. Initially, this strategy drew wide popular support, as ten years of multiparty politics had failed to tackle the country's economic and political woes—especially amidst a health crisis caused by the coronavirus pandemic.[21] Clearly, correctivist frames are important for understanding trends of power consolidation in dictatorships but also during periods of authoritarian relapse, especially in the context of a surge in populist leaders globally—topics for future investigation.

New normative ideas, authoritarian regeneration, and decay

Scholars of authoritarian politics have shown that ruling parties emerging out of revolutionary movements are particularly robust as they tend to have a stronger leadership and are more cohesive, amongst other factors.[22] However, these scholars say little about how incumbents seek to generate authoritarian stability once this revolutionary legacy fades, and what determines whether their attempts are successful. The dominant perception is that these parties gradually become less relevant, especially if their leaders personalize their rule.[23] Whilst the previous section explains how new incumbents use correctivist frames to fortify their rule, this book identifies another ideational strategy through which leaders—once they have established personalist power—try to regenerate authoritarian legitimacy and stability to protect their own interests. This strategy consists of incumbents' strategic creation of new normative priorities to redefine a party's wider goals and raison d'être—not only or even necessarily out of ideological conviction but crucially for their own personal benefit.

---

[20] Heba Saleh, 'Tunisia's Populist President Promises Elections Next Year', *Financial Times*, 14 December 2021, https://www.ft.com/content/d4a25b46-d681-4bcc-9ce3-eaec463dd4b3, last accessed 20 December 2021.

[21] St Antony's College, 'The Tunisian Political Crisis; The end of Democracy?', YouTube, 10 November 2021, https://www.youtube.com/watch?v=Rfbi8upb-gk, last accessed 12 August 2022.

[22] Samuel P. Huntington and Clement H. Moore (eds.), *Authoritarian Politics in Modern Society: The Dynamics of Established One-Party Systems*, New York: Basic Books, 1970; Benjamin Smith, 'Life of the Party: The Origins of Regime Breakdown and Persistence under Single-Party Rule', *World Politics*, 2005, 57, 3, pp. 421–451; Steven Levitsky and Lucan A. Way, *Competitive Authoritarianism: Hybrid Regimes after the Cold War*, Cambridge: Cambridge University Press, 2010; Steven Levitsky and Lucan A. Way, 'Not Just What But When (and How): Comparative-Historical Approaches to Authoritarian Durability', in James Mahoney and Kathleen Thelen (eds.), *Advances in Comparative-Historical Analysis*, Cambridge: Cambridge University Press, 2015, pp. 97–120.

[23] Alongside the literature cited in note 22, see Immanuel Wallerstein, 'The Decline of the Party in Single-Party African States', in Joseph La Palombara and Myron Weiner (eds.), *Political Parties and Political Development*, Princeton, NJ: Princeton University Press, 1966, pp. 201–214.

Amongst other examples, in the mid-twentieth century, several personalist leaders who had led their countries to independence adopted socialism as a main referent for their parties, at a time when their rule was beginning to decline. In 1964 in Tunisia, President Habib Bourguiba renamed the ruling Neo Destour the Socialist Destourian Party to signal a wider change in the party's ideological underpinnings and priorities. In Algeria in 1976, independence figure Houari Boumediene issued a National Charter to launch the country's 'era of socialism' and called upon the National Liberation Front to undergo vast ideological and structural renewal to realize this new political chapter.[24] Notably, socialism initially truly invigorated the leadership of Bourguiba and Boumediene; as new people flocked to the ruling parties, their representatives were bestowed with greater responsibilities and new prerogatives.

Anne Meng has found that personalist leaders in sub-Saharan Africa— once their leverage dwindled—have similarly created new 'rules and structures that govern the distribution of power and resources'.[25] In the process, some incumbents have even empowered rival elites, who subsequently constrained their rule.[26] The present book identifies the ideational backdrop to such regime transformations, showing that leaders create new normative priorities to legitimate wider structural changes. These new normative priorities need to resonate with followers in that they find them credible and in tune with their values and identities. If they don't, the regime may become a breeding ground for internecine contention, which makes both leadership change and regime collapse more likely.

This book illustrates that in Tunisia, depending on the specific domestic and international context, Ben Ali promoted a variety of new normative prerogatives—ranging from security reinforcement, to ostensible economic liberalization, to selective political innovations, including the advancement of women's rights. This ideational work legitimated wider structural changes, such as the strengthening of presidential prerogatives and of the security apparatus. It also gave rise to new actors, including technocrats and lumpen activists. There was, in fact, continuous internal regime renewal under Ben Ali. This even bestowed some substance to his claim to instigate 'political

---

[24] A copy of the National Charter of 30 July 1976 is available at http://www.joradp.dz/JO6283/1976/061/FP714.pdf, last accessed 7 February 2022.
[25] Anne Meng, *From Personalized Rule to Institutionalized Regimes*, Cambridge: Cambridge University Press, 2020, p. 12.
[26] Ibid.

change'—though any reforms were, of course, meant to ultimately fortify Ben Ali's own power base.

The literature on authoritarian upgrading in the Arab world has highlighted the adaptability of authoritarian regimes—typically in the context of dictators' ostensible liberalization efforts beginning in the 1990s.[27] One of Ben Ali's key ideologues himself lauded that '[the RCD] always knew how to change and adapt. It was always able to renew its discourse and support base.'[28] This book shows that these reforms were part of a wider authoritarian regeneration toolkit, and it details the relation between ideational and structural innovations. It also uncovers how the specific strategies incumbents pursue depend on the distribution of power in the regime. Whereas leaders advance correctivist frames in contexts where ruling parties constrain their rule, typically when they first assume office, they promote new normative ideas once they already possess ample leverage. These two practices offer valuable new pathways for identifying, scrutinizing, and comparing processes of authoritarian regeneration and decay—across countries and times.

In addition, the book has shown why some attempts at authoritarian regeneration are successful whereas others fail, as well as why some that are initially successful may exhaust themselves over time—possibly even destabilizing a regime from within. It proposes that authoritarian regimes enter a state of decay if dictators' normative priorities do not resonate with followers in that the latter deem these priorities as not credible or desirable, even after any promotional strategies leaders may have pursued. Some normative priorities may also exhaust themselves as an ideology loses wider appeal—such as when the collapse of the Soviet Union laid bare the limits of its socialist approach—or because of changing domestic political circumstances. For example, a regime's security prerogatives are only credible if followers believe there is, in fact, a tangible security threat. In Tunisia, the defeat of the Islamist opposition exposed Ben Ali's persistent bolstering of the security apparatus as purely self-serving.

In a similar vein, the claim to political liberalization made by many longtime Arab dictators in the 2000s was not credible to many, let alone to ruling party followers, who had been witnessing firsthand incumbents' accumulation of

---

[27] Steven Heydemann, 'Upgrading Authoritarianism in the Arab World', Brookings Institution Saban Center Analysis Paper No. 13, 2007; Oliver Schlumberger, *Debating Arab Authoritarianism: Dynamics and Durability in Nondemocratic Regimes*, Stanford, CA: Stanford University Press, 2007.

[28] Sadok Chaabane, 'Tahawwul al-Sabi' min November wa-l-Tajdid al-Fikri li-l-Tajammu' al-Dusturi al-Dimuqrati' ['The 7 November Transition and the Intellectual Renewal of the Constitutional Democratic Rally'], in *Markaz al-Dirasat wa-l-Takwin, Muntadayat al-Fikr al-Siyasi 2008–2009* [*RCD Centre for Studies and Training, Political Thought Forums 2008–2009*], Tunis: RCD Publications, 2009, p. 47.

greater personal powers.[29] Ben Ali's failure to renew his regime at the time, including its ideological underpinnings and objectives, resulted in a legitimacy crisis. This book argues that ruling parties cease to be self-reinforcing if the authority and legitimacy of the incumbent have come under threat— even where parties still offer some perks and privileges, at least to selected constituents. In Tunisia, some disgruntled followers began to pursue acts of internecine contention to display their discontent, specifically at the local and regional levels, though these were only a minority and proceeded mostly inconspicuously. Ben Ali responded by bolstering his security capacities. This book, in fact, has shown that internecine contention may result in authoritarian reinforcement, as leaders seek to shield themselves from any challengers. But it does make regime change and breakdown more likely—especially during moments of political crisis and turmoil.

Internecine contention and regime collapse

This book has illustrated that during the Arab Uprisings, contention within the RCD burst out into the open and contributed to the collapse of the Ben Ali regime. Indeed, many grassroots and even some mid-level followers participated in the protest movement (some advocating for internal reforms, others seeking regime collapse), whereas local and regional representatives frequently engaged in 'passive resistance' to signal to the powerbrokers in Tunis that they too wanted political change. Their contention undermined any efforts of the RCD Secretary General to organize large-scale rallies in favour of Ben Ali. Importantly, internecine contention exposed Ben Ali as a straw man, who had lost support amongst wide sections of his own party. This deeply unsettled even loyal figures in the elite, who feared being trapped on a sinking ship. In this context Prime Minister Mohamed Ghannouchi took over power on 14 January 2011.

Notably, contention within ruling parties was not limited to Tunisia, though these trends have not been investigated in depth. Indeed, those countries that saw the largest protests during the Arab Uprisings were the region's republics, and, with the exception of Libya, they all had ruling parties. According to the dominant literature, these parties should have defended their regimes. Instead, they became major sites of internecine contention. In Yemen, the political

---

[29] For more information on leadership succession dynamics in the Arab republics, see Roger Owen, *The Rise and Fall of Arab Presidents for Life*, Cambridge, MA: Harvard University Press, 2012.

upheaval 'brought longstanding divisions within the GPC to the surface'.[30] In particular, the GPC split into two camps, one supporting incumbent Ali Abdullah Saleh and his son, whom he had hoped to groom as a successor; the other, led by former Prime Minister Abdul Kareem al-Eryani, challenging their political domination and increasingly personalist rule.[31]

In his study of Egypt's Kerdasa neighbourhood in Cairo, Hani Awad remarked on a 'struggle between the old and new "guard"' within the NDP leadership in the 2000s. He found that longtime NDP figures were replaced by 'amateurs with no history of public service' and who supported President Hosni Mubarak and his son Gamal whom he sought to groom as a successor.[32] Those party leaders who tried to resist their sidelining were 'subjugated and humiliated, mostly by the security services'. As a result, the police found almost no allies amongst the old guard in Kerdasa during the Egyptian revolution.[33] Such passive resistance may have been a more general trend, as other scholars remarked that during the Arab Uprisings 'the NDP faded from existence'[34] and that 'ruling party politicians stood by and watched events from the sidelines'[35] rather than countermobilizing for the regime. Much of the conflict within Egypt's NDP and Yemen's GPC were owing to the Presidents' efforts to groom a family member as a successor, a trend reminiscent of the Tunisian scenario.

In Syria, the Ba'th party emerged as a particular target of the protesters and later of the rebels, with many senior and mid-level Ba'thists being assassinated. In 2012, party loyalists even created a militia, the Ba'th Battalions, to counter the protest movement.[36] However, contention also erupted inside the party, as countless rank-and-file members and even some leaders resigned their membership and either engaged in passive resistance or outright joined the revolution.[37] In June 2012, President Assad promoted popular Ba'th figure Riadh Hijab as Prime Minister, probably with the aim of strengthening his support amongst party activists and reunifying the membership base. But only

[30] Tik Root, 'A Shake Up in Yemen's GPC?', *Foreign Policy*, 22 February 2013, https://foreignpolicy.com/2013/02/22/a-shake-up-in-yemens-gpc/, last accessed 18 September 2018.

[31] Ibid.

[32] Hani J. D. Awad, 'Forgotten as History: Politics and Space in the Cairo Peri-Urban Fringe', DPhil thesis, University of Oxford, 2018, pp. 209–210.

[33] Ibid., pp. 210–212.

[34] Joshua Stacher, *Adaptable Autocrats: Regime Power in Egypt and Syria*, Stanford, CA: Stanford University Press, 2012, p. 158.

[35] Jason Brownlee and Joshua Stacher, 'Change of Leader, Continuity of System: Nascent Liberalization in Post-Mubarak Egypt', *American Political Science Association Newsletter*, 2011, 9, 2, p. 5.

[36] Aron Lund, 'The Ba'th Battalions Move into Damascus', *Carnegie Middle East Cener Diwan*, 13 January 2014, https://carnegie-mec.org/diwan/54167?lang=en, last accessed 1 February 2022.

[37] Aron Lund, 'The Ba'th Party and the War in Syria: An Interview with Sami Moubayed', *Carnegie Middle East Center Diwan*, 17 November 2013, http://carnegie-mec.org/diwan/53490, last accessed 18 September 2018.

two months later, in August 2012, Hijab decided to switch sides and backed the revolution.[38] Nevertheless, as the case of Syria shows, internecine party contention does not necessarily lead to regime collapse, especially if some sections continue to fervently defend the regime. Moreover, ruling parties are only one regime institution, even if a central one, and others, such as the security apparatus, matter as well (sometimes even more), alongside wider domestic factors and foreign alliances—all of which in Syria helped tilt the balance of power in favour of Assad.[39]

Beyond the Arab world, contention within ruling parties has contributed to the collapse of regimes during major revolutionary episodes. These include the wave of prolonged mobilization that culminated in the dissolution of the Soviet Union in 1991. Indeed, Mark Beissinger found that 'the tide [of protests] created enormous divisions within Soviet institutions . . . and the lines of battle frequently crossed the state–society divide.'[40] Communist activists sometimes took on a role in the protest movement. For example, during a major demonstration on 25 February 1990 in Moscow against the political dominance of the Communist Party, 22% of those who took to the streets themselves hailed from the Communist Party.[41] In Romania, six party veterans wrote an open letter in which they criticized President Nicolae Ceauşescu upfront, 'denouncing his excesses, his erratic economic policies, and the general deterioration of Romania's international image.'[42] In Azerbaijan, the First Secretary of the Communist Party admitted that some officials in his country 'turned out themselves to be organizers of disorders.'[43] In addition, in East Germany, the party 'began to unravel and disintegrate,'[44] and frictions between rival factions burst out into the open. Some grassroots activists charged that their leaders were 'dogmatic, conservative, and incapable of change', whilst senior officials insisted that 'a growing number of party members . . . must be excluded from

---

[38] Ian Black, "Syria's Prime Minister Confirms Defection to "Join Revolution of Freedom"', *The Guardian*, 6 August 2012, https://www.theguardian.com/world/2012/aug/06/syria-prime-minister-confirms-defection, last accessed 1 December 2021.

[39] Moreover, unlike the other Arab republics, Syria was not facing a succession crisis, Bashar al-Assad having successfully assumed the presidency after his father, Hafez, passed away in 2000.

[40] Mark R. Beissinger, *Nationalist Mobilization and the Collapse of the Soviet State*, Cambridge: Cambridge University Press, 2002, p. 97.

[41] Ibid., p. 98.

[42] Vladimir Tismaneanu, *Stalinism for All Seasons: A Political History of Romanian Communism*, Los Angeles: University of California Press, 2003, p. 227.

[43] Quoted in Mark R. Beissinger, *Nationalist Mobilization and the Collapse of the Soviet State*, Cambridge: Cambridge University Press, 2002, p. 97.

[44] Rasma Karklins and Roger Petersen, 'Decision Calculus of Protesters and Regimes: Eastern Europe 1989', *Journal of Politics*, 1993, 55, 3, p. 607.

the party because they stood against the general line of the party, negated the success of the socialist state, and [damaged] the party.[45]

Clearly, internecine contention played a major role in the disintegration of the Soviet Union, though this trend has not been investigated in greater depth.[46] Areas for further enquiry might include party followers' multiple reasons for supporting the protests, their ranks and objectives, and their specific contentious actions and their effects. The literatures on social movements and revolutions have, indeed, largely focussed on the political opposition, neglecting contention within the regime camp, including ruling parties.[47] And research on coups has centred on elite dynamics, disregarding how revolts amongst wider party ranks may, in fact, incite senior officials to turn against their leader.[48] This book sheds new light on contentious politics, elite coups, and regime breakdown more generally. It proposes that not anti-regime protests per se but internal contention may be the final straw that breaks a regime's back—possibly amid wider mass unrest. If a significant phenomenon, contention within ruling parties undermines any efforts at countermobilizing for the regime and fosters insecurity even amongst loyal elites, who may turn against their own leader—possibly staging a coup and advocating for wider regime change—in order to save their own skin. This is precisely what happened in Tunisia on 14 January 2011, the day the Ben Ali regime collapsed.

Implications for future research

The book is an in-depth study of the Ben Ali regime and although I included some comparative elements, scholars will naturally have to further test and develop many of its key propositions and the extent to which they hold across a variety of cases and over time. An interesting avenue for future research would be to explore similar trends of contention in other political institutions,

---

[45] Steven Pfaff, *Exit-Voice Dynamics and the Collapse of East Germany: The Crisis of Leninism and the Revolution of 1989*, Durham, NC: Duke University Press, 2006, p. 57.

[46] In addition to the literature cited above, Valerie Bunce has investigated the 'subversive' nature of Soviet Union institutions, such as leadership succession struggles that ultimately destabilized the system. See, for details, Valerie Bunce, *Subversive Institutions: The Design and the Destruction of Socialism and the State*, Cambridge: Cambridge University Press, 1999.

[47] Recently, a new literature on state-mobilized movements has emerged; however, it focuses on how dictators use social movements to realize their goals, not on internecine contention. See, for details, Grzegorz Ekiert, Elizabeth Perry, and Xiaojun Yan (eds.), *Ruling by Other Means: State-Mobilized Movements*, Cambridge: Cambridge University Press, 2020.

[48] Milan W. Svolik, *The Politics of Authoritarian Rule*, Cambridge: Cambridge University Press, 2012; Barbara Geddes, Joseph Wright, and Erica Frantz, *How Dictatorships Work*, Cambridge: Cambridge University Press, 2018.

such as local councils or legislatures, and their effects on regime stability and collapse. This could involve scrutinizing how contention in various authoritarian institutions may overlap and influence each other, as well as the political opposition, with possibly cumulative effects. Another exciting path for future investigation would be to study incumbents' ideational strategies of power fortification within different types of dictatorial regimes. This would allow scholars to gain a more fine-grained understanding of the role of ideology, norms, and questions of authority and legitimacy in processes of power consolidation and regeneration in distinct authoritarian systems, as well as when and why these may cease to be effective.

This book built on historical institutionalists' concern for institutional change, as well as on the literature on authoritarian upgrading in the Arab world—both of which investigate the adaptive and transformative nature of regimes and their institutions. However, many scholars pursuing this line of research do not distinguish between formal and informal institutions, which 'hampers the investigation of their respective effects', as has been noted in a related study.[49] This book differentiated between formal and informal rules and practices in authoritarian regimes and explored the specific natures of both, where and how they intersect, possibly condition each other, and their causal roles in processes of authoritarian regeneration and collapse. Amongst other trends, it showed that formal authoritarian institutions, if void of normative substance, are but hollow structures that can easily be challenged, including by actors from within the regime's own ranks. Future research will benefit from differentiating more systematically between different kinds of institutions and their specific effects to gain a deeper understanding of authoritarian regimes' adaptive, transformative, and at times contradictory potentials—including the causal roles some play in their own breakdown.

At a broader level, this book highlights once again the importance of conducting research beyond 'where the light shines',[50] that is, beyond the immediately visible and obvious. Ever since the Arab Uprisings, dozens of books have appeared on the protest movement and the political opposition, uncovering entirely new information on key actors and dynamics. However, phenomena that did not fit into this frame of 'people power' were commonly cast aside or outright ignored. In Tunisia, indeed, it was not even necessary to search far beyond 'the light' to understand that there was an entirely different

---

[49] Ivan Ermakoff and Marko Grdesic, 'Institutions and Demotions: Collective Leadership in Authoritarian Regimes', *Theory and Society*, 2019, 48, 2, p. 565.

[50] This expression is borrowed from Lisa Anderson, 'Searching Where the Light Shines: Studying Democratization in the Middle East', *Annual Review of Political Science*, 2006, 9, 1, pp. 189–214.

narrative amongst ex–Ben Ali officials about the regime's collapse. Ben Ali himself affirmed in 2012 that he only intended to drop his family in Jeddah and that his 'plane returned to Tunisia [without him] . . . in breach of his clear orders'.[51] The same year, some recorded phone conversations between Ben Ali and senior officials were published in Tunisian media outlets in which he sought to convince them to help him return to Tunis, though these recordings only made it into the international news a decade later.[52] Tunisian researchers have also been preoccupied with reconstructing some of the events inside the regime during the uprisings, and their findings were crucial for this book.[53] It is difficult to understand how these publicly available resources have failed to inform mainstream political science debates, other than through scholars' need to adhere to dominant disciplinary preoccupations or possibly research bias in that some may prefer to focus on groups and movements they identify and sympathize with, notably pro-democracy revolutionaries.

In fact, the collapse of a dictatorship—when followed by the establishment of democratic politics—offers a rare opportunity to conduct research into many different aspects of authoritarian politics. Typically, indeed, during the period immediately after the regime breakdown, many documents are published detailing its inner workings. Regime opponents are able to talk freely, often for the first time. In some cases, former regime officials are willing to testify as well. Whilst access to leadership levels can sometimes be difficult, regional and local figures are easier to reach and—because they tend to be less tainted by the party propaganda typical of officials in capital headquarters—often provide even more valuable insights into the regime's internal dynamics and set-up, including key points of conflict and contention. These resources offer unique insights into various facades of authoritarian rule.

Not only scholars but also policy-makers and political activists will benefit from a more accurate understanding of the complex processes leading to the collapse of dictatorships—during the Arab Uprisings and beyond. Indeed, as many have missed the key role regime figures themselves played in the

---

[51] 'Tasrih al-Ra'is Bin Ali—20 Huzayran 2011' ['Declaration of President Ben Ali—20 June 2011'], published via his lawyer, Akram 'Azuri, Beirut, 20 June 2011.

[52] Emir Nader, 'Secret Audio Sheds Light on Toppled Dictator's Frantic Last Hours', BBC News, 14 January 2022, https://www.bbc.co.uk/news/world-africa-59972545, last accessed 28 February 2022.

[53] Amongst the most notable publications which have been cited in this book are Abdelaziz Belkhodja and Tarak Cheikhrouhou, 14 Janvier: l'Enquête, Tunis: Apollonia Editions, 2013; interview in the presence of Mustafa Kamel El-Nabi, Tahar Boussema, Mohamed Dhifallah, Sonia Temimi, and Abdellahf Fourati, 'Témoignage du Colonel Major M. Samir Tarhouni sur le Déroulement des Événements du 14 Janvier 2011 à l'Aéroport de Tunis Carthage', in Abdeljelil Temimi (ed.), L'Observatoire de la Révolution Tunisienne, Tunis: Fondation Temimi Pour la Recherche Scientifique et l'Information, 2015.

fall of authoritarian regimes, they have, as a result, subsequently underestimated their persistent strength and willingness to make a political comeback. In Tunisia, many ex-regime officials re-emerged a couple of years after the uprisings. Initially, they were mostly officials who were less politically tainted, typically those who had been marginalized by Ben Ali in the 2000s. They included Beji Caid Essebsi, President between 2014 and 2019. Importantly, the rise of these figures paved the way, in a second step, for many senior Ben Ali officials to stage a comeback, including those who had supported him until the very end. They include Abir Moussi, a key party figure who defended the RCD after the uprisings and who became a central political player beginning in the late 2010s.[54] Internal regime dynamics and contention are, in fact, key to better understanding the resilience of old regime figures and their networks and, as such, should be central themes in future research on democratic backsliding.

I would like to finish on a set of open questions that I have not succeeded in answering in this book. When I first began my investigation of the Ben Ali regime, I was determined to solve all the mysteries behind its sudden collapse in 2011 during the Arab Uprisings. However, I soon realized that this was not possible. This is not because of a lack of data—there is plenty available. Rather, the challenge is that many key actors began to panic in the face of the political turmoil. Their decisions were highly contingent and did not always make sense to the scholarly eye looking for generalizable patterns and some degree of rationality. These include Ben Ali's own actions. Why did he decide, on 14 January 2011, to step onto the plane to accompany his family to Saudi Arabia? We know that it was a spontaneous decision—he had not planned on taking that plane—so what if he hadn't? Would he have been ousted anyway? If so, how? Or can we envision a scenario in which he would have managed to weather the turmoil and to stay in power? If he had done so, how would this have affected the trajectory of the Arab Uprisings in other countries, where the protesters sought to emulate the successful Tunisian example?

The Ben Ali regime certainly was vulnerable and in crisis, so it may have been just a matter of time before it collapsed, especially in the face of mounting internecine contention. However, some incumbents have managed to stay in power, sometimes for decades, despite regime decay and growing opposition to their rule, prominent examples including Mao Zedong and

---

[54] See, for details, Anne Wolf and Raphaël Lefèvre, 'Revolution under Threat: The Challenges of the "Tunisian Model"', *Journal of North African Studies*, 2012, 17, 3, pp. 559–563; Anne Wolf, 'Former RCD Officials Stage a Comeback in Municipal Elections in Tunisia', *Journal of North African Studies*, 2018, 23, 4, pp. 551–556.

Fidel Castro. This book has demonstrated that dissent and contention make regime breakdown much more likely—especially if they erupt within its own ranks—but they do not automatically cause that outcome. Many studies of successful revolutions suffer from retrospective determinism in that they assume a change in the political order was inevitable. But moments of political turmoil and contingency heighten the agency of key actors, whose decisions—not always rational—may change the trajectory of events, sometimes in unintended ways. As a result, the final outcome of revolutionary episodes is unpredictable. And it is worth exploring how things could have gone differently.

In the case of Tunisia, a pressing question is whether elite actors would have moved against Ben Ali had he not boarded that plane on 14 January but stayed in Tunisia. We cannot answer this with any certainty, of course. But I do believe it is safe to say that any elite action against Ben Ali on the ground would have been less likely. This is because it would have carried much greater risks: Ben Ali still had large parts of the security apparatus under control, despite individual instances of defection. Moreover, Tunisia does not have a tradition of violent elite battles and coups, much unlike some of its neighbours. Ben Ali himself ousted his predecessor in a bloodless coup d'état. And any move against Ben Ali on the ground would likely not have been smooth and peaceful. In fact, this book has shown that elite actors decided to challenge Ben Ali on 14 January 2011 because they believed they had an opportunity to do so without great costs and wanted to save their own skins, not because they had a longstanding plan to overthrow him. They even sought to conceal the very fact that a coup had taken place by perpetuating the false narrative that Ben Ali had 'fled', to suggest that their takeover was a matter of invoking the constitution.

During my decade-long investigation into Tunisian politics, I have come across a myriad of opinions on these remaining questions, and I leave it up to the reader to make up their mind on them. Revolutionary episodes are inherently contingent, and nobody can claim to be able to explain every single of their features. But what I can say with much certainty and what I would like to finish on is that despite Ben Ali's coercive muscle and contingent political contexts, ultimately, it was his legitimacy and authority inside the regime that explained his rise to power and personalist rule, and—once they diminished and internecine contention grew—crucially contributed to the decay and sudden collapse of the dictatorship.

Selected Bibliography

Interviews

Abidi, Samir. Interviewed in Tunis, 30 June 2016.

Ammar, Habib. Interviewed in Gammarth, 27 July 2017.

Amroussia, Sami. Interviewed in Gafsa, 23 June 2016.

Baccouche, Hedi. Interviewed in Tunis, 28 September 2015 and 22 July 2017.

Ben Ali, Nesrine. Interviewed via Viber, 6, 10, 13, and 16 February 2017.

Ben Miled, Mounir. Interviewed in Tunis, 24 May 2016.

Boughattas, Anis. Interviewed in Tunis, 29 January 2017.

Chaabane, Sadok. Interviewed in Tunis, 20 July 2017.

Chaabouni, Tarek. Interviewed in Tunis, 1 October 2015.

Chaouch, Ali. Interviewed in Tunis, 11 February 2017.

Cheikhrouhou, Mahmoud. Interviewed in Tunis, 1 July 2016.

Chelbi, Afif. Interviewed in Tunis, 22 September 2015.

Chettaoui, Nabil. Interviewed in Tunis, 29 June 2016.

Chiboub, Afif. Interviewed in Tunis, 13 February 2017.

Daly, Abderrazek. Interviewed in Sidi Bouzid, 25 June 2016.

Djilani, Hedi. Interviewed in Tunis, 6 February 2017.

Elloumi, Faouzi. Interviewed in Tunis, 28 September 2015.

Ghannouchi, Mohamed. Interviewed in Tunis, 2 August and 2 October 2015.

Ghariani, Mohamed. Interviewed in Tunis, 27 May 2016, 8 February and 20 and 22 July 2017.

Hachicha-Charchour, Naila. Email interview, 15 April 2017.

Jegham, Mohamed. Interviewed in Tunis, 19 July 2017.

Jeridi-Trabelsi, Nejia. Interviewed in Tunis, 4 February 2017.

Kaaniche, Adel. Interviewed in Tunis, 26 July 2017.

Karoui, Hamed. Interviewed in Tunis, 1 February 2017.

Mannai, Dhamir. Interviewed in Tunis, January 2014.

Marzouki, Moncef. Interviewed in Tunis, May 2015.

Mdhafer, Zouhair. Interviewed in Tunis, 10 February 2017.

Mebazaa, Fouad. Interviewed in Tunis, 30 May 2016.

Mohsen, Abbes. Interviewed in Tunis, 21 and 22 July 2017.

Morjane, Kamel. Interviewed in Tunis, 26 May 2016.

Mourou, Abdelfattah. Interviewed in La Marsa, July 2013.

Moussi, Abir. Interviewed in Tunis, 31 May 2016.

Nasfi, Hassouna. Interviewed in Bardo, 24 May 2016.

Neffati, Chedli. Interviewed in Tunis, 2 February 2017.

Rouissi, Moncer. Interviewed in Tunis, 21 July 2017.

Saada, Ryadh. Interviewed in Tunis, 24 July 2017.

Sebri, Akram. Interviewed in Tunis, 26 May 2016.

Turki, Khayem. Interviewed in Tunis, February 2014.

Zarrouk, Naziha. Interviewed in Tunis, 30 January 2017.
Zouari, Abderrahim. Interviewed in Tunis, 9 February 2017.

Pseudonymous interviews

Abdelaziz. Interviewed in Gafsa, 23 June 2016.
Abderrazek. Interviewed in Gafsa, 23 June 2016.
Adel. Interviewed in Tunis, 2 February 2017.
Ahmed. Interviewed in Tunis, 8 February 2017.
Alaa. Interviewed in Bardo, September 2015.
Amine. Interviewed via Skype, 3 June 2016.
Anis. Interviewed in Sidi Bouzid, 25 June 2016.
Anouar. Interviewed in Sousse, 27 July 2017.
Aymen. Interviewed in Bardo, 6 October 2015.
Aziz. Interviewed in Monastir, 25 July 2017.
Bochra. Interviewed in Tunis, 24 February 2017.
Brahim. Interviewed in Bardo, September 2015.
Ezzeddine. Inteviewed via Skype, 12 June 2016.
Fawzi. Interviewed via Skype 3 June 2016.
Foued. Interviewed in Tunis, 30 September 2015.
Habib. Interviewed in Tunis-Bab Souika, September 2015.
Hamdi. Interviewed in Tunis, 5 February 2017.
Hamza. Interviewed in Ras Jebel, Bizerte governorate, 9 February 2017.
Hedi. Email interview, 30 May 2016.
Houda. Interviewed in Sidi Bouzid, 25 June 2016.
Khalid. Interviewed in Sidi Bouzid, July 2016.
Khalil. Interviewed in Jendouba, 29 May 2016.
Larbi. Interviewed in Tunis-Bab Souika, September 2015.
Mohammed. Interviewed in Monastir, 27 July 2017.
Naoufel. Interviewed in Tunis, 24 July 2017.
Nejib. Interviewed in Tunis, 29 June 2016.
Sadok. Interviewed in Ras Jebel, Bizerte governorate, 9 February 2017.
Sahbi. Interviewed in Tunis, 24 May 2016.
Salma. Interviewed in Sidi Bouzis, 25 June 2016.
Sami. Interviewed in Monastir, 25 July 2017.
Samia. Interviewed in Tunis, 29 September 2015.
Selim. Interviewed in Regueb, Sidi Bouzid governorate, 27 June 2016.
Souhail. Interviewed in Sidi Bouzid, 25 June 2016.
Tayeb. Interviewed in Sidi Bouzid, 25 June 2016.
Youssef. Interviewed on Skype, 3 June 2016.
Zakaria. Interviewed in Gafsa, 24 June 2016.

Party and regime publications

'Arrestation à Titre Préventif de Quelques Personnalités', *L'Action*, 7 November 1987.
'Biographie du Président Zine El Abidine Ben Ali', *L'Action*, 7 November 1987.
'Le Premier Alinéa de l'Article de la Constitution de la République Tunisienne', *L'Action,*
    7 November 1987.

'Changement dans la Légalité Constitutionnelle', *L'Action*, 8 November 1987.

'Communiqué de la Direction du Parti Socialiste Destourien', *L'Action*, 8 November 1987.

'Dans le Respect de la Légalité et de la Constitution', *L'Action*, 8 November 1987.

'La Cellule Destourienne de l'Agence TAP: L'Ère Nouvelle Sera une Ère de Labeur, de Réalisation, de Sérénité et de Renforcement des Acquis Républicains', *L'Action*, 8 November 1987.

'Une Manifestation Spontanée de Soutien au Président Zine El Abidine Ben Ali', *L'Action*, 8 November 1987.

'Les Secrétaires Généraux des Comités de Coordination Expriment Leur Appui au Président Ben Ali', *L'Action*, 10 November 1987.

'La Motion du Règlement Intérieur: Garantir la Cohésion et l'Unité des Rangs pour Préserver les Acquis', *Le Renouveau*, 1 August 1993.

Salem Cheikh, 'Parti du Bon Pied', *Le Renouveau*, 29 July 1998.

'Dans le Vif du Salut', *Le Renouveau*, 31 July 1998.

'Attachement à Préserver les Acquis et à Concrétiser les Objectifs du Changement', *Le Renouveau*, 1 August 1998.

Dermech, Abdelkrim, 'Le Rassemblement Gagnera sous la Conduite de Ben Ali le Pari de l'"Ambition"', *Le Renouveau*, 1 August 2003.

Chaabane, Sadok, *Ben Ali, Bâtir une Démocratie: De la Lutte des Croyances à la Compétition des Programmes*, Tunis: Maison Arabe du Livre, 2005.

'La Jeunesse Tunisienne: Détermination Renouvelée à Relever le Défi', *Le Renouveau*, 30 July 2008.

'Le RCD Par les Chiffres', *Le Renouveau*, 30 July 2008.

Chaabane, Sadok, 'Tahawwul al-Sabi' min November wa-l-Tajdid al-Fikri li-l-Tajammu' al-Dusturi al-Dimuqrati' ['The 7 November Transition and the Intellectual Renewal of the Constitutional Democratic Rally'], in *Markaz al-Dirasat wa-l-Takwin, Muntadayat al-Fikr al-Siyasi 2008–2009 (RCD Centre for Studies and Training, Political Thought Forums 2008–2009)*, Tunis: RCD Publications, 2009, pp. 45–57.

Mdhafer, Zouhair, 'al-Tahawwul al-Dimuqrati wa-Khususiyyat al-Nizam al-Intikhabi fi Tunis' ['Democratic Transition and the Electoral System Specificities in Tunisia'], in *Markaz al-Dirasat wa-l-Takwin, Muntadayat al-Fikr al-Siyasi 2008–2009 [RCD Centre for Studies and Training, Political Thought Forums 2008–2009]*, Tunis: RCD Publications, 2009, pp. 13–45.

Ouederni, Ahmed Iyadh, 'al-'Alaqa bayn al-Tajammu' wa-l-Dawla fi Zil al-Ta'addudiyya al-Siyasiyya' ['The Relationship between the Rally and the State in Light of Political Pluralism'], in *Markaz al-Dirasat wa-l-Takwin, Muntadayat al-Fikr al-Siyasi 2008–2009 [RCD Centre for Studies and Training, Political Thought Forums 2008–2009]*, Tunis: RCD Publications, 2009, pp. 3–13.

'Année Internationale de la Jeunesse: La Consécration d'une Démarche Avant-Gardiste', *Le Renouveau*, 19 December 2010.

'M. Mohamed Ghariani Préside un Meeting à Sidi Bouzid', *Le Renouveau*, 25 December 2010.

Reports, development indicators, and legal resources

Al-Nizam al-Dakhili li-l-Tajammu' al-Dusturi al-Dimuqrati [Statute of the Constitutional Democratic Rally], copy received from private archives in Tunis.

'Further Information on UA 219/91 (MDE 30/20/91, 28 June 1991)—Tunisia: Death Penalty', Amnesty International, 10 October 1991, https://www.amnesty.org/en/documents/mde30/024/1991/en/, last accessed 13 February 2018.

'Tunisia: Prolonged Incommunicado Detention and Torture', Amnesty International, 4 March 1992, https://www.amnesty.org/en/documents/mde30/004/1992/en/, last accessed 5 November 2017.

Author transcript of the court hearing of Rachid Ammar, record number 11-3-55, dated 25 January 2011.

Al-Nashra al-Shahriyya li-l-Ihsa'iyyat [*Monthly Bulletin of Statistics*], al-Ma'had al-Watani li-l-Ihsa' [National Institute for Statistics], September 2012.

'Al-Yawm al-I'lami hawla al-Tasarruf fi al-Amwal wa-l-Mumtalakat al-Musadara: Min al-Musadara ila al-Tasarruf' ['Media Day on Disposal of Confiscated Funds and Property: From Confiscation to Disposal'], al-Lajna al-Wataniyya li-l-Tasarruf fi al-Amwal wa-l-Mumtalakat al-Ma'niyya bi-l-Musadara aw al-Istirja' li-Fa'idat al-Dawla [National Committee for the Disposal of Funds and Property Designated for Confiscation or Disposal for the Benefit of the State], Ministry of Finance Publications, November 2013.

Rijkers, Bob, Caroline Freund, and Antonio Nucifora, 'All in the Family: State Capture in Tunisia', World Bank, Policy Research Working Paper No. 6810, March 2014.

Video files

St Antony's College, 'The Tunisian Political Crisis; the end of Democracy?', YouTube, https://www.youtube.com/watch?v=Rfbi8upb-gk, last accessed 9 August 2022.

Rideaudur, 'Sakhr El Materi ne Sait pas Parler Arabe—13 Janvier—Tunisie' [in Arabic], YouTube, 16 January 2011, https://www.youtube.com/watch?v=dCTJROhdm70, last accessed 9 August 2016.

TUNISIEINFOS, 'Haqiqat Kull Ma Jara dakhil Qa'at Jalsat Tafasil Ma Jara' ['The Truth of Everything that Happened in the Courtroom, the Details of What Happened'], YouTube, 3 March 2011, https://www.youtube.com/watch?v=B6ylHKlfNm8, last accessed 25 August 2016.

Tounssihor, 'Saida Agrebi Bras Droit de Leila Ben Ali', YouTube, 16 April 2011, https://www.youtube.com/watch?v=BjGyXL69v2Y, last accessed 3 May 2017.

Amjadrus, 'The Last Speech of Bin Ali' [in Arabic], YouTube, 17 January 2011, https://www.youtube.com/watch?v=kANXV_onYhQ, last accessed 23 September 2018.

US embassy in Tunis cables

'Tunisia Celebrates 7 November; Elections Next April; National Pact Signed', Wikileaks, 8 November 1988, 88TUNIS11598_a, confidential.

'Anonymous Communiqués Allege RCD Discontent with Ben Ali', Wikileaks, 18 May 2005, 05TUNIS1047_a, confidential.

'Succession in Tunisia: Finding a Successor or Feet First?', Wikileaks, 9 January 2006, 06TUNIS55_a, secret.

'Corruption in Tunisia Part II: The Anatomy of Exploitation', Wikileaks, 29 June 2006, 06TUNIS1630_a, confidential.

'Corruption in Tunisia Part IV: The Family's Holdings', Wikileaks, 5 July 2006, 06TUNIS1672_a, confidential.

'Womens' "NGO": Less Hijab, More Ben Ali', Wikileaks, 1 November 2006, 06TUNIS2679_a, confidential.

'Ben Ali Announces New Policies to Facilitate Business', Wikileaks, 24 November 2006, 06TUNIS2798_a, unclassified.

'Ambassador's Courtesy Call with Minister of Defense', Wikileaks, 4 January 2007, 07TUNIS29_a, secret.

'RCD VP Lauds Party Influence, Bemoans Opposition Weakness', Wikileaks, 26 June 2007, 07TUNIS841_a, confidential.

'2006/2007 Terror Cell in Tunisia: What Happened and Why', Wikileaks, 24 January 2008, 08TUNIS75_a, secret.

'Appeal Court Reduces Sentences of Some "Soliman" Terrorists', Wikileaks, 22 February 2008, 08TUNIS168_a, confidential.

'Tunisia: What Succession Scenario?', Wikileaks, 9 May 2008, 08TUNIS493_a, secret.

Memoirs and testimonies

Ammar, Habib, *Parcours d'un Soldat: Entre le Devoir et l'Espoir*, Tunis: Simpact, 2016.

Ben Ali, Leila, *Ma Vérité*, Paris: Éditions du Moment, 2012.

Ben Salem, Moncef, *Mudhakkarat 'Alim Jami'i wa-Sajin Siyasi: Sanawat al-Jamr* [*Memoirs of an Academic Scholar and Political Prisoner: The Years of Fire*], n.p. [Tunisia]: self-published, December 2013.

'Istintajat al-Qira'a al-Naqdiyya li-Masarat al-Hukm min Sanat 1955 ila Sanat 2010' ['Conclusions from the Critical Reading of the Trajectories of Governance from 1955 until 2010'], Association of Former Tunisian Parliamentarians, July 2017, private archives in Tunis.

Kourda, Sami, *Le 'complot' de Barraket Essahel: Chronique d'un calvaire*, Tunis: Sud Éditions, 2012.

El Materi, Moncef, *De Saint-Cyr au Peloton d'Exécution de Bourguiba*, Tunis: Arabesques, 2014.

'Tasrih al-Ra'is Bin Ali—20 Huzayran 2011' ['Declaration of President Ben Ali—20 June 2011'], published via his lawyer, Akram 'Azuri, Beirut, 20 June 2011.

'Témoignage du Colonel Major M. Samir Tarhouni sur le Déroulement des Événements du 14 Janvier 2011 à l'Aéroport de Tunis Carthage', in Abdeljelil Temimi (ed.), *L'Observatoire de la Révolution Tunisienne*, Tunis: Fondation Temimi Pour la Recherche Scientifique et l'Information, 2015.

Books, chapters, journal articles, and policy briefs

Al-Arabi al-Zuraibi, Muhammad, *al-Regueb min al-Tahrir ila al-Ta'mir* [*al-Regueb: From Liberation to Reconstruction*], Tunis: Dar Al-Qalam Publishing, 2016.

Albrecht, Holger, and Oliver Schlumberger, '"Waiting for Godot": Regime Change without Democratization in the Middle East', *International Political Science Review*, 2004, 25, 4, pp. 371–392.

Alexander, Christopher, *Tunisia: From Stability to Revolution in the Maghreb*, Abingdon: Routledge, 2016.

Aleya-Sghaier, Amira, 'The Tunisian Revolution: The Revolution of Dignity', in Ricardo Larémont (ed.), *Revolution, Revolt and Reform in North Africa: The Arab Spring and Beyond*, Abingdon: Routledge, 2014, pp. 30–52.

Allal, Amin, ' "Revolutionary" Trajectories in Tunisia: Processes of Political Radicalisation, 2007–2011', *Revue Française de Science Politique*, 2012, 62, 5, pp. 821–841.

Allal, Amin, and Vincent Geisser, 'La Tunisie de l'Après-Ben Ali', *Cultures & Conflits*, 2011, 83, pp. 118–125.

Anderson, Lisa, 'Political Pacts, Liberalism, and Democracy: The Tunisian National Pact of 1988', *Government and Opposition*, 1991, 26, pp. 244–260.

Anderson, Lisa, 'Searching Where the Light Shines: Studying Democratization in the Middle East', *Annual Review of Political Science*, 2006, 9, 1, pp. 189–214.

Awad, Hani, 'Forgotten as History: Politics and Space in the Cairo Peri-Urban Fringe', DPhil thesis, University of Oxford, 2018.

Barrie, Christopher, 'The Process of Revolutionary Protest: Development and Democracy in the Tunisian Revolution of 2010–2011', Working Paper, 28 August 2018, https://osf.io/preprints/socarxiv/eu5b4/, last accessed 9 August 2022.

Beissinger, Mark R., *Nationalist Mobilization and the Collapse of the Soviet State*, Cambridge: Cambridge University Press, 2002.

Beissinger, Mark, Amaney Jamal, and Kevin Mazur, 'Explaining Divergent Revolutionary Coalitions: Regime Strategies and the Structuring of Participation in the Tunisian and Egyptian Revolutions', *Comparative Politics*, 2015, 48, 1, pp. 1–21.

Belhadj, Souhaïl, *La Syrie de Bashar Al-Assad: Anatomie d'un Régime Autoritaire*, Paris: Belin.

Belkhodja, Abdelaziz, and Tarak Cheikhrouhou, *14 Janvier: L'Enquête*, Tunis: Apollonia Editions, 2013.

Bellin, Eva, 'The Robustness of Authoritarianism in the Middle East: Exceptionalism in Comparative Perspective', *Comparative Politics*, 2004, 36, 2, pp. 139–157.

Blaydes, Lisa, 'Rebuilding the Ba'thist State: Party, Tribe, and Administrative Control in Authoritarian Iraq, 1991–1996', *Comparative Politics*, 2020, 53, 1, pp. 93–115.

Blaydes, Lisa, *State of Repression: Iraq under Saddam Hussein*, Princeton, NJ: Princeton University Press, 2018.

Boix, Carles, and Milan Svolik, 'The Foundations of Limited Authoritarian Government: Institutions, Commitment, and Power-Sharing in Dictatorships', *Journal of Politics*, 2013, 75, 2, pp. 300–316.

Bredoux, Lénaïg, and Mathieu Magnaudeix, *Tunis Connection: Enquête sur les Réseaux Franco-Tunisiens sous Ben Ali*, Paris: Éditions du Seuil, 2012.

Brinks, Daniel M., Steven Levitsky, and Maria Victoria Murillo, *Understanding Institutional Weakness*, Cambridge: Cambridge University Press, 2019.

Brownlee, Jason, *Authoritarianism in an Age of Democratization*, New York: Cambridge University Press, 2007.

Brownlee, Jason, Tarek E. Masoud, and Andrew Reynolds, *The Arab Spring: Pathways of Repression and Reform*, Oxford: Oxford University Press, 2015.

Bueno de Mesquita, Bruce, Alastair Smith, Randolph M. Siverson, and James D. Morrow, *The Logic of Political Survival*, Cambridge, MA: MIT Press, 2003.

Bunce, Valerie, *Subversive Institutions: The Design and the Destruction of Socialism and the State*, Cambridge: Cambridge University Press, 1999.

Cantori, Louis, Tim Jacoby, Sheila Carapico, Samer Shehata, Ellen Lust-Okar, Banu Bargu-Hasturk, Glenn E. Robinson, and Ebtesam Al-Kitbi, 'Political Succession in the Middle East', *Middle East Policy*, 2002, 9, 3, pp. 105–123.

Capoccia, Giovanni, 'When Do Institutions "Bite"? Historical Institutionalism and the Politics of Institutional Change', *Comparative Political Studies*, 2016, 49, 8, pp. 1095–1127.

Cavatorta, Francesco, and Lise Storm, *Political Parties in the Arab World: Continuity and Change*, Edinburgh: Edinburgh University Press, 2019.

Charrad, Mounira M., 'Central and Local Patrimonialism: State-Building in Kin-Based Societies', *Annals of the American Academy of Political and Social Science*, 2011, 636, 1, pp. 49–68.

Chehabi, H. E., and Juan J. Linz (eds.), *Sultanistic Regimes*, Baltimore, MD: Johns Hopkins University Press, 1998.

Chomiak, Laryssa, 'The Making of a Revolution in Tunisia', *Middle East Law and Governance,* 2011, 3, pp. 68–83.

Chouikha, Larbi, and Éric Gobe, *Histoire de la Tunisie Depuis l'Indépendance*, Paris: La Découverte, 2015.

Clark, Victoria, *Yemen: Dancing on the Heads of Snakes*, New Haven, CT: Yale University Press, 2010.

Collombier, Virginie, 'Gamal Moubarak et le Parti National Démocratique ou la Stratégie du Désastre: Comment Ceux qui Prétendaient Préparer la Succession Présidentielle ont Précipité la Chute du Régime', *Outre-Terre*, 2011, 3, 9, pp. 333–345.

Cook, Steven A., *Ruling But Not Governing: The Military and Political Development in Egypt, Algeria and Turkey*, Baltimore, MD: Johns Hopkins University Press, 2007.

Daoud, Zakya, 'Chronique Tunisienne (1989)', *Annuaire de l'Afrique du Nord*, 1991, 28, Paris: CNRS, pp. 679–712.

Daoud, Zakya, 'Chronique Tunisienne (1990)—Annexes Documentaires', *Annuaire de l'Afrique du Nord*, 1992, 29, Paris: CNRS, pp. 777–914.

Dix, Robert H., 'Why Revolutions Succeed and Fail', *Polity*, 1983, 16, pp. 423–446.

Ekiert, Grzegorz, Elizabeth Perry, and Xiaojun Yan (eds.), *Ruling by Other Means: State-Mobilized Movements*, Cambridge: Cambridge University Press, 2020.

Erdle, Steffen, *Ben Ali's 'New Tunisia' (1987–2009): A Case Study of Authoritarian Modernization in the Arab World*, Berlin: Klaus Schwarz, 2010.

Ermakoff, Ivan, *Ruling Oneself Out: A Theory of Collective Abdications*, Durham, NC: Duke University Press, 2008.

Ermakoff, Ivan, 'The Structure of Contingency', *American Journal of Sociology*, 2015, 121, 1, pp. 64–125.

Frantz, Erica, and Elizabeth Stein, 'Countering Coups: Leadership Succession Rules in Dictatorships', *Comparative Political Studies*, 2017, 50, 7, pp. 1–29.

Gana, Nouri (ed.), *The Making of the Tunisian Revolution: Contexts, Architects, Prospects*, Edinburgh: Edinburgh University Press, 2013.

Gandhi, Jennifer, *Political Institutions under Dictatorship*, Cambridge: Cambridge University Press, 2010.

Gandhi, Jennifer, and Adam Przeworski, 'Authoritarian Institutions and the Survival of Autocrats', *Comparative Political Studies*, 2007, 40, 11, pp. 1279–1301.

Gause, Gregory, 'Why Middle East Studies Missed the Arab Spring', *Foreign Affairs*, July/August 2011, 90, 4, pp. 81–90.

Geddes, Barbara, 'What Do We Know about Democratization after Twenty Years?', *Annual Review of Political Science*, 1999, 2, pp. 115–144.

Geddes, Joseph Wright, and Erica Frantz, *How Dictatorships Work*, Cambridge: Cambridge University Press, 2018.

Gehlbach, Scott G., and Philip Keefer, 'Investment without Democracy: Ruling-Party Institutionalization and Credible Commitment in Autocracies', unpublished manuscript, University of Wisconsin, Madison, 2008.

Geisser, Vincent, 'Le Président Ben Ali en Campagne contre les "Médias Sataniques"', *Annuaire de l'Afrique du Nord*, 2002, 38, Paris: CNRS, pp. 381–387.

Geisser, Vincent, and Éric Gobe, 'Des Fissures dans la "Maison Tunisie"? Le Régime de Ben Ali Face aux Mobilisations Protestataires', *L'Année du Maghreb*, 2007, 2, Paris: CNRS, pp. 353–414.

Giugni, Marco, Doug McAdam, and Charles Tilly, *How Social Movements Matter: Social Movements, Protest and Contention*, Minneapolis: University of Minnesota Press, 1999.

Gobe, Éric, and Michaël Bechir Ayari, 'Les Cadres Supérieurs de la Fonction Publique Tunisienne: Réalités d'une Condition Socioprofessionnelle', *Cahiers du Gdr Cadres*, 2004, 8, pp. 87–100.

Goldstone, Jack, 'Towards a Fourth Generation of Revolutionary Theory', *Annual Review of Political Science*, 2001, 4, pp. 138–187.

Goodwin, Jeff, and Theda Skocpol, 'Explaining Revolutions in the Contemporary Third World', *Politics and Society*, 1989, 17, 4, pp. 489–509.

Grewal, Sharan, 'A Quiet Revolution: The Tunisian Military after Ben Ali', Carnegie Endowment for International Peace, 24 February 2016.

Hale, Henry E., 'Regime Change Cascades: What We Have Learned from the 1848 Revolutions to the 2011 Arab Uprisings', *Annual Review of Political Science*, 2013, 16, pp. 331–353.

Haugbølle, Rikke, and Francesco Cavatorta, 'Will the Real Tunisian Opposition Please Stand Up? Opposition Coordination Failures under Authoritarian Constraints', *British Journal of Middle Eastern Studies*, 2011, 38, 3, pp. 323–341.

Heydemann, Steven, 'Upgrading Authoritarianism in the Arab World', Brookings Institution Saban Center Analysis Paper No. 13, October 2007.

Hibou, Béatrice, *The Force of Obedience: The Political Economy of Repression in Tunisia*, Cambridge: Polity, 2011.

Hinnebusch, Raymond A., *Syria Revolution from Above*, London: Routledge, 2002.

Hostrup Haugbølle, Rikke, and Francesco Cavatorta, ' "Vive La Grande Famille Des Médias Tunisiens": Media Reform, Authoritarian Resilience and Societal Responses in Tunisia', *Journal of North African Studies*, 2012, 17, 1, pp. 97–112.

Jebnoun, Noureddine, *Tunisia's National Intelligence: Why 'Rogue Elephants' Fail to Reform*, Washington, DC: New Academia Publishing, 2017.

Joffé, George, 'Shame-Faced No Longer?', *Journal of North African Studies*, 2020, 25, 2, pp. 159–166.

Kalyvas, Stathis N., 'The Decay and Breakdown of Communist One-Party Systems', *Annual Review of Political Science*, 1999, 2, pp. 323–343.

Kamrava, Mehran, *Fragile Politics: Weak States in the Greater Middle East*, London: Hurst, 2016.

Khechana, Rachid, 'Les Médias Tunisiens Face à la Prépondérance de l'Etat Partisan', *Confluences Méditerranée*, 2009, 2, 69, pp. 99–105.

Khiari, Sadri, 'De Wassila à Leïla, Premières Dames et Pouvoir en Tunisie', *Politique Africaine*, 2004, 3, pp. 55–70.

King, Stephen J., *Liberalization against Democracy: The Local Politics of Economic Reform in Tunisia*, Bloomington: Indiana University Press, 2003.

Kurzman, Charles, *The Unthinkable Revolution in Iran*, Cambridge, MA: Harvard University Press, 2009.

La Palombara, Joseph, and Myron Weiner (eds.), *Political Parties and Political Development*, Princeton, NJ: Princeton University Press, 1966.

Labiadh, Salem, *Tunis: al-Thawra fi Zaman al-Haymana* [*Tunisia: The Revolution during Times of Domination*], Tunis: Mu'assassat al-Hasad, 2013.

Lamloum, Olfa, 'Le Zaim et l'Artisan ou de Bourguiba à Ben Ali', *Annuaire de l'Afrique du Nord*, 1998, 37, Paris: CNRS, pp. 377–395.

Larif-Beatrix, Asma, 'Chronique Tunisienne (1998)', *Annuaire de l'Afrique du Nord*, 1990, 27, Paris: CNRS, pp. 743–757.

Levitsky, Steven, and Maria Victoria Murillo, 'Variations in Institutional Strength', *Annual Review of Political Science*, 2009, 12, pp. 115–133.

Levitsky, Steven, and Lucan A. Way, *Competitive Authoritarianism: Hybrid Regimes after the Cold War*, Cambridge: Cambridge University Press, 2010.

Leys, Simon, *The Chairman's New Clothes: Mao and the Cultural Revolution*, London: Allison & Busby, 1977.

Lust-Okar, Ellen, *Structuring Conflict in the Arab World: Incumbents, Opponents, and Institutions*, Cambridge: Cambridge University Press, 2005.

Lutterbeck, Derek, 'Tool of Rule: The Tunisian Police under Ben Ali', *Journal of North African Studies*, 2015, 20, 5, pp. 813–831.

Al-Madani, Tawfik, *al-Mu'arada al-Tunisiyya, Nash'atuha wa-Tatawuruha* [*The Tunisian Opposition, Its Birth and Evolution*], Damascus: Ittihad al-Kuttab al-Arab, 2001.

Al-Madani, Tawfik, *Suqut al-Dawla al-Bulisiyya fi Tunis* [*The Collapse of the Police State in Tunisia*], Beirut: Arab Scientific Publishers, 2011.

Magaloni, Beatriz, *Voting for Autocracy: Hegemonic Party Survival and Its Demise in Mexico*, New York: Cambridge University Press, 2006.

Magaloni, Beatriz, and Ruth Kricheli, 'Political Order and One-Party Rule', *Annual Review of Political Science*, 2010, 13, pp. 123–143.

Mahoney, James, and Kathleen Thelen (eds.), *Advances in Comparative-Historical Analysis*, Cambridge: Cambridge University Press, 2015.

Mahoney, James, and Kathleen Thelen (eds.), *Explaining Institutional Change: Ambiguity, Agency, and Power*, Cambridge: Cambridge University Press, 2010.

Mair, Peter, *Party System Change: Approaches and Interpretations*, Oxford: Oxford University Press, 1997.

Mayer, Robert, 'Strategies of Justification in Authoritarian Ideology', *Journal of Political Ideologies*, 6, 2, 2001, pp. 147–168.

Meng, Anne, *From Personalized Rule to Institutionalized Regimes*, Cambridge: Cambridge University Press, 2020.

Meng, Anne, 'Winning the Game of Thrones: Leadership Succession in Modern Autocracies', *Journal of Conflict Resolution*, 65, 5, 2021, pp. 950–981.

Meyns, Peter, and Dani Wadada Nabudere (eds.), *Democracy and the One-Party-State in Africa*, Hamburg: Institut für Afrika-Kunde, 1989.

Moore, Clement H., *Tunisia since Independence: The Dynamics of One-Party Government*, Berkeley: University of California Press, 1965.

Morse, Yonatan L., *How Autocrats Compete: Parties, Patrons, and Unfair Elections in Africa*, Cambridge: Cambridge University Press, 2019.

Mouldi, Lahmar (ed.), *al-Thawra al-Tunisiyya* [*The Tunisian Revolution*], Doha: Arab Center for Research and Policy Studies, 2014.

Murphy, Emma C., *Economic and Political Change in Tunisia: From Bourguiba to Ben Ali*, London: Palgrave Macmillan, 1999.

O'Donnell, Guillermo, *Bureaucratic Authoritarianism: Argentina, 1966–1973, in Comparative Perspective*, Berkeley: University of California Press, 1988.

Omelicheva, Mariya Y., 'Authoritarian Legitimation: Assessing Discourses of Legitimacy in Kazakhstan and Uzbekistan', *Central Asian Survey*, 35, 4, 2016, pp. 481–500.

Onoma, Ato Kwamena, *The Politics of Property Rights Institutions in Africa*, Cambridge: Cambridge University Press, 2010.

Owen, Roger, *The Rise and Fall of Arab Presidents for Life*, Cambridge, MA: Harvard University Press, 2012.

Panebianco, Angelo, *Political Parties: Organization and Power*, Cambridge: Cambridge University Press, 1988.

Pepinsky, Thomas, *Economic Crises and the Breakdown of Authoritarian Regimes: Indonesia and Malaysia in Comparative Perspective*, New York: Cambridge University Press.

Perkins, Kenneth J., *A History of Modern Tunisia*, Cambridge: Cambridge University Press, 2008.

Perthes, Volker, *Arab Elites: Negotiating the Politics of Change*. London: Lynne Rienner, 2004.

Pfaff, Steven, *Exit-Voice Dynamics and the Collapse of East Germany: The Crisis of Leninism and the Revolution of 1989*, Durham, NC: Duke University Press, 2006.

Pierson, Paul, 'Power and Path Dependence', in James Mahoney and Kathleen Thelen (eds.), *Advances in Comparative-Historical Analysis*, Cambridge: Cambridge University Press, 2015, pp. 123–146.

Puchot, Pierre, *La Révolution Confisquée. Enquête sur la Transition Démocratique en Tunisie*, Paris: Sindbad, 2012.

Al-Qayzani, Tarik, *al-Hizb al-Dimuqrati al-Taqaddumi* [*The Progressive Democratic Party*], Tunisia: Dar Muhammad for Publishing, 2011.

Roberts, Adam, Michael J. Willis, Rory McCarthy, and Timothy Garton Ash (eds.), *Civil Resistance in the Arab Spring: Triumphs and Disasters*, Oxford: Oxford University Press, 2016.

Rudebeck, Lars, *Party and People: A Study of Political Change in Tunisia*, London: Hurst, 1967.

Sadiki, Larbi, 'Wither Arab "Republicanism"? The Rise of Family Rule and the "End of Democratization" in Egypt, Libya and Yemen', *Mediterranean Politics*, 2010, 15, 1, pp. 99–107.

Sarotte, Mary Elise, *The Collapse: The Accidental Opening of the Berlin Wall*, New York: Basic Books, 2014.

Sartori, Giovanni, *Parties and Party Systems: A Framework for Analysis*, Cambridge: Cambridge University Press, 1976.

Sassoon, Joseph, *Anatomy of Authoritarianism in the Arab Republics*, Cambridge: Cambridge University Press, 2016.

Sassoon, Joseph, *Saddam Hussein's Baath Party: Inside an Authoritarian Regime*, Cambridge: Cambridge University Press, 2012.

Schlumberger, Oliver, *Debating Arab Authoritarianism: Dynamics and Durability in Non-Democratic Regimes*, Stanford, CA: Stanford University Press, 2007.

Silva, Patricio, 'Technocrats and Politics in Chile: From the Chicago Boys to the CIEPLAN Monks', *Journal of Latin American Studies*, 1991, 23, 2, pp. 385–410.

Skocpol, Theda, *States and Social Revolutions*, Cambridge: Cambridge University Press, 1979.

Slater, Dan, *Ordering Power: Contentious Politics and Authoritarian Leviathans in Southeast Asia*, Cambridge: Cambridge University Press, 2010.

Smith, Benjamin, 'Life of the Party: The Origins of Regime Breakdown and Persistence under Single-Party Rule', *World Politics*, 2005, 57, 3, pp. 421–451.

Springborg, Robert, *Mubarak's Egypt: Fragmentation of the Political Order*, Abingdon: Routledge, 2018.

Sraieb, Noureddine, 'Tunisie: Chronique Intérieure (1992)', *Annuaire de l'Afrique du Nord*, 1994, 31, Paris: CNRS, pp. 955–995.

Stacher, Joshua, *Adaptable Autocrats: Regime Power in Egypt and Syria*. Stanford, CA: Stanford University Press, 2012.

Svolik, Milan W., *The Politics of Authoritarian Rule*, Cambridge: Cambridge University Press, 2012.

Taubman, William, *Khrushchev: The Man and His Era*, New York: Norton, 2003.

Thabti, Adel, *al-Ittihad al-'Am al-Tunisi lil-Talaba* [*The General Tunisian Student Union*], Tunis: MIPE, 2011.

Tharwat, Mohamed, *'Asr al-Jumhuryat al-Malakiyya* [*The Era of Monarchical Republics*], Cairo: al-Dar al-Thaqafiyya lil-Nashr, 2002.

Tuquoi, Jean-Pierre, and Nicolas Beau, *Notre Ami Ben Ali: L'Envers du 'Miracle Tunisien'*, Paris: La Découverte, 1999.

Valbjørn, Morten, 'Reflections on Self-Reflections: On Framing the Analytical Implications of the Arab Uprisings for the Study of Arab Politics', *Democratization*, 2015, 22, 2, pp. 218–238.

Von Soest, Christian, and Julia Grauvogel, 'Identity, Procedures and Performance: How Authoritarian Regimes Legitimize Their Rule', *Contemporary Politics*, 23, 3, 2017, pp. 287–305.

Wallerstein, Immanuel, 'The Decline of the Party in Single-Party African States', in Joseph La Palombara and Myron Weiner (eds.), *Political Parties and Political Development*, Princeton, NJ: Princeton University Press, 1966, pp. 201–214.

Wedeen, Lisa, *Ambiguities of Domination: Politics, Rhetoric, and Symbols of Domination in Contemporary Syria*, Chicago: University of Chicago Press, 1999.

White, Gregory, *A Comparative Political Economy of Tunisia and Morocco: On the Outside of Europe Looking In*, Albany: State University of New York Press, 2001.

Willis, Michael, *Politics and Power in the Maghreb: Algeria, Tunisia and Morocco from Independence to the Arab Spring*, London: Hurst, 2012.

Wolf, Anne, 'An Islamist "Renaissance"? Religion and Politics in Post-Revolutionary Tunisia', *Journal of North African Studies*, 2013, 18, 4, pp. 560–573.

Wolf, Anne, ' "Dégage RCD!" The Rise of Internal Dissent in Ben Ali's Constitutional Democratic Rally and the Tunisian Uprisings', *Mediterranean Politics*, 2018, 23, 2, 245–254.

Wolf, Anne, 'Former RCD Officials Stage a Comeback in Municipal Elections in Tunisia', *Journal of North African Studies*, 2018, 23, 4, pp. 551–556.

Wolf, Anne, *Political Islam in Tunisia: The History of Ennahda*, New York: Oxford University Press, 2017.

Wolf, Anne, and Raphaël Lefèvre, 'Revolution under Threat: The Challenges of the "Tunisian Model"', *Journal of North African Studies*, 2012, 17, 3, pp. 559–563.

Zederman, Mathilde, 'Contrôle Social et Politique de la Diaspora Tunisienne: Un Autoritarisme à Distance?', in Amin Allal and Vincent Geisser (eds.), *Tunisie: Une Démocratisation au-dessus de Tout Soupçon?*, Paris: CNRS Editions, 2018, pp. 395–412.

Zouaoui, Ridha, *al-Thawra Al-Tunisiyya, Thawrat al-Hamish 'ala al-Markaz* [*The Tunisian Revolution: The Power of the Marginalized*], 'Ala' al-Din: Sfax, 2012.

Index